ROCHESTER CATHEDRAL, 604–1540

An Architectural History

ROCHESTER CATHEDRAL, 604–1540

An Architectural History

J. Philip McAleer

UNIVERSITY OF TORONTO PRESS
Toronto Buffalo London

ISBN 0-8020-4222-8

Printed on acid-free paper

Canadian Cataloguing in Publication Data

McAleer, J. Philip (John Philip), 1935–
    Rochester Cathedral, 604–1540 : an architectural history

    Includes bibliographical references and index.
    ISBN 0-8020-4222-8

    1. Rochester Cathedral (Rochester, Kent, England).   2. Church
    architecture – England – Rochester (Kent).   3. Rochester (Kent,
    England) – Buildings, structures, etc.   I. Title.

    NA5471.R7M33 1999   726.6'09422'323   C98-931662-9

University of Toronto Press acknowledges the financial assistance to its
publishing program of the Canada Council for the Arts and the Ontario
Arts Council.

This book has been published with the help of a grant from the Humanities
and Social Sciences Federation of Canada, using funds provided by the
Social Sciences and Humanities Research Council of Canada.

University of Toronto Press acknowledges the financial support for its
publishing activities of the Government of Canada through the Book
Publishing Industry Development Program (BPIDP).

Canadä

In memory of my parents,
John Hugh McAleer (1905–1970) and
Catherine Helen Swan McAleer (1910–1989)

Contents

Illustrations

PLANS

DOCUMENTS

Preface

Until excavations are carried out – particularly in the crypt and nave – any architectural history of Rochester Cathedral must remain tentative in many respects, especially with regard to those aspects concerning the pre-Gothic history of the building. Parts of the building seen during the extensive repairs carried out in the last quarter of the last century are not only not visible today, but were often unrecorded in any pictorial form at that time. The primary record is the notes of James Thomas Irvine (1825–1900) relating to his role as clerk of the works, during the restoration of the cathedral between 1871 and 1878 under the direction of Sir George Gilbert Scott (1811–78). These papers, formerly in the West Kent Archives Office in Maidstone, are now on deposit in the Rochester upon Medway Studies Centre (formerly the Medway Area Archives Office, now recently redesignated the Medway Archives and Local Studies Centre), Civic Centre, Strood, Rochester, Kent.[1] Even so, Irvine's records do not always provide clear and conclusive evidence for the conceptions about the early history that were derived from the fabric as uncovered in those years: crucial aspects were not drawn at all; others were not described or rendered precisely enough to eliminate any doubts about the validity of the interpretations put forward; and, most surprising, photography was not used to document any of the discoveries.

The major published accounts, most obviously the study of W.H. St John Hope (1854–1919), the only major comprehensive architectural history of the building,[2] are now over or nearly a hundred years old. They record observations that, again, often can no longer be confirmed by direct observation, and conclusions from this same 'evidence' that now, in some cases, seem untenable. This is particularly true of Hope's fundamental history, which, at certain points, especially regarding the early Romanesque building, is based on premises that can no longer be accepted with confidence, and that skew the later portions of his account.

Hope's theories and conclusions, however, have been generally, and rather uncritically, accepted by most later writers. But then these later writers have been relatively few in number. Since the publication of Hope's work, scholarly investigation about Rochester – especially the cathedral fabric – seems to have ceased almost entirely. Only one paper challenging one of Hope's (major) conclusions has been published. Otherwise, in histories of the Romanesque and Early Gothic, his work remains the essential reference and basic authority.

The fact that the major architectural histories of Rochester date to near one hundred years ago may of itself be sufficient excuse to attempt another. And it may appear all the more plausible and necessary in the light of the many publications on medieval architecture in Britain that have appeared, not only since 1900, but particularly since the middle of this century, indeed, since about 1970. The wealth of new information alone may be considered appropriate justification for re-examining the architectural history of Rochester. In addition, the methodology of recent, if not of contemporary, architectural history returns us to Hope's work and provides another reason beyond the mere passage of time that encourages a reinvestigation. In his account, Hope made no attempt to place the various building periods of the cathedral fabric in a larger architectural context. He did not attempt to test any of his hypotheses about the evolution of the building, the reconstruction of its early form, or the chronology he proposed by recourse to architectural parallels. Indeed, he was actually heavily dependent upon the theories of Irvine, not only with regard to aspects of the fabric he could not see, but also with regard to still visible remains. Hope seems to have accepted many of Irvine's ideas and conclusions rather uncritically; this may have been because he was – when he first turned his attention to Rochester – at the beginning of his career.

The particular nature of this study, which is primarily architectural history in the traditional and, in the view of some current scholars, narrow definition, is a reflection both of the circumstances in which it originated and of my own interests and inclinations.

Initially, I was asked to take over the authorship of the chapter on the medieval fabric of the cathedral for the volume that was eventually to appear as *Faith and Fabric: A History of Rochester Cathedral 604–1994* (Kent History Project, 4: Woodbridge [Suffolk] 1996). Initially, I agreed to deal only with the Romanesque phases; then, as work progressed and the years passed, my role was enlarged to include responsibility for all of the medieval fabric. The intended context of my study determined its focus on the material fabric and the consequent archaeological approach, with an emphasis on stylistic development, for other contributors to the aforementioned volume were to deal with other aspects of the cathedral's history. This approach, however, seemed appropriate to the particular nature of the building in question as well as to the character of the earlier studies and the problems of interpretation both presented. It was also one to which I am very sympathetic, since, in dealing with art and architecture, the context I always find the most interesting and revealing is the formal tradition to which a work belongs, and the continuous imaginative transformation of that tradition by the creators of each individual work of art. And it is, of course, those forms that draw us back to particular works of art or architecture again and again, for the visual and emotional enjoyment they offer. From this pleasure also springs, especially in the case of buildings, an interest to know what the original structure was like, since so few have survived intact and unaltered.

Nevertheless, in my study of Rochester, I have not deliberately rejected a contextual approach so much as I have failed to find any significant political, social, economic, or religious events – with perhaps one exception – that seemed to touch directly on the cathedral and that would or could explain not only its particular forms and appearance, but even when or why work stopped or started when it did (basic facts not always easy to determine with precision). As my knowledge of architectural history – whatever its limitations – is, I believe, stronger than my knowledge of the political, social, economic, and religious developments and events over the 450 years that encompass the standing fabric of the cathedral, I believe the interested reader is better served by my traditional approach. That approach might well be defined in the words of a more distinguished colleague in the preface to his work of architectural history: 'The approach adopted in this book is archaeological in the nineteenth-century sense, a tradition traceable from Willis via Bilson to Pevsner, in which the eye is the primary tool.'[3] It therefore adheres to the traditional methodology and subject matter of art and architectural history, what has been termed the 'visual taxometry of art,' the analysis and history of style per se.[4] In the case of Rochester, it seemed especially appropriate to focus on the building itself in a situation where the building is our major document.

This study was not begun with the intention of demolishing Hope's history. Nevertheless, in the course of studying the building and reading that history, and particularly as a result of the examination of Irvine's papers, doubts began to arise about the validity of many of Hope's conclusions. Thus, it seemed important and useful to question much of this received wisdom about medieval Rochester, because of the dubious nature of some of the basic 'evidence' and of our current knowledge of the evolution of the Romanesque and Gothic styles, even if definite and definitive answers cannot in many instances be given until careful archaeological investigation of the fabric takes place. It is hoped, however, that the questions raised may serve as a guide to future investigators.

Because of the close scrutiny to which the cathedral was subjected by the nineteenth-century historians, it is probably impossible to observe any feature that has not been previously noted. One can, however, differ in the interpretation of the place of many of these features in the successive phases of building and rebuilding. I have been able to examine all aspects of the fabric of the building as it now stands in order to confirm – so far as is now possible – what has been reported and to form the basis for my interpretation of its history. Whenever my observations have disagreed with those made by Hope or others, I have so indicated in the notes.

Aside from the obvious problems created by the continual process of rebuilding and alteration, destructive acts of nature, and human neglect, another difficulty in composing a history must be mentioned: the three major restorations to which the cathedral was subjected in the nineteenth century. The problem is not so much that of detecting the restorations as it is of deciding what it was the restorations replaced, or on what evidence the often drastic rebuilding was based. Thus, 140 years later, I find myself echoing the sentiments expressed by Arthur Ashpitel (1807–69) in the opening paragraph of his paper on Rochester Cathedral,[5] perhaps one of the first attempts at a serious study:

The architect and antiquary has great difficulties in treating of this most interesting cathedral. First, from the paucity of the records concerning its history, compared with the stores of leiger books, chartularies, and chronicles possessed by some collegiate bodies; and secondly, from the numerous alterations and restorations, – attempted with the best motives it is true, but executed at a time when the subject was not at all understood. From this cause the external character of the work is often entirely changed; and those indications of additions to, or alterations from, the original design – those slight matters which in an untouched building catch the eye, and guide the observer to such important results, are here quite obscured or obliterated – those tests which have been so successfully applied elsewhere are here entirely lost. It is then with considerable diffidence the following remarks are offered. However defective they may be, the building itself is of such great interest, that any attempt, however imperfect, to throw light on its foundation and history, must necessarily be of some value.

Amen!

Bedford, Nova Scotia
1 January 1998

Acknowledgments

This study would not have been possible without the generous help of a number of people at Rochester. I wish to thank, particularly, the former dean, the Very Rev. John R. Arnold (1978–89), now Dean of Durham, and his successor, the Very Rev. Edward F. Shotter, as well as the Chapter, for allowing me access to all parts of the cathedral for study on more than one occasion. The patience and guidance of the vergers must also be gratefully recorded: special gratitude, I think, must be expressed to Knowler Jennings and, especially, to the late Michael Ratcliffe, whom I pestered most often. The continued interest of Anneliese (Mrs John) Arnold in the progress of my research has also been much appreciated. Nor should the generous hospitality, on occasion, of Canon Richard Lea and his wife, Rosemary, be overlooked.

I must also make known the degree of my indebtedness to Mary R. Covert. She very kindly and most helpfully made a good deal of the primary and secondary material that she had gathered for her projected PhD thesis on the cathedral available to me in photocopy form. Living and working, as I do, in a provincial area without any adequate library resources, having this collection of material at hand in my study was an invaluable convenience. Nonetheless, I must also register my appreciation to Gwen Ling, a librarian at the then Technical University of Nova Scotia, for her obliging zeal in tracking down my awkward interlibrary loan requests over the last decade, and also to the always helpful staff of the Kent County record office in its various locales and constantly changing nomenclature during the same period.

In addition, thanks are due to Nigel Yates, editor of *Faith and Fabric: A History of Rochester Cathedral 604–1994* (Woodbridge 1996), for his patience in dealing with my overly long contribution to that volume and his encouragement to seek publication of the full study elsewhere, and to T.W.T. Tatton-Brown, archaeological consultant to the cathedral since 1986, for reading several drafts of this study and discussing a few specific problems such as the types of stone used in the cathedral.

Finally, particular appreciation must be rendered to the Friends of Rochester Cathedral for a well-timed grant that allowed the purchase of photographs of some of J.T. Irvine's drawings preserved in the Dean and Chapter records, and to the dean of the Faculty of Architecture of the former Technical University of Nova Scotia, Thomas Emodi, for a similarly well-timed allocation of funds to employ one of our undergraduate students, Wesley E. Wollin, to produce computer-aided graphic renderings of my drawings of profiles and of several plans, as well as to cover the cost of preparing the index. Thanks also to Ruth Pincoe for preparing the index.

One last obligation, unfortunately a sad one, remains to be stated. It is with considerable regret for friendship lost that I would like to supplement the dedication of this study to my parents with one to the memory of Michael Ratcliffe (1965–95), a verger of the cathedral from 1987 to his untimely death, and to John F. Bishop (1931–95), for many a good ride on his Honda Gold Wing to and from the cathedral and around Kent in the course of my research.

Abbreviations

AB	*Art Bulletin*
Ant. Jnl	*The Antiquaries Journal*
Arch.	*Archaeologia*
Arch. Cant.	*Archaeologia Cantiana*
Arch. Jnl	*Archaeological Journal*
BAACT	British Archaeological Association Conference Transactions
BL	British Library, London
BM	British Museum, London
B. mon.	*Bulletin monumental*
BE	*The Buildings of England*
Cong. arch.	*Congrès archéologique*
CUL	Cambridge University Library
DoE	Department of the Environment
EH	English Heritage
EHR	*English Historical Review*
HBM	Historic Buildings and Monuments (Scottish Development Department)
Jnl BAA	*Journal of the British Archaeological Association*
Jnl SAH	*Journal of the Society of Architectural Historians*
Med. Arch.	*Medieval Archaeology*
MPBW	Ministry of Public Buildings and Works
MW	Ministry of Works
NMR	National Monuments Record
RCHM	Royal Commission on Historical Monuments
RDCL	Rochester Dean and Chapter Library
RIBA	Royal Institute of British Architects (London)

RMSC   Rochester upon Medway Studies Centre (Strood)
            (now Medway Archives and Local Studies Centre)
RS   Rolls Series: Rerum Britannicarum Medii Aevi
            Scriptores *or* Chronicles and Memorials of Great
            Britain and Ireland during the Middle Ages
VCH   *Victoria County History (The Victoria History of the
            Counties of England)*

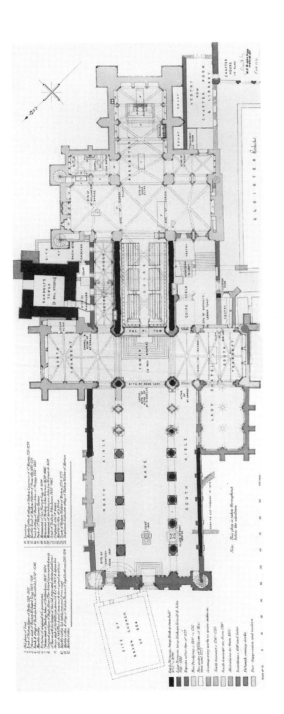

1 Historical plan of cathedral by W.H.St.J. Hope, from *Arch. Cant.* 23 (1898), pl. II (photo: by permission of Society of Antiquaries of London)

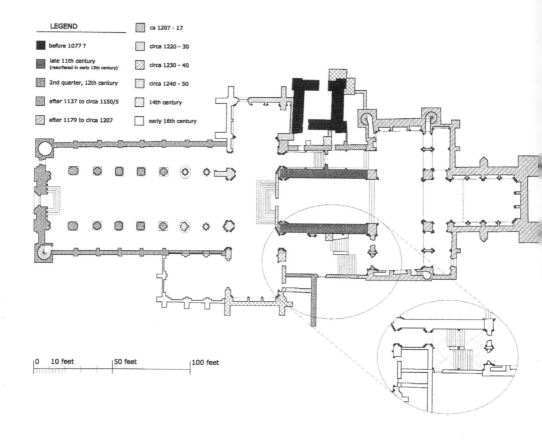

0   10 feet   50 feet   100 feet

2 Plan of cathedral (post-medieval alterations, additions, and rebuilding
   omitted) with author's suggested building phases and intended form of
   south choir aisle (drawing: W.E. Wollin)

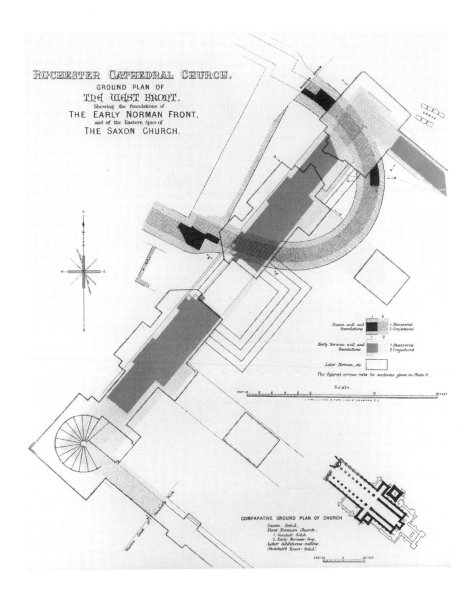

3 Remains of apsidal structure discovered under north half of (Romanesque) west façade in 1888, from *Arch. Cant.* 18 (1889), pl. I (photo: by permission of Society of Antiquaries of London)

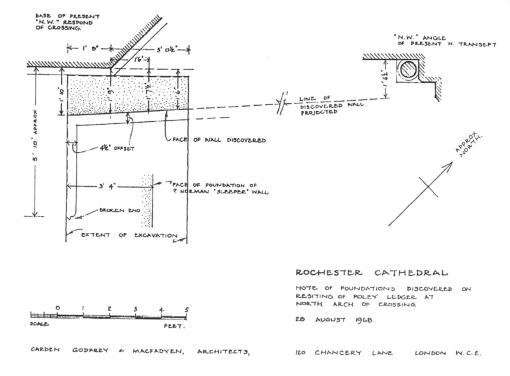

BASE OF PRESENT
"N.W." RESPOND
OF CROSSING.

"N.W." ANGLE
OF PRESENT N. TRANSEPT

LINE OF
DISCOVERED WALL
PROJECTED

FACE OF WALL DISCOVERED

4½" OFFSET

3' 4"

FACE OF FOUNDATION OF
? NORMAN "SLEEPER" WALL

BROKEN END

EXTENT OF EXCAVATION

APPROX.
NORTH.

ROCHESTER CATHEDRAL

NOTE OF FOUNDATIONS DISCOVERED ON
RESITING OF POLEY LEDGER AT
NORTH ARCH OF CROSSING

28 AUGUST 1968.

SCALE   FEET.

CARDEN GODFREY & MACFADYEN, ARCHITECTS,   120 CHANCERY LANE   LONDON W.C.2.

4 Plan of foundations uncovered in 1968 east of (Gothic) northwest crossing
pier (Carden, Godfrey & Macfadyen, Architects)

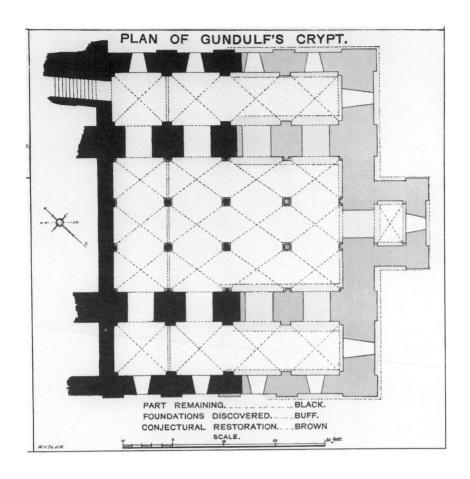

PLAN OF GUNDULF'S CRYPT.

PART REMAINING............................BLACK.
FOUNDATIONS DISCOVERED..........BUFF.
CONJECTURAL RESTORATION.....BROWN
SCALE.

5 Plan of Romanesque crypt as restored by Hope, from *Arch.* 49 (1886), pl. I
(photo: by permission of Society of Antiquaries of London)

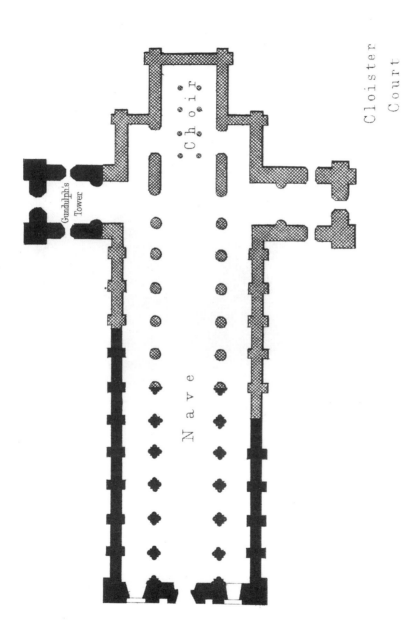

6 Plan of Romanesque cathedral as restored by A. Ashpitel, from *Jnl. BAA* 9 (1854), pl. 29 (photo: by permission of Society of Antiquaries of London)

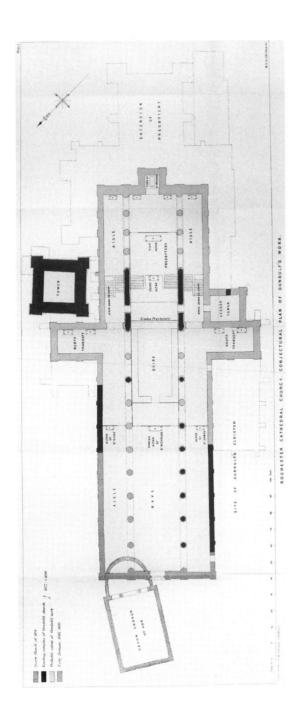

7 Plan of early Romanesque cathedral as restored by Hope, from *Arch. Cant.* 23 (1898), pl. I [photo: by permission of Society of Antiquaries of London]

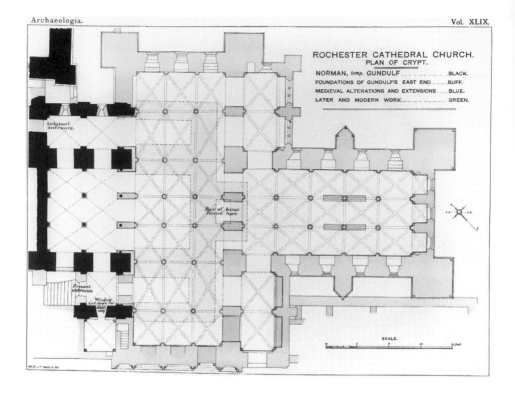

ROCHESTER CATHEDRAL CHURCH.
PLAN OF CRYPT.

NORMAN, *temp.* GUNDULF_____BLACK.
FOUNDATIONS OF GUNDULF'S EAST END_____BUFF.
MEDIEVAL ALTERATIONS AND EXTENSIONS_____BLUE.
LATER AND MODERN WORK_____GREEN.

8 Plan of remains of Romanesque crypt and Early Gothic extension by
  Hope, from *Arch.* 49 (1886), pl. II (photo: by permission of Society of
  Antiquaries of London)

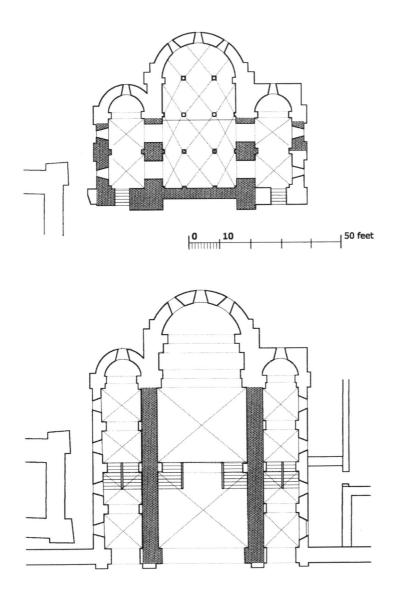

0 10   50 feet

9 Plan of early Romanesque crypt as restored by author (drawing: WEW)

10 Plan of eastern termination of the early Romanesque cathedral as restored by author (drawing: WEW)

11 Profiles of capitals and base mouldings (JPM/WEW):

A. south nave arcade, fourth (quatrefoil) pier from east, base
B. south nave arcade, fifth (twelve-shafted) pier from east, base
C. west front, interior, arcading, north side, north shaft, base
D. crypt, presbytery section, east responds, base
E. crypt, round columns in presbytery section, base
F. crypt, column base
G. crypt, west wall, respond north of south aisle, base
H. presbytery, north side, shaft base
I. north choir aisle, north wall, shaft base
J. responds of east side of crossing and at west end of choir aisles, bases
K. major transept, north arm, west respond, base
L. southwest crossing pier, base
M. south transept/nave aisle respond, base
N. north and south nave arcades, western piers, east responds, base and plinth
O. north nave arcade, second pier from east (western Gothic pier), west shafts, base
P. south choir aisle, east portal (screen), base of shaft
Q. south choir aisle, west portal, shaft base
R. south nave arcade, second pier from east, west face, base
S. 'Chapter house' ('Bishop Hamo's') doorway, base
T. Lady chapel, entrance arch, base
U. Lady chapel, wall shaft, base
V. crypt, capital
W. south choir aisle, east portal (screen), capital

12 Profiles of door jambs (JPM/WEW):
A. south choir aisle, east doorway (screen)
B. south choir aisle, west portal
C. south choir aisle, cloister portal
D. west front, northwest doorway
E. minor transept, south arm, west wall, portal to 'vestry'
F. major transept, south arm, portal in east wall

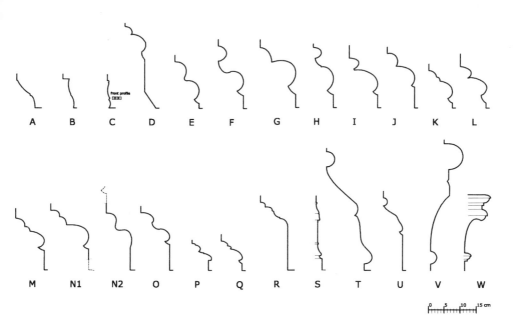

A   B   C   D   E   F   G   H   I   J   K   L

M   N1   N2   O   P   Q   R   S   T   U   V   W

0 5 10 15 cm

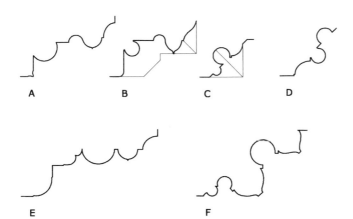

A   B   C   D

E   F

0 5 10 15 cm

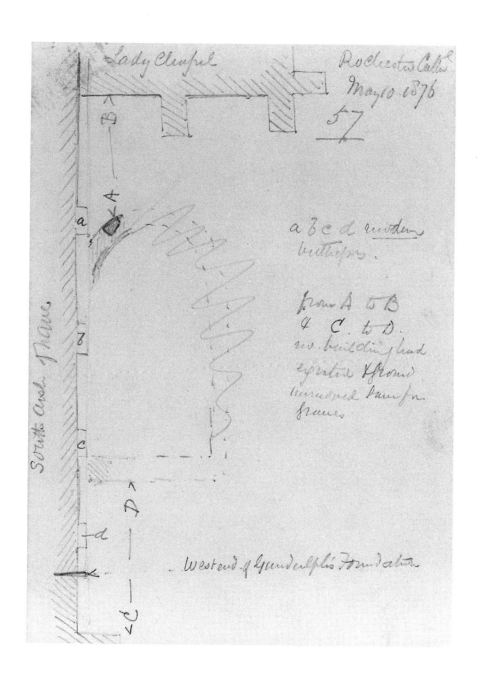

The handwritten annotations in the sketch read:

Lady Chapel

Rochester Cath.
May 10 1876

57

South end Nave

a b c d wooden
buttresses.

from A to B
& C. to D.
no building had
existed & from
burned dam for
frames.

West end of Gundulph's Foundation

13 J.T. Irvine: sketch of foundations uncovered outside south aisle of nave
in March 1876 (RMSC, DRc/Emf 77/26)

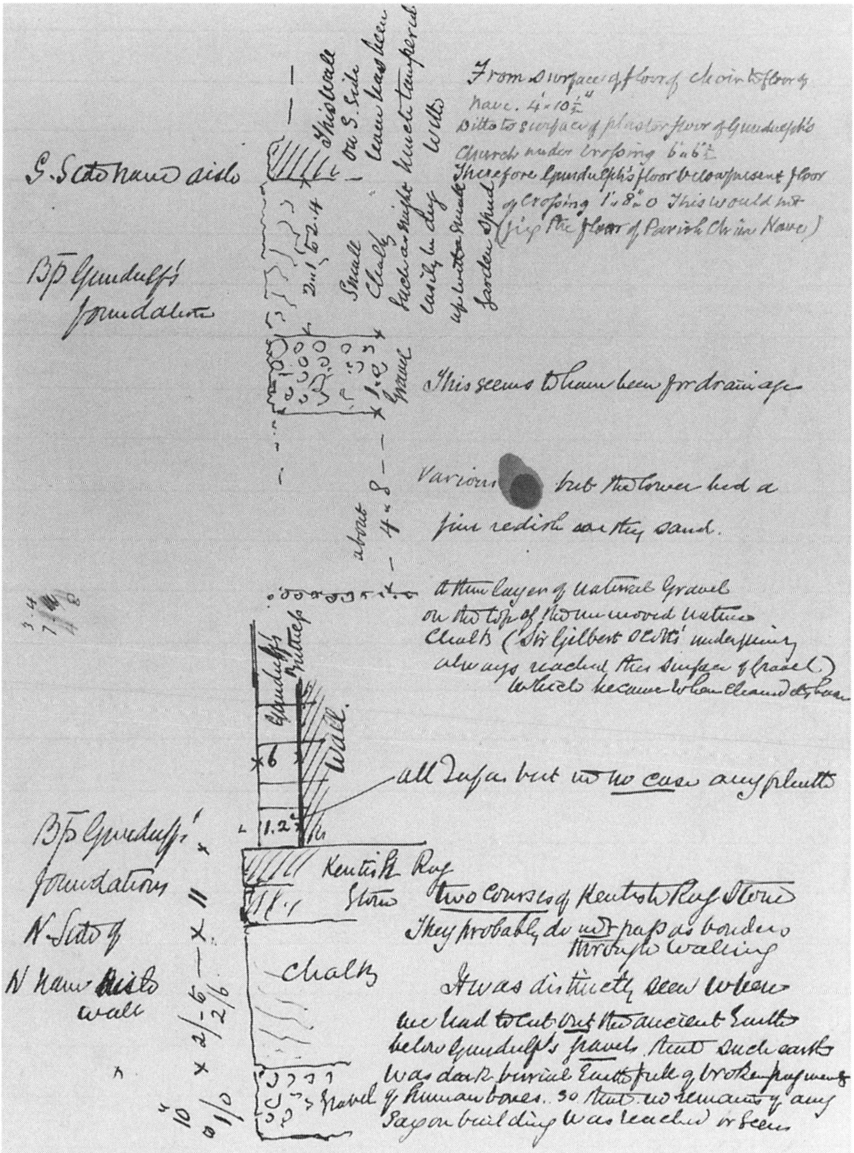

[Handwritten field notes and section drawing of foundations, with marginal annotations]

S. Side of nave aisle

Bp Gundulf's foundation

This scale on S. Scale. Seam has been...

Small Chalk

This seems to have been for drainage

Various ... but the tower had a fine reddish sea stiff sand.

all Infra but in no case any plinth

Bp Gundulf's foundations

N. Side of N nave aisle wall

Kentish Rag Stone — two courses of Kentish Rag Stone. They probably do not pass as bonders through the walling

Chalk

It was distinctly seen when we had to cut out the ancient earth below Gundulf's gravel. That such earth was dark burial earth full of broken pavements & of human bones. So that no remains of any Saxon building was reached or seen

From surface of floor of choir to floor of nave. 4'.10½"
Ditto to surface of plaster floor of Gundulf's Church under crossing 6.6½
Therefore Gundulf's floor below present floor of crossing 1'.8"0 This would not...
(= the floor of Parish Ch. in Nave)

Here the Concrete of Sir Gilbert's underpinning rests on the unmoved native Chalk. If ancient excavations were found they were always cleared out to bottom before being filled with Concrete.

14 Irvine: south and north nave aisle walls, section of foundations (RMSC, DRc/Emf 77/36)

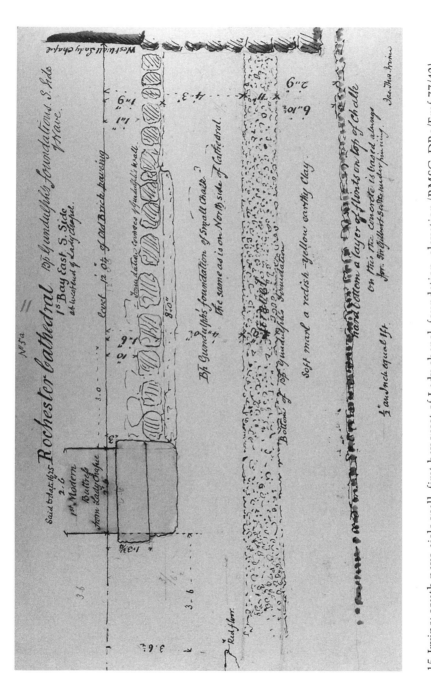

15 Irvine: south nave aisle wall, first bay west of Lady chapel, foundation, elevation (RMSC, DRc/Emf 77/42)

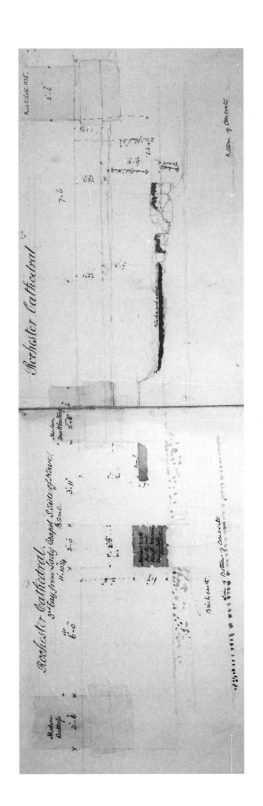

16 Irvine: south nave aisle wall, second and third bays west of Lady chapel, foundation, elevation (RMSC, DRc/Emf 77/41)

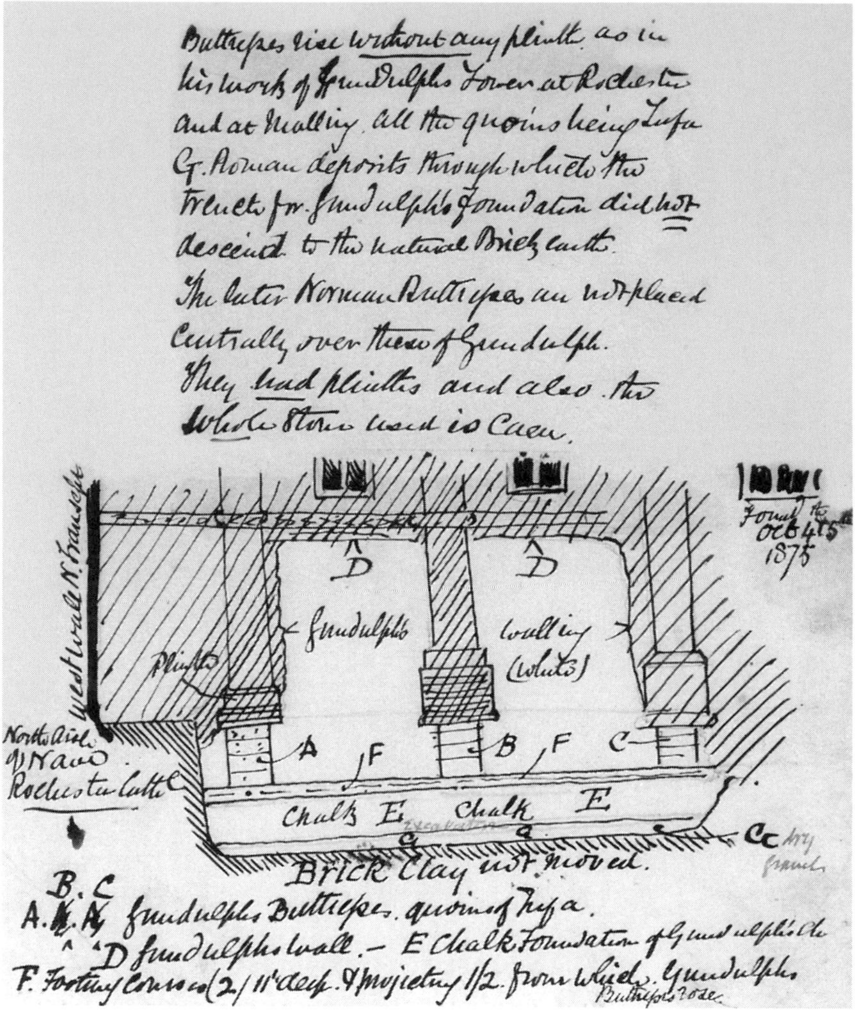

Buttresses rise without any plinth, as in
his work of Gundulph's Tower at Rochester
and at Malling, all the quoins being Tufa
& Roman deposits through which the
Trench for Gundulph's foundation did not
descend to the natural Brick earth.

The later Norman Buttresses are not placed
centrally over these of Gundulph.

They had plinths and also the
whole stone used is Caen.

Found the Oct 4th 1875

West wall of N. Transept

North Aisle
of Nave
Rochester Cath.

Plinth

D   D

Gundulph's   walling (white)

A   F   B   F   C

Chalk E   Chalk   E

Brick Clay not moved.

Cc dry gravel

B. C
A. A. Gundulph's Buttresses. quoins of Tufa.
D Gundulph's wall. – E Chalk Foundation of Gundulph's the
F. Footing Courses (2/ 11" deep & projecting 1/2. from which Gundulph's Buttresses rose.

17 Irvine: north nave aisle wall, three eastern bays, elevation (RMSC, DRc/
Emf 77/16)

to have been right about his square end
for I have found a cross wall 8 feet
thick but projecting from this is a
feature he did not find, namely a
small square chapel.

centre line of crypt

I am going to follow this out to the end—
for it is utterly contrary to what one expected.
    Re the rest of the church I have
arrived at the following chronology:—
    (1) Gundulph's Tower.
    (2) Gundulph's church —
    (3) The Nave
    (3a) Nave alterations } (1) recasing of Gundulph's work
        (2) north side of north arcade) (3) Rebuilding of
        Triforium — with old material — by Ernulph — Also
        the West front + ornamentation of nave aisles
    (4) First Early English alterations — comprising the
        lower parts of the choir aisles, the east end
        of the nave aisles, + the bases of the Tower piers

18 Hope: detail from letter of 20 October 1881 to Irvine with plan of
rectangular chapel at east end of crypt (RMSC, DRc/Emf 77/81)

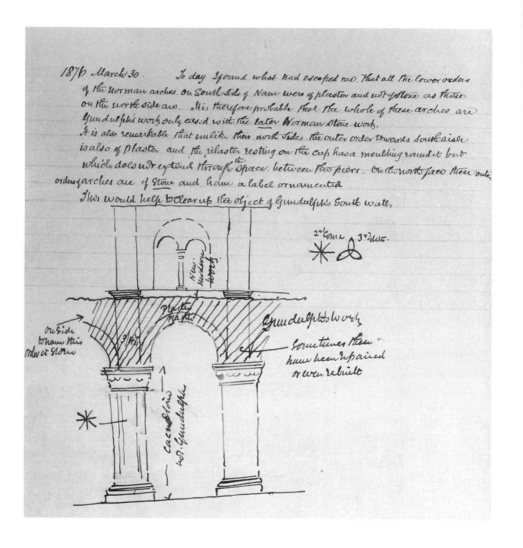

1876 March 30. To day I found what had escaped me, that all the lower orders of the Norman arches on South side of Nave were of plaster and not of stone as these on the north side are. It is therefore probable that the whole of these arches are Gundulph's work only cased with the later Norman stone work.

It is also remarkable that unlike their north sides, the outer order towards south aisle is also of plaster and the pilaster resting on the cap has a moulding round it but which does not extend through space. between the piers. On the north face these outer orders of arches are of stone and have a label ornamented.

This would help to clear up the object of Gundulph's South wall,

19 Irvine: draft of letter of 30 March 1876 to G.G. Scott with reference to south side of south nave arcade (RMSC, DRc/Emf 77/17)

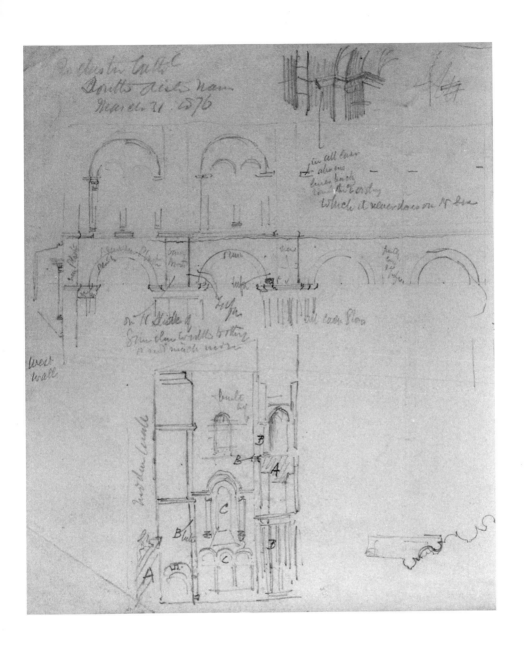

20 Irvine: sketch, dated 31 March 1876, of west bays of aisle face of south
nave arcade (RMSC, DRc/Emf 77/18)

21 North tower, exterior, north face (JPM)

22 North tower, interior, south wall and southwest angle, ca. 1925 (Guildhall Museum, Rochester, AF 68)

23 North tower, interior, northeast angle, ca. 1925 (Guildhall Museum,
Rochester, AF 69)

24 Crypt, view towards northwest (nave and north aisle) (JPM)

25 Crypt, northeast Gothic respond incorporating Romanesque respond capital (vault Romanesque) (JPM)

26 Crypt, north aisle facing west with blocked entrance stairway (photo: source unknown)

27 Crypt, interior of window in east bay of north aisle (JPM)

28 Crypt, exterior of window in west bay of north aisle (JPM)

29 Crypt, Romanesque pier and respond at west end of south aisle (wall to
left of respond Early Gothic) (JPM)

30 Crypt, Gothic angle respond at east end of south aisle (wall and arch to
right of respond modern) (JPM)

31 South nave aisle, exterior, three western bays (JPM)

32 South nave clerestory, exterior, remains of blind arcading at west end
(adjacent to turret) (JPM)

33 North nave aisle, exterior, eastern bay and easternmost buttress (JPM)

34 Nave, interior, view towards west from crossing (JPM)

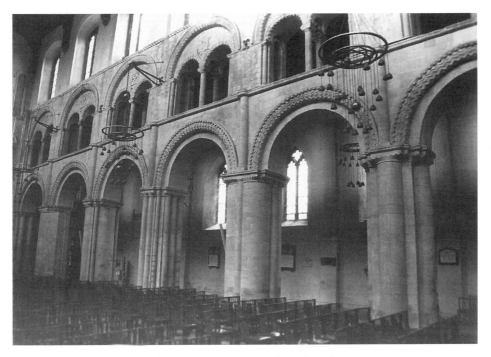

35 North nave arcade, remaining Romanesque bays (JPM)

36 North nave arcade, second storey arcades, detail, bays six and seven from
east (JPM)

37 South nave arcade, second pier from east, north face showing juncture between early (left) and later (right) Gothic (JPM)

38 North nave arcade, fifth pier from east, base (JPM)

39 North nave aisle, interior, view to west (JPM)

40 North nave aisle, interior, view of aisle wall from transept (JPM)

41 West façade from southwest (JPM)

42 West façade, detail, south half (JPM)

43 West façade, detail, nave end, two lowest registers of arcading at south
(JPM)

44 West façade, detail, south aisle end, window (JPM)

45 West façade, detail, tympanum of west portal (JPM)

46 West façade, interior, blind arcading to north of west portal (JPM)

47 West façade, interior, remains of arcading north of inserted Perpendicular west window (JPM)

48 South nave aisle, interior, west end (JPM)

49 Presbytery, exterior, east façade, detail (JPM)

50 Presbytery, exterior, north elevation (JPM)

51 North arm of minor transept, exterior, east face (JPM)

52 Presbytery, exterior, north elevation, detail, base of buttress (JPM)

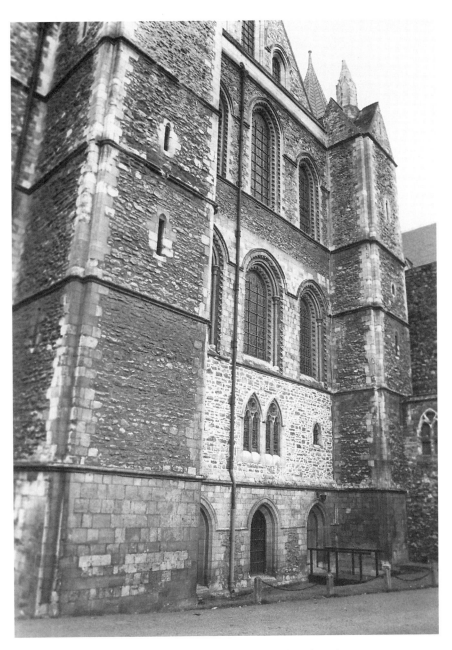

53 North arm of minor transept, exterior, north face (JPM)

54 North arm of major transept, exterior, north face (JPM)

55 North arm of major transept, exterior, west face (JPM)

56 Exterior, south elevation of choir, minor east transept and presbytery
(JPM)

57 Exterior, surviving fragment (vestry) of west range of cloister (JPM)

58 South arm of major transept, exterior, east clerestory (JPM)

59 South arm of major transept, exterior, south face (JPM)

60 South arm of major transept, exterior, west clerestory (JPM)

61 Crypt, interior, view of section under presbytery (JPM)

62 Crypt, interior, view to north of section under minor transept (JPM)

63 Presbytery, interior, north elevation (JPM)

64 North arm of minor transept, interior, east elevation (JPM)

65 South arm of minor transept, interior, east elevation (JPM)

66 North arm of minor transept, interior, south chapel (JPM)

67 South arm of minor transept, interior, north chapel (JPM)

68 South arm of minor transept, interior, detail of bases and plinth of shafts
(JPM)

69 Minor east transept, interior, vaults viewed towards north (JPM)

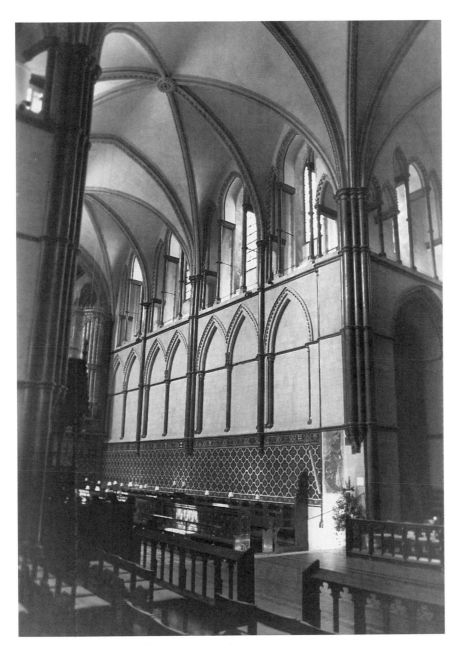

70 Choir, interior, north elevation viewed from minor transept (JPM)

71 Choir, interior, shaft and bases at east end of south wall (JPM)

72 North choir aisle, interior, view to east (JPM)

73 South choir aisle, interior, view to east (JPM)

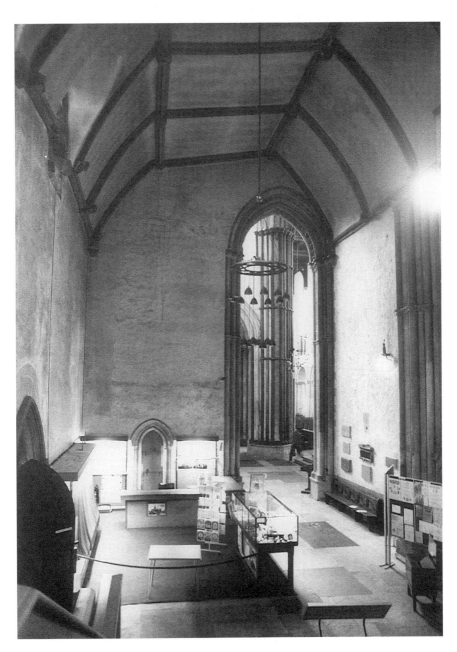

74 South choir aisle, interior, view to west (JPM)

75 South choir aisle, interior, eastern end of south wall (JPM)

76 South choir aisle, interior, south wall, line of 'quoins' above right jamb
   of portal (JPM)

77 South choir aisle, interior, middle of north wall with respond, tomb attributed to Bishop John de Bradfield and pier buttress (JPM)

78 South choir aisle, interior, northeast section with entrance to crypt and wooden vestry enclosure above (JPM)

79 South choir aisle, interior, remains of intended vault above ceiling (JPM)

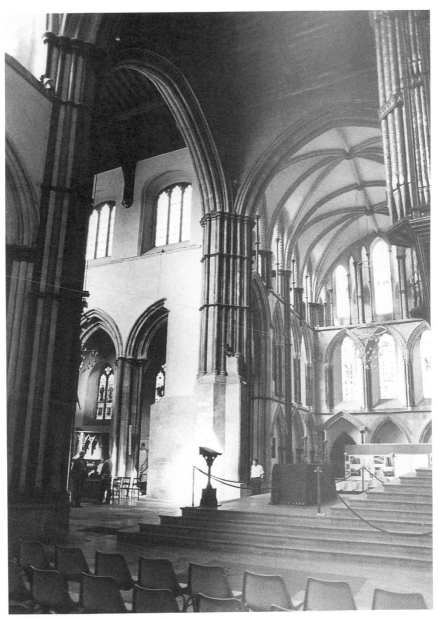

80 Interior, east end of north nave arcade, northwest crossing pier and north
   arm of major transept (JPM)

81 North major transept arm, interior, east elevation (JPM)

82 North major transept arm, interior, west elevation (JPM)

83 North major transept arm, interior, detail of vaulting of clerestory (JPM)

84 South major transept arm, interior, east and south elevations and vault
   (JPM)

85 South major transept arm, interior, west clerestory (JPM)

86 Nave, interior, southwest crossing pier, north face (JPM)

87 Nave, interior, northwest crossing pier, south face (buttress wall to left) (JPM)

88 North aisle, interior, north nave arcade from east end (buttress wall at left) (JPM)

89 Nave, interior, south arcade, first two piers from east (JPM)

90 Nave, interior, north arcade, first two piers from east (JPM)

91 Nave, interior, north arcade, first pier from east, detail, base viewed from west (JPM)

92 Nave, interior, north arcade, second pier from east, detail, base viewed from west (JPM)

93 North arm of minor transept, detail of portal in west wall (JPM)

94 South choir aisle, south jamb of portal-screen (JPM)

95 South choir aisle, south jamb of portal in west wall (JPM)

96 Exterior east jamb of portal from south choir aisle to north cloister
walk (JPM)

97 South jamb of portal at west end of north nave aisle (JPM)

98 Portal attributed to Bishop Hamo de Hethe, detail, left (north) jamb
(JPM)

99 Portal attributed to Bishop Hamo de Hethe, detail, arch (JPM)

100 Exterior, window in penultimate west bay of north nave aisle (JPM)

A

B

C

101 Interior, north major transept arm, stone vault, bosses (C.J.P. Cave:
NMR AA52/6516–18; RCHME, © Crown copyright)

    A. oak leaves and acorns sprouting out of mouth of bovine head
        (boss at centre of south bay) [6516]

    B. 'Green Man': oak leaves and acorns (boss of transverse rib
        between bays) [6517]

    C. foliage (boss at centre of north bay) [6518]

A

B

C

102 Interior, south major transept arm, wooden vault, bosses (Cave: NMR
AA52/6519–22, 6538; RCHME, © Crown copyright)

A. 'Green Man' (boss at centre of north bay) [6519]
B. four small heads with leaves and acorns (boss between northern
and middle bays) [6520]
C. dragon with foliage (boss at centre of middle bay) [6521]

D

E

D. branches and foliage (boss between middle and southern bays) [6522]
E. dog's head sprouting foliage (boss at centre of southern bay) [6538]

103 Interior, north choir aisle, vault boss (Cave: NMR AA52/6530; RCHME, © Crown copyright)

A

B

C

104 Wooden bosses of ceiling in south choir aisle: a–e, facing south, east to
west, as seen from below; f–l, facing north, west to east, as seen from
below (Cave: NMR AA52/6523, 6531–7, 6539–42; RCHME, © Crown
copyright)

    A. 'Green Man' (terminal boss, east end of south rib) [6523]
    B. multi-petalled flower with leaves [6539]
    C. coiled dragon [6540]

D

E

F

D. four-petal flower with diagonally positioned heads [6541]
E. 'Green Man' (terminal boss, west end of south rib) [6542]
F. 'Green Man' (terminal boss, west end of north rib) [6537]

G

H

I

G. four-petal flower with diagonally positioned leaves [6536]
H. winged 'Green Man' [6535]
I. face with tongue sticking out [6534]

J

K

L

J. flower and radially arranged foliage [6533]
K. four small faces peering out of surrounding foliage [6532]
L. 'Green Man' (terminal boss, east end of north rib) [6531]

105 Lady chapel, exterior, south wall (JPM)

106 Lady chapel, interior, view to west (JPM)

107 Lady chapel, interior, east wall with entrance arch (JPM)

108 Lady chapel, interior, detail, northeast corner (JPM)

ROCHESTER CATHEDRAL, 604–1540

Introduction

The cathedral of Rochester is a small building, one of the smallest of the English medieval cathedrals, yet its constructional history is one of the more complicated, owing in part to meagre and possibly not very reliable documentation. Its constructional history has also perhaps been reconstructed as more complicated than it indeed may have been owing to an uncritical acceptance of the slight documentation and what might be regarded as a misreading or, at least, a questionable interpretation of the surviving physical evidence.

The heretofore accepted chronology for the cathedral has recognized five major phases and three minor ones. They have been defined as follows:

(a) A small church consisting of an apse and oblong nave, possibly separated by a triple arcade, dating from the period of the foundation of the see in 604. It remained in use until the Norman Conquest and for nearly two decades thereafter.

(b) A new building in the Romanesque style begun by the second Norman bishop in the 1080s that remained unfinished at the time of his death in 1108. The plan of its eastern arm has been reconstructed as consisting of a large aisled crypt under the eastern half of a presbytery of six or seven bays: both crypt and presbytery were straight-ended with, in addition, solid walls separating the presbytery from the aisles for most of their length; asymmetrical towers flanked the presbytery. A transept may not have been included, but if present, it was at most of an extraordinarily narrow form, scarcely wider than an ordinary nave bay; as a result, there was no proper crossing and, therefore, no central tower. There then followed a 'normal' nave and aisles that, however, remained incomplete; a simple wall with a single portal served as a west façade. A cloister was thought to have been located immediately south of the nave.

(c) During a second phase of construction in the early twelfth century, the east end and the nave were rebuilt, the latter completed with an entirely new façade. A new cloister and monastic buildings were now built south of the choir.

(d) As a result of fires in 1137 and 1179, an undetermined amount of rebuilding took place on each occasion at the east end. As a consequence of the latter fire, at least the south arm of the transept was rebuilt following the earlier form.

(e) About 1200, a new building campaign began that resulted in the almost total replacement of the late eleventh-century crypt (and any twelfth-century alterations) and the upper eastern arm by about 1227. The new crypt extended under the entire enlarged eastern arm. The new work took the form at both levels of a straight-ended, unaisled presbytery, a minor transept with two chapels in each arm, and an aisled choir that at the upper level retained the solid walls of the first Romanesque presbytery. A major transept was included, its north arm finished by circa 1240, the south arm probably only by 1280. A projected crossing tower was never completed above the level of the roofs of the four adjacent limbs. The reconstruction of the nave was begun but was halted after just two bays had been rebuilt.

(f) Late in the second quarter of the fourteenth century, a crossing tower was raised. It received bells and probably a spire.

(g) The Romanesque nave clerestory was replaced in the fifteenth century when a gigantic west window was inserted in the west front.

(h) No other major work was carried out on the cathedral until circa 1500 when a structure was built opening off the west side of the south arm of the major transept. It was intended to serve as the nave to an established altar to the Virgin in the transept (the so-called Lady chapel). At the time of the Dissolution, it was still incomplete, as its vaults had not been constructed.

Of the construction phases outlined above, the following elements were thought to remain:

(a) the foundations of the apse and east end of the nave walls of the Saxon church (located under the existing west front);

(b) the two west bays of the crypt and the solid side walls of the choir, plus one of the flanking towers;

(c) the nave piers (encasing the earlier piers) and gallery and west front;

(e) all of the thirteenth-century crypt, and the presbytery, minor transept, choir, and major transept;

(f) until the mid-eighteenth century, the spire; until the early nineteenth century, the central tower;

(g) the rebuilt clerestory and west window (the tracery of which was renewed in the nineteenth century);

(h) the incomplete Lady chapel.

This study will argue the following:

(a) The small apsidal structure partially uncovered under the west front is probably *not* the Saxon cathedral of 604.

(b) The first Romanesque church consisted of a small aisled crypt, probably apsidally ended; a four-bay presbytery with solid walls between it and the aisles, probably all terminating in apses; a transept of normal proportions, probably without east chapels, but with a crossing and tower; a nave, probably with a three-storey elevation (of unknown design), terminating in a sectional façade.

(c), (d) The nave of the *completed* eleventh-century building was rebuilt, most likely as a result of the fire of 1137, but in any case certainly during the 1140s rather than the period 1115–25; the amount of reconstruction – if any – at the east end is now impossible to determine as to its extent or form.

(d), (e) A major rebuilding began shortly after the fire of 1179 at the east end in the new Gothic style, with work on the south arm of the major transept nearing completion by about 1240. Neither arm of the transept received its vaults at this time. Rebuilding of the nave arcade was begun but was halted after only two bays.

(f) In the second quarter of the fourteenth century, the major transept was vaulted – the southern arm in wood – and the central tower received its belfry stage, probably capped by a spire.

(h) The existing incomplete Lady chapel may have been preceded by an earlier structure of which the entrance arch
alone remains.

It is therefore evident that the major revisions offered here concern the form and chronology of the (two) Romanesque phases and
the dates of the Gothic rebuilding. With respect to the former, a
modest plan more typical of the period is proposed for the first
eleventh-century church with a (partial?) rebuilding dated late in the
second quarter rather than in the first quarter of the twelfth century.
With regard to the latter, redating affects both ends, with work starting a decade or two earlier than previously considered (1180/90 versus 1200), and completed much earlier in the thirteenth century,
certainly a decade before the middle of the century (1240 versus
1280 or later). The fourteenth-century date for the construction of
the major transept vaults has not been hitherto recognized; nor has
the possibility of an earlier phase for the Lady chapel been considered.

As a result, the position of Rochester in the development of the
Romanesque and Gothic in Britain is slightly altered. Previously,
Rochester was considered to have been the earliest church in England to have had a long straight-ended choir, one possibly with a
small projecting east chapel. With the elimination of that reconstruction, whether dated to the late eleventh century or the early
twelfth, Rochester no longer plays a role in the development of the
straight east end in English Romanesque. In other respects it remains of considerable interest: one of the few crypts not in the
context of an ambulatory and radiating chapel plan; one of a small
number of early churches with solid side walls rather than an arcade
to the presbytery; one of the more spectacular displays of the late
Romanesque tendency to indulge in a variety of pier designs. The
early Gothic rebuilding remains of interest for its unique aisleless
presbytery, as an early example of the double east transept plan, and
for its inclusion of a vast crypt, one of the latest, if not the last, in
Britain.

The later work in the building, more fragmentary in nature, although not without an impact on the perception of the whole, is
typical of similar exercises in maintenance and modernization at
other cathedral and abbey churches. The vaulting of the major transept and the construction of the belfry in the fourteenth completed

the work of the previous century after a hiatus of a hundred years; the insertion of tracery in various windows during the fourteenth and fifteenth centuries was, in contrast, less a desirable 'necessity' than a matter of cosmetics and fashion. The fifteenth century saw two major projects: the rebuilding of the nave clerestory and roof, and the insertion of the west window: were they a matter of maintenance or fashion? Whatever the reason, the results were standard rather than being in any way exceptional, their very ordinariness compounding the lamentable loss of the Romanesque design of the clerestory, not to mention the centre of the west façade. As to the sixteenth century, on the other hand, the construction of the Lady chapel, if it had been completed, would have produced one of the most charming and attractive of such Perpendicular chapels.

The Pre-Conquest Church

Historical Précis: Personages and Events

The diocese of Rochester,[1] which was later to be the smallest and poorest of the medieval English dioceses, had the honour of being the first established after Canterbury, although, admittedly, it was an honour shared with London. In 604, (Saint) Augustine, archbishop (597–604) of Canterbury, consecrated Mellitus bishop (604–19) of London and Justus bishop (604–24) of Rochester – Dorubrevis (Durobrivae) or Hrofaescaestrae – in the kingdom of Aethelberht (560–616) of Kent.[2] Rochester, on the banks of the river Medway, is only twenty-four miles from Canterbury. It was in an area – West Kent – that perhaps had not long been under the authority of the royal house of Aethelberht and which then may have also included Surrey.[3] From the late seventh century, the kingdom of Kent came increasingly under the domination of the Mercian kings, then the kings of Wessex, finally becoming part of the kingdom of Wessex in 827.[4]

The land apparently granted by Aethelberht to the new church at Rochester comprised approximately the southern half of the roughly twenty-three and a half acres enclosed by the Roman walls that may date from the early third century. This suggests that, at the time the cathedral was founded, the city was virtually abandoned, its population much reduced ever since the mid-fifth century. A Saxon cemetery dating to the fifth or sixth century, which has been found southeast of the city, is evidence for some modest continued habitation. The establishment of the see probably contributed to the revival of the fortunes of the city, although nothing is known about it except for traces of Saxon cemeteries dating to the seventh and, possibly, eighth centuries.[5]

For the years between its founding and the conquest of England by William, Duke of Normandy (1035–87), the surviving documents are mainly charters concerned with (royal) grants of land during the period 734 to 1012. With respect to the vicious Danish raids of the ninth and tenth centuries, to which Kent in general and Rochester upon the broad Medway in particular were vulnerable, there are no specific indications of their impact. The Danish siege of Rochester in 885, when the city was relieved by King Alfred (871–88), had followed an earlier slaughter of its inhabitants in 842 (when London suffered similarly). Renewed attacks on Kent began again in 980 and became frequent between 991 and 1016: Rochester endured a second Danish siege in 999. The Danes were not the only menace, for the Mercians had ravaged Kent and destroyed the city in 676, causing the then bishop, Putta (669–76), to abandon his diocese (he was translated to Hereford, 676–88). There were further invasions by the kings of Wessex in 686–7. Even as late as 986, King Aethelred II (978–1016) of Wessex is recorded in the 'Anglo-Saxon Chronicle' as having laid waste the diocese of Rochester. Yet there is no contemporary testimony as to how the cathedral fabric was affected. The city and its major buildings surely must have suffered some damage on these various unfortunate occasions.

There is equally scant evidence regarding the nature of the cathedral community between its foundation and 1076/7 when, just before the appointment of the first Norman bishops (Arnost and Gundulf) and the subsequent establishment of a monastic chapter, there were only four or five canons. It was unlikely ever at any time to have been monastic, although some of the bishops may have been monks, especially during the late tenth and early eleventh centuries.[6] A charter of 803 was witnessed by five priests and a deacon of Rochester, as well as the bishop, Waermund (781/5–803/4);[7] another of 889 was witnessed by the bishop (Swithwulf, 868/80–893/6), and an ealdorman, a minister, three priests, an archdeacon, and a deacon, all most likely members of the Rochester community.[8] Equally little is known about the relations between Rochester and Canterbury before the Conquest, although it is significant that at the time of the Domesday survey the value of the estates held by the archbishop in West Kent exceeded those of the bishop in his own diocese.

The Documentary Evidence

Documentary references to a pre-Conquest church at Rochester are few and, as is often the case with early sources, are not specific about the plan, size, date of construction, or the various possible alterations or rebuildings that might have occurred over a period of more than 450 years. The earliest reference is provided by Bede (ca. 673–735) in his 'History of the English People.' In that work, he mentioned that a church at Rochester was built by King Aethelberht of Kent and dedicated to Saint Andrew: 'Augustine consecrated Justus in Kent itself, in the city of Dorubrevis ... and in it King Aethelberht built the church of the apostle St. Andrew.'[9] Bede repeated the same information when he recounted the burial of Paulinus, the third bishop (625–44): 'Paulinus ... was buried in the sanctuary ['secre-tarium'] of the church of the blessed apostle Andrew, which King Aethelberht had built from its foundations at Rochester [in the same city of Hrof].'[10] It has been considered that Bede's statement that Aethelberht built the church from the foundations ('a fundamentis') implied a stone, not a wooden, building.[11] The 'Liber Temporalium' describes the donations of King Aethelberht, comprising the south-eastern part of the Roman city, to his church at Rochester in the time of the first bishop, (Saint) Justus: 'In this church of Roffa the holy Justus sat as first bishop, and he ordained priests to serve God in it, for the sustenance of which priests king Aethelberht gave a piece of land which he called Priestfield, to the end that the priests serving God might have and hold it forever. He also endowed the church with Doddyngherne, and with the land from the Medway to the east gate of the city of Roffa on the south part, and with other lands without the city wall towards the north part.'[12] If authentic, the earliest and only surviving charter from this period (and before 734), dated 28 April 604, records an additional grant of land at Southgate, the southwestern quarter of the city, to St Andrew's at Rochester, in the name of Aethelberht.[13]

It has been assumed that Aethelberht's building survived until the Conquest,[14] although it is likely that the early church at Rochester was at least damaged, if not destroyed, during the numerous periods of turbulence between 604 and 1066. For instance, Aethelberht's building may have suffered when Rochester and Kent were laid waste by Aethelred, king (675–704) of the Mercians, in 676.[15] Further dam-age or destruction would not be surprising during the chaotic years of the ninth and tenth centuries, or even as a result of the siege of

Rochester by Aethelred II, the Redeless, in 986.[16] Yet no record of any later building or rebuilding exists. Nonetheless, that the earliest church survived intact and unaltered may be doubted.

The Archaeological Evidence and Its Interpretation

Remains of a building that have been identified with Aethelberht's construction were brought to light in 1888, during the course of work underpinning the existing west front (see figs. 1, 3).[17] Some additional facts were obtained by excavation and probing a few years later, in 1894.[18] The curve of an apse was traced east and west of the west wall of the present building's north aisle (its location has been marked on the floor of the cathedral). Not a regular semicircle in plan, it measured twenty-four feet six inches (7.4676 m) wide, with a depth of nineteen feet (5.7912 m).[19] A sleeper wall apparently existed across the chord of the apse. Traces of the beginning of a nave were also found, suggesting a width for it of twenty-eight feet six inches (8.6868 m); it may have been forty-two feet (12.8016 m) in length. The foundations, four feet (1.2192 m) thick and about four feet six inches (1.3716 m) deep, were composed of concrete with an aggregate of small pebbles and Kentish rag. The walls, about two feet four inches (0.7112 m) thick, but preserved to a maximum height of one foot eight inches (0.5080 m) only at one point, were constructed of tufa, Kentish rag, and reused Roman brick.[20] The axis of the building inclined much more to the northeast than that of the existing cathedral, which is oriented to the southeast.

The identification of the building as a church was partly based on the presence of Anglo-Saxon graves, with the same orientation, located to the east and south of the structure.[21] The attribution of these remains to a church of the early seventh century has also been generally accepted because of the similarity of the basic forms – apse, sleeper chord wall, and wide nave – to those of the other, presumably early, churches of Canterbury and elsewhere in Kent,[22] some of which are also characterized by the reuse of Roman material. St Pancras, Canterbury,[23] and the churches at Lyminge[24] and Reculver,[25] where apses or traces of apses survive, afford the closest parallels, the latter two additionally suggesting that the sleeper wall may have supported a triple arcade.[26]

That this small apsidal building alone served as the cathedral and parish church of Rochester until the Conquest has been doubted. W.H.St.J. Hope (1854–1919) pointed out that the apsidal structure uncovered in 1888 appeared rather insufficiently large – he calculated it could have held only 250 persons kneeling – for its dual function.[27] Consequently, although no other church than the cathedral is mentioned as being in Rochester during these centuries,[28] he suggested that foundations discovered outside the south aisle wall of the present building in 1876, when that wall was being underpinned, belonged to a second, larger church. Part of what was thought to be the curve of an apse and a wall a short distance to its west had been encountered at that time, along with remains of a floor of red *opus signinum* both east and west of (within) the purported curved wall (figs. 1, 13, 16).[29] They were uncovered by J.T. Irvine (1825–1900), who was supervising the work under the direction of Sir G.G. Scott (1811–78), during the restoration of 1871–8.[30] According to Irvine, there was no evidence of other walls further east or west. Hope's interpretation was much more positive than can be justified by Irvine's description of what was found; the eastern piece of masonry was so badly decayed that Irvine was actually most uncertain if it formed part of the curve of an apse or not.[31] By contrast, the fragmentary curve shown by Hope in his plan implies an arc greater than the total width of the adjacent Romanesque nave.[32]

Beyond recording the two walls on his plan, Hope did not speculate about the specifics of the plan or exact size of his candidate for a second larger cathedral church. Since the distance between the putative curved wall and the wall west of it, as shown by Hope, is a distance equal only to two bays – bays five to seven – of the existing aisle wall (to which the fragmentary western wall was perpendicular), it is much shorter than the length ascribed even to Aethelberht's purported church; presumably, Hope considered this to be the apse of a building similar in plan to the smaller apsidal structure to the northwest. Unfortunately, Hope did not consider the possible significance of the *opus signinum* floors found east of the east fragment as well as west of it (where it was covered by black wood ash), and Irvine did not provide any additional observations about the possible chronological relation between these as well as to the west fragment. The possibility that the floors and either segment of wall may belong to some Roman building cannot be ruled out.[33]

Aside from the discrepancies in the recording and interpretation of the fragmentary walls, it may be doubted on other grounds whether these remains belonged to a Saxon church. An attempt in the 1930s to recover these remains found no trace of the apse, and only a short length of what might have been the wall that was supposedly west of it.[34] Until further evidence is forthcoming, then, Hope's suggestion must be set aside.[35]

It must also be admitted that there is no secure evidence on which to base the identification of the remains of the apsidal building at the west end of the north nave aisle as those of the early cathedral. Bede informs us that the ninth bishop, Tobias (693–726), was buried in 'the chapel [porticus] of St. Paul the Apostle which he had built within the church of St. Andrew as his own burial place.'[36] Curiously, Hope interpreted *porticus* as an axial *apse*, rather than in its now accepted sense as a lateral rectangular chamber. Furthermore, he identified the 'porticu sancti Pauli apostoli' as the *eastern* apse of a church that also had a western one. It was in the western apse that he thought the high altar of Saint Andrew and the tombs of the sainted third and fourth bishops, Paulinus and Ithamar (644–55), were placed.[37] In postulating the early church at Rochester as double apsed, he had the church at Lyminge, rather than the Saxon cathedral at Canterbury, in mind as a model.[38] In any case, at this time, the apse would have been reserved for the clergy, the altar, therefore, standing west of the chord of the apse, with burials preferably outside the church or in a porticus.[39]

A comparison with Lyminge and Reculver might suggest that the extension of the curve of the apse beyond the semicircular at Rochester implied the existence of a porticus at the junction of nave and apse, since it could be argued that the apses at the former buildings were stilted because they were overlapped by porticus, one on the north at Lyminge, one on each side at Reculver. However, as the porticus at both churches may well have been later additions,[40] the stilting of their apses cannot be taken as an intentional accommodation for porticus, and, consequently, the shape of the apse at Rochester cannot be taken as an argument for the existence of a porticus of which the foundations have not survived or have not been located. In any case, as Tobias added his porticus in the early eighth century, the shape of the apse cannot have any significance, unless it is assumed that the early builders were being very far-sighted.

Nevertheless, the southwest angle of a rubble wall with shallow foundations, overlaid by some of the 'Anglo-Saxon' burials, *was* found nine feet (2.7432 m) from the line of the supposed (south) nave wall (due west of the existing west portal's south jamb) and perpendicular to it (fig. 3).[41] It could have formed the angle of a porticus, nineteen by seventeen feet (5.7912 x 5.1816 m) externally,[42] overlapping the apse, but the graves discovered overlying it imply that it had but a short life, even if it could or should be considered as a later addition to the apsidal structure.

Alternatively, in light of the excavated remains of the apse, it could be presumed that the porticus in which Tobias had been buried opened off the nave as at St Pancras, Canterbury, rather than overlapping the apse and nave as at Lyminge and Reculver. Yet no evidence of a porticus in this location was recognized during the later nineteenth-century investigation, despite a deliberate search for it.[43]

Since there is no evidence of the porticus in which Bishop Tobias was buried, these remains, then, cannot be identified as belonging to the early cathedral with any certainty. Indeed, the apparent lack of porticus – the one documented feature – would argue strongly against it.[44] An additional complication in accepting the apsidal structure as the remains of the early cathedral is the fact that an unspecified number of 'bodies' was found near the sleeper wall, which seemed to have been cut away to accommodate them.[45] As there was apparently no evidence that the burials were of significant individuals, that is, saintly bishops, the presence and location of these bodies also suggest that the building may not have been the cathedral.[46] Indeed, their presence suggests the possibility that the building may already have been disused or a ruin at the time the burials were made.[47]

More recently, a much larger and later structure has been proposed by C.A.R. Radford (1900–98) as the cathedral church, on the basis of even slighter evidence.[48] Short lengths of two walls meeting at an oblique angle, uncovered north and east of the existing north-west crossing pier, have most improbably been identified as belonging to a large late-tenth-century building.[49] Only four feet eight inches (1.4224 m), with a maximum revealed width of one foot ten inches (0.5588 m), of the wall running north–south were uncovered: it rose to a maximum preserved height of one foot (0.3048 m) above an offset four and one half inches (11.43 cm) wide representing the top of the foundation that was excavated to a depth of one foot (0.3048 m) only (fig. 4). The north face of the foundation was traced eastwards for a length of four feet (1.2192 m) before it broke off. The L-plan wall was identified as late Anglo-Saxon by Radford because 'it was embedded in a chalk foundation of c. 1100.'[50] The east–west section was interpreted as the 'north side of [a] ... crossing,' the north–south stretch as the west wall of a transept 'irregularly set out,' and narrower than the 'crossing':[51] the basis for either conclusion is not self-evident from the remains, which could just as well have formed an exterior angle, or even an interior angle between two walls unrelated to a crossing or transept. If taken as solid walls they would seem to be incompatible with the idea of a crossing or a nave with aisles.[52]

Radford's association of the L-plan fragment of wall and foundation with a cruciform building 'probably with an aisled nave,' crossing, 'small transepts' (i.e., narrower than the crossing but sixteen feet [4.8768 m] square], and an eastern arm 'of about the same size' appears to derive from his observation that the 'nave and quire of the 12th century were of the same width, but about four feet (1.2192 m) narrower than the central crossing.'[53] He therefore concluded that these peculiarities of the Romanesque church were possibly based on a late Saxon structure, as in the case of Sherborne Abbey (Dorset), where, following A.W. Clapham (1883–1950), he dated the pre-1066 core to circa 1000. This phase of Sherborne Cathedral, as it then was, is now dated to a rebuilding between 1045 and 1058, its eastern 'crossing' of the so-called salient type in which the four arms of nave, 'transepts,' and chancel were slightly narrower than the crossing.[54] The type is better and more concretely exemplified in the church of St Mary at Stow (Lincolnshire), where the 'crossing' and 'transept arms' date no earlier than circa 1034 to 1049.[55] In other words, this type of plan, with a square central bay, in some instances surmounted by a tower, and four narrower radiating arms, is a late development in Anglo-Saxon architecture, one that continues into the 'Overlap.'[56] Consequently, even if Radford's observation about the relationship of the Romanesque nave and choir to the crossing is correct, to accept his conclusions based on the L-plan wall, in the light of our present knowledge of the evolution of Anglo-Saxon architecture, would mean postulating a large-scale rebuilding of the cathedral at Rochester sometime within two decades of the Conquest. Such a large-scale rebuilding at this period would seem most unlikely in view of the documented rebuilding of the cathedral that was undertaken within twenty years after the Conquest.[57]

As another parallel, Radford offered the church of St Botolph at Hadstock (Essex), which he dated to the late tenth or early eleventh century; it is now dated circa 1050–80.[58] This building had an *aisleless* nave with lower flanking 'wings' at its east end entered through wide arches (rebuilt); as the wings (north only surviving) form spaces segregated from the nave and separated from each other by the nave space, a true transept and crossing were *not* formed. Admittedly, the L-plan segment of wall at Rochester could have formed the south-western inner corner of a flanking north wing as at Hadstock, although a more appropriate comparison for Radford's purposes might have been the late-tenth/early-eleventh-century church of St Mary-in-Castro at Dover (Kent),[59] also with an aisleless nave, but with a tower over its east end (a cross wall and the east wall forming a square bay with the side walls) and with wings and chancel much narrower and lower than the nave. Although either of these churches might well constitute more plausible models, with regard to form as well as scale, for a hypothetical eleventh-century pre-Conquest building at Rochester, the L-shaped fragment of walling cannot be easily placed in that period.

The construction of the wall reportedly consisted of 'rubble built of flint and Kentish rag set in a hard brown mortar'; the composition of the foundation was not described. Aside from the apsidal structure, there are no other purported Saxon structures with which to compare it in this respect. G.M. Livett (1859–1951) described the mortar of the small bits of *in situ* 'Early-Norman' walling as 'a fine yellow sand mortar.'[60] A further problem is raised by Radford's statement that the floor level of this tenth-century structure was fifteen to sixteen inches (38.1–40.64 cm) below the modern pavement: Hope, earlier, had identified the level of the early Romanesque church ('Gundulph's church') as twenty inches (50.8 cm) below the present pavement in the crossing.[61] A building of this magnitude, therefore, cannot be accepted, even hypothetically, on the basis of such slight remains that were as poorly documented as any uncovered in the previous century.[62] Without further excavation, and in the absence of comparative material from elsewhere in the building, it is both rash and futile to speculate about the significance of this isolated segment of wall.[63]

Conclusions

Because of the lack of correspondence between the meagre remains partially excavated at the west end of the existing building and the single specific feature mentioned by Bede, it is decidedly incautious to accept the small apsidal structure as the cathedral building erected by King Aethelberht in 604. Possibly that structure served as a funerary or cemeterial chapel, but as conclusive evidence for its date and for that of the nearby burials was not brought forth, its function must remain in doubt. The remains of a second larger church, as identified by Hope, to the south of the existing nave, must also be discounted. And it seems that the masonry uncovered near the present northwest crossing pier is more likely to be associated with a Romanesque structure than, as in Radford's interpretation, a large Saxon one of the tenth century.[64]

It is therefore necessary to conclude that the location of the pre-Romanesque cathedral building has not been identified. It may be that it lay in the vicinity of the east end of the present building, possibly to one side or the other. If the new building had been begun alongside the old Anglo-Saxon cathedral, it would have allowed the latter (sufficiently repaired) to remain in use as a chapel – or possibly as the chapter house. Although the body of the third bishop, Paulinus, buried 'in secretario,' had been translated to an unspecified location in the new (Romanesque) cathedral, as early as circa 1088,[65] there is no reference to the translation of the body of Tobias, who seems to have been buried in a (or the) porticus of the (old) cathedral. If the cast end of the new building was to occupy the site of the old Saxon church, then the saints buried in it would have had to have been temporarily translated while awaiting final translation into their new home. However, there is no record of such a series of translations. Indeed, the sainted fourth bishop, Ithamar, was not translated until as late as 1128,[66] but there is no reference as to where he – or any of the other early bishops – was originally buried. Of course, if the old cathedral had been retained for use as a chapter house, Tobias's body could have continued to rest there for years after the translation of Paulinus, whose cult – it might be noted – was more venerable than that of Ithamar.[67] Unfortunately, when a new chapter house was built by Bishop Ernulf (1115–24),[68] whether or not it was on the site of the old cathedral, we hear of no translations; moreover, the chapter house was certainly begun and possibly finished four years before Ithamar's translation. Thus, it would seem that the little information available about the site of the burial and the translation of the relics of the early bishops does not help resolve the enigma of the location of the pre-Conquest cathedral church and the date of its final destruction: they remain problems yet to be solved.[69]

TWO

The Free-Standing Tower

Historical Précis

The earliest structure surviving above ground at Rochester may be the remains of a free-standing tower[1] that now bears the name of the second Norman bishop, Gundulf (1076/7–1108), the builder of the first Romanesque church.[2] It is located a short distance from the north choir aisle wall,[3] between the arms of the major and minor transepts of the early Gothic church (ca. 1180/90–ca. 1240), which obviously have been planned around it (fig. 1). The attribution of the tower to Gundulf appears to be 'modern,' for none of the medieval texts associates the tower with him: indeed, the association may only date from the early eighteenth century.[4] Certainly, by the mid-sixteenth century, the tower had not yet acquired his name, and even then, and for the next two centuries, it was referred to variously as the 'three-bell steeple' or the 'five bell tower.'[5]

The tower was a ruin from at least the end of the seventeenth century, its interior open to the sky until it was restored, roofed and furnished in the early 1920s.[6] A good deal of the interior surfaces of the walls were then relined in brick and two wooden floors were inserted. The interior of the tower is now covered with such heavy coats of (white) paint that it is difficult to ascertain some of its structural phases or original features with absolute certainty.[7]

The Physical Evidence

Exterior

The massive tower is bare of any architectural details, except for broad but shallow clasping angle buttresses, and two setbacks of the wall between them (fig. 21).[8] The upper setback is stronger than the lower, but neither are marked by a proper chamfer or any other moulding. The fabric of the tower is Kentish rag with a sparing use of ashlar for quoins as is best seen in the original northwest angle buttress.[9] Two large buttresses, with setbacks and chamfered ashlar quoins, were later added at the northeast angle.[10] A simple pier buttress has also been placed, possibly at a somewhat later date, against the south face of the original southeast angle buttress.

Owing to later alterations, the location of the original entrance to the tower is uncertain. Entrance is now made from the north choir aisle of the cathedral by way of a tunnel cut through rubble to a crude opening broken through the west end of the south wall (figs. 1, 22) or, from the exterior, through a much better made, wider opening at the east end of the north wall (figs. 21, 23), now appearing like a deep recess and containing a small modern doorway. The date of these two entrances is problematical. Brick arches (one pointed, one segmental) support the crude barrel vault of the opening broken through the south wall; its existence cannot be documented earlier than the late nineteenth century.[11] That in the north wall features flat jambs with quoins at the interior angles and a rebated jamb at the west exterior angle, yet it is covered by a brick vault of depressed curvature. A portal in this location was reportedly discovered in the late eighteenth century,[12] but its present form appears to be due to an enlargement and remodelling carried out in the late nineteenth century.[13] Another smaller opening has been forced through the west side above ground level; in recent times it was used as a coal shute, and is now blocked.[14]

The original windows are either blocked up or greatly altered. The most visible windows are the two on the north face (fig. 21): the lower (ground floor) window is a narrow slit with a (later) flat head of one block, its ashlar jambs chamfered; the wider upper (first floor) window has its original semicircular arch of rubble. The east window, now obscured from outside owing to recent construction,[15] has flint rubble jambs and also retains its original semicircular arch.

That the tower was somewhat higher than it is at present is indicated in an engraved view of 1781/3 published by F. Grose (ca. 1731–91).[16] It shows large pointed arches springing from corbels at the top of a windowless third stage. The corbels and arches were probably added in order to support a parapet or, more possibly, an upper chamber that probably served as a belfry.[17] These elements, constituting roughly the upper third of the tower's height, were demolished in the early nineteenth century.[18] The rubble fill now occupying a good deal of the space between the south wall of the tower and the wall of the north choir aisle, through which the south entrance tunnel has been cut, probably accumulated at that time.[19]

Interior

On the interior, the tower possesses neither vaults nor a newel-stair. The space is now divided into two major stages reflecting the original disposition. The ground stage has been further subdivided into two, in a fashion reflecting modern expediency rather than an ancient arrangement. A modern floor has been inserted at the level of the original first floor, for which the evidence is two deep pockets for joist ends, and a horizontal one for a wall plate, preserved at the south end of the east wall.[20] In the eighteenth century, traces of a second floor, approximately twenty-five feet (7.62 m) above the first, reportedly were visible.[21]

The three windows of the original ground stage are still preserved (in what is now the first floor or choir robing room): all were of single splay opening towards the interior. The north and east windows also display the imprint of the plank formwork for their arched heads, which are in the form of splayed barrel vaults. At some later period, an opening was broken through the middle of the south wall (fig. 22), presumably in order to form an entrance from floors that had been placed in the space (perhaps first in the fourteenth century) between the tower and the early-thirteenth-century north choir aisle wall; the worn steps, now giving the appearance of a stepped sill, are due to this function. At the upper level, the original first floor (now the second floor or choir practice room), there is a window – that visible from the exterior – in the north wall that is now glazed. There is no evidence of a window in the west wall, which is well preserved; in contrast, the east wall has been rebuilt from a level lower than the window sill in the north wall. The opening in the south wall (now partially glazed, and serving as a fire exit) has also been broken through at a later period, as an off-axis 'extension' of the lower opening (fig. 22).

It is at the original first-floor level, and now visible only from the interior of the tower, that another entrance is encountered. It is in the form of a straight-sided tunnel-like passageway, with a horizontal rather than a splayed vault, that pierced the west wall.[22] Clearly part of the initial construction, it is located at the south end of the wall; its outer end is now blocked by the east wall of the shallow chapel of the later Gothic transept. It could have formed an – or the only – original entrance way, as its threshold is at the original first-floor level. An exterior wooden staircase, of course, would have been needed to reach it.

The Problem of Its Function and Date

The purpose of the Rochester tower is not known and its date is uncertain: both aspects have been the subject of some debate. It has been considered as initially defensive in function, as part of the city walls, or as intended for use as a stronghold or treasury.[23] It has also been claimed that it served as a bell tower from the middle of the twelfth century.[24] Most recently it has been asserted that the tower was built in the mid-twelfth century as a bell tower,[25] thus severing any connection with the 'traditional' attribution of the tower to Gundulf.

Indeed, at an early stage in his research, W.H.St.J. Hope (1854–1919) queried if the tower had been built by Gundulf: 'What evidence is there that Gundulph built it at all? His castle-wall, his work in the nave, at Malling Abbcy, Town Malling Church & St. Leonard's Tower are all distinguished by a rude but most decided herring-bone work. This I do not find at all distinctly in the north campanile [sic]. Neither do I find the curious niches existing at Malling Abbey, Darent [sic] Church & St. Leonard's.'[26] But he was moving in the opposite direction, for at that time Hope was apparently considering whether the tower might not be pre-Gundulf in date. That it preceded Gundulf's church he was, at least, certain, 'or: why should windows have been put in on all four [sic: Hope incorrectly assumed that originally there was a window in the south side] sides.' Despite his later attribution of the tower to Gundulf, his querulous observation is still a strong argument for placing the tower earlier than the Romanesque church, and possibly even prior to Gundulf's arrival at Rochester.[27] Admittedly, Hope's query should have been formulated in reverse: if the tower postdates the Romanesque church, why was it placed so close to the north choir aisle wall, and to the east wall of the north arm of the transept, that it must have blocked much of the light reaching any windows in those walls? And why was it not aligned with the existing walls? The questions are similar even if it is considered that the tower was built by Gundulf instead of in the mid-twelfth century.[28] If it preceded the church, it could be asked why Gundulf in building the tower did not anticipate the effect of its location on the layout of the church *or*, alternatively, why he laid out his church so awkwardly close to the tower?

The uncomfortable proximity of the tower to the north choir aisle and, particularly, to the east wall of the north arm of the transept (fig. 1),[29] and its lack of alignment with these walls, argue strongly that the tower preceded the church; otherwise, if erected at a later date, that is, after the Romanesque church had been completed, it surely would, and could, have been located a few feet further north, so as not to block any north choir aisle windows, and could as well have been positioned further east, reflecting the presence of a fully formed transept chapel.[30] If built by Gundulf, its location suggests that either he did not have the erection of a new cathedral church in mind at the time the tower was constructed, or a curious lack of foresight on his part.

Of the Kentish buildings mentioned by Hope, none – with one exception – sheds much light on the date and function of the north tower. Indeed, the only feature held in common by these buildings is their bare, unarticulated, unornamented 'style' and the occasional and sporadic use of herringbone work. The latter cannot be taken as an indication of Gundulf's patronage as it is now recognized as a feature found in late Anglo-Saxon as well as post-Conquest buildings.[31] It may only serve as an indicator of an early date (i.e., the late eleventh century). The small patch of 'herringbone' work visible in the south aisle of the cathedral may not even belong to the Gundulfian building as, according to the notes of Irvine made at the time the aisle wall was underpinned in 1876, the typical Gundulfian foundations were partly missing in these bays.[32] The niches of the west front of Malling Abbey – Gundulf's church is now mostly destroyed – most likely belong not even to a mid-twelfth-century construction of the façade but to an eighteenth-century 'restoration.'[33]

Only the chancel of the small church of St Margaret at Darenth survives.[34] Covered by a groin vault, it lacks any architectural feature in common with the tower. On the exterior, the only ornamental motif is not niches (as implied by Hope) but a tiny scallop pattern that appears on the edge of the east window arches. Of the parish church at West Malling, only the tower remains, as is the case with a related building not mentioned by Hope, the parish church at Dartford. That of St Mary at West Malling is buttressed at the west angles, and rises sheer without any setbacks or string-courses.[35] It is essentially windowless except for large belfry openings on three sides (there is a pair of openings on the north; the south opening is larger than the west one). The tower at Holy Trinity, Dartford, which may originally have been detached, is divided into three stages by thin string-courses.[36] It possesses a newel-stair that, however, rises only to its second floor. Windows occur on three sides at the first-floor level and four at the second, all smaller than the belfry openings at St Mary, West Malling. Neither tower has any ornamental details.

The Rochester tower has been frequently compared to another Kentish building usually associated with Gundulf, despite a lack of documentation: St Leonard's Tower, just outside West Malling.[37] Although limited in extent, the architectural details of this tower are slightly richer than those of the others. Like the Rochester tower, there are broad but shallow pilaster buttresses at the angles, with, in this case, two chamfered setbacks (only the lower one is continuous). More notably, there are four shallow flat-backed niches on both the east and south faces; they are not pierced for windows. Significantly, a spiral-stair – a feature conspicuously lacking at Rochester – was located in the northwest angle.[38] The distribution of windows is quite different from the towers of the parish churches at West Malling and Dartford: there are three large windows at ground-stage level (one is lacking on the south face) and five at the first stage (two are found in the east face). These windows are also larger, more numerous, and somewhat differently distributed from those of the north tower at Rochester. Internally, they have stepped sills.

There is, however, one specific feature that links St Leonard's Tower with Rochester's. At St Leonard's, there is a similar tunnel-vaulted passageway piercing the east wall that appears to have been the only entrance. Now blocked on the exterior, it was situated on the side of the tower built above a rock ledge, so it too must have been approached by a flight of wooden stairs. Such tunnel-like first-floor entrances approached by exterior wooden staircases are characteristic of castle construction of the late-eleventh and early-twelfth centuries: such for example was the case at the White Tower in London (firmly associated with Gundulf, who, if not the 'architect,' was 'principal overseer'),[39] and the castles at Colchester (probably by

1086) and later at Rochester (soon after 1126).[40] There is no evidence that St Leonard's Tower was ever used as a bell tower, although a small chapel seems to have been built near it in the later twelfth century. The nature of their entrances makes it most likely that both towers were built as small keeps.[41] Unfortunately, there is no way of precisely dating St Leonard's Tower, for the association of the tower with Gundulf is modern.

Conclusions

The possible, even likely, absence of any ground-level entrance and the provision for access by an external wooden staircase may well argue for its initial function as a defensive stronghold. The austerity of the basic form – the absence of any standard decorative motifs associated with the Romanesque style – as well as the lack of an internal newel-stair,[42] and even, possibly, the omission of a stone vault, suggest the tower could be very early post-Conquest in date: it is difficult to accept a date even as late as circa 1100,[43] let alone 1150 as has been proposed.[44] The only conventional Romanesque and non-Anglo-Saxon feature is the clasping angle buttresses.

An early post-Conquest, pre-Gundulf, date for the tower means that the builders of the Romanesque cathedral were presented with a *fait accompli* around which they had to work, and explains the awkward relationship of the tower to the church. If it was built after the east end of Gundulf's church was completed, or as late as circa 1150, its awkward proximity to the church is unexplained and difficult to understand.

The history and form of the tower may be reconstructed as follows. Sometime in the uncertain decade preceding Gundulf's appointment as bishop a tower was built in order to serve as a small keep. It was of two stages with clasping angle buttresses as its only feature in addition to two slight setbacks. Small windows, splayed internally, were placed in the middle of the east, north, and west walls of the ground floor stage. At first-floor level, windows were located only in the east and north sides, with the entrance approached by a wood staircase at the south end of the west wall. Internally, it was subdivided by a wooden floor and served by a wooden staircase.

The tower was probably converted or adapted for use as a bell tower in the second quarter of the thirteenth century when the reconstruction of the Romanesque church had progressed as far as the major transept. At that time, the remodelling of the crossing piers made it expeditious to dismantle the Romanesque crossing tower. Indeed, the bells may have been removed even earlier, once work on the new transept had begun. As a result, the north tower was increased in height by the addition of one stage, that windowless stage (depicted in Grose's engraving of 1781/3) provided with a floor and an external arched corbel table and, very likely, a wooden bell chamber above.[45] Because the construction of the new transept blocked the entrance to the tower, a new entrance was made at ground level at the east end of the north wall. It was about the time of the conversion of the tower to serve as a belfry that the buttresss were added at the northeast angle: perhaps the additional weight aggravated or revealed an existing weakness in the structure at that point.

As a new belfry was not constructed over the thirteenth-century crossing until the mid-fourteenth century, these temporary measures saw long service. Even with the completion and hanging of four new bells in the central tower, it appears three bells remained in the north tower until the late middle ages.[46]

THREE

The Late-Eleventh-Century Romanesque Building

Historical Précis: Personages and Events[1]

Somewhat exceptionally, after the Conquest, the last Saxon bishop, Siward, was allowed to retain his office until his death in 1072/4. His successor, Arnost, a monk of Bec and prior of Saint-Étienne at Caen, died a few months after his appointment (1075). Gundulf (ca. 1023–1108), also a monk of Bec who had served at Saint-Étienne, was subsequently appointed in 1076.[2] He was a close friend of the Lombard, Lanfranc, archbishop of Canterbury (1070–89), himself formerly of Bec and former abbot of Saint-Étienne, and also of (Saint) Anselm of Aosta, abbot of Bec and later archbishop of Canterbury (1093–1109). Over fifty at the time of his appointment, Gundulf served his diocese, two archbishops, and three kings energetically for the next thirty years. He acted as a mediator in the revolt against King William II Rufus (1087–1100) in 1088, and actively supported Archbishop Anselm, who twice was forced to flee into exile as a result of disputes with William Rufus (over church synods and reform, 1087–1100) and King Henry I (1100–35) (regarding lay investiture, 1103–6). In addition to his diplomatic skills, it is also attested that Gundulf was unusually skilled in building.[3] He was requested by King William I to build a keep at London,[4] and later by William Rufus to erect the fortifications at Rochester.[5] The exact nature of his role, especially with regard to the former construction, is far from clear, and it has been suggested that his position may have been that of an efficient administrator rather than that of 'architect' or master builder.[6] In contrast to the great keep ('White Tower') at London, Gundulf's castle at Rochester probably consisted of no more than a walled enclosure of stone with a ditch on three sides and perhaps one mural tower and a gate tower.[7] It most likely replaced one of the motte and bailey type, with timber palisades and a wooden tower built soon after the 1066 conquest.[8]

By 1083 Lanfranc and Gundulf had determined to establish a monastic community at Rochester. This was a highly unusual decision, for monastic chapters at cathedrals had no continental parallels, although at the time of the Conquest they existed in England at Canterbury, Winchester, and Worcester.[9] The establishment of a chapter at Rochester parallels the similar act at Durham,[10] and both were then followed by many others during the next decades. The original foundation is supposed to have been for twenty-two monks. As no customary for Rochester survives, it is presumed that Rochester followed the customary created by Lanfranc for his monks.[11] This was a version of the rule of Saint Benedict similar to that practised at the great French abbey of Cluny. The first prior was Ernulf (later to be bishop, after being prior of Canterbury, 1096–1107, and abbot of Peterborough, 1107–14), and the second Ralph, who also had been a monk at Saint-Étienne, Caen (and who in 1107 became abbot of Battle).[12]

The major historical events within the proximity of Rochester, subsequent to the speedy conquest of Kent by the Duke of Normandy, were the conflicts of Odo (1030/5–97), bishop of Bayeux and earl of Kent, with his half-brother, the new king, William I, and subsequently with his nephew, William II. William I arrested and imprisoned Odo in 1082, for reasons not entirely clear. In 1087, Odo initiated a revolt against the newly crowned William Rufus in support of the claims of his older brother Robert Curthose, Duke of Normandy (1087–1106; d. 1134).[13] It is now difficult to assess to what extent the activities of the earl of Kent affected the construction of the cathedral that was begun during these turbulent years. William Rufus did, however, restore to Rochester the manor of Lambeth, and bestowed the church of St Mary of Lambeth, in order to compensate for the damage *he* caused to the cathedral during Odo's rebellion in 1088.[14] The decade of the 1090s was rather quieter in Kent as the cathedral advanced towards completion.

The Documentary Evidence

William of Malmesbury (ca. 1080–ca. 1143), writing sixty years or so after the event, in his 'Gesta Pontificum Anglorum,' circa 1125, described the church at Rochester at the time of the death of its last Anglo-Saxon bishop, Siward, as 'utterly forsaken, miserable, and waste, from lack of all things within and without.'[15] The 'Textus Roffensis,' in the main, generally dated to circa 1122/3, informs us that during his long episcopate, Gundulf 'built entirely anew, as it appears today, the church of St. Andrew, which was almost ruined by age.'[16] Construction of the new cathedral, however, may not have begun immediately. Indeed, it probably was not actually started until as late as 1082/3,[17] at which time Lanfranc introduced the twenty-two monks in place of the secular canons that, at Gundulf's arrival, were only about five in number.[18] Although the archbishop had been able to regain most of the property formerly alienated from the see in 1076,[19] and the next year even returned some of the income to Rochester in order to help re-establish its fortunes, other property regained in 1076 was not returned until 1083. At the latter date Lanfranc also made additional gifts of his own land and others he had newly purchased. Gundulf had also apparently acquired property between 1077 and 1083. Thus, it would appear that it was only by 1083 that the cathedral's finances were sufficiently re-established on a predictable and secure footing that would justify the considerable undertaking of replacing the small and no doubt shabby Saxon church with a new much larger Romanesque one.

The Standing Physical Evidence

Very little of the first post-Conquest building as initiated by Bishop Gundulf is visible today, although much has been written about it. Of the early Romanesque church, the only obviously recognizable part that has survived later reconstruction is the crypt (fig. 24), although it is not complete (and at present is not completely accessible).[20] Still visible are the two western bays of a crypt that once extended at least one bay further east. They are divided into a nave (twenty-six feet nine inches [8.1534 m] wide) and aisles (ten feet nine inches [3.2766 m] wide) by thick walls, with plain arched openings (five feet six inches [1.6764 m] wide) allowing lateral communication. The nave retains six bays of original groin vaulting (with elliptical curves to the groins), supported on two slender monolithic columns, and coursed, half-column wall responds (fig. 24). On each side at the east, the capital only of one more wall respond can be seen imbedded in the Gothic masonry (fig. 25), implying that there was at least one more pair of free-standing columns.

The profile of the base mouldings consists of a torus above a quarter curve.[21] The capitals are neither conventional volute nor cushion/scallop, but are a more primitive cushion type with a straight-sided abacus above.[22] One capital, in the southwest corner, is an upside-down base. In the aisles, the responds are flat pilasters with quirked and chamfered imposts. The stone of the capitals, bases, and monolithic shafts has been identified as Barnack limestone from Northamptonshire, but is more likely Marquise limestone from near Boulogne (Pas-de-Calais); the bulk of the construction, including the coursed wall responds and the aisle pilasters, is of tufa.[23]

Entrance to the crypt was by stairways situated in the presbytery aisles: a blocked doorway at the west end of the north aisle of the crypt is still visible (fig. 26). Two of the original windows, although altered, remain on the north (figs. 27, 28),[24] and one – later enlarged to a doorway – on the south. The east edge of an external flat pilaster buttress is also visible on the south, to the west of the former window.

One other probable feature of the early church is simultaneously visible and invisible. The solid side walls of the existing choir, covered by Gothic arcades on their inner sides and plaster on their aisle faces, are generally considered to be survivals from the presbytery of the church erected by Gundulf. Their fabric has never actually been investigated.

The Archaeological Evidence

At various times in the nineteenth century, buried parts of the structure were uncovered or otherwise investigated. The motivation for most of these incursions was the necessity of repairs rather than mere curiosity or even the desire for knowledge as a result of methodical archaeological investigation. Consequently, some additional information supplementing the paltry remains visible above ground has been acquired about the crypt, the presbytery, the foundations of the nave aisle walls, and the west front. Not all of the discoveries were well documented and the interpretations of some of the results can be questioned.

As a result of boring carried out by A. Ashpitel (1807–69) in 1853,[25] the supposed eastern limit of the crypt, in the form of 'foundations of a huge rubble wall ... upwards of eight feet [2.4384 m] thick,' reportedly was found at a distance east of the surviving portion of the crypt, which suggested a total original length for it of four bays and that it ended in a straight east wall. In 1881, W.H.St.J. Hope

(1854–1919) conducted further investigations and claimed to have discovered a projecting rectangular chapel, nine feet [2.7432 m] wide by six feet six inches [1.9812 m] long, to the east. He also confirmed the wall discovered earlier by Ashpitel, but determined that it had extended across the aisles as well (fig. 5).[26]

The floor of the eleventh-century presbytery was supposedly found in 1872 when a tunnel for the wind trunks of the organ bellows was made under the supervision of J.T. Irvine (1825–1900).[27] Of plaster on mortar, it was a *sloping* surface five feet four inches [1.6256 m] (at the east) to six feet seven inches [2.0066 m] (at the west) below the present choir floor (therefore, one foot eight inches [0.5080 m] below the floor of the present crossing). There were two single six-inch [15.24 cm] steps at widely spaced intervals. At the east, the floor butted up against the west face of the crypt's west wall, thus indicating that the eastern half of the presbytery had a raised floor.[28] When the northwest exit from the crypt was investigated, it was seen that the descending stair was deflected to the north, apparently in order to allow for the placement of an ascending stair in the aisle rising to a level over the crypt.[29]

In the area of the crossing, a section of wall running east–west was uncovered in 1968, a short distance to the east of the present north-west crossing pier (fig. 4).[30] C.A.R. Radford (1900–98), identified it as 'a chalk foundation of c. 1100.' Also described as 'a sleeper wall of chalk blocks,' approximately two feet (0.6096 m) only of its north face were preserved. In addition, an L-shaped section of another wall, embedded in the chalk foundation, which Radford dated to the late tenth century, might also be reconsidered as a possible product of the late eleventh or early twelfth century.[31] Only the east and north faces were uncovered; the north-south arm was traced for four feet eight inches (1.4224 m), while the east–west arm broke off after four feet (1.2192 m) from the angle. It was constructed of flint rubble and Kentish rag set in a hard brown mortar; less than a foot (0.3048 m) of walling remained above the top of its foundation, the two distinguished by a setback of four and one-half inches (10.16 cm).

The process of underpinning the nave aisle walls in 1875–6, also supervised by Irvine, produced evidence of the foundations of the church associated with Gundulf.[32] As described and published by G.M. Livett (1859–1951), they apparently belonged to two different campaigns of construction, with an unaligned break on either side of the nave: in the south aisle wall, at the end of the penultimate bay;

and after three bays in the north aisle.[33] To the east of these 'breaks,'
the foundation trenches – best preserved on the north side – had
been filled first with a foot-deep [0.3048 m] layer of dry gravel, then
by two and a half feet [0.7620 m] of chalk; a footing of two courses of
Kentish ragstone eleven inches [27.94 cm] high followed (fig. 14).[34]
On the south side (figs. 15, 16), only a fragment of the footing course
remained at the east, and no trace of the original aisle wall.[35] On the
north (fig. 17), the eleventh-century wall was preserved in the three
eastern bays for a height of three feet [0.9144 m], with the lower
parts of three buttresses that projected about six inches [15.24 cm].[36]
They were cut off by the plinths of the (later) buttresses now visible
on the exterior of the wall in these bays.[37] In addition, a drawing of
Irvine, which does not seem to have been known to Livett or Hope,
of the fifth bay from the east (fourth bay from the west) records
Gundulfian gravel and chalk foundations in that bay.[38] In this connection, a reported observation by D.A. Alexander (1768–1846) in
1802, when work on the middle bays of the north aisle wall was
being carried out, is of particular interest. He found that the wall,
('only') six feet (1.8288 m) below the surface, was built 'on Chalk
and other loose uncemented rubble, on a stratum of loose ground' –
a description that seems to fit the foundations attributed to Gundulf's
phase of building.[39]

The foundations revealed (in 1888) under the western bays of the
aisle walls, as again reported by Livett, were of a rather different
character. In the western two-thirds of the southwest bay, instead of
a foot of gravel, there was a double layer of flints laid in and covered
by sand mixed with some lime; this was followed by four layers of
chalk and sand; the trench was greater in depth than in the case of
the so-called Gundulfian foundations of loose gravel and small chalk.[40]
The foundations in the west bay on the north side were found to be
slightly different: a bed of mortar three inches (7.62 cm) thick was
first laid down; then there followed five sequences of alternating
layers of flints and 'red sandy mould,' finishing with a layer of flints
and mortar on which the foundation footing of two courses of Kentish
rag was placed.[41] However, Irvine's description of the foundations in
the west bay of the north aisle differs considerably from Livett's:
Irvine recorded foundations, like those at the *east* end of the wall,
consisting of a foot (0.3048 m) of loose gravel followed by two feet
three inches (0.6858 m) of 'small chalk,' and differing only from
'Gundulph's' by the absence of a footing course of Kentish rag before

the wall proper began.[42] At the same time, Livett reported that loose chalk was found under the west respond of the south arcade, and that the foundations of the ('Early-Norman') north arcade remained and were later used to support the 'Later-Norman' respond.[43]

The underpinning of the west front in 1888 is notable for having revealed an earlier Romanesque one (fig. 3).[44] It was a simple west wall, with pilaster buttresses at the angles and in the line of the nave arcades. There was a single, central west portal of three orders. The west wall was plastered down to its footing on the interior and survived to a maximum height of two feet six inches [0.7620 m]. The foundations under the west front varied in some respects from those found further east in the west bays of the nave aisles. They consisted of alternating thin layers of mortar, flints, and 'mould' followed by two courses of Kentish rag.

Historiography

The several plans of the east end that have been restored over the crypt have been either rather eccentric, to say the least, or precocious, to say the most. Ashpitel reconstructed a plan (fig. 6) in which the western quarter of the presbytery was defined by solid side walls, followed by a single arcade and an aisleless, two-bay extension.[45] Thus, for unexplained reasons, only a quarter of the existing solid side walls of the choir – and that quarter the second from the east – was utilized in his restoration or dated to Gundulf's church. The presbytery aisles, only two bays in length, were straight-ended and, together with the open eastern bay of the presbytery, formed a rectangular ambulatory from which projected the aisleless flat-ended extension positioned over the eastern two and a half bays of the four-bay crypt. In his restored plan of the main level of the cathedral, Ashpitel showed four pairs of small columns in the area of the cross aisle and eastern extension that he labelled the choir; it is not clear if these are a reflection of the similar columns in the crypt or an intention to indicate a hall church arrangement at this level. The latter interpretation would seem to conflict with his identification of this space as the choir.

Hope also restored the presbytery with solid side walls, which, however – again for some unstated reason – were shown in his plan (fig. 7) only half as long as those still existing; they were continued eastwards by four arches corresponding to the bays of the crypt, for a total length equal to six bays (seventy-six feet [23.1648 m]).[46] There was a small projecting chapel at the east, internally nine feet [2.7432 m] square and two-thirds the height of the eastern elevation. He suggested that the chapel was designed to receive the relics of the third Saxon bishop, Saint Paulinus.[47]

The form of the eastern arm suggested by Hope for Gundulf's building, a long aisled presbytery, with solid walls in its western portion and a crypt under its longer eastern section, ending in a straight east wall across the entire width, was strongly challenged by F.H. Fairweather (d. 1950).[48] His main argument was that the rectangular termination was most unlikely in the late eleventh century and was more appropriate for the third quarter of the twelfth. He attempted to show that a plan normal in all respects for the late eleventh century – that is, an apse in echelon scheme with a short choir based on that of Christ Church, Canterbury – could fit on the site.[49] As a result, he dated the 'square east end' of the crypt to post-1137 and further hypothesized that the crypt may have been begun by Bishop Ernulf (1115–24) but was not completed until repairs following a fire in 1137 were carried out.[50] Indeed, according to Fairweather, even the solid side walls of the presbytery 'mostly' belong to this later period, since he thought that the relatively short walls of Gundulf's presbytery had been extended eastwards and refaced; even then, he considered the core of the north wall more likely to be eleventh-century than that of the south.[51]

Following the east arm, in his plan, Ashpitel had incorporated the so-called Gundulf's Tower as the north arm of a transept, balanced by a second identical tower on the south (fig. 6).[52] There was, consequently, a very narrow oblong 'crossing,' the eastern piers of which were in effect the solid side walls of the presbytery. Curiously, the west ends of the 'piers' were not aligned with the east walls of the transeptal towers.

Other aspects of the plan proposed by Hope (fig. 7) were similar to Ashpitel's insofar as he too accepted a narrow, rectangular, towerless 'crossing' that, however, he associated with transept arms only fourteen or fifteen feet [4.2672 or 4.572 m] wide; he admitted he knew of no parallel for such a narrow transept.[53] Hope also balanced Gundulf's tower by a smaller one on the south – an idea, it seems, he partly derived from Ashpitel;[54] its north and west walls, he claimed, had formed the choir's south aisle wall and the east wall of the south transept arm, respectively. A line of tufa quoins still visible above the west jamb of the existing (Gothic) portal from the south choir aisle to the cloister was considered by Hope to be the only above-ground remains of this south tower, representing a section of its east wall (fig. 76).

Fairweather also rejected Hope's restoration of an oblong crossing and narrow (or possibly low) transept-like extensions in favour of a more conventional solution.[55] By exhaustively demolishing Hope's somewhat curiously backward reasoning behind his attachment to the idea of a narrow, towerless crossing, Fairweather argued for a square crossing with transept arms shallower than the present Gothic ones and with an apsidal chapel in each.

There has been less disagreement about the form of the nave that followed, although it may be questioned if anything remains to be seen of it. In Ashpitel's plan (fig. 6), the 'transept' bay was followed by a nave of eleven bays, but he suggested no other details. Remaining from Gundulf's nave, Hope specifically enumerated: three bays of the nave north aisle wall, up to the first string-course, with the bases of three buttresses (one no longer visible); four and a half bays of the nave south aisle wall, to an uncertain height; and five bays of the south nave arcade as high as (but not including) the triforium passage (later altered by the addition of a new outer order on the nave side, and the recasing of the piers) (fig. 7).[56] According to Fairweather, the work remaining from the first Romanesque church consisted of a cut-down portion of the north choir aisle wall; the free-standing north tower; the foundations of the three east bays of the north nave aisle wall; the south nave aisle wall from the west wall of the (later) Lady chapel to just short of the southwest façade turret; and bays three to seven of the south nave arcade.[57] Both Hope's and Fairweather's conclusions were partly based on the observations of Irvine as reported by him and Livett.

The Hitherto Accepted Plan Re-examined

As is so often the case, attention has focused more on the form of the east end of the building than on the western limb. Ironically, although Hope's plan for the eastern arm has been generally accepted, his early date for the long straight-ended aisled presbytery and crypt has been rejected by some later writers. Except for Fairweather's, there has been no other alternative proposal regarding the form of the eastern termination of the eleventh-century church.

On the other hand, there has been little further discussion concerning the plausibility of an early date for the form Hope proposed and no examination of the 'logic' of the form whether early or late. Thus, regarding the form of its eastern arm, Guldulf's church has been placed in limbo. The area of the transept and Hope's notions about it have received even less attention. As to the nave, again Hope's thesis that it remained unfinished by Gundulf or that Gundulfian work is encased in later work has been subject to scant re-examination.

The interpretations outlined in the preceding section may be questioned in almost all respects, both with regard to forms as well as to dates. Hope's reconstruction of the plan of the crypt and the date he assigned to it, the basis for his presbytery, as well as Fairweather's late dating of the existing earliest part of the crypt, do not stand up under scrutiny. So too, the conclusions Irvine based on the foundations he uncovered in the area of the transept and nave aisles, and his observations about the nave arcade, may be challenged. This is all the more necessary because Irvine's sometimes peculiar notions were accepted by Livett and, especially, by Hope, and, as a consequence, by other later writers. Alternative solutions may be proposed on the basis of the same evidence supplemented by other information, observations, and comparisons. However, as a result, it will be seen that Fairweather's Gundulfian church, consisting of a solid-walled presbytery of two bays with an apsidal termination, flanked by aisles also ending in apses, a square crossing with transept arms, and an eight-bay nave, that is, his 'normal' plan with the exception of the apsidal chapels in the transept arms, perhaps comes closest to the probable solution for the first Romanesque church.

Crypt

Neither Ashpitel nor Hope has left any precise account of his investigations in the crypt, at what specific points and intervals the boring was conducted, and just exactly how it was performed. So it is impossible to be sure that they were not perhaps encountering sleeper walls or foundations for the Gothic piers. The form of the early crypt, as determined by the boring conducted by Ashpitel and then by Hope, may be questioned owing to the existence of other slightly more concrete evidence. There is a curious and possibly significant anomaly present at the juncture of the early work with the later Gothic 'extension.' At this point, there are no signs of Romanesque pilaster responds on the aisle sides of the remaining easternmost pair of piers (fig. 30), as there are on the piers at the west: the existing responds are Gothic from the ground up to their abaci, which are set at a higher level than the Romanesque respond imposts (fig. 29). Yet, the vault that springs from them is the original Romanesque groin vault of this bay. The absence of Romanesque responds at the east end of the aisles suggests that the aisles may originally have ended at this point in semicircular apses, rather than continuing with one or more bays with piers identical to those at the west. No proper excavations have ever been carried out at the junction between the Romanesque and the Gothic extension – and none at all in the aisles.[58] Thus, a more conventional form similar to that proposed by Fairweather – for other reasons – must still be considered a possibility.

Despite Hope's repeated claims that he carefully traced the outline of the foundations of the chapel projecting from the east end of the crypt (fig. 5), the exact nature and extent of Hope's excavation is not at all clear. Unfortunately, his investigations were not documented by plans or sections, let alone by photography.[59] The only specific description of what he found is contained in a letter to Irvine in which he stated: 'The walls sprang directly from the present floor line but a trench was previously cut which was first filled in with rubble flints & liquid mortar, but the latter is of the poorest quality' (fig. 18).[60] Curiously, the quality of the foundations was later upgraded by Hope when he characterized them as being 'somewhat better' than the earliest Norman foundations elsewhere, and described them as 'being composed of flint *and small chalk*, with some mortar, *and no gravel*, laid in dark earth with oyster shells in it' (emphasis added).[61] The absence of gravel and the presence of layers of flints and mortar were characteristic of the foundations of the first west front and the western bays of the north aisle (as reported by Livett), but chalk was not utilized in either of these two types of foundations. On the other hand, mortar is not reported as a constituent element of the earlier work as uncovered in the eastern bays of the nave aisles, or in the west bay of the south aisle.[62] Consequently, the foundations encountered by Hope in the crypt do not correspond to any of the nave foundations, whether identified as Gundulf's or 'Early-Norman' (in either case dated before 1100). The most that can be concluded, and that cautiously, is that they fall between the two groups in the nave, which, chronologically considered, would appear to be nonsense.[63]

Recently, in 1994, a very limited excavation in the crypt, which should have encountered the eastern limit of the foundations of the chapel, found no evidence of it. Evidence of Hope's trenching along the eastern axis of the crypt was encountered and the rubble and yellow mortar foundations of the early Gothic work were exposed.[64]

Fairweather's rejection of Hope's dates – rather than his form – resulted in an equally implausible and unacceptable solution, namely, a twelfth-century date for a long straight-ended crypt considered as the continuation of the existing (western) bays. In so doing, he argued that the entire east end, in the form proposed by Hope, straight-ended choir *and crypt*, as well as the (now vanished) crossing, transept, *and* the two eastern bays of the nave arcade, all belong to the twelfth century, the product of a rebuilding (mentioned above) begun by Ernulf but not completed until after a fire in 1137.[65] Aside from an unexplained gap of thirteen years when work either ceased or proceeded very slowly, his attribution of the surviving western bays of the crypt lying under the eastern half of the present choir to the period of Ernulf (and later) is stylistically impossible. These bays compare favourably in several of their details, notably the capitals, with the undercroft of the great dormitory erected at Christ Church, Canterbury, by Archbishop Lanfranc – a construction certainly of circa 1080.[66] The west bays of the Rochester crypt undoubtedly belong to the first Romanesque church.

Presbytery

The plan of the crypt, in all probability, would have determined the plan and elevation of the presbytery of which there is no surviving fabric except for the existing solid side walls – if the presumption that they date to this period is correct. Of course, precedents or parallels for this particular feature need not have included crypts in their structure. The peculiar aspect of the presbytery plan as restored by both Ashpitel and Hope is that neither author includes the full extent of the solid side walls as they exist at present in his restoration. In addition, in neither instance do the solid walls extend for the full length of the restored presbytery, although in both cases the proposed presbyteries are as long (Ashpitel) or longer (Hope) than the solid walls as they are today. In Ashpitel's plan (fig. 6), the short section of solid wall is succeeded by an open bay and then the (roughly) two-bay aisleless extension. The eastern cross aisle thus created did not form an ambulatory since Ashpitel placed the choir in the area east of the space enclosed by the solid walls (which may also have been occupied by two rows of four columns). In Hope's plan (fig. 7), the solid walls, pierced by doors and equal to three bays of the aisle, are followed by four arcaded bays ending against the east wall with its tiny projecting chapel; four additional altars are lined up against the east wall.

Other than whatever may be deduced from the supposed form of the crypt, there is no remaining evidence for the form of the presbytery at the main level. If there was a long, aisled, straight-ended presbytery, except for the solid side walls, it was totally swept way by the early Gothic rebuilding following a fire in 1179.

Transept

Hope's reconstructions, of either a narrow transept with tall narrow arches between the nave and the transept arms, as he thought more likely, or low extensions opening off aisles separated from the nave by a continuous arcade, are even more unusual than his proposals for the plan of the presbytery. His views about the form of the transept were greatly dependent upon the observations and opinions of Irvine who, in 1872, thought he had uncovered the foundations of the east and south walls of the south arm of the eleventh-century transept, and the footing of a supposed angle buttress below the line of a series of 'tufa quoin-stones' still visible slightly west of the axis of the present south transept façade (fig. 59).[67] Footings and tufa stones, even though the latter were thought to 'pertain to a later rebuild,' were taken as indicating the southwest angle of the early Romanesque transept arm, which, accordingly, would have been about two-thirds the width of the existing one.[68]

Either of Hope's proposals for the form of the transept are more problematic and, ultimately, even less likely than his proposals for the presbytery. Neither Hope nor Irvine before him seems to have considered that the footing and line of ashlar stones in the face of the south transept arm may have marked the junction of a west wall associated with the west range of the cloister against the transept.[69] Of the west range of the cloister, only the line of its east wall is now visible, with a squarish room at its south end that retains Romanesque angle responds for a ribbed vault.[70] After the Dissolution, the west range had been adopted to domestic needs (prebendary houses), and it may be that 'tenement,' then in the possession of one John Heath, which is described in the Parliamentary Survey of 1649 as consisting of 'a Kitchyn, a Woodhouse, a Cellar and Three upper roomes with a Garden butting upon the Library towards the East, and doth conteyne by estimation one hundred foott in Length and fourtie foott in Breadth.'[71] It is clearly a structure of substantial width, wider than the cellarer's building as later reconstructed by Hope.[72] Possibly re-built or remodelled, the 'tenement' seems to have remained in use until the early nineteenth century, when it appears on a plan of the precinct, drawn by Alexander and dated March 1801,[73] as a range projecting south from the west half of the south choir aisle and overlapping the south transept façade for rather more than half its width. A narrower structure extended westward from the cloister range, thereby forming a narrow court parallel to the remainder of the transept façade and to the south wall of the (late Perpendicular) Lady chapel.[74]

The east face of the north half of the range of domestic structures appears in a drawing by W. Alexander (1767–1816).[75] The section at the very north end, overlapping and parallel to the east face of the transept arm, and covered by a lean-to roof rising against the east wall to the sill of the present clerestory windows, may be a surviv-ing bay of the twelfth-century western range. A small semicircularly arched window, under a larger semicircular arch, with a string at impost level and one below, remains in the upper level of the north-ern half of the wall.[76] That this section of wall was a bay of the twelfth-century west range seems more likely than that it belonged to a (rectangular) chapel, for the window as depicted by (W.) Alexander seems too high up to have served a chapel.[77] It is this east wall of the putative twelfth-century range that may explain the 'quoins' yet visible on the inner face of the south choir aisle wall (fig. 76), while its sloping roof explains the shorter easternmost lancet window of the later (thirteenth-century) aisle wall to its east.[78] Unfortunately, the remaining remnants of this bay have been altered out of all recognition, apparently even before the restoration by Sir G.G. Scott (1811–78) (fig. 57).[79] Whether the penultimate or ultimate northern bay of that west range, its presence proves that, if there was a tower on the site, as Ashpitel, Irvine, and Hope suggested, it had been taken down no later than the second quarter of the twelfth century.

The northward extent of the west cloister range also suggests that, if the earlier Romanesque transept had a chapel, it was a small one: there is just barely room for a small chapel in the angle between the end of the range and the choir aisle. If there had been a larger, strongly projecting chapel opening off the middle of the east wall of the transept arm, it would have occupied the site of the end bay of the west range (as identified above) and part of what is now the adjoining Gothic aisle, and therefore would have to have been demolished in order to make way for the northward completion of the cloister range. In order to accommodate transept chapels of the usual apsidal projecting type, as part of his normal late-eleventh-century plan, Fairweather found it necessary to relocate the east wall of the transept slightly west of its present position.[80] However, this shift both ignored and contradicted the evidence, at least as supposedly found and interpreted by Irvine, that the eleventh-century east wall of the south arm of the transept is under the later existing one.[81]

Yet Fairweather perhaps more correctly pointed out that the foundations of the south and east walls of Hope's – and Irvine's – theoretical south tower were too slight to have actually supported a tower. They were at the most four feet [1.2192 m] thick, creating an internal space of nineteen feet by about seventeen feet [5.7912 x 5.1816 m], compared to walls seven feet [2.1336 m] thick bounding an internal space nineteen feet [5.7912 m] square in the north (Gundulf's) tower.[82] Fairweather suggested that they had supported walls forming an open court around an apsidal chapel projecting from the south transept arm, in the space between the junction of the west range of (Ernulf's) cloister with the transept arm and the original south choir aisle wall.[83] R. Gem suggested that these foundations may be evidence of a rectangular transept chapel – a form that he proposed was in keeping with the straight termination of the choir and its projecting rectangular chapel.[84] Because it now appears that the west range overlapped at least half the length of the transept arm, the existence of any chapel such as Fairweather or Gem proposed in this location is unlikely.

However, it should not be overlooked that Fairweather proposed a normal crossing with a tower and was probably right in these respects. Evidence for a regular crossing actually had been uncovered by Irvine in the form of a broad respond, three feet nine and one-half inches [1.1557 m] wide, projecting twenty-one inches [53.34 cm], with re-entrant angles, directly under the later Gothic respond at the northwest end of the presbytery.[85] Fairweather had used this respond as part of his argument that a regular crossing with a tower existed before 1200; he dated the respond anytime after 1135.[86] Since no base mouldings were uncovered, there is no reason why the simple pilaster form of the respond could not, indeed, date to the late eleventh century.[87] The presence of a pair of responds in this position also argues that the east wall of the Romanesque transept underlies the later Gothic one – an equation that Fairweather seems to have forgotten.

With regard to Radford's 'sleeper wall of chalk blocks' (fig. 4), his identification of it with the 'type of foundation belong[ing] to the oldest Norman work dating from the late 11th and early 12th century' is not supported by the description given by Livett regarding the four types of foundations found under the Romanesque nave aisles and west front, none of which used chalk *blocks*, and all of which apparently used footing courses of Kentish rag.[88] Aside from dating, Radford offered no interpretation of the significance of this sleeper wall except for the implication that it related to the definition of the crossing of Gundulf's church; strangely, he did not use its presence to counter Hope's reconstruction of a narrow transept.[89] As, according to Radford's interpretation, an earlier wall imbedded in the sleeper wall had an offset that marked a floor level '15–16 in. [38.1–40.64 cm] below the modern pavement,'[90] the level of the sleeper wall itself would appear to be well above the floor level of this area of Gundulf's church, which as calculated by Hope was twenty inches (50.6 cm) below the floor of the present crossing.[91] If Hope's calculations are correct, and also Radford's observations in this respect, it would suggest that the earlier wall could belong to the later twelfth century and, consequently, the chalk foundations to the thirteenth.

A date in the later twelfth century for that earlier (L-plan) wall (which Radford dated to the late tenth century) also seems to be a more likely (even if ultimately equally problematic) possibility because of its composition of 'rubble built of flint and Kentish rag set in a hard brown mortar.' This does not correspond to the small bit of walling preserved on the Gundulfian or Early-Norman foundations that – according to Livett – employed a 'fine yellow sand mortar,' although the early work did use Kentish rag for the faces of rough walls with flints inside.[92]

Nave

From the evidence of the foundations of the nave aisles as recorded by Irvine (figs. 14–17), it is clear that none of the standing sections of the aisle walls date to Gundulf's building.[93] This is especially obvious on the south side where the footing course of ashlar remained only in the bay immediately west of the present Lady chapel. An area of plaster, roughly fifty-one and one-half by thirty-two inches (1.308 x 0.8128 m), at the base of the wall in the penultimate bay, adjacent to the western respond, has been removed to reveal some roughly laid masonry including six stones set on end. This was identified as part of Gundulf's south aisle wall by Professor Robert Willis (1800–75),[94] but this identification conflicts with the evidence of the foundations as reported by Irvine (figs. 15, 16), since the characteristic footing of two courses of Kentish rag were missing under the four western bays of the wall.[95] On the north side (fig. 17), foundations attributable to the early church along with three feet [0.9144 m] of wall remained in the first three bays at the east end, and additional Gundulfian-type foundations were recorded by Irvine in the fifth bay from the east and in the western bay, and by (D.A.) Alexander under the rebuilt middle bays.[96] The latter foundations, along with the evidence for the sleeper wall of the south arcade and the foundations for the responds of the north arcade, suggest that, contrary to the conclusions of Hope and Livett, the north aisle was also actually built by Gundulf. This might be taken as some evidence for the contrary position that he at least intended to complete the nave (and probably did so).

Irvine claimed that the arches of the south arcade are of Gundulf's time, 'with a later-Norman order substituted on the nave side,' and that, therefore, the piers on this side are all the early ones recased.[97] The suggestion that the piers had been recased was made primarily because the inner or lower order towards the nave and both archivolts towards the aisle are unmoulded (they are now covered over with plaster). But it also was prompted by Irvine's discovery of the use of tufa, as opposed to Caen stone alone, in some of these arches, and for the spandrels and some of the rear pilasters.[98] However, an examination of Irvine's sketches (figs. 19, 20) reveals that the use of tufa was sporadic and not exclusive, for the presence of Caen stone is also noted. The appearance of tufa in the spandrels could just as well be explained by its reuse; although the material may have been characteristic of the early phase (but with only foundations remaining how can one be certain?), its use or appearance is not confined to work of that date.[99] Most significant, Livett himself had identified work in the north aisle wall in which tufa was present as 'undoubtedly Later-Norman work' by which he meant work associated with the existing west front.[100] Fairweather emphasized instances and possibilities of the reuse of tufa in twelfth-century work and in later periods as well.[101] Irvine noted the use of Caen stone in two of the pilasters (the second and third from the west): it is difficult to think of reasons why certain pilasters would have been rebuilt in the twelfth century while other pilasters (such as the westernmost one) and the spandrels remained untouched.[102]

Furthermore, if the original piers were recased, it might be expected that they would be thicker than the arcades they support: such is not the case, for the existing arcades, centred on the piers, all 'fit' and correspond in scale.[103] In order to accept these theories, it is necessary to postulate that the Gundulfian piers were stripped of their original casing, that the outer orders of the arches facing the nave were also removed, as well as, presumably, the facing of the spandrels between them – although the spandrels towards the aisle remained intact. This work was then followed by the recasing of the piers and the construction of new outer orders and sprandrels only towards the nave. It is difficult to imagine that much labour or material was thus saved, or for what reasons this cumbersome process might have been undertaken, particularly as it would seem that the orders and sprandrels towards the aisle had to be temporarily supported until the casing of the piers was rebuilt. An additional argument against the notion that the piers of the south arcade are the eleventh-century ones recased in the twelfth is the fact that they all stand on low chamfered plinths identical to those under the piers on the north side for which an early date has never been suggested. Finally, it might seem rather surprising that the twelfth-century builders apparently felt it necessary to restrain themselves in the design of the north arcade by using plain lower orders to nave and aisle, thus matching those on the south, before indulging in a display of chevron ornament on the outer orders. If symmetry was of importance, it seems more likely that they would have also rebuilt the lower order to the nave and the upper one towards the aisle on the south.

The erection of the south arcade by Gundulf was explained as necessary to provide a boundary for the monastic cloister, although, strictly speaking, only the south aisle wall was required for that purpose. The fact that there was no evidence for any cloister portals in the supposed Gundulfian south aisle wall was neither mentioned nor considered. More to the point, there is no physical evidence that Gundulf's monastic buildings *were* next to the nave rather than, as they certainly were later, next to the choir.[104] Indeed, the area south of the nave seems inappropriate for a cloister and associated monastic buildings as the ground rises fairly sharply to the south,[105] being the lowest slope of Boley Hill.[106] Even if the ground level is higher today than in the late eleventh century, there is no likelihood of its having been a relatively level area as apparently existed – and still exists – to the east, the site of the surviving monastic buildings.

Suggested Reconstruction and Chronology

We might begin by dating 'Gundulf's' Tower prior to the appointment of Gundulf as bishop, so that it was a *fait accompli* around which he had to build his new cathedral. In addition, perhaps Gundulf found it desirable or necessary to build his church on a restricted site *between* the tower and the Saxon church. The later was reportedly not in good condition when the new building was begun, but no doubt it would have had to have continued to serve the community for some years until the sanctuary of the new church was ready to accommodate services.[107]

That new building was no doubt a modest one. It is difficult to resist resolving the dichotomy between the archaic or retardative feature of the solid presbytery walls with the precocious feature of the aisled straight east end by suggesting that the presbytery – and crypt – of Gundulf's church ended in an apse flanked by apsidally terminated aisles that could have been flat on the exterior (fig. 10). The aisled crypt, therefore, would have been a small one of two straight bays plus an apse, located under the eastern half of a four-bay presbytery (fig. 9).

The remainder of Gundulf's church was relatively conventional, including a transept and crossing of normal proportions, a lightly built nave with thin walls and a wooden roof, and concluding with a façade of the sectional type. Its single unconventional feature may have been the lack of chapels to the transept, although there is the slight possibility that shallow apsidal or rectangular ones were placed in the angles between transept arms and choir aisles.

There is no consecration recorded in the lifetime of Gundulf, except that implied by the translation of the relics of the sainted third bishop, Paulinus, circa 1088,[108] which, depending upon when the church was begun, in 1077 or in 1082/3, could signify either the completion of the crypt and the presbytery above or of the crypt alone. Unfortunately, it is not known whether the relics of Saint Paulinus were placed in the crypt or in the presbytery.[109] If construction started as early as 1077, it is surprising that the translation did not take place sooner; if the relics were not placed in the crypt, one wonders what its purpose was initially. In any case, the tomb of Paulinus, wherever located, never became the focus of a significant pilgrimage. Construction proceeded rather slowly if it took eleven years (1077–88) to build the crypt and presbytery. This rate of progress should be compared to the *seven* years (1070/1–1077/8) it reportedly took Lanfranc to completely rebuild his cathedral church.[110] At Worcester Cathedral, it appears that the entire east end, comprising a large crypt, presbytery, transept, and the east bays of the nave, was constructed in only five years, 1084–9.[111] This suggests that 1082/3 is a plausible beginning date for the construction of an east end consisting of a crypt and presbytery that could have been completed by 1088.

The plausibility of the date of 1088 for the translation of the relics of Paulinus marking the completion of the presbytery does, nevertheless, raise the interesting question of its coincidence with the suppression of the rebellion of Bishop Odo of Bayeux and the subsequent recompense of Rochester for damage to the cathedral as a consequence by the king, William Rufus. Without knowing the exact sequence of events – was the translation before or after the damage was perpetrated? – it would seem that the structure may have been little affected, for it is nowhere else mentioned. The lack of comment might appear particularly odd if the translation had preceded the damage, for then it might be expected that the relics but recently translated would have been endangered by the actions of the king's men in the course of putting down the insurrection. If the translation took place after the rebellion was terminated, then any damage to the fabric clearly seems to have been limited in extent.

The parochial altar in the nave was in use by 1107, the year before Gundulf's death.[112] Livett, therefore, suggested that the nave was completed circa 1095–1100.[113] For some reason, Livett insisted upon a distinction between Gundulf's work and what he termed 'Early-Norman,' even though he dated the latter to the lifetime of Gundulf, well before his death in 1107. The distinction seems to have been occasioned by the change in foundation construction, noted first in 1875–6 in the aisles, and again in 1888 at the west front.[114] Although he took pains to point out the similarities between them,[115] he assumed a greater significance for the change than it actually need have, as it could simply indicate a different building campaign. Apparently for Livett, it was important to make a distinction between Gundulf's work – that is, the monastic part of the church, presumably paid for (in this case) by the bishop (and archbishop) and under his supervision – and 'Early-Norman' work – that is, work on the nave as a parish church, which was not the concern of the bishop, and which was paid for by the parishioners.

The interpretation of the significance of the difference in the construction of the foundations at the west end of the nave is somewhat complicated by the apparent conflict between Livett's observations and Irvine's memory, with regard to the west bay of the north aisle.[116] If Irvine's memory is correct, then it would appear that the west front was a final separate phase of construction, the length of the nave and its form perhaps not having been absolutely decided upon when the nave foundations were laid before its construction.

Differences between the foundations at the east and west ends of the nave, as one might expect, were also fundamental to Hope's interpretation of the extent of building under Gundulf.[117] Hope maintained that the south nave arcade and aisle were *never completed* and that the north arcade was never begun. Therefore, 'the parishioners had to be content with a temporary building, occupying probably the six western bays of the nave.'[118] However, it seems quite out of character that Gundulf would have drawn the line so sharply and not provided for his parishioners. To have left them almost literally out in the cold is quite contrary to the picture of Gundulf portrayed in the 'Vita Gundulfi,' as a caring bishop, concerned about the poor and pensioners, one easily moved to fits of weeping.[119] Furthermore, Hope did not seem to be paying attention to his own conclusions, for the space west of the three bays of the nave occupied by the monks' stalls and the two bays 'raised sufficiently high to serve as buttresses to the work east of them' lacked both a north arcade and north aisle wall, and possessed but four bays of the south arcade – carried no higher than the arches – with the accompanying bays of the aisle perhaps roofed in; as well, there was a west wall unattached to any structure to the east! Clearly, such an incomplete structure could not even have been temporarily enclosed in order to serve as a parochial church. For his part, Hope never explained – if the nave was never properly completed – why the remains of the west front were plastered on the interior.[120] Indeed, he never explained who began the west front, even if it is accepted that it remained incomplete. Considering that the west front was plastered on the interior, it does not seem rash to conclude that the building begun by Gundulf was completed, if not well before, certainly by the time of his death.

Liturgical Arrangements

The evidence is very slight regarding the liturgical arrangements that prevailed in the early church. In the course of the tunnelling under the existing choir floor, Irvine thought he had uncovered traces of 'some sort of a screen' standing further east than the existing stone one, that is, on the *east* side of the east crossing arch.[121] Hope accepted Irvine's findings – and interpretation – completely at first, concluding that consequently the monk's choir had not extended into the nave (there being no crossing in his view).[122] Later, he decided that the area between the screen and the west wall of the crypt – twenty-seven feet (8.2296 m) long – would have been too small, and that the monks' stalls must therefore have extended westwards into the nave, occupying the eastern three bays of his ten-bay nave.[123] Consequently, he placed four altars against the east wall, the two east bays forming a retrochoir; the high altar was positioned against a screen between the retrochoir and a two-bay presbytery; and the two (or three) bays enclosed by the solid side walls contained the 'quire' altar positioned between flights of steps leading up to the presbytery; the monks stalls followed in the next three bays (fig. 7).

Irvine, it will be recalled, also reported encountering several levels of plaster flooring in the course of his excavation in the choir.[124] The lowest level, which he, and then Hope, associated with Gundulf's church, consisted of three sections created by two single six-inch (15.24 cm) steps, eleven and one-half feet (3.5052 m) apart. The western section of the presbytery was at the same level as the nave floor; the eastern third was a slightly sloping surface that abutted the west face of the west wall of the crypt well below the level of the crypt vaults (over five feet [1.524 m] below the present choir floor). There was no evidence of steps leading from the middle of the presbytery to the raised section (regardless of its shape) over the crypt, which Irvine therefore thought may have been accessed by means of stairs at the sides. In his restoration (fig. 7), Hope did place pairs of flights of steps flanking a 'quire altar' placed against the west wall of the crypt as Irvine suggested.[125]

Assuming the plan here suggested, and using Lanfranc's Christ Church as an analogy, one can suggest that the high altar was placed in the raised apsidal section of the presbytery, with the matutinal or daily altar placed in the lower section rather forward of any stairs leading up to the sanctuary. Because of the longer presbytery at Rochester compared to Canterbury, where the matutinal altar was placed in the crossing, the monks' stalls may have occupied the area under the crossing and perhaps only the first rather than the first three bays of the eight-bay nave.[126] Presumably there would have been a rood loft separating the monastic from the parochial parts of the church. Gundulf was reportedly buried in front of the altar of the Crucifix, which may well then have been in the second bay of the nave.[127] Further west, a second screen probably separated it from the parochial altar of St Nicholas.

Its Place in Late-Eleventh-Century Architecture

Despite the fact that so little remains of it, the first Romanesque church at Rochester is of interest not only because it was the first, and an early building following the Conquest, but because of the remains of its crypt. Crypts were not uncommon in the period, although it was far from true that every large church had one. They were generally found at major buildings and were frequently associated with an ambulatory plan. Examples are the Benedictine abbeys of Bury St Edmunds, Canterbury St Augustine, Evesham, and Gloucester, and the cathedrals of Winchester and Worcester.[128] There may also have been a large crypt at Old St Paul's, London.[129] In all cases, the crypts extended under the entire eastern arm, which included an ambulatory;[130] all date before 1100.[131] The crypt of the new choir at Christ Church, Canterbury, begun circa 1096 by Prior Ernulf (1096–1107), was the last of this series.[132]

In Normandy, crypts are found at the cathedrals of Rouen, begun before 1037, and Bayeux, begun circa 1046–9, and at La Trinité, Caen, circa 1090. In the last case, the crypt does not extend under the aisles and is associated with a choir that has solid side walls.[133] The immediate model for Rochester, however, may have been the much smaller crypt of Lanfranc's cathedral at Canterbury, which was confined to the area – exclusive of the aisles – of the short sanctuary of two bays that, it should be noted, terminated apsidally.[134]

The other probable remains of Gundulf's church – albeit heavily disguised – are the feature of the solid side walls to the presbytery, rather than arcades open to the aisles. There are a few known parallels for this feature in England, the most notable example being Edward (1042–66) the Confessor's abbey church at Westminster, circa 1055. Others were Lincoln Cathedral, begun 1072/3; Old Sarum Cathedral, begun 1075/8; St Albans Abbey, begun after 1077; Whitby Priory, late eleventh century; and Blyth Priory, begun after 1087/8.[135] Except for St Albans,[136] all are known only from excavation and are associated with the apse in echelon plan type. Two surviving examples in Normandy are found at the abbey churches of La Trinité, Caen, circa 1059–66 (as already mentioned),[137] and Cerisy-la-Forêt, circa 1090–1100(?),[138] in both cases once again associated with the apse in echelon arrangement. At the former church, the presbytery was later extended over an added aisleless crypt, resulting in a combination of two features exceptional for the region.[139] Lanfranc's cathedral seems to be the single English building uniting solid side walls in the presbytery with a crypt of equal length beneath. As all the parallel examples date from the late eleventh century, it is extremely likely that the existing length of the solid side walls dates to this period and equally unlikely that short solid walls were extended in the twelfth century, as is implied by the restorations of Ashpitel and Hope, and as is explicitly stated by Fairweather, who dated much of their fabric after 1137![140]

The results of less concretely founded speculation suggest that the first Romanesque church at Rochester may have been even more interesting or significant than it seems simply on the basis of the scant visible or visitable remains. As has been seen, Hope's attribution of his discovery of a long straight-ended aisled presbytery to the late-eleventh-century building has been rejected on developmental grounds. As Fairweather's study made clear, such an apparently original form could not have been anticipated at Rochester, which should have been, in theory, a miniature version of Canterbury. Innovation or invention were not to be expected at the minor see, especially considering the close relationship between Gundulf and Lanfranc.[141] If the restoration of an aisled, straight-ended presbytery is correct – and, as has been seen, there is considerable room for doubt – it becomes the earliest of a general type that was to have greater currency in the following century.[142] With the exception of Rochester, all examples of the tendency towards straight or flat east walls among major buildings occur after circa 1110, that is, twenty-five or more years later, and are generally less problematic: thus, Hereford Cathedral, circa 1107/15, and Southwell Minster, circa 1108/14; and for the rectangular ambulatory type, Chertsey Abbey (where the choir walls may have been solid), circa 1110, and Old Sarum, perhaps begun shortly after 1110 by Bishop Roger (1107–39). However, examples of a type similar to that proposed by Hope in his final solution for Rochester, that is, arcades and aisles terminating against a straight east wall, and therefore without an ambulatory, occur only after the middle of the twelfth century: for instance, Holy Cross, Winchester, circa 1160; Bardney Abbey, circa 1175; Ripon Minster, 1170s; St Frideswide, Oxford, circa 1175; the rebuilt east arm of Waltham Abbey, 1177; and Brinkburn Priory and Jervaulx Abbey, circa 1190–1200 and circa 1195, respectively.[143] The straight east wall continues as a 'favorite formula' after 1200, as seen at the abbeys of Whitby, circa 1220, and Rievaulx, circa 1230, and the cathedrals of Ely, circa 1235–52, and Lincoln, circa 1256–80. There is, of course, no parallel among these buildings for Hope's small rectangular eastern chapel. Similarly, the odd combination of solid side walls at the west and arcades at the east, as restored by Hope, is without parallels and is unique.

Rectangular chancels had, of course, appeared before in England in the pre-Romanesque period, and are found in all periods of Anglo-Saxon architecture from the earliest to the decades immediately before the Conquest, from the Old Minster of 648 at Winchester (Hampshire) and the early Northumbrian churches – Monkwearmouth, Jarrow, Escomb – to Breamore (Hampshire), circa 1000, St Lawrence, Bradford on Avon (Wiltshire), eleventh century, and St Mary, Stow (Lincolnshire), circa 1050.[144] Although apsidal sanctuaries seem to have been characteristic of the early Kentish churches, the meagre evidence from parish churches of the late Saxon period and the Saxo-Norman overlap in Kent suggests flat-ended chancels were typical.[145] These earlier rectangular sanctuaries were relatively modest and simple in form, usually associated with small aisleless naves.[146]

It is into this context that Gundulf's one documented foundation, the nunnery abbey church at Malling, fits. It has been suggested that it might have had a straight termination to its aisleless presbytery, as well as a small projecting rectangular chapel, and therefore would support Hope's hypothetical termination for the presbytery at Rochester. A small rectangular chapel, fifteen by twenty-one feet [4.572 x 6.4008 m] externally and eleven feet [3.3528 m] wide internally, was uncovered there in 1932.[147] According to F.C. Elliston-Erwood, the area between the chapel's foundations and the east side of the crossing, some twenty-five feet [7.62 m] long, had been completely destroyed by the installation of modern service facilities, so there was no evidence for the form of the presbytery to which it was presumed the chapel was attached and no secure evidence for the date of the chapel. He concluded, on the basis of a chronology derived from a likely sequence of typological evolution, that the original sanctuary was apsidal, and that the rectangular chapel was a twelfth-century addition. Nonetheless, it must be admitted that the dating of the chapel can be argued either way: as a late-eleventh-century original or as a later extension in the twelfth century. The form and chronology of the east end has not been resolved by more recent excavations.[148] But even if the original presbytery had been flat-ended, it would not have been remarkable; and lacking aisles and a crypt it was hardly dependent upon Rochester. The important – and unique? – element is the projecting chapel, which was rather larger – and therefore more plausible – than the one proposed by Hope for Rochester.[149]

At the same time, the few slightly earlier or roughly contemporary developments on the Continent display significant differences and do not afford convincing evidence of being models or sources of influence for Rochester. The abbey church of Saint-Bertin, circa 1045/6–1065/81, at Saint-Omer (Pas-de-Calais), the late-eleventh-century abbey, later collegiate church, of Notre-Dame at Nesle (Somme) and also Saint-Hildevert, Gournay-en-Bray, near Rouen (Seine-Maritime), of the early twelfth century, have been suggested as possible prototypes.[150] At Saint-Bertin, a nearly square aisled sanctuary of five bays, raised over a crypt, was accessible only from a pair of staircases in the crossing that flanked the axial entrance to the crypt;

namely, the aisle did not communicate with the transept. In a somewhat similar fashion at Nesle, the aisles of the short oblong sanctuary (also over a crypt) were similarly closed off from the transept; three small chapels occupied the bases of a towered structure at the east end.[151] Of these two buildings, the *plan* of Saint-Bertin is more similar to that proposed by Hope for the eastern half of Rochester's presbytery than that of Nesle. Unfortunately, nothing is known of the elevation of Saint-Bertin; nonetheless, the spatial configuration must have been very different, so much so as to preclude any likely influence. At Gournay, the short (three-bay) aisled choir (partly rebuilt in the later twelfth century), which opens directly off a conventional transept, is more comparable to the later aisled flat-ended English presbyteries cited above. The simplicity of its plan and the uncomplicated relationship of its few major spatial volumes – there is no crypt – places it as distant typologically from Nesle or Saint-Bertin as those later English buildings. Moreover, the appearance of the flat-ended choir is as unexpected and difficult to explain at that time in that part of France as would be a similar plan thirty years or so earlier at Rochester.[152]

This unexpected, unconventional form of the east end, if indeed it actually existed, is a contrast with the conservative, almost old-fashioned, character of the presbytery with its solid side walls in the place of arcades. It does seem difficult, therefore, to reconcile the archaic feature of the solid side walls to the presbytery at Rochester, which has been characterized, albeit from the twelfth-century point of view, as a 'retarded and unimpressive design,'[153] with the forward-looking features of the straight ending encompassing nave and aisles of equal length. Owing to the proximity of Canterbury and, most particularly, the close association between Lanfranc and Gundulf, evidenced especially by Lanfranc's patronage of the rebuilding of Rochester, a presbytery of four 'bays' (twice the length of that at Canterbury), terminating apsidally, and placed above an aisled crypt of the same plan – but shorter in length – seems a more logical, a more understandable form for the east end of Rochester as initially constructed under Gundulf. There is no compelling reason why Rochester at that early date should have had a presbytery six (or seven) bays long, with a crypt of almost equal size, both considerably larger than those of the metropolitan cathedral.

By comparison with the east limb, the transept, nave, and especially the west front were more standard, except for the vexing issue of chapels – their absence or presence and shape – in the transept arms. Judging from the existing north arm of the Gothic major transept, a shallow chapel could have been accommodated in the space between the Romanesque arm and the north tower, perhaps partly housed in the thickness of the wall. Equally, on the south side, a shallow chapel could have fitted between the end of the west range and the south aisle wall. In form, the chapel could have been either apsidal or rectangular. The latter is a possibility for the period as the first Romanesque church at Lincoln, begun by Bishop Remigius (1067–92) in 1072, is thought to have had rectangular eastern chapels opening off its transept arms.[154] At Lincoln, however, there were no constraining factors, so the chapels are much larger than they could possibly have been at Rochester. Since the choir at Lincoln has been reconstructed as one of three bays with solid side walls and an apse, it offers a further precedent and parallel for Rochester.[155] On the other hand, as a parallel for their absence at Rochester, transept chapels were probably also lacking at the nunnery church founded at Malling by Gundulf.[156]

With regard to the nave, there is no evidence for either the shape of the arcade piers or the design of the elevation. The façade was of the basic sectional type, one not unusual for the period, and did not anticipate in any particular way the unique aspects of the later (existing) west front belonging to the beginning of the third quarter of the twelfth century.

Conclusions

The form of the church built under Gundulf's episcopacy is – especially with regard to its eastern half – very uncertain. It is difficult not to agree with A.W. Clapham (1883–1950), who more than sixty years ago concluded: 'The form [of the early church] suggested by Sir William Hope rests on little or no evidence and is neither reasonable nor probable.'[157]

The problem begins with the plan and size of the crypt. Because the investigations carried out by Ashpitel and then by Hope were so poorly recorded, their conclusions are open to doubt. Indeed, in both cases, there really is no documentation at all. Ashpitel gives no indication of just how and, more important, exactly where the boring was done: did the boring perhaps actually disclose sleeper walls laid down by the builders of the *Gothic* crypt? As the form Hope proposed for the crypt is essentially without precedent and at least eight decades earlier than any similar examples, further doubts justifiably may be raised.

Hope's reconstruction of a small projecting eastern chapel is even more dubious and lacking in parallels. Again, in a similar fashion, it may be questioned whether Hope's excavation in the area between the later two Gothic piers of the crypt may not actually have come across the foundations for these piers (figs. 8, 18): surely the digging of the trenches for the foundations of these massive piers would have effectively destroyed the fabric of the 'chapel' – if it had existed. It also may be asked, if this site was that of the original chapel, perhaps the repository of relics, whether it would have been completely discarded, its existence apparently totally ignored in the rebuilding?[158] A less rhetorical question might focus on the absence of Romanesque responds at the east end of the crypt aisles and ask whether the presence of Gothic ones could indicate that the original termination of the crypt lay just beyond.

Unless and until more conclusive excavations are carried out, a small crypt underlying the eastern half of a longer presbytery, both of triapsidal termination, seems more probable and plausible. This solution gains further credibility from a comparison with the metropolitan church, a comparison which also reveals that Rochester was not an exact copy of that model. Gundulf's sanctuary would have been longer than that of Lanfranc's Canterbury (roughly four bays to two). The sanctuaries of both buildings were characterized by solid side walls. Although the fabric of the existing solid walls has not been investigated, parallels in the late eleventh century, and the lack of any from the subsequent period, suggesting that the form went out of fashion, also indicate that the full length of the existing walls is correctly attributed to Gundulf's period.

Hope's reconstruction of a rectangular towerless 'crossing' and extraordinarily narrow transept arms (or of no crossing at all) must also be discarded. As even he admitted, there are no parallels for such a truly bizarre form. Since this seems to be an idea he rather inherited from Irvine – and Ashpitel? – and for which there is no archaeological evidence, it should be dismissed. In this instance, Irvine's somewhat puzzling discoveries outside the south wall of the transept and the rather inconclusive investigation under its east wall can be replaced in the argument by the responds attached to the inner faces of the west ends of the solid side walls of the choir, which indicate the line of the east wall of the transept and the possibility of a regular crossing.

With regard to the nave, little can be said, as no information remains except for the evidence of its width and length as revealed by the foundations of the aisle walls and the first west front. That there was but a single west portal is of some interest, for this was and was to be typically English, as opposed to the custom or preference for three west portals that developed in the Île-de-France in the twelfth century, based perhaps on earlier precedents, primarily in Normandy.

The plan proposed here is, then, that of a rather modest building, one generally conventional for the period, and perhaps appropriate to its position as a small diocese in the shadow of Canterbury, yet of a dignity befitting its historical importance. Its most significant features would be the existence of a crypt and, in particular, the length of its presbytery, the latter anticipating later developments that were to become so characteristically English.[159]

FOUR

Alterations and Rebuilding in the Twelfth Century

Historical Précis: Personages and Events

Upon the death of Gundulf in 1108, Ralph d'Escures, a former abbot of Séez in Normandy, was appointed bishop. His tenure was brief as he was translated to Canterbury in 1114. Ralph's successor was Ernulf, a former prior of Christ Church (1096–1107) and abbot of Peterborough (1107–14). Already aged, he died in 1124.[1] His successor, John, was the nephew of the former bishop, Ralph, who had just recently died as archbishop of Canterbury (1114–22). John was not a monk but had served as archdeacon to his uncle at Canterbury. The period between the death of John in June 1137 and the appointment of Walter, archdeacon of Canterbury and brother to the archbishop, Theobald (1138–61), in January 1148 is one of some confusion. Between 1137 and 1140 the see was under the care of another John, the bishop of Séez (d. 1144), who was a supporter of King Stephen (1135–54). The situation was not regularized until 1142, when Archbishop Theobald appointed Ascelin (1142–8), a former sacrist of Christ Church and the prior (1139–42) of Dover Priory. His reign of less than six years was disputatious. One dispute involved the bishop and the monks against the archdeacon (Robert Pullen), while a second was between the monks and the bishop. By contrast, the long tenure of thirty-three years of Bishop Walter (1148–82) was placid and has left little trace in the records. It has been remarked that '[a]ll about him there were great events, not least the dramatic life and death of Archbishop Thomas Becket [1162–70], but Walter's part in them appears slight or conventional.'[2]

Although all the bishops, with the exception of John of Séez, were remembered for having made generous gifts to the priory in the form of service-books, vestments, and plate, only Ernulf is credited with any construction during this period. His patronage affected not the church but rather the monks' offices, as it is specifically stated that he built the chapter house, dormitory, and refectory.[3] The lack of any additional references to the rebuilding of the church is all the more remarkable in light of a devastating fire that reportedly swept Rochester in 1137, shortly before the death of Bishop John of Canterbury. The damage to the church is nowhere specifically indicated, but the effect of the fire on the new monastic buildings of Ernulf was apparently severe, for the monks were forced to seek temporary shelter elsewhere.

The major event towards the middle years of the century, the civil war (1138–47) between King Stephen and his cousin, the Empress Matilda (1102–67), the daughter of King Henry I (1100–35), was relatively sparing of Kent, for most of the conflict raged in a great arc around southeast England, from Winchester to Gloucester to Lincoln (and London).[4] At some time early in this period, the priory became heavily in debt to Stephen's chief captain in this region, William of Ypres:[5] could this have been due to some rebuilding that must have been necessary after the 1137 fire?[6]

The Physical Evidence

As has been discussed in the previous chapter, only the two west bays of the crypt of the church begun by Bishop Gundulf (1076/7–1108) remain visible today. Consequently, the existing nave and west front form the most obvious and conspicuous Romanesque remains. They clearly date from the advanced twelfth century, not the late eleventh, and therefore are the result of a later rebuilding that obviously replaced the nave of the structure begun and most probably finished by Gundulf. Because they still exist, it might be thought that the nave and west front present fewer problems of interpretation than does the largely destroyed late-eleventh-century building. Such, however, is not the case for, although some attention has been focused on them, there has been, historically, little agreement about the precise date of their construction. Furthermore, there is ample evidence that the builders' initial intentions were altered in the course of construction, even if the exact sequence of events is not now easy to determine. Nor are the reasons for the changes always apparent. The extent of any alteration or rebuilding in the twelfth century is also problematic, for a complete rebuilding of the original church east of its nave has been suggested.[7] These building campaigns, the one – east end – hypothetical and the other – nave and west front – actual, are all the more problematic because there is a total lack of documentation pertaining to either of them.

Rebuilding, Repairs, Restoration

The later medieval alterations to the Romanesque fabric of nave and façade are readily apparent. All the aisle windows, as is indicated by their pointed arches, if not by their tracery, have been replaced. So too, the entire clerestory on both north and south has been rebuilt. And most conspicuously, as seemed to happen to every earlier west front in England, a large window was inserted in the Perpendicular period and style. There are, however, other alterations that are less apparent. During the eighteenth century, the cathedral was subjected to a number of no doubt necessary repairs, and in the nineteenth century to three bouts of restoration: first under the supervision of L.N. Cottingham, primarily 1825 to 1830, then, 1871 to 1878 under the direction of Sir G.G. Scott, and finally by J.L. Pearson, 1888 to 1894.[8] Repairs as early as the seventeenth century, and then during the eighteenth century and early years of the nineteenth, were mainly concerned with the aisle walls. Cottingham's work was primarily confined to the west window and gable, Scott's to the underpinning of the aisle walls. It was the last of these restorations, Pearson's, that particularly affected the exterior appearance of the west front.

Perhaps more conspicuous than the alterations to the west front is the loss of much of the fabric of the aisle walls (fig. 1). The remaining bays of the south aisle wall, from immediately west of the Perpendicular addition ('Lady chapel') up to the southwest angle turret, are largely the result of necessary conservation work carried out in 1664.[9] About the same time, the north aisle wall was rebuilt from the buttress on the west of the third bay from the east (the joint is on the east side of the buttress) to the seventh bay, above the inserted Perpendicular door and window (the buttress to the west was rebuilt in 1802).[10] It appears that the Gothic windows in this wall were reset during the seventeenth-century rebuilding as only that in

the fifth bay has been entirely renewed. No doubt, when the clerestory was rebuilt, the pitch of the aisle roof was lowered and, consequently, the aisle wall was raised several feet above the termination
of the buttresses, as can be seen in bays one to three and eight (the
seventeenth-century section was rebuilt to a height equal to the
bays to its east and west). The original Romanesque height of the
wall was at a level equal to the second string of the (rebuilt) northwest turret.

Nothing original is visible on the exterior of the south aisle except
the (restored) lower courses of four buttresses (fig. 31).[11] The top
three to four feet (0.9144 to 1.2192 m) of this wall were rebuilt in
1801 (fig. 31, 41, at right); work at the same level on the north side,
carried out in 1802, is of a (deliberately) different character.[12]

In contrast to the aisle walls, the Romanesque design of the façade
now appears complete, except for the obvious destruction wrought
by the intrusion of the Perpendicular great west window (fig. 41). It
was, however, subjected to considerable deconstruction and restoration during the eighteenth and nineteenth centuries. Only at the end
of the last century was it returned more or less accurately to its late-
medieval appearance.[13] Much of this work of subtraction and addition affected the four turrets, collectively one of the façade's most
conspicuous features. Actually, the angle turrets are small stair-towers because they contain unusually ample newel-stairs within.[14]

Of the angle stair-towers, only the lower two registers of the southern one are original: its upper stages were removed between 1772
and 1816 and rebuilt during the restoration of 1888. The north angle
tower has been twice rebuilt from the ground up. In the 1760s it was
torn down and then rebuilt but only to a height equal to the north
aisle.[15] During the restoration of Pearson that work was completely
taken down and the tower rebuilt: its reconstruction and the octagonal stages of the southern one were based on early engraved views.[16]
As to the turrets in the line of the nave arcades, only the southern
one is original for the north turret had been rebuilt in the Perpendicular period. That rebuilding was removed and replaced by a copy
of the south turret during the restoration begun in 1888.[17]

The arrangement of graduated arcades (figs. 41, 42), which reflected
the original slope of the roofs over the aisles, had survived only on
the south side, where it had been incorporated under a horizontal
parapet that was the result of the flatter roof placed over the aisle in
the course of the Perpendicular alterations. On the north side, the

graduated arcade had disappeared during the 1760s' rebuilding of the north angle stair-tower; it was replaced by an arcade of three tall bays, the centre one with an ogee arch.[18] The original design was also restored between 1888 and 1894.[19]

On the interior, alterations to the nave design are even more obvious (fig. 34). In addition to the replacement of the Romanesque clerestory and roof in the Perpendicular period (fifteenth century),[20] the easternmost bays were lost altogether owing to an aborted project, begun in the middle decades of the thirteenth century, to rebuild the entire nave (fig. 34, in foreground). In the aisles, not only have all the Romanesque windows been replaced, but the eastern three bays on the south have effectively been completely removed by the construction, at the beginning of the sixteenth century, of a large structure (now generally identified as the Lady chapel) opening off the west side of the south transept arm. The several rebuildings of the northwest angle stair-tower seem to have affected the penultimate west bay of the north aisle as well. Internally, this bay lacks the flat string-course of the six bays to the east (including the three rebuilt in the 1660s); furthermore, there is no respond between it and the west bay and there are no details to the inner jambs of a blocked fifteenth-century portal that may well have been reset. As the interior surfaces of the walls are heavily plastered, the different phases of work have effectively been disguised.

Exterior

The standing Romanesque fabric of the aisles is now limited to portions of the north aisle wall.[21] It consists of the remains of two buttresses and three bays of a decorated string-course placed below the level of the window sills at the east end of the aisle (fig. 33), as well as a length of decorated string-course in the western bay. The buttresses, of the shallow pilaster type, are executed in ashlar (Caen stone): the eastern one rises to, or near, its original height; the western has been truncated at the string-course (also Caen stone). The walling between the buttresses is executed in Kentish rag. The section of string-course at the west end of the aisle, which is carved with lozenges decorated with pellets, has been reset, no doubt when the northwest angle stair-tower was rebuilt in 1892–4, at a higher level than the section remaining *in situ* at the east end of the same wall.[22]

Of the exterior design of the Romanesque clerestory, only a hint remains. At the west end, on the south side adjacent to the stair-tower at the end of the nave arcade, there is an angle-shaft that is best explained as the terminal shaft of a bay of blind arcading (fig. 32), one of a series that would have flanked the clerestory windows.

The exterior of the façade is characterized by the clear and emphatic articulation of its five components: the two large stair-towers at the angles of the aisles, the terminal walls of the aisles, and the end wall of the nave (figs. 41, 42). The articulation is achieved by setting back the walls of the aisles, thus throwing the nave end and the stair-towers into prominent relief. Rather unusually, no buttresses are used. Originally, there was only one west portal, the central one – the north aisle portal is a later (late-thirteenth-century) insertion – which is flanked by shallow arched recesses. A taller shallow recess enbracing a window was placed in each aisle end wall.

The surfaces are decorated with registers of arcading that were not continuous in design or level, but that were symmetrically disposed on the five planes (fig. 41). Three registers are on the nave end: the archivolts of the central portal interrupt the lowest; the later Perpendicular window has displaced most of the two upper ones. An additional three registers of arcading are found on the turrets that rise out of the angles of the nave end and that originally flanked a steeply pitched gable. On each aisle end, a band of arcades, gradated in height, corresponded to the original slope of the aisle roof. Each angle stair-tower received four registers of arcading different in height and detail from those of the nave end.

The decorative motifs of the nave end are rich and varied (fig. 43). They include a series of upright five-pointed leaves in the lower arcade (as restored), each encircled by its own stem on the north side, with more organic leaf-circles on the south; a diaper pattern consisting of four-petal flowers set within a pelleted circle; a twisted cable motif on a string-course along with a bar/lozenge chain design; a zigzag with small bosses between the zigs on the lintels under the small tympana; a trellis diapering; and, finally, a large bar/lozenge chain. The small tympana had (reading from north to south) a pair of opposed birds; a man holding a fish;[23] a bird with its tail under it; a symmetrical rinceau; a bird with its tail under it (badly eroded); and a symmetrical rinceau. In addition, it is notable that the shafts of the lowest register, consisting of tall narrow bays of arcading, lack bases and instead stand on strongly projecting corbels carved with a variety of grotesque figures. Two of the shafts of this register – one each side of the portal arch – are spirally cabled, each differently arranged. The arches of this lowest arcade are carved with various lobed leaves, usually each leaf under a C-shaped arc;[24] the arches over the small tympana have a chevron design; and those of the third tier, also decorated with chevron, share their supports with billet-decorated intersecting arcading above them. On the lowest register of the turret proper, the wall behind the arcades is filled with circles possessing prominent boss-like centres; jambs and arches are chevroned, while the string-course below is billet-carved and the one above has a crenellated or fret motif. Shaft-rings are found on the arcades of the uppermost tier.

Other motifs appear in the recesses of the aisle ends (fig. 44): the wall area below the window is composed of square stones laid diagonally; the string below the window is of linked squares; and a sawtooth design parallels the roll of one arch adjacent to a label bearing dogtooth.[25] A number of similar and additional decorative patterns formerly surrounded the arch of the Perpendicular west window.[26] The several diaper patterns – consisting of large and small squares, encircled four-petalled flowers, cusped lozenges, fretwork, and elaborate four-petal flowers – probably were reset during the installation of the window, one or some derived from the original gable or from between the registers of arcading.[27]

As to the portal proper, the two column figures, a lintel carved with the figures of the twelve apostles and a tympanum bearing a depiction of Christ in a mandorla with the symbols of the four evangelists, are notable and well-known features (fig. 45). In addition to the figurative sculpture of column figures, lintel, and tympanum, there are a number of other distinctive features worthy of note. The shafts of the three outer orders employ shaft-rings that were not simple mouldings but were carved with various motifs, all now badly eroded.[28] On the northern shafts, they seem to be (outer order to inner): human figures and a monster's encircling tail; vine and leaf; and undecipherable. On the southern shafts (inner to outer) are found vine and leaf; a bust in a medallion flanked by birds; and foliage-encircled monsters (restored). Shaft-rings are also found under the column figures and are thus at a much lower level than those of the plain shafts: the shaft-ring below the male figure (north) is carved with medallions with a figure visible within one, and that below the female figure (south) with winged bird-dragons.

The capitals of the shafts are also richly carved: in most cases their underlying form is that of the cushion type. On the north shafts, the decorative motifs are (outer to inner): three tiers of simple pointed leaves;[29] a human figure between two harpies; foliage rinceau; opposed bird-dragons;[30] and harpies (on the jamb half-shaft).[31] On the south, there are (inner to outer): three figures in a rinceau (on the jamb half-shaft);[32] an angel and an eagle in scalloped-shaped fields; circular rinceau, with an ox and a lion; and circular rinceau.

The five orders of the portal are all richly carved with deeply undercut motifs of similar but varying patterns. Reading from the outer order to the inner, they are: symmetrically patterned foliage, frequently alternating with birds that reach back to their tails;[33] irregular repetition of symmetrical foliage, including backward-facing birds on the north half, with a series of foliage rinceau spread over two voussoirs (three pairs), followed by eleven voussoirs of human heads spouting foliage;[34] loops of foliage containing birds or animal or human heads; individual voussoirs carved with nearly identical leaf patterns; a twisted cable moulding; and backward-facing harpies (not clasping their tails), with some symmetrical leaf patterns interspersed.

Interior

On the interior, the original details of the north aisle wall consist of only two eastern buttress-like responds, accompanied by a stretch of decorated string-course extending over three bays (fig. 40). The form of the responds up to the string-course is that of a shallow pilaster (like the exterior buttresses); above that level, for an equal height, they gain slender angle-shafts; a third section is again a plain pilaster, shallower than the lower part. The three bays of the string-course at the east end of the north aisle are carved with a kind of double or overlapping zigzag with rosettes in the resulting lozenge-shaped centres. A section of decorated string also remains in the west bay of the south aisle. The pattern on this string-course is quite different from that preserved on the north, as it is a type of double scale pattern with raised edges and small circles at the junction of the scallops.

The rebuilding of the western bays of the north aisle included the re-creation of the responds, although in a simpler form. Consequently, chamfered plinths are preserved under the first, fourth, fifth, and sixth (counting from the east) responds. The south wall was, perhaps, only refaced rather than rebuilt, but because the inner face of the wall is completely plastered, it is impossible to know how much, if any, may be original work. It is worthy of note that all of its responds have a much stronger projection than those in the north aisle, and no evidence of any chamfered plinths remains.

Of the nave arcade, five pairs of piers plus the west responds survive, along with the second-storey arches (figs. 34, 35).[35] The basic design is quite unexceptional: compound piers support an arcade of two orders; the second-stage openings consist of a superordinate arch of one order encompassing a pair of arches of one order. The latter spring from a pair of shafts in the middle (which appear as a single shaft, the second shaft being nearly invisible because it is placed towards the aisle) and a single angle-shaft at each side. Continuous string-courses are placed at the bottom of the second stage and of the (destroyed) clerestory. Taken all together, however, these elements constitute one of the more unusual and curious nave designs in twelfth-century architecture. Three features in particular are remarkable. Each pair of piers is of a different design; there is neither vault nor floor separating the two stages in the aisles (figs. 39, 40); and a passageway runs through the thickness of the second-storey arcade wall. Other features of interest are (figs. 35, 36) the half-shafts that once rose up the wall from the level of the nave pier abaci to the clerestory (they now stop at the floor of the second stage) and the diaper patterns applied to all the tympana in the second storey.

The two easternmost twelfth-century piers of both arcades were rebuilt as the first phase of the aborted project – begun about the middle of the thirteenth century – to replace the Romanesque nave.[36] From east to west, the remaining pier designs are: a square core with a large half-shaft on each face;[37] a quatrefoil shape created by round columns at the angles with half-shafts in between on each face;[38] a cruciform core with two half-shafts on the north and south faces, three on the east and west faces, and re-entrant shafts (fig. 38); an oblong core with a half-round pier on the wider east and west faces flanked by shafts, and a large half-shaft to north and south; and, the simplest in form, an elongated octagon (long axis east–west).[39] The west responds consist of two half-shafts engaged to a broad pilaster flanked by angle-shafts.[40]

These florid designs all rise from plinths that are square and simply chamfered,[41] except for the four western ones of the north arcade, which are embellished with spurs of a leaf design (fig. 38).[42] The base mouldings consist of a rather wide, shallow, collar-like scotia over a torus (figs. 11a–b). In contrast, the southeastern half-Romanesque/half-Gothic pier has a more elaborate base (figs. 37, 11a), consisting of two thin rolls above a narrow quarter-hollow: its plinth has been remodelled to an octagonal form.

The spandrel of each bay was bisected by a single shaft that formerly continued into the second stage (fig. 36). The pier designs are so eccentric and complex that in no case could these shafts have been coordinated with a similar element of the piers, except in the case of the eastern remaining pair, which is the simplest and most conventional in design.

The mouldings and decoration of the arcade arches are reasonably uniform and consistent (figs. 35, 36), including also the use of multi-scallop capitals. Within the decorative details, there are indications of the sequence of the work, if a general tendency towards more complex forms is accepted as a line of development. Thus, all the capitals on the north main arcade have more numerous scallops than those on the south, and became progressively richer from east to west. The four western piers on that side also are the only ones to bear spurs on their base plinths, although it is the spandrel above the westernmost pier on the south that received a pair of sunk roundels with chevroned frames. The abaci are all uniform, with a roll inserted between the straight and hollow chamfered sections. The inner or lower order of each arcade is unmoulded (those on the south are plastered over), while each outer order bears a chevron design, identical on north and south; the label received a large nail-head motif. Finally, a string-course consisting of a broad fillet and a roll runs under the second stage.[43]

In a less conspicuous fashion than in the case of the piers, the diaper patterns of the tympana of the second storey are also subject to variation rather than strict repetition (fig. 36).[44] Although the designs are similar, all are individual arrangements that are not disposed in pairs; generally those on the south are somewhat simpler. On the south side, the designs are (east to west): squares with articulated four-petal rosettes;[45] squares with raised flat four-petal rosettes; lozenges with raised borders and sunk four-petal rosettes; squares with eight-petal rosettes alternating with squares subdivided into four squares; squares with sunk lozenges; and lozenges with raised borders and four-petal rosettes. The central medallions are also varied, and, with one exception (third bay), they are all based on a pattern of leaves/stem/flower. On the north side, the diaper patterns are (east to west): squares with large round raised rosettes; squares with four-petal rosettes, each bearing a smaller one in a central circle; four squares arranged to form a pattern with diagonal fleur-de-lis, some with a central rosette; squares subdivided into four small squares with two patterns, diagonal fleur-de-lis and eight-petal rosettes; lozenges with flat four-petal flowers; and lozenges with four-petal rosettes, chip carved. The medallions of the four north–east bays are the most similar of any; the tympana of the second, fourth, and fifth (east to west) bays on the south are the most neatly arranged. The chamfered labels are decorated with a scallop pattern.

As actually executed, the second-storey arcade displays the same uniformity in design as the nave arcade, since the tympana patterns, despite their variety, do not show any significantly richer effects at the west than the east. The only progression revealed is the appearance of a few varied leaf capitals replacing the multi-scallop type in the last three bays on the south and the last two on the north.

The interior design of the west wall at Rochester has been gravely affected by the insertion of the Perpendicular west window; although traces of the original arrangement remain, they are not fully revealing of all its particulars.[46] The central portal is flanked by two registers of three arcades equivalent to the nave arcade in height (figs. 46, 11c). Preserved at the sides of the west window are the first bays of two additional registers, the lower one of which only roughly corresponds to the height of the second storey of the nave (fig. 47). It would seem that the lower arcade was originally an open passageway rather than blind as in the case of the upper one.[47] There is no evidence for the size or shape of the Romanesque west window, although it has been suggested that it may have been round.[48]

The end walls of the aisles were also decorated with blind arcading (fig. 48); three bays are found below the window that has a single order of jamb shafts and a moulded arch. A smaller opening above, with unmoulded jambs, gives onto a wall passage and faces a tiny window in the outer skin of the wall (fig. 44, at top). At the angle, the mass of the stair-tower intrudes into the space of the aisle, with the inner corner articulated by an angle-shaft. A chamfered string-course wraps around the intrusion at the level of the capitals of the aisle end window, with a second one twelve courses higher up that marks the original height of the aisle wall; the angle-shaft stops below it. A large portal in the east face of the (southwest) angle tower gives access to the stairs within. Like the aisle end window and blind arcading, the portal's jamb-shafts have small multi-scallop capitals but its arch is distinguished by a fret motif.

The unseen internal arrangements of the façade are perhaps as interesting as the visible ones of its wall faces. The spacious, generously proportioned newel-stairs of the angle stair-towers lead up to a passageway in the thickness of the wall that crosses the front below the sills of the upper aisle-end windows; the passage corresponded to the (lost) register of arcading immediately above the central portal's arch.[49] This wall passage also gave access to the passageways through the second-stage arcades.[50] At the junction with the nave arcades, narrow newel-stairs lead to the higher levels. At clerestory level, in addition to the entrance to the clerestory passageway, there is also evidence of a second passageway across the west front. It would have been behind the uppermost level of internal (blind) arcading, and must have been supported above the lower passageway by means of a series of small vaults. The stair vice continued up to yet another passageway across the front, this at the level of the gable, and to the exit to the nave roof eaves. The well-formed exits from the newel-stairs are preserved at all levels on both sides.[51]

The Documentary Evidence for a Chronology

There is no documentary testimony relating explicitly to the construction of either the existing nave or the façade. As a result, the dates that have been assigned to them – especially to the nave – have varied. For the building history of the cathedral in the middle decades of the twelfth century, there are two events that should either have been reflected in or had an impact on the structure, but their exact significance is now difficult or even impossible to determine. The first is the record of a consecration in May 1130, during the tenure of Bishop John I (1125–37).[52] The other event was a devastating fire in 1137.

No work on the cathedral is credited in the surviving texts to Gundulf's successor, Ralph d'Escures, or to his successor, Ernulf, or to his successor, John, although it is recorded – as previously mentioned – that Ernulf was responsible for building the dormitory, chapter house, and refectory.[53] The records are equally silent regarding the episcopates of John (of Séez) II, Ascelin, and Walter, the very period (1137 to 1182) during the earlier part of which (1137 to 1160 at the latest) the nave and west front were totally reconstructed.

Although a reconstruction of the church, in whole or in part, begun under Ernulf could explain or account for a consecration in 1130 (six years after his death), that date need not be explained by new construction, as it seems more usual than not for final consecrations of completed buildings to take place well after all construction was finished.[54] Indeed, it seems a new choir could be brought into use without any dedication other than the celebration of the first Mass.[55] The dedication at Rochester was held four days after the new choir of Christ Church, Canterbury, was consecrated: the service was led by the archbishop of Canterbury, William of Corbeil (1123–36), and attended by thirteen bishops (two from Normandy) and King Henry I. It was only two years before the dedication, in 1128, that the body of the fourth bishop, Ithamar (644–55), had been translated (from an unknown location).[56] The 1130 consecration at Rochester, coming as it did a few days after that at Canterbury, can be regarded simply as a matter of convenience, rather than as marking a significant event in the constructional history of the building.

The fire of 1137, according to Gervase of Canterbury, was devastating: 'On the third of June, the church of St Andrew, Rochester, was burnt, and the whole city, together with the offices of the bishop and monks.'[57] Whatever the actual extent of the destruction to the east end of the church, which it is now impossible to determine, it seems likely that the nave was rebuilt after this event, and was then immediately followed by the present façade.

Historiography

Despite the lack of documentary testimony, Bishop Ernulf was credited with the remodelling and completion of the nave by W.H.St.J. Hope (1854–1919), as well as an extensive reconstruction and rearrangement of the presbytery, and this attribution of the nave to him has been perpetuated in the subsequent literature. Hope's hypothesis would mean that practically the entire church had been rebuilt or, at least, extensively remodelled, in a period of eleven years or less, work beginning possibly within less than a decade after the death of its founder.[58] The exact amount of time elapsed depends upon just when Gundulf's building campaigns are thought either to have stopped or to have been completed: as has been discussed,[59] there is no definite evidence for the dates concerning these alternative views, which range between 1095 and 1107.

Hope's attribution of this work to Ernulf was partly tied up with his idea that the nave of the church begun by Gundulf had not been fully completed within Gundulf's lifetime.[60] According to Hope, the architectural evidence for new work at the east end consisted of 'various fragments of mouldings that have been found in the [Gothic] quire and presbytery,' along with some stones with a diaper lozenge (later reused in the buttressing wall built under the east arch of the nave north arcade), possibly from a choir screen, as well as a second-floor level in the choir, about a foot or two (0.3048 or 0.6096 m) above that associated with Gundulf's.[61]

Hope was, of necessity, rather vague about the form of the east end as supposedly reconstructed under Ernulf. Presumably, the basic form of the east end of Gundulf's church – as it had been 'discovered' and reconstructed by Hope – was perpetuated or maintained. This long, flat-end aisled presbytery was, as has been discussed, attributed *de novo* to Ernulf (though not completed until after the fire of 1137) by F.H. Fairweather (d. 1950), a dating and attribution that were more or less accepted by A.W. Clapham (1883–1950).[62] Because nothing of it is standing, or is even to be seen, and the architectural fragments associated with it by Hope are now missing, nothing further about the east end can be said in this context. But it would indeed seem strange if such an extensive rebuilding had effectively vanished with scarcely a trance.[63]

Building Phases

The western arm of the church, the only part of the structure still standing that dates to the twelfth century, was the product of two successive building phases, each of which reveals changes in the design intentions.[64] The two phases are, first, the nave arcade and aisle walls, and, second, the west façade. The major change in the design of the nave was the decision to give up the idea of vaulting the aisles, which then affected the form of the second storey of the elevation. The major change in the design of the façade was to abandon the intention to construct two western towers in favour of a new variant of the established sectional façade type.

The rough or uneven surface of the spandrels around the arches on the aisle side of the north arcade suggest that there was once preparation for, or at least the intention to erect, vaults over the aisle at this level (fig. 39).[65] The spandrels on the aisle side of the south arcade are smoother, more finished, and suggest that the idea of vaulting the aisles was given up before the arches of this arcade were constructed. The aisle side of the south arcade also lacks the chevron decorated order and label with a radial zigzag found on the north arcade; in addition, there is a chamfered string-course under the gallery sill. On both sides, however, pilasters rise from the arcade capitals into the gallery level.

Judging from the height and the wide span of the arches, if the existing design can be taken as a reflection of the original intentions, a type of gallery was anticipated in which the arcades opened into the space between the aisle vaults and the lean-to roof above them. It would have been either a false gallery, if there was neither exterior wall nor windows (hence, a low dark space lighted only from the nave), or a low gallery (as at Durham Cathedral), if there was a low exterior wall (i.e., one not equal in height to the arcade) and small external windows. Other subdivided gallery arches of similar proportions are found at Christchurch Priory (Hampshire), and the cathedrals of Chichester (Sussex) and Hereford.[66]

The decision to abandon vaulting certainly affected the design of the second storey in one other respect. As a result of the elimination of the aisle vaults, a passageway through the second-storey piers was included in the construction of what can now best be termed the 'pseudo-gallery.'[67] It also became necessary to carry up the aisle walls higher than was first planned: this is both evidenced by and accounts for the extension to each of the original (eastern) responds in the north aisle.

Hope thought that the space between the upper and lower arches of the arcade of the pseudo-gallery was originally open, as in the eastern nave bays at Romsey Abbey (Hampshire), of the 1140s.[68] He considered the stones with the diapering to be a later insertion, because of irregularities in the coursing of the pattern, 'many of them being chopped up to fit them in.'[69] The irregularities, however, seem the result of carelessness because they occur in the lower courses, immediately above the double arches, not at the outer circumference where they would be expected if the space had been filled in later.

The existing west front was not built with the aisle walls and nave arcades.[70] There is a vertical joint visible at the end of each arcade: nor is the coursing continuous across the responds and the west wall.[71] This suggests that the arcades were built while the first façade was still standing, and that it was only replaced as the last phase of work. The features of the upper part of the aisle end wall, above the lower string-course and the arch of the window, additionally confirm that when the façade was built all intention of constructing vaults or a gallery at arcade level had been given up: the aisle end wall is designed as a response to a single tall space equal to nave arcade and second-storey openings.[72] The enlarged scale of the western piers further suggests that there had been some thought of erecting a pair of west towers. This implication appears to have been confirmed during the underpinning of the north aisle wall (1875–6), and later of the west front (1888), when large blocks of (reused?) tufa were found. They were interpreted as the beginning of foundations for a west tower.[73]

Proposed (Revised) Chronology

First of all, it must be stressed that there is no remaining physical evidence of any work at the east end of the building that can be attributed to Ernulf.[74] The stones with the lozenge pattern, which Hope and others at that time thought were similar to work associated with Ernulf at Canterbury and elsewhere at Rochester, that is, the chapter house,[75] are now dated to the second not the first quarter of the century. The work at Canterbury, the north passage to the crypt, has since been assigned to circa 1150.[76] A slightly earlier date of circa 1140 is also now recognized for the west wall of the Rochester chapter house.[77] With the disappearance of the moulded stones, and the redating of the lozenge pattern, the slight concrete evidence for Ernulf's choir has vanished.

It is, of course, conceivable that Ernulf, during his ten-year episcopate, enlarged the presbytery of the cathedral as had been recently accomplished at Canterbury, that latter work initiated when he had served as prior there. If this was the case, Ernulf's work at Rochester was formally very different from that at Canterbury, for the so-called Glorious Choir consisted of an extension almost as long as the nave of Lanfranc's church, terminating in an ambulatory and radiating chapels and including a crypt under the whole of it.[78] If the straight eastern termination postulated by Ashpitel and then Hope, with or without a small eastern chapel, represented the work of

Ernulf, then the new work consisted of an *extension* to Gundulf's crypt and presbytery. As the solid side walls are still in evidence, Ernulf clearly did not replace Gundulf's presbytery as a result of a desire to 'modernize' it, that is, to construct a conventional presbytery with arcades for its full length. In this case, the resultant increase in size was not appreciable, certainly not in any way comparable to the difference in scale between the new 'Glorious Choir' and Lanfranc's presbytery at Canterbury. The increase at both levels really amounted only to replacing a curved apse by a rectilinear one. The effect on the aisles at crypt and main level would have been somewhat greater but hardly dramatic: two square bays replacing an apse. As a result, it is difficult to retroactively justify such an alteration. The reason, moreover, for additional building or rebuilding at that time at Rochester is less than obvious. The reason is unlikely to have been in order to accommodate more monks; it is said the number had been increased by Gundulf during his episcopate from the initial twenty-two to sixty and no doubt his long presbytery with the choir in the crossing and first bay of the nave was planned as sufficient accommodation. There is no recorded increase in the size of the monastic community during the period between 1108 and 1114.

There is always the possibility that the purported straight-ended presbytery was the result of modifications made following the 1137 fire. In this case, for the same reasons as outlined above, the new work would represent a modestly scaled extension to Gundulf's long presbytery, a replacement of the apse by two rectilinear bays.

There is little or no evidence to suggest any rebuilding in the area of the transept at this time. The walls briefly revealed in 1968 that were dated by C.A.R. Radford (1900–98) to the late tenth century and circa 1100, and that have been discussed in earlier chapters,[79] appear to have been at a level above that of the floor of Gundulf's church.[80] This would suggest that the L-plan segment of wall might date to the mid-twelfth century. However, its composition as reported, 'flint and Kentish rag set in a hard brown mortar,' does not match that of the twelfth-century work, especially with regard to the use of a brown mortar: G.M. Livett (1859–1951) described the 'Later-Norman' mortar as being grey and shelly.[81] Once again, there seems to be nothing quite comparable to it elsewhere in the building to help with the dating and so it is necessary to fall back upon the evidence of the levels. Nor does the sleeper wall of chalk blocks (or the chalk foundation) of 'circa 1100' correspond to any of the foundation types uncovered in the nave in the 1870s or 1880s, none of which used chalk *blocks*.[82] Owing to the limited extent of the walls uncovered and, especially, to the limited amount of information available about them, and because even less is known about the nature of the foundations and possible sleeper walls under the nave arcade and crossing piers, it is incautious, even futile, to attempt to speculate about their possible significance.[83]

The major problem with the date for the nave proposed by Hope also involves the question of style: the nave, judged by its decoration, is more likely to be post–1125, or even post–1135, than pre-.[84] The date of the nave, of course, relates to the date of the west front that was regarded by Hope as a continuation of Ernulf's work in the nave, built or completed under Bishop John I, therefore presumably before 1137.[85] By contrast, the west front has been dated by other authorities at no earlier than circa 1150; more usually it has been dated even later, circa 1160–70.[86] Clapham, more sensibly, but without any discussion, dated the nave to 1140–50,[87] which considerably narrowed the gap between it and the date assigned by others to the west front. Recently, although specifically with regard to the west portal, the date appears to have settled at circa 1160.[88]

Stylistically, there are many features of the nave design that could occur earlier but that, in combination, produce an ensemble more typical of the period after 1115–24/1124–37 than before. This is true of the variable pier types that have numerous successors in the second half of the century – frequently among the larger parish churches, as well as of the multi-scallop capitals of the nave arcade piers, of the chevron design of the arches,[89] and of the diapered tympana; all look towards the massed decorative effects common after the 1140s, exemplified by the arcading on the inside and outside of Rochester's own façade.

The use of a different design for each pair of piers at Rochester is preceded only by the choir of the then abbey of Peterborough (Northamptonshire), begun in 1118, and perhaps in the nave of Castle Acre Priory (Norfolk); the latter may be slightly earlier or just contemporary with Rochester. The variation in pattern at the former is rather inconspicuous. At Castle Acre, the effect is quite flamboyant, for the variation from pier to pier was compounded by coordinating the opposed faces, with the result that each pier was actually made up of two designs. Later examples of changing pier patterns are found in small churches such as Whaplode (Lincolnshire), circa 1150, Orford

(Suffolk), circa 1170, and, especially, the abbey hospital(?) – now the parish church of St Thomas a Becket – of Ramsey (Huntingdonshire), circa 1170–80. Symmetrical alternation of two or more types also occurs more frequently later in the century, as at the monastic infirmaries of the cathedrals of Ely (Cambridgeshire), circa 1175, and Norwich (Norfolk), late twelfth, or in parish churches such as Wisbech Church (Cambridgeshire), late twelfth.[90] As most later variation in pier forms was limited to a few forms and involved some kind of rhythmic sequence, Rochester remains exceptional, if not unique, in the pattern of its piers.[91]

The multi-scallop capitals of the piers also support a post-Ernulf date, that is, at least after 1125: in Rochester they appear in the great hall of the keep begun by Archbishop William of Corbeil some time after 1127.[92] The later date of post–1137 is buttressed by several other features found at the west end of the nave, such as the leaf spurs on the north arcade pier plinths and the chevron roundels of the southwest arcade spandrel. The latter is a motif that appears in a somewhat more elaborate form on the upper stage of the minor transept stair-turrets at Christ Church, Canterbury.[93] These stair-turrets were completed by Prior Wibert (1153–67), who also built the great gate where the same motif appears.[94] Leaf spurs are also found at some of Wibert's other Canterbury work: a surviving base of the open arcade of the undercroft of his Aula Nova and the bases of his now mostly destroyed cloister.[95] While the work carried out during Wibert's years as prior does not generally offer exact parallels for the work at Rochester in the nave and on the west front, it is similar in spirit.[96] This is due, especially, to the use of diverse patterns and enriched arcading such as, for example, ornamented string-courses, including the zigzag, as on the Canterbury vestiarium, and diaper patterns on the jambs between shafts and in horizontal rows on wall surfaces, as in the minor transept stair-turrets of Christ Church. Chevron-decorated arches of various types also abound at Canterbury.

Beak-like spurs had occurred on the shaft bases of the chapter-house doorway at Rochester that also has another motif found on the interior shaft bases of the west portal, one of the flanking arcade bases, and both bases of the exterior north aisle arch. This motif is a band of pyramidal studs (fig. 11c). The reappearance of this motif at the west front again suggests that it may have been begun during the late 1140s, the date now generally accepted for the decorative features of the east range of the cloister.[97] Outside of Kent, spurs decorate the bases of the nave arcade piers at Melbourne Church (Derbyshire), a building that has been (conservatively?) dated to circa 1136–57, and in the crypt of Archbishop Roger Pont l'Évêque, circa 1160, at York Minster.[98]

A motif of some prominence at Canterbury after circa 1150, and which consequently achieved widespread popularity in Kent, appears on the inside of the west front. This motif is the fret, found only in the nave around the arch of the doorway into the southwest stair-tower (fig. 48). Its presence there, but not elsewhere in the nave, can be taken as evidence that the west front was certainly in construction during the 1150s.[99]

The construction of the nave during the 1140s agrees with a time-frame of the 1150s for the façade, to which it is closely related stylistically, and suggests that the current date of circa 1160 for the façade portal could be pushed back to 1150–5. The record of two bells being placed in a 'major tower' some time during this period by Prior Reginald (1146–54)[100] allows the further hypothesis that the central tower was rebuilt – or, perhaps, was simply carried one storey higher than the roofs – at the time work on the western half of the nave was progressing to a conclusion.

Liturgical Arrangements

The evidence for the liturgical arrangements at the east end after the rebuilding of the nave are slight. It has been suggested that the rood screen separating the monastic from the parochial church was placed at the third pair of nave piers west of the crossing.[101] The monks' stalls were consequently thought to have been located in the western half of the crossing and first two nave bays, with, in the presbytery, the matutinal altar positioned between the first and second bay, and the high altar at the end of the third bay. As a result of the acceptance of Hope's straight east end, but with continuous solid side walls, doors communicating between the aisles and presbytery were placed in the fourth bay, with the fifth and final bay occupied by four subsidiary chapels formed by altars placed against the east wall.[102]

This reconstruction both confuses 'evidence' from the existing twelfth-century nave (the hypothetical location of the rood screen) with the eleventh-century church (the hypothetical flat-ended presbytery) and ignores the evidence of floor levels from the excavation of J.T. Irvine under the modern floor of the Gothic choir. In particular, the suggestion that there were three levels in the presbytery created by a flight of five steps under the east crossing arch and additional flights of four steps in both the first and second 'bays,' contradicts Irvine's findings, especially regarding the lowest level identified with Gundulf's church.[103] It will be recalled that the excavation produced indications of only *two* six inch (15.24 cm) steps, separated by eleven and one-half feet (3.5052 m), stepping up from the west end of the choir, which was at the same level as the nave floor, to a sloping surface that abutted the west face of the west wall of the crypt well below the level of the crypt vaults (over five feet [1.524 m] below the present upper floor level). The existence of a second floor, *uniform* in level, two feet above the lowest level of the floor associated with Gundulf's building, was also ignored: Irvine reported that this plaster floor covered only the centre, which he took as indicating the presence of stalls along either side of the solid-walled choir (this was revealed at the west end of the choir; the eastern extent of the stalls was not traced).[104] Hope – if not Irvine – identified this level with rebuilding due to Ernulf,[105] but this level and arrangement may be the ones that prevailed after whatever rebuilding or repair was necessitated by the fire of 1137. However the evidence produced by the tunnelling should be interpreted, none of the plaster floor levels reportedly uncovered by Irvine permits a restoration involving three flights of stairs within the choir. Yet it must be said that, if Irvine's report that the extent of the second floor level implied the presence of stalls is correct, it then suggests that the choir may have been moved further east, perhaps removed from the east bay of the nave, and this might then provide an argument for a modest eastward extension by Ernulf. However, neither the modest length of the extension nor the fact that the presbytery was still at two strongly differentiated levels would really seem to allow for the relocation of some stalls east of the crossing.

A vision recounted in the 'Miracula S. Ithamari Ep[iscopi].' may describe the rood at the time of the completion of the nave: a horizontal beam supporting a cross and boxes containing the relics of the saints.[106] It is perhaps of greater interest that the author of the 'Miracula,' which was probably composed in the decade or two following 1130, refers to the existing building as if it were that erected by Gundulf unaltered (as it may well have been if the 'Miracula' was composed before the fire of 1137); he makes no mention of Ernulf.

Although his mission was no doubt to emphasize the venerability of the relics by associating them with the earlier bishop who possessed a reputation for great piety and devotion to the (Anglo-Saxon) saints,[107] the narrative might well have made additional reference to Ernulf's accommodation of the relics in his remodelled sanctuary – if that had, indeed, been the case. Instead, the author recounts only the two translations of the relics by Gundulf, first from their (unspecified) original place of burial to a 'testudo' on the north side of the church and then to a position in the presbytery accessible to many where they were placed in a 'theca inestimabilis thesauri.'[108]

Determining the extent and location of the monks' choir in this period becomes yet more complicated and fraught with uncertainty, when a third floor level encountered in the course of the 1872 tunnelling is taken into account.[109] This level, which was one foot ten inches (0.5588 m) above the second (two feet nine inches [0.8382 m] below the present), would appear to have been continuous over the entire width of the choir. It was attributed by Hope to either post-1137, or post-1179; if post-1137, it might suggest that the stalls had not yet at that time been moved east of the crossing.

The Position of the Twelfth-Century Rebuilding with regard to Contemporary Architecture

Presbytery

The plan of the straight-ended presbytery in the form postulated by Hope has already been discussed in the previous chapter.[110] If that plan was either the result of an extension carried out by Ernulf or a consequence of the 1137 fire, it would at either time, but especially at the earlier date, still be a rather remarkable occurrence. The small projecting oblong chapel would continue, of course, to be quite extraordinary, although it may be recalled that recent – admittedly limited – excavation did not produce evidence confirming Hope's reported discovery.[111]

Nave[112]

Throughout its course, English Romanesque displayed an interest in varied pier design.[113] This is demonstrated by the many examples of alternating pier systems: subtle, as in the case of the nave of Ely Cathedral – where, after 1107, the forms alternate between two versions of the compound type, one with shafts, the other with shafts and segments of round piers[114] – or at Worksop Priory (Nottinghamshire) – where the nave piers (ca. 1180), like those of the choir of Christ Church, Canterbury (ca. 1175–9), alternate between round and octagonal; or more obvious, as at Durham Cathedral, begun in 1093, with its boldly contrasting forms of compound and round piers.[115] The nave of Durham, circa 1110–28, displays an attitude that is intensified at Rochester: the round piers are decorated with three different geometric patterns – trellis, horizontal zigzag, and vertical cabling/fluting – arranged in pairs across the nave, so there is, in effect, more than simple alternation. There was a similar combination of alternation and variety in the nave arcade at Lindisfarne Priory (Northumberland) in the 1120s or 1130s. Both Durham and Lindisfarne were preceded by the much smaller round piers belonging to the undercroft of Lanfranc's dormitory at Canterbury, which were carved with a variety of geometric patterns (chevron, spiral, lattice).[116] At Rochester, all the piers may be described as compound, and there is no alternation or use of geometric patterns; instead, the theme of constantly varying designs has been taken up and made into the controlling principle (figs. 34, 35).[117]

The predominance of the pier design in the design of the elevation at Rochester is as unusual in a Romanesque context as it is common in the early Gothic (figs. 34, 35).[118] On the other hand, precedents for diapered tympana extend back to the late eleventh century: Rochester's, which are the most elaborate of any, may be at the end of the series (fig. 36).[119]

West Façade

The richness of the nave arcade was matched, if not exceeded, by the west front, although the insertion of the Perpendicular window has diminished the effect (fig. 41). Despite the fact that the west front is modest in scale and in its basic architectural form, it is not without impact owing to its richly arcaded and decorated surfaces. Nor is the fundamental form without interest with respect to the history of façade design in this century, as it is neither of the two standard types that predominated during this period – the sectional façade and the twin-tower façade[120] – although it is closer to the former than the latter. Nevertheless, the façade of Rochester has been the object of scholarly attention and interest less because of its architectural form than because of the figurative sculpture of its central portal. Consequently, the west front has been dated less on the basis of its architectural style than on the style of the column figures and tympanum. The sculpture ensemble as a whole has never been the subject of a thorough analytical study, but the dating of the west portal, although variable, has never been placed earlier than 1150–60, while, until recently, dates after 1160 have been favoured.[121]

The application of numerous registers of arcading may be paralleled by the destroyed façade of Hereford Cathedral (complete by 1150?), and the façades of Castle Acre, St Botolph's at Colchester (Essex), Croyland Abbey (Lincolnshire), and Malmesbury Abbey (Wiltshire), all generally dated to the period between 1150 and 1170.[122] It is a reflection and an expression of the increasing taste for rich surface effects in the developing Romanesque style in England, and elsewhere, which reached a full, if not absolutely definitive formulation by mid-century.[123]

The notable sculptural adornment of the façade centres on the west portal with two column figures, one male and one female; a tympanum with Christ in Majesty supported by two angels and surrounded by the beasts of the Evangelists; a lintel with the seated Apostles; and archivolt voussoirs carved with a variety of motifs – foliage, birds, and masks in the main – as has been described (fig. 45). The six small tympana under the arches of the second tier of arcading complete the ensemble (figs. 42, 43). All of these features have been traced to various regions of France, in terms of their type, style, and subject matter, and are features with few parallels in England.[124]

Of these features, the two column figures have attracted the greatest attention, as they constitute a unique survival in Britain from this period.[125] Such figures are, of course, characteristic of the early Gothic portals of churches in northeastern France, from their initial appearance at the abbey church of Saint-Denis (Seine-St-Denis), circa 1135–40, and at Chartres Cathedral (Eure-et-Loir), circa 1145, which suggests a *terminus post quem* for the Rochester façade. In England, the use of column figures in this period was most unusual. Among the major churches, those at Rochester were paralleled at Lincoln alone where they are known only from eighteenth-century engravings.[126] Just one other smaller-scale example survives, from Minster-in-Sheppey (Kent),[127] while another that formerly graced a window of the Moot Hall in Colchester (Essex) is, again, known only from an eighteenth-century drawing.[128]

Sculptured tympana are frequently found in the portals of English Romanesque parish churches, but are uncommon occurrences in the design of major church west portals (fig. 45). Carved tympana were part of the portal ensemble, along with column figures, of the French churches already alluded to; however, the iconography employed in the Rochester tympanum is characteristic of examples from Burgundy rather than the Île-de-France.[129]

A third region of France is implicated in the case of the archivolt voussoirs (fig. 45). The distinctive arrangement of the motifs in a radial fashion on the orders has been traced to the Poitou.[130] It should be noted that the mode in which the sculpture is applied to the voussoirs of the Poitevin churches most often mentioned in comparison with Rochester, the west façade of Notre-Dame-la-Grande, Poitiers (Vienne), and the south transept portal at Aulnay-de-Saintonge (Charente-Maritime), produces a very different effect from that seen at Rochester. In the west French buildings, the original planar surface of the vertical outer face of the archivolt is maintained – despite the deeply undercut carving, and is further emphasized by the retention of the right angle between the two voussoir faces; the horizontal inner plane is *not* carved. By contrast, at Rochester, where the outer plane is not flat and the right angle between the planes is eliminated (the inner plane is reduced to a narrow band), the sculpture is placed on a diagonal surface.[131]

The same general region also seems to be the origin of the small tympana under the arcades (fig. 43), even though they do not seem to have been a common phenomena there. Small tympana bearing motifs similar to some at Rochester are found at several prominent Poitevin churches, notably, once again, Notre-Dame-la-Grande at Poitiers and the two former priory churches of Parthenay-le-Vieux (Deux-Sèvres) and Villesalem (Vienne).[132] As a motif, small tympana are found as far afield as on the façades of churches at Ronsenac (Charente) in the neighbouring Angoumois, and Jussy-Champagne (Cher), to the east in Berry. In the west French buildings, the small tympana are associated with pairs of subarches placed under the larger lateral arches of a tripartite design that includes the central portal. Thus, the way they are placed at Rochester is distinctively different, and the compositional ensemble in which they take part in the west of France is not repeated at Rochester.[133]

The other features of the façade sculpture have drawn very little, if any, comment – the non-column-figure shafts of the portal,[134] the portal capitals,[135] the lintel,[136] and the corbels, capitals, and other decorative motifs of the arcading.[137]

In contrast to the sculptural enrichment, the basic design of the façade is not paralleled by the façade types of any of the regions with which the sculptural motifs have been associated.[138] Only one French building, the cathedral of Le Mans (Sarthe), seems to offer any similarities.[139] In its original form, it had a pronounced, clearly articulated turret at each of its western corners: the wall in between them was flat, all in one plane. There was a central portal only, with – perhaps significantly vis-à-vis Rochester – shallow flanking recesses; however, there were no recesses on the aisle ends. The façade also lacked registers of arcading, no doubt because of its relatively early date, circa 1120.[140]

The basic organization of the façade of Rochester, in its departure from the standard sectional type, may have been anticipated in England only by one other building. In the design of the façade of the priory church at Lindisfarne, circa 1130, the flat wall of the sectional façade, punctuated and defined by shallow pilaster buttresses at the angles and in the line of the nave arcades, was replaced by prominent stair-towers flanking a flat field. The slope of the aisle roof was also hidden by a wall rising to a horizontal line. Anticipating Rochester, the use of pilaster buttresses to articulate the three major divisions (nave and side aisles) and to hide small stair vices was abandoned at Lindisfarne. As noted earlier, at Rochester, changes in plane, in order to achieve articulation, were substituted and, following Lindisfarne, small stair-towers at the angles were adopted, although it would seem the slope of the aisle roof was revealed. Formally, both of these façades are early manifestations of changes in façade design that are heading in the direction of the screen façade, as fully revealed a century later at Salisbury Cathedral (Wiltshire). Between Rochester and Lindisfarne, on the one hand, and Salisbury, on the other, lie the façades of buildings such as Croyland and Malmesbury abbeys.[141] Architecturally, then, the façade of Rochester is significant for its rejection of either of the two then standard façade-types, the sectional façade and the twin-tower façade, and for the introduction and emphasis of different features. Allied to this, of course, is the decorative treatment of nearly the entire surface with registers of arcading, an important and distinctive aspect of façade design in England during the later twelfth and the thirteenth centuries. Ironically, with regard to the future of façade design in England, the façade of Rochester is more significant for its architectural form than for the appearance of figurative sculpture centring on the west portal, which, as it turned out, had little future in the British Isles.

One other, less visible, aspect of the façade deserves comment. On the basis of comparisons with several other nearly contemporary and later buildings, the prominent newel-stairs and the lowest arcaded passageway across the interior of the front may have had a specific liturgical function (fig. 47). That is to say, this lowest passage, which was open to the nave through an arcade, corresponds to the second register of arcading on the west face (fig. 41) and may therefore have had only small slit windows opening to the exterior. If it did, it bears a resemblance to the arcaded passageway between the central portal and the west windows found at Salisbury a century later. That passageway, and a similar but enclosed one at Wells Cathedral (Somerset), has been assigned a role in the Palm Sunday liturgy.[142] Specifically, choristers were stationed in it to sing the response to the hymn 'Gloria, laus et honor' as the cathedral clergy and congregation, assembled in front of the church, prepared to re-enter the cathedral. The choristers were meant to be heard, not seen – hence there were only narrow apertures towards the exterior, hidden behind sculpture at both Wells and Salisbury.[143] The amplitude of the newel-stairs ('stair-towers') at Rochester, more than necessary for the utilitarian purpose of providing access for maintenance, would be appropriate for use by choristers in long robes.

At least two other Romanesque buildings in England may have had west front wall passages with a similar function. As mentioned above, the earlier façade of Lindisfarne Priory, despite its smaller scale, had small stair-towers like those at Rochester at the angles. They led to a passageway across the west wall, open to the nave through five arcades. A single wide doorway gave access from the passage to a small chamber (now destroyed) placed over the projecting orders of its portal-porch, under a double-pitched roof.[144] A second example, perhaps contemporary with Rochester, and closer geographically, is at St Botolph's, Colchester. As at Rochester, the relevant level has not survived complete, but there is clear evidence of an arcaded wall passage above the west portal that opened to the west by small slit windows and that, therefore, could have served a similar liturgical function.[145]

Conclusions

It would be gratifying to reconcile some of the conflicting interpretations of the building history as presented by earlier scholars, but the concrete evidence permits only the statement of several possible alternatives.[146] The first possibility, for which there is neither stylistic nor textual evidence, is to accept the modern attribution of a partial or complete rebuilding of the east end, either perpetuating or introducing a long choir with a straight east wall, to Ernulf, and then to assume that this east end was relatively undamaged in the fire of 1137, which did, however, necessitate the rebuilding of the nave.[147] In this case, it might seem rather surprising that Ernulf's chapter house and dormitory were badly damaged while his lengthened presbytery escaped unscathed, were it not for the fact that the presbytery would not have extended as far east as the east range of the cloister, and perhaps was vaulted.

Another possibility is that Gundulf's building was badly damaged by the fire of 1137, including the east end, which was possibly less severely affected than the nave. The long apsidal presbytery and crypt were then rebuilt or remodelled, including a short extension involving three aisles all ending in one flat wall – forming the first example of its type, but one not so far separated in years from the next, Holy Cross, Winchester (Hampshire), circa 1160, as it would be if dated to circa 1080. Rebuilding after 1137 also eventually produced the nave and west front we now have. This interpretation therefore assigns no work in the church proper to Ernulf, but rather postulates a nearly total rebuilding of the church during the two decades following the fire of 1137.[148] Such an extensive rebuilding between 1137 and 1150/55 (the suggested date of the west portal and front) would seem to be a rather – if not remarkably – speedy accomplishment, considering the repairs and rebuilding necessary in the cloister.

A third possibility is (a) to regard the evidence for a straight cast end as a fiction – until more positive evidence is forthcoming – and (b) to assume that the original Gundulfian east end, which consisted of solid side walls to the presbytery and an apsidal termination, was undamaged in the fire and rebuilding only of the nave was required. This possibility may gain a certain plausibility if two factors are considered. Even if Gundulf's church had a relatively long presbytery triapsidal in form (that is, four bays versus Hope's presbytery of seven bays), Ernulf's chapter house and dormitory would still have been detached from the church at some distance further east. There-fore, they could have been damaged without necessarily involving equally serious damage to the east end of the church (as was possi-bly the case in the first alternative). In addition, if one considers that Gundulf's presbytery with its solid side walls may well have been vaulted, its preservation would be less surprising. Gundulf's nave on the other hand must have been wooden-roofed and perhaps suffered the consequences.

The character of the work undertaken after the fire of 1137 – the rather slight nature of the nave aisle walls, and the several changes of plan – might be explained by the need to restore the monastic offices at the same time. Funds had to be divided between church and monastery. Any extension of the crypt and presbytery, if it did indeed take place at this time, might of necessity have been modest. While the rebuilding of the nave, owing to the abandonment of the aisle vaults, proved in some ways equally modest, surface decoration seems to have been called forth in order to compensate for a reduced splendour of scale or complexity of structure.

Epilogue

According to Gervase of Canterbury (d. ca. 1210), a second fire of 1179 was equally disastrous as the first: 'On the fourth of the ides of April, a sad accident happened to the church at Rochester. For this church of St Andrew with its offices, and this city, was consumed by fire and reduced to a cinder.'[149] His authority may be suspect, as his claim that the church was reduced to cinders is manifestly not the case.[150] Even so, a second account also tells us that 'the church of Rochester, with all the offices and the whole of the city within and without the walls, was burnt a second time on the 11th of April.'[151] It is difficult to judge what the extent of the damage *actually* was: obviously the nave and west front were little affected.[152]

The degree to which this fire affected the east end has been con-sidered minimal. Hope, following Irvine, thought that only repairs were necessary. During the repairs of Irvine to the transepts in 1872, some mouldings were recovered that Irvine thought resembled work at Canterbury dated to 1175–9.[153] These three pieces, in which pronounced rolls and hollows were augmented by dogtooth, billet, and chevron occurring individually, rather than together as at Canterbury, with equal likelihood could be related to rebuilding in the cloister under the patronage of Bishop Gilbert Glanville (1185–1214),[154] rather than to repairs to the transept carried out post-1179. In addition, Irvine recorded that 'an ancient floor of plaster ... was cut through' one foot (0.3048 m) below the present stone paving in St Edmund's Chapel (the south choir aisle), or eleven and one-half inches (0.2921 cm) below the stone floor in the south transept; it was discovered during the laying of gas pipes in 1876.[155] He went on to note: 'The plaster floor in the transept bore strong marks of fire being discoloured to some depth. Masses of lead which had poured down in a melted state from the burning roof above were found run into and sunk into its surface.' Is this evidence of the severity of the fire in 1179? Irvine also reported that the 'plinth of the large square buttress at the top of the stairs down into the crypt from St. Edmund's chapel had stood on this floor.' The buttress in question certainly belongs to the Gothic rebuilding and dates well after 1227, and although one might expect its footings to have been cut through the plaster floor, especially as the floor must pre-date 1179, it is difficult to understand how its plinth could have *stood* on this floor, unless it was a matter of the plinth having been carried down below its contemporary floor level. In any case, it has generally not been considered that this fire may have been the primary cause or motivation behind the erection of the Early Gothic east end now existing.[156]

FIVE

The Early Gothic Rebuilding

Historical Précis: Personages and Events[1]

The end of one century and the beginning of the next were linked by the overlapping episcopate of Gilbert Glanville, 1185 to 1214.[2] His episcopate was one of the stormier ones in terms of the relationship between bishop and monks in the history of Rochester – or possibly it is just one of the better documented. His appointment seems to have had the support of King Henry II (1154–89) and formed part of a plan to replace the monks by a college of secular canons, as the previous bishop, Waleran (1182–4), had perhaps planned to do.[3] The king's death (at Chinon [Touraine], 6 July) put an end to such ideas at Rochester, as well as at the cathedral priory of Canterbury.

As an expert in canon and civil law, Bishop Gilbert was much away from his cathedral church. Gilbert preached the Third Crusade with Archbishop Baldwin (1185–90) at Geddington (Northamptonshire) in 1188 and was in favour with King Richard I, Coeur-de-Lion (1189–99). After Richard's capture (by Duke Leopold V of Austria) and subsequent imprisonment in Germany by the emperor, Henry VI (1190–7), from February 1193, Gilbert worked hard for his release, which was achieved a year later (February 1194).

His relationship with King John (1199–1216 [at Newark]) was less happy. The death of Hubert Walter, archbishop (1193–1205) of Canterbury, had eventually resulted in an interdict being imposed by Pope Innocent III (1198–1215) because John had refused to accept the papal nominee, Stephen Langton, as archbishop. All but two of the English bishops went into exile. Already, in 1207, Bishop Gilbert had fled to Scotland in order to avoid persecution; the next year he went to Rome. During the interdict, 1209–13, all ecclesiastical property, both spiritualities and temporalities, was seized by the king; subsistence allowances were granted to the clergy.[4] The losses of the clergy are considered to have been 'exceedingly heavy.' Only the threat of an invasion under the leadership of the French king, Philip Augustus (1180–1223), which was promoted by Innocent III, brought John to submission in May 1213; Langton and his bishops returned.

With the lifting of the interdict, the years of turmoil were not yet over. At Runnymede, on 15 June 1215, John had been forced to capitulate to the demands of his barons by issuing Magna Carta. Innocent, however, annulled the Charter, suspended Archbishop Stephen Langton (1207–28), excommunicated the baronial rebels, and imposed an interdict on London. In 1215, King John laid siege to the castle of Rochester and his troops and followers are said to have pillaged the priory.[5] By March 1216 John had hemmed in the barons in London. The future King Louis VIII (1223–6) of France landed in Kent in response to the barons' offer of the crown to him. At this point John died; his successor was the infant, King Henry III (1216–72), thus necessitating a regency (until Henry came of age in 1227). It was left therefore to Hubert de Burgh, who was shortly to become grand justiciary of England (1219–30), to destroy Louis's fleet and reinforcements on 24 August 1217.

Beginning in the late twelfth century, in the election first of Waleran, then of Gilbert, as bishop, the monks of Rochester attempted to assert their independence from Canterbury and the right to elect their bishop in their chapter.[6] Bishop Benedict of Sawston (1215–26), precentor of St Paul's and the choice of the Rochester monks, was consecrated at Oxford in an attempt to evade the domination of Canterbury. Yet upon the death of Bishop Henry Sandford (1227–35), Archbishop (Saint) Edmund of Canterbury (1234–40) refused to accept the election by the prior and chapter of Richard Wendene, rector of Bromley; after three years of litigation, the will of the Rochester monks finally prevailed. Although Pope Gregory IX (1227–41) confirmed the election and upheld the right of the Rochester monks to elect their bishop in chapter, Wendene's successor, Bishop Lawrence of St Martin (1251–74), waged unsuccessful litigation to secure the further independence of Rochester from Canterbury. Nonetheless, thereafter, it would seem, the monks routinely petitioned the archbishop for, and received, licence to elect upon the death of their bishop.

In contrast with the election of the bishops, which was often disputatious, primarily because of the relationship with Canterbury, the priors were elected without royal or even episcopal interference, although the monks often complained of episcopal abuses and interference in other matters, such as the rights of presentation to benefices or the appointment of priory servants. Interestingly enough (and perhaps an indication of Rochester's modest position in the ecclesiastical hierarchy in Britain), after 1189 no monk or prior left Rochester to rule elsewhere. According to the 'Custumale Roffense,' written circa 1300, by a monk of Rochester, John de Westerham (later prior, 1320–1), there were eight principal obedientiaries at Rochester, all of whom were elected by chapter, although five(*) were approved by the bishop: a subprior (responsible for the maintenance of discipline), a precentor or cantor, an almoner(*), a sacrist(*), a chamberlain(*), a cellarer(*), an infirmarer(*), and a warden of the chapel of St Mary ([of the Hospital of St Mary in Strood, founded by Gilbert ca. 1192/4] whose duties were combined with those of a feretrar), plus the prior. There was no anniversarian, no pittancer, no feretrar – despite the existence of three shrines (of Saints Paulinus [625–44], Ithamar [644–55], and William of Perth [?–1201]) – and never a treasurer.[7]

The little evidence for the financial situation of the priory during the last years of the twelfth century and the first half, even three quarters, of the thirteenth does not suggest that it was a propitious time for a major building campaign. For instance, the priory had apparently incurred huge debts as a result of the legal battle with Bishop Gilbert and his successors that had lasted well into the second half of the thirteenth century. Even as late as the ninth decade of the century, the situation was still of sufficient gravity that Archbishop John Peckam (1279–92) accused the prior, John de Rainham (1262–83), of maladministration and debt, and removed him from office.[8] Against this background, the murder just outside Rochester in 1201 of one William, a baker from Perth, who was on pilgrimage to the Holy Land, would seem to have been most fortuitous.[9] Offerings from his shrine are said to have allowed for the rebuilding of the east end and choir by 1227.[10] However, his cult seems to have taken off rather slowly compared to other contemporary ones in the wake of Thomas Becket's murder (1170) at Canterbury and subsequent canonization (1173). William of Perth was canonized only in 1256,[11] whereas Gilbert of Sempringham, who died in 1189, was canonized in 1202; Wulfstan of Worcester (d. 1095), who began to work miracles in 1201, was canonized in 1203; and Bishop Hugh of Lincoln, who died in 1200, was admitted to the calendar in 1220.[12] The flow of pilgrims to the shrine of William may have diminished rather rapidly from whatever height it had achieved earlier in the century, as the income does not seem to have been sufficient to allow for the completion of the main transept in the 1240s.

Within this period, the most notable events that might be expected to have had some direct impact on the fabric of the cathedral were the fire of 1179; the flight and exile of Bishop Gilbert; the Interdict; the sack or pillaging of the cathedral by King John; and the invasion of Kent by the French dauphin, Louis. Except for the first, all the other events define the decade 1207 to 1217.

The New Work

The effect of the fire of 1179, seemingly as severe as that of 1137, which reportedly devastated the city, monastery, and cathedral of Rochester, is difficult to assess, as the cathedral was supposedly completely consumed, which is obviously not true, as the surviving nave and west front testify.[13] However, it may have been the east end in particular that was gravely damaged (having perhaps escaped significant damage in the fire of 1137), and it was this event that may have led to the complete rebuilding – involving a considerable extension – of the east end, a building phase otherwise unexplained by any of the surviving sources. At the same time, there is little evidence that any effort had once again to be expended upon either the repair or the extensive rebuilding of the monastic offices,[14] although Bishop Gilbert is credited with having arranged for the completion of the cloister in stone, presumably between 1185 and 1207.[15]

The new work at the east end completely replaced all the Romanesque structure east of the nave proper, except for the solid side walls of the late-eleventh-century presbytery and the two bays of the crypt under its eastern half of the same date (figs. 1, 8). The rebuilding represented a very significant enlargement, even granting the possibility of an earlier six- or seven-bay, aisled, straight-ended eastern arm. The work consists of an aisleless presbytery of two double bays with a straight east wall, an aisled minor east transept extending two bays on either side of the crossing, a new clerestory and vaults over the former presbytery, which now became the choir, choir aisles of four bays, and a major east transept – the arms projecting more boldly than in the case of the minor one – with a towered crossing.[16] Rather unexpectedly, it included a greatly enlarged crypt (fig. 8), one coextensive with the area of the presbytery and minor transept.

The Physical Evidence

Exterior

The presbytery (figs. 49, 50) is characterized by massive turret-like buttresses at its eastern angles that, however, do not contain newel-stairs in their lower half, and by a strongly projecting buttress placed in the middle of each side wall, quite unlike any other used in the construction of the east end because of its four-sided (demi-hexagonal) form (fig. 52). Each elevation consists of three tiers of windows corresponding to the crypt, main ('ground') floor, and clerestory. In the case of the east façade (fig. 49), the design is particularly neat, with the lower level of three windows of equal size succeeded at clerestory level by one with a tall central window flanked by a lower one, a composition that is repeated on a smaller scale in the (recessed) gable. Its neatness may be due to the fact that it is partly the work of Sir G.G. Scott, carried out during the restoration of 1867–76.[17] There seems to have been some evidence for the upper clerestory–level lancets, but the gable design is most probably entirely Scott's.

Externally, the new work is extremely plain; the walls are of Kentish rag rubble with limestone ashlar used for such elements as angle quoins, string-courses, and a wide band at the level of the lower windows.[18] Specifically, ashlar masonry occurs in bands equal to the level of the crypt window arches (spandrels) and the full height of the lower windows, but is not used at the level of the upper windows. It also appears in the crypt level of the eastern turrets, in all of the polygonal buttresses up to the level of the apex of the lower window arches – above which it is used only for the diagonal faces – and for all of the narrow flat buttress between the transept chapels.

There are six string-courses above the crypt: at main floor level; at the sill and impost levels of the lower windows; at the sill and impost levels of the upper windows (the last not continued over the buttresses); and below the parapet. They are each composed of a scotia under a downturned roll, and are undecorated; all appear on the side elevation, creating an unusually consistent and tidy appearance (fig. 50).[19] The turrets and buttresses have bases for angle shafts that were abandoned by the time the level of the first string-course was reached (fig. 52).[20]

The crypt windows are of two orders, both of a hollow chamfer, with a double chamfer label, lacking any decorative motifs. The windows of the lower level of the east front have a jamb-shaft between two continuous orders decorated with dogtooth, while those of the north side have only the outer order of dogtooth; the upper level (clerestory) has a double surround of dogtooth (fig. 50). It appears that all the windows, including those of the crypt, have been completely restored except for the lower part of the outer order decorated with dogtooth of the four lower windows of the presbytery north wall, which still retain the tracery inserted in them during the Perpendicular period.

The eastern aisles of the minor transept, which internally form two chapels in each arm, have smaller flat-faced buttresses with chamfered angles between the bays, and – on the north arm only – a miniature turret-like buttress at the angle (fig. 51). The chapel blocks terminate in east-facing gables. The chapel windows, like the lower windows of the east front, have been restored with a jamb-shaft between rows of dogtooth. (The south elevation of the presbytery and the lower part of the east face of the south arm of the minor transept are obscured by the later structure now serving as the chapter house and library [fig. 56]; the presbytery's south elevation is visible from a small court between it and the library.)

The north arm of the minor transept is also characterized by large turrets at its exterior angles that, in this case, each contain newel-stairs beginning at ground level (fig. 53). There are no balancing turrets at the exterior angles of the south arm, no doubt owing to the claustral buildings that once adjoined (fig. 56). The façade of the north arm between the angle turrets is divided into four registers by string-courses continued from the turrets. The lowest contains two windows of the crypt and, in the westernmost bay, a portal. (The present condition does not allow a judgment as to whether the western bay was originally a window.) The second level was originally blank, but a pair of small (restored) two-light windows with Geometric tracery, associated with the tomb recess of Bishop Walter de Merton (1274–7), has been pierced through the middle,[21] as well as a small cusped lancet to the west. The third and fourth registers each have three lancets; three lancets have also been placed in the (restored) gable (as on the east front).[22]

The exterior face of the south minor transept arm, completely refaced by L.N. Cottingham during restoration work carried out from 1825 to 1830, was divided into three nearly equal registers by two string-courses (fig. 56).[23] Before restoration, the lowest register retained traces of five arches (abbba), the central three pierced by windows to the crypt; the heavy wall piers of the arcade now take the form of a strongly projecting triangle of three shafts engaged against a pilaster with chamfered jambs.[24] The second level has three windows, the wider central one with a nearly semicircular arch, a shaft between two orders of large dogtooth on the jambs, and a continuous label. They are flanked by narrow, equally tall bays with keyhole-shaped arches. Traces of two more similar blind bays were once visible on either side of the three-light window, with elaborate Curvilinear tracery, inserted in the south wall of the southeast chapel.[25] The third tier possesses only three windows, the middle one tallest and widest; not surprisingly, their two orders are decorated with a dogtooth pattern. A small oculus is now placed in the (restored) gable, again with a continuous label.[26]

The exterior elevation of the north choir aisle is mostly hidden by the north ('Gundulf's') tower. A massive, strongly projecting, flat-faced buttress, apparently constructed when the aisle was remodelled in the fourteenth century, now divides it into two sections and forms the pier for a flyer (it is 'balanced' by an equally massive pier buttress later added against the south face of the south choir wall). In addition, there is evidence of an earlier, original buttress having been partly ripped away between bays three and four.[27] Otherwise, no work of the Early Gothic period is visible on the exterior of the aisle, for the thirteenth-century lancets have disappeared, seemingly replaced by short windows at the top of the wall with simple sub-Perpendicular tracery.

On the exterior of the choir, the north clerestory windows are all restored: they differ from those of the west face of the minor transept's north arm only in the lack of a label, as is also true of the east windows of the major transept's north arm. The uppermost string-course is at the same level on the west face of the minor arm and the choir; yet, although of the same design, it is placed at a higher level on the east face of the major arm. The choir's south clerestory windows (fig. 56), more easily visible than those on the north, are lancets with unmoulded and undecorated frames, lacking any string-course or label.[28]

The major transept arms had strongly projecting, flat-faced buttresses with three setbacks placed at right angles at each exterior angle. Owing to the north tower's proximity, an unusually shallow chapel, with a slender north-facing lancet, opened off the north arm. There is no similar balancing chapel in the south arm, an asymmetry again perhaps due to the presence of the twelfth-century west range of the adjoining cloister.[29]

The exterior details of the major transept are less plain than on those parts to the east. The north front is divided by string-courses into three stages (fig. 54).[30] In the lowest, at the west end, there is a heavily restored portal of two orders (plus moulded inner jambs) with jamb-shafts ('water-holding' bases, squat bell capitals), moulded arches, and (restored) head stops to the moulded label. On the second stage, there are three lancet windows with blind bays in between and flanking them, forming a continuous arcade of seven bays with detached shafts (abacaba). The three windows of the upper (clerestory) level are also set in a continuous arcade of seven stepped bays (abcdcba). The gable, set back behind a straight parapet, is filled with three oculi that have heavy moulded frames and recessed plate-like quatrefoils within.[31] The east face of the arm is effectively invisible because of the proximity of the north tower; only the clerestory can be seen. The west face, also of three stages, has two lancet windows in the second stage flanked and separated by blind arches in the north bay, while each of the clerestory-level bays has two lancets with a blind arch between and (restored) Purbeck shafts (fig. 55).[32]

The south façade of the major transept is a simple design, again of three stages (fig. 59). The lowest is bare; the second is mostly filled by the three equally broad two-light windows ('Y' tracery) with two orders of jamb shafts; the third is occupied by the similarly designed frames of five lancets stepped in height.[33] The recessed gable is dominated by an inlaid cross executed in flint checker work placed above a horizontal band, also of checker pattern, bearing three shields.[34] The lower part of the east face was originally overlapped by the west range of the cloister (fig. 57); at clerestory level there is a flat pilaster buttress between each bay. The east clerestory windows are now filled by simple two-light (restored) Geometric tracery: the lights have but one pair of cusps and support a pointed quatrefoil (fig. 58). The west face below its clerestory has been altered by the addition of the structure now known as the Lady chapel; at the upper level, a single deep buttress is placed only in the line of the nave aisle wall. The window tracery on this side is very different from that on the east (fig. 60). A shaft-like mullion, with base and capital, divides each clerestory window into two lights; the pointed arches lack cusping, while the otherwise solid spandrel between them is pierced by an oculus with a quatrefoil within.

The medieval crossing tower has been twice replaced, first in 1826 by Cottingham and again in 1904 by C.H. Fowler (1840–1910), so it is known only from engraved views before 1830.[35] They show the stage corresponding to the steeply pitched roofs to have been decorated with bays of tall, shallow, trefoil-headed arcading, characterized by a lack of capitals or imposts as well as shafts. There were flat buttresses at the angles, with one slight setback.

Interior[36]

The crypt extends under all of the presbytery and the new minor transept with its eastern chapels (figs. 8, 61, 62). The major spaces, corresponding to transept and presbytery, are subdivided into three equal aisles by slender monolithic columns supporting ribbed vaults. Massive rectangular piers mark the position of the eastern crossing piers above, and form support for three arches across the entrance to the eastern arm.[37] Smaller piers (in terms of their north–south thickness) mark the division between the transept chapels. Half-shafts, also monoliths, are engaged on the walls and sides of the piers as responds. The crypt was well lighted by three windows in each terminal wall, four in each side wall of the section under the presbytery, with additional ones in the transept chapels (now all altered). Altogether, there was provision for seven altars: two in each transept arm, and three at the east wall of the east ('presbytery') arm.[38] Small piscinas appear in the north- and southeastern chapels, and the southeast chapel of the north arm: two have trefoil arches and one a semicircular arch (that in the south wall of the south chapel at the east).

The columns are round and octagonal. They alternate in the section under the presbytery (fig. 61); in the section under the transept, the west row is all round, but in the east row only those in the line

of the crossing are round, thus o, r, o, o, r, o (fig. 62).[39] Their capitals
are of the moulded bell type, with two rolls at the top separated by a
chamfered moulding (fig. 11v). Their bases are characterized by double
rolls that in most cases are separated by a narrow hollow (fig. 11f).
(In contrast, the bases of the responds against the east wall of the
presbytery section and of the round columns in that area, as well as
of the responds against the west wall of the transept section, have
only two rolls [figs. 11e, g].) There is one aberrant capital and one
aberrant base in the 'crossing' area, on different shafts: they each
have an unusually large roll. The ribs all have a simple hollow
chamfer profile; the diagonal ribs – except in the window recesses –
are semicircular. Wall ribs are used in the east arm, and in the
chapel bays. Bases, shafts, and capitals were all originally of oolitic
limestone,[40] while the ashlar facing of the walls and the vault ribs
are a mixture of Caen and Reigate freestones.[41] The abaci, and the
string-course at the same level around the outer walls, all of a simple
roll, are of Purbeck in the eastern arm of the crypt and of Bethersden
marble in the transept,[42] being one of the occasional appearances of
this stone in the building in place of Purbeck.[43] All the piers have
chamfered angles with triangular bar stops.

The walls erected above the crypt are anything but thin and their
substantial thickness is everywhere revealed in the interior elevation of the presbytery, which is divided into two unequal stories
(fig. 63).[44] The lower two-thirds of the wall are treated as a tall
continuous arcade, with a single order of Purbeck shafts, forming a
deep recess around each window that also has an order of limestone
shafts.[45] Triple or single shafts are placed between the window arcades corresponding to the major or minor divisions of the main
(sexpartite) vault. There are four windows in the long side walls, two
tiers of three on the east wall (the lower east windows have two
orders of non-Purbeck shafts and capitals).[46] Except for the capitals
of the wall arcade, Purbeck – or sometimes Bethersden – is used
everywhere, for bases, shafts, shaft-rings, strings, and capitals. In
front of each window of the clerestory, which includes a wall passage, there is a triplet of stepped arches decorated with dogtooth
rising from thin Purbeck shafts. The central arches are very wide,
the flanking ones quite narrow, with the lateral jambs springing
from shafts half the height of those between the arches. Lintels of
Purbeck, extending from the capitals straight back into the wall,

form supports for a series of pointed barrel vaults over the walk-
way.[47] The vault – two sexpartite bays – springs from about halfway
up the height of the clerestory.

The minor transept elevation continues the basic two-storey division of the presbytery (fig. 64).[48] On the east side, where the arcades
form the openings of the chapels, the sides of the heavy piers are
treated as flat sections of walling with two orders of shafts at the
entrance. Three tall blind arcades continue across both the end walls
and onto the west walls. Continuous string-courses are found at the
base of the window sills (continued as rings over the shafts), at the
level of the abaci, and below the sill of the clerestory passageway,
where they are again continued over the vaulting shafts. The lower
windows have two orders of limestone shafts; in addition, limestone
is used for the capitals of the wall arcades, again as in the presbytery.
Otherwise Purbeck, as in the presbytery, is everywhere used for
shafts. There are no clerestory windows on the east side, there being
only an arcaded passageway fronted by a series of equal-sized arches
with single shafts continued from the west bay of the presbytery.
There is one small asymmetry (due to Cottingham's restoration?)
between the outer bays of each arm: the southeast bay has three
arches, the northeast bay four. The lack of clerestory windows on
this side of the transept is explained by a large room built over each
block of chapels: the windows of these rooms are at clerestory level
on the exterior (fig. 51). The interior wall of each towards the
presbytery bears two large bays of blind arcading: otherwise the rooms
are bare.[49] The outer bays of the west clerestory have a triple arcade,
while the inner ones have a triple arcade plus two lower arches.
Each of the three clerestory windows on the north (and south) has a
triplet of arches of equal height – the lateral arches absurdly narrow
– in front of it.

Throughout the presbytery and minor transept, the bases of the
shafts – in Purbeck (or Bethersden) – are composed of a scotia between two tori, rather Attic in form, and a straight-sided, high, disk-
like element (figs. 68, 11h). They are raised on a continuous plinth
of distinctive shape that forms a bench along the walls or piers
between the shafts. The plinth, executed in limestone, flares out
towards the top and is capped by a half roll. The capitals are of the
moulded bell type; the arches are moulded in thin rolls and hollows
with an outer label carved with billet. In the transept, as in the
presbytery, the lower wall arches have billet-decorated labels, while
dogtooth is used on the clerestory arcades.

In the south wall of the south arm, there are two semicircular archways, the east one leading to an ascending stair and the room located above the east aisle chapels, the west to descending steps that exited, not into the crypt, but into a room, constructed at this time, that opens off the south aisle of the eleventh-century crypt; it is located under the descending stairs from the minor transept arm to the lower level of the south choir aisle.[50] Both mural stairways are now blocked.[51] One ascending vice in the north arm is reached through a door in the north wall of the northeast chapel; the second opened directly off the main space in the northwest corner (the doorway is now blocked).[52]

In the choir, instead of the usual arcade and some type of gallery, there is a solid wall on each side supporting the clerestory level.[53] The solid walls are no doubt correctly considered to be the remains of the presbytery walls of the earliest Romanesque ('Gundulfian') church, refaced (fig. 70).[54] Above a dado left bare to accommodate the choir stalls, the wall is decorated with bays of blind arcading,[55] on a pattern of two per section of vaulting above, except at the east end, next to the minor transept, where an increased thickness of wall eliminates one bay of the blind arcade. These projecting sections are actually the ends of the west walls of the minor transept's arms: a vertical joint, masked in part by a nook-shaft, marks the eastern limit of the surviving eleventh-century solid choir walls. Details of the arcading are similar to those found in the minor transept and presbytery: Purbeck shafts, moulded capitals, and billet-decorated labels. Each of the four clerestory windows on each side is fronted by a stepped triple arcade, on the arches of which dogtooth appears. In contrast to the presbytery, the clerestory windows rise much higher into the lunette area under the vaults. As in the presbytery, Purbeck lintels spanning the passageway, from shaft capitals to window wall, support transverse pointed barrel vaults. The vault springs from a level well above the clerestory sill, and Purbeck shafts, corresponding to the ribs, rise up the elevation, singly or in triplets from corbels. String-courses, continued from the west wall of the minor transept, are found at the level of the blind arcading's imposts and clerestory sill, crossing the vaulting shafts as rings.

The new work was entirely vaulted. The projecting bays of the presbytery received two bays of sexpartite vaulting, with a regular quadripartite vault constructed over the narrower western bay in the line of the transept chapels; the latter also received (square) quadripartite vaults. A large, quadripartite vault is found over the nearly square crossing, enriched by a boss consisting totally of deeply undercut foliage (now gilded) (fig. 69). The minor transept arms are covered by sexpartite vaults – the intermediate transverse rib in each one deflected to meet the apeces of the diagonal ribs.[56] There are no heavy arches defining the crossing; instead, there are only thin ribs: as a result, the vaulting bay of each arm extends to include the thickness of the crossing piers, thereby enlarging the vault bay from an oblong to a square. Thus, the vertical division in the elevation, on the east between the chapels, on the west between the choir aisles and the projecting bay, no longer corresponds to the axis of the vault bay. If the vault area had been made oblong, two more or less equal divisions would have been possible, thus allowing the intermediate rib to transverse the arm on a straight (unbroken) line (fig. 1).

Sexpartite vaults were extended into the choir in two unequal bays where the transverse ribs are decorated with a bold dogtooth (fig. 70); there are two bosses following on from the earlier one in the east crossing, making the choir vaulting the richest in the eastern arm. The bosses each have a tire-like frame, the eastern one decorated with dogtooth, surrounding a rosette of four lobed leaves in a '+' plan; in the more complex western one, there is a swirl of long stemmed lobed foliage deeply undercut, somewhat similar in form to that of the eastern crossing.[57]

Compared to the presbytery and minor transept, the choir is somewhat more decorative in character, the decoration taking the form of lobed 'stiff-leaf' foliage – found at the ends of the long tapering corbels to the wall shafts and above the central shafts of each pair of blind arches – and the enriched ribs of the vault.[58] Carved heads are included on one corbel on the south (the easternmost), two on the north (the western and eastern ones, the head on the latter female), and the southeast crossing shafts (accompanied by foliage); three descending animals are found on the middle corbel on the north side; the richest foliage is found under the east crossing shafts.

Both the choir aisles have been extensively altered since first built, the south – which may never have been completed according to the original plan – more so than the north. In the north aisle, stairs in the western half of the third bay from the east lead up to the higher level of the two eastern bays because of the aisle bays of the late-eleventh-century crypt beneath them. The early Gothic construction included single wall shafts that, rising from a (stepped) bench at the base of the wall, divide the length of the aisle into four square bays (fig. 72).[59] Because of the proximity of the north tower, the north aisle initially must have been rather dark. The inside of the exterior wall bears traces of the jamb of a single lancet window in the west bay, while the jambs of two lancets, and segments of depressed (pointed) arches, are exposed in the east bay.[60] This suggests that, initially, the two middle bays may have been blind, since windows in them would have been directly opposite the north tower, so little light would have reached them. The pair of windows in the east bay is opposite the wide space between the tower and (new) minor transept north arm, hence taking advantage of the brighter location; the single window in the west bay corresponded to the narrower gap between the tower and the north arm of the (still standing?) Romanesque transept or of the later Gothic major transept (in the latter case, the gap partially closed by its shallow east chapel). In their stead, a series of clerestory-like windows has been inserted at the top of the wall, along with the existing vault. The latter has transverse and longitudinal ridge ribs and bosses that place its construction in the fourteenth century. Two small unpretentious portals – their jambs and arches have a simple continuous chamfer – were inserted, perhaps at different dates, one in the western bay and the other smaller one in the second bay from the east.[61]

The south choir aisle presents a very unusual appearance, consisting as it now does of one space equal to the full length of the minor transept arm for the entire distance between the transept arms, major and minor (figs. 73, 74).[62] At its east end, there are two sets of stairs, the one on the north descending to the crypt, and that on the south ascending to the raised floor level of the south arm of the minor transept. The descending stairs are provided with a rich portal at their bottom forming the crypt entrance; two orders of shafts, with moulded capitals, rise from a base of two rolls on a circular plinth; the inner arch is almost straight-sided; Bethersden rather than Purbeck is used for shafts, bases, capitals, and inner arch, with the outer moulded pointed arch of Reigate stone.

The west face of the east wall is filled by two tall blind arches with Purbeck bases, shafts, and capitals to the pairs of angle-shafts on each jamb (fig. 73). The wall under the south arch is pierced by a small doorway.[63] Between them rises a limestone shaft crossed by the Purbeck abacus and shaft-ring. The west wall to the south of the tall arch opening into the south arm of the major transept is bare except for a very small portal in its centre (fig. 74). The arch, with shafts flanking a flat axial surface, employs limestone for bases, shafts, and capitals, with Purbeck used only for the abaci.

The north wall – the solid south side wall of the late-eleventh-century presbytery – has three features: at a point one-third its length from the east, there is a tall Purbeck shaft that rises to the ceiling (fig. 78); at two-thirds of its length, there is a strongly projecting respond (fig. 74, at right); between the two, in the middle of the wall, there is a massive rectangular buttress (fig. 77). This last feature partially blocks the stairs descending to the crypt. The respond consists of a flat axial surface flanked by shafts – three to the west, two to the east – retaining shaft-rings and moulded capitals, plus a corbel head, all in limestone (figs. 74 [at right edge], 77). The details correspond in type and level to the responds of the arch between the aisle and the major transept's south arm. The buttress has chamfered angles and, on its south face near the top, a blind arch with Purbeck shafts and abaci, moulded limestone bases and capitals, and Purbeck upper string (fig. 77).[64]

The lower half of the eastern two-thirds of the south wall displays (from east to west) traces of two segmental arches, a trefoil arch and the portal to the cloister, which has the voussoirs of an earlier semi-circular arch revealed above it (fig. 75).[65] Above these features, at the east end of the wall there is a lancet with double shafted jambs, similar to those in the minor transept, and, in the middle third of the wall, there are two additional lancet windows of unequal length, that at the west being half the length of the one immediately to its east; neither has jamb-shafts. A line of quoins has been revealed above the west jamb of the cloister portal rising to the sill level of the short lancet window. In contrast to the eastern two-thirds, the western third of the wall is blank. The entire space is covered by an asymmetrical ceiling of three east–west sections with ribs and bosses of wood.[66]

Behind the blank featureless wall, between the line of quoins and the east wall of the south transept arm, there is a small room, probably a remnant of the Romanesque west range of the cloister, which occupies the place of the south tower that W.H.St.J. Hope (1854–1919) theorized Gundulf had erected there.[67] It was formerly entered from the major transept's south arm by a simple doorway (twenty-four and one-half inches wide [62.23 cm]) with a sill raised thirty-three inches (83.82 cm) above the transept floor, and continuous mouldings. The south wall of this small room rather puzzlingly

contains two tall arches on its north face, consisting of two chamfered orders, with three shafts of Bethersden marble against a polygonal pier between them. There are polygonal moulded limestone
(Reigate) capitals; unfortunately, the bases are so eroded that no
trace of mouldings survive between a torus at the bottom of the
shaft and a straight-sided plinth-like section.[68] The bases are set (on
a modern cement plinth) about forty-four inches (111.76 cm) above
the surface of the pavement in the adjoining south aisle.

In contrast to the minor transept and presbytery, the elevation of
the north arm of the major transept was conceived of as three storeys
or stages (figs. 80, 81), with the exception of the arches leading to
the choir or nave aisles and the arched opening to the eastern chapel.
On the east side in the north arm (fig. 81), the wall is divided into
two halves by a group of three Purbeck vaulting shafts. The chapel
arch fills the north half; on the south, the narrow section of wall
between the tall aisle arch and the vaulting shafts is filled by two
arches, one above the other, the lower forming a shallow recess, the
narrower upper one enframing a small (blocked) window.[69] Because
of the free-standing tower to the north, there was no space for the
transept arm to have an eastern aisle for chapels as in the minor
transept. Instead, there is a single shallow oblong chapel lighted
only by a slender lancet in its narrow north wall.[70] The jamb shafts
of this window bear the only capitals carved with stiff-leaf foliage in
the entire building, although elaborate, fully developed stiff-leaf had
appeared on the choir corbels.[71]

The lower two stages on the north and west are each of the same
height and are filled by three large bays of arcading, the lower ones
blind, the upper ones forming a continuous arcade over deeply splayed
windows. The western bay of the north wall is occupied by a portal:
the Purbeck shafts of its tall inner jamb support a broad, almost
straight-sided, pointed arch. The bases and shafts of the lower window zone are of Purbeck, the moulded capitals of limestone; in the
blind arcades below, the capitals are Purbeck. The upper level – on
all three sides – is a clerestory with a wall passage: as further east, it
is fronted by a triple arcade, except across the north wall where the
gradated units (4/3/4), with Purbeck shafts and capitals, read continuously, only separated by thin piers formed at the junction of the
units. Dogtooth makes its only appearance in the north arm in the
clerestory where, rather distinctively, the centre arch in each bay of
triplets on the east and west sides is straight-sided (fig. 82).

The arch to the north nave aisle is curious, for it projects up into the clerestory level; that is, it is much taller than the nave arcades and aisle were to be (fig. 82). To correspond to the actual height of the nave arcade and aisle, an arch was inserted under it – with capitals and arch mouldings of the same profile as the upper arch. It is doubtful that there could ever have been the intention of making the nave arcade or aisles as high as this arch. It seems designed to reflect the tall choir aisle arch rising to the clerestory sill on the east side – in itself unusually tall because of the uniform level of the vaults maintained above the aisle stairs. The springing point of this aisle arch is coordinated with that of the second stage arches, but being so much wider, its arch rose much higher, thus breaking into the clerestory sill.

The construction of the supports for the vaults over the clerestory passageway – which are effectively pointed barrel vaults – differs significantly from that used in the choir and presbytery. In the north arm, lintels of Purbeck extend from the compound piers between the windows to the exterior wall (fig. 79). An arch springs from their inner end, its other end rising from head corbels placed next to the splayed jamb of the window opening; this arch thus crosses the passageway diagonally. Consequently, a small pocket of vaulting is created between it, the wall, and the lintel.

It is also interesting to observe that, in the construction of the east wall of the north transept arm (and of the north choir aisle wall), no attempt was made to arrange access to the north tower; it is especially surprising that no connection was made at clerestory level. A small rectangular aperture at the north end of the clerestory passage, with its sill well above the floor of the passage, looks into the space above the vault of the east chapel. The west face of the west wall of the tower is visible from a level below its upper set-back: it is completely solid and undisturbed. Indeed, it was as a result of the construction of the transept arm and chapel that the 'tunnel' through the upper level of the tower's west wall was blocked up.[72]

The south arm of the transept does not match the north arm, nor did it before the later alterations as a result of the addition of the so-called Lady chapel on its west side (fig. 84).[73] The original interior elevation of the south major transept arm continued the design of the presbytery and minor transept: tall bays of arcading nearly filled the wall below the clerestory. On the east side, the arch to the south choir aisle was originally followed by two narrow arches; three similar arches rising over windows are on the south wall, and two more were on the west wall plus the arch to the south nave aisle (fig. 85). At a later date, the two original tall blind arches of its east elevation were converted into a single wide arch like that opening into the shallow chapel in the north arm. In the south arm, only the vaulting shafts – as well as their bases, shaft-rings, and capitals – are of Purbeck, which is also used for the bases, shafts, and capitals of the clerestory arcade.

The three lower windows of the south wall (under the arcades), rather surprisingly, are broad lancets subdivided by 'Y' tracery (fig. 84): the central mullions and jambs all bear shafts – the bases, shafts, capitals, and arch mouldings all being of limestone.[74] The clerestory design on the east side, continuing the wall passage, has a triple arcade on the interior with a very wide central bay, still with dogtooth – the only appearance of this motif in the south arm – on the outer arch moulding forming a kind of label. The windows are now filled with (restored) late Geometric tracery consisting of two pointed and cusped lights, with a pointed quatrefoil above (fig. 58).[75] The south clerestory has five graduated lancets and an internal arcade of five arches: the spandrels are not pierced. The western clerestory alters the design by introducing a single wide window of two lights, with a quatrefoil above, and an inner 'screen' that repeats the design: a centre shaft supports a kite-shaped spandrel pierced with a quatrefoil (fig. 85; cf. fig. 60).[76] The window jambs and central mullions are only chamfered, not moulded, with the curious detail of labels over the windows supported on stops formed by either foliage or human heads. The free-standing shafts of the screening arcade have rings, a feature lacking on the south and west sides.

Rather curiously, neither transept arm was provided with a newel-stair: their clerestories could have been gained only via those of the nave, for they do not connect with those of the choir. The central tower – of which only the lowest stage corresponding to the abutment of the roofs was built in the thirteenth century – therefore, was (and is) reached from an approach over the choir or transept (or intended nave?) vaults, for which purpose a small doorway with a pointed arch was placed in the middle of each side. Since the interior walls of this stage are of rough masonry, a lantern clearly never was intended; a wooden floor or vault would have been necessary to close it from view from below.[77]

The final work on the transept – the vaulting of the arms – was not carried out at this time. That the intention was to vault the transept is apparent from the stone springers that were at all points everywhere put in place. Eventually, these springers would determine the type of vault constructed a century later, both in the profile of the ribs as well as in the number and disposition of the ribs.[78]

It is apparent that there was also an intention to replace the Romanesque nave as well, although work never progressed beyond the first two bays (fig. 80). The opposing faces of the west crossing piers consist of plain masonry to a height of about fourteen feet (4.2672 m), probable evidence of a screen that had been constructed between them in order to separate the monastic and parochial parts of the church (figs. 86, 87). Above this, the piers bear the normal shafting, of Purbeck, complete with bases.

On the west side of the northwest crossing pier, there is a massive buttress almost completely filling the first arcade bay. On its north face, it bears a heavily moulded arch springing from Purbeck capitals atop Purbeck shafts – only the west one remains – and triple scotia bases (fig. 88). The arch mouldings are similar to those of the lower arcade in the north arm of the major transept, although the capitals are more elaborately profiled. The label over the arch had a stop at the west end in the form of a female head, the face of which is now missing. The northwest angle of the buttress is shaped as a filleted roll and it is interesting to observe that the Purbeck block of the west capital extends to become part of this angle roll. Both faces of the wall under the arch contain a considerable amount of reused Romanesque ashlar distinguished by two patterns, a pellet-decorated woven lattice and the 'X' of a trellis design. There are four blocks of the lattice pattern on the south face and seven on the north, which has, in addition, six blocks with the 'X' pattern. This pattern is similar to one on the chapter house and that on some (reset) blocks formerly on the west front.[79] Some blocks of each pattern, along with some plain ones with diagonal tooling, have been reddened by fire.

The new Gothic arcade was to be taller than the Romanesque arcade, the arches rising into the level of the old pseudo-gallery openings, but falling well short of equalling the height of the lower two storeys of the Romanesque elevation (figs. 34, 90). Only the first pair of piers on each side of the nave arcade and one of the second pair (that on the north) were fully completed – the first examples of true Gothic pier design in the building (figs. 89, 90).[80] They have a lozenge-shaped core, with eight, widely spaced, attached shafts of (a rather rusty-coloured) Purbeck,[81] which rise from a plinth of Purbeck shaped to follow the curves of the Purbeck bases of the shafts (fig. 91). The bases are double-deckers, with either triple rolls or a roll/hollow/roll (torus/scotia/torus) (northwest pier), separated by a low straight-sided element from a lower set of roll/hollow/roll mouldings (figs. 11n, o). The axial shaft towards the nave lacks a capital: rather there is a continuation of the abacus as a shaft-ring as if it were intended ultimately to relate the shaft to vaulting.[82] On the north side, the second pier, of the same plan as the first pair, was rebuilt up to the springing of the third (Romanesque) arch (fig. 90). The east face relates to the new tall arcade, the west face to the lower Romanesque arch, with moulded capitals appearing in place of the original scalloped ones. The corresponding pier in the south arcade was perhaps only partially rebuilt at this time, for, although the east half is early Gothic, the west half imitates a Romanesque form (fig. 37). The tooling and jointing of the masonry, however, as well as the capital decorated with oak leaf, indicate that it is a replacement carried out in the fourteenth century, and not a genuine Romanesque survival. In contrast to the first pair of Gothic piers, the shafts of the second ones are in coursed stone.[83] Unlike the first pair of piers, the second stand on octagonal plinths that have been partly made up from the Romanesque ones (fig. 92). The west parts are of Caen limestone with the larger part of Reigate sandstone. The base mouldings are again of Caen. The arch profile of the few nave arcades completed, featuring rolls with fillets, corresponds to the crossing arches – north, south, west – and the arch from the south transept arm to the aisle.

Both aisles retain indications of the intention to cover them with ribbed vaults: the springers of the projected ribs are found on both the north and south piers, and at the arch between the south aisle and the transept arm (figs. 88, 89).

The Documentary Evidence for the Traditional Chronology

There are only six references that may be taken as documenting the progress of the Gothic (re)construction with any degree of precision. The two most important ones are those recording the entrance into the new choir in 1227,[84] and a consecration in 1240 (5 November).[85]

Surprisingly, there is no record as to when work actually began. Several other references may indicate or relate to the new construction at the east, and its rate of progress, but they are frustratingly vague and it is not, in fact, absolutely clear as to which part of the church they actually refer. Thus, Ralph de Ros, prior from before 1193 to circa 1203, or perhaps later, to 1208,[86] is said to have 'caused the great church to be covered in and for the most part to be leaded,' while Elias, who was probably sacrist in 1203 and who is mentioned as prior in 1214 and 1215,[87] also 'caused the great church to be leaded.'[88] That the crypt and at least the presbytery were completed by 1214 has been inferred from the burial of Bishop Gilbert in that year, 'on the north side of the church.'[89]

The remaining reference relates to the western half of the construction: 'Richard de Eastgate, monk and sacrist [of Rochester], began the north aisle [arm] of the new work towards the gate of St. William, which brother Thomas de Mepeham nearly completed. Richard de Waldene, monk and sacrist, made the south aisle [arm] towards the court [curia]. William de Hoo, sacrist, made the whole choir from the aforesaid aisles [arms] from the oblations to St. William.'[90] Unfortunately, we do not have the inclusive dates of tenure for these individuals in the position of sacrist, and the dates that are available suggest a different order than that implied by the sequence of names in the text. William of Hoo became prior in 1239, and resigned in 1242;[91] it appears that Richard of Eastgate succeeded him (in 1239?) as sacrist; one Adam was sacrist in 1254.[92] Thomas of Meopham is mentioned as sacrist in 1255;[93] there are no recorded dates for Richard of Walden.

Historiography

A. Ashpitel (1807–69) was one of the first to attempt an outline history of the development of the cathedral. Although brief, as has been seen in previous chapters, his paper contained ideas that later seem to have influenced J.T. Irvine (1825–1900) and Hope. For the Gothic rebuilding, he saw a simple history: 'The two transepts differ in design – one [the south] is at least forty years later than the other. The north transept is of very early English work ... Much of the same character, but little later, if any, is the beautiful choir. Its aisles, eastern transepts, lady chapel, and crypt, are evidently all of one date, all from one plan, all erected at the same time, and all the production of one hand and mind.'[94] Ashpitel's chronology contained the seed of an idea that later resurfaced: a great gap in time between the erection of the two arms of the major transept. Without explicitly so stating, he seems to have believed that work began with the north arm of the major transept soon after 1201 (murder of William of Perth), proceeded to the reconstruction of the entire eastern arm, which was finished by 1227, the recorded year of entry into the choir, and was followed by the south arm of the transept, which was complete by the dedication of the church in 1240. William of Hoo was consequently given credit for the choir, choir aisles, minor transept, presbytery, and crypt! And he may have begun the south arm of the transept as well.

In his first attempt at a history of the cathedral,[95] Hope outlined a sequence of construction that also began with the crossing (left incomplete), proceeded with the choir aisles, then moved to the minor transept and presbytery (attributed to William of Hoo), which were *followed* by the choir, north arm of the major transept, and, finally, its south arm. The first work to be carried out after the fire of 1179 was the destruction of the first two bays of the nave in order to lay the bases of the four crossing piers of the intended tower, which were carried up a few feet before work stopped, apparently as a consequence of the murder of William of Perth, after which event work shifted to the choir aisles. The minor transept and new presbytery were erected outside of the Gundulfian straight-ended presbytery, and it was only after they were carried high enough for the north arm at least to receive a wooden ceiling that the two east bays of Gundulf's work were taken down *and the new crypt vaulted*. The work outside the old presbytery was sufficiently complete by 1214 to receive the burial of Bishop Gilbert. Work on the choir, the solid side walls of which Hope thought William of Hoo had intended to pierce with arcades, did not proceed immediately, *perhaps from lack of funds*, and when resumed the style had changed: 'the coarse workmanship and extravagant use of marble columns' of the minor east transept and presbytery were replaced by work 'of much better execution and superior design.' This work was completed by 1227. As soon as funds permitted, the north arm of the major transept was taken in hand: 'it appears to date from *circa* 1250.' It was only 'towards the end of the thirteenth century' that the south arm of the major transept, which had been rebuilt after the fire of 1179, was 'altered.' About this time the north transept was vaulted, but perhaps not the south, and the rebuilding of the nave was commenced. Shortly after, the east wall of the south arm was altered, and the south choir aisle assumed its present shape, as a result of partially destroying the (putative) south tower. The northern half of the area formerly occupied by this tower was added to the space of the aisle, which then received its curious lopsided wooden ceiling after the south wall had been completed.

This chronology may be compared to the more complicated building sequence subsequently proposed by Hope for the choir, aisles, major transept, crossing, and the beginning of the nave, involving four (or five?) architects. Apparently under the influence of Professor Robert Willis (1800–75), Hope accepted the fact that the rebuilding began with the presbytery and minor transept. He, however, continued to hold that this work was begun outside Gundulf's east end, and that it was only when the new work could be enclosed by a roof that the two east bays of the old presbytery were taken down and the new work provided with floors by vaulting the crypt.[96] While the former premise is most likely, the latter is implausible. The new work was finished – or at least roofed in – by the time of the burial of Bishop Gilbert in 1214. The next phase was the renovation of the choir after sufficient time had elapsed for the accumulation of funds from the offerings at the shrine of William to pay for it. Hope continued to regard the work of the choir as 'better and of superior design' to the work east of it. Thereafter, his sequence may be outlined as follows:

(1) the limestone bases and shafts of the arches to the choir and the nave aisles from the transept (of the south nave aisle arch, only the pier respond bases), the east and west responds of the crossing piers, and the north choir aisle, by one master different from the designer of the choir (therefore the third master mason);

(2) the responds of the crossing piers towards the choir, and the arches of the choir aisles with the clerestory bay above, by the master mason of William of Hoo (the second master mason);

(3) the north arm of the major transept, including the construction of the arch to the nave aisle and of the northwest crossing pier (on earlier bases), by a fourth master mason under sacrist Richard of Eastgate;

(4) the beginning of the nave, with the bases of two new piers on each side, the solid buttress against the northwest pier, and the

responds and piers of the first bay, by the designer of the north arm of the transept (the fourth master mason);

(5) the 'second pair of piers' in the nave and the two arches on either side, including preparation for vaulting the aisles (abandonment of marble shafts [for the second time]), by a new master mason – the fifth;

(6) the south arm of the major transept, including the southwest crossing pier (above bases laid down earlier) and the north, south, and west crossing arches, by the fifth master mason under Richard of Walden;

(7) the vaulting of the north arm of the major transept;

(8) the alterations in the south arm of the major transept, that is, the replacement of the two blind arches by the east chapel recess;

(9) the enlargement of the south choir aisle – as a result of removing the north half of the supposed south tower of Gundulf – and the construction of a door to the vestry (which was formed from the remaining south half of the tower) resulting in the renovation of the east clerestory of the south arm of the transept (originally, because of the tower, the two south bays were blind);

(10) the vaulting of the south arm of the major transept – in wood; and

(11) the raising of the central tower above the level of the roofs (belfry stage) and spire (1343).[97]

The dating of the phases of the new work was still derived from a certain few of the documentary references with little thought for plausibility, with the dates for the later phases in particular vaguely defined. Thus, the 'new quire was finished and used for the first time in 1227' and 'the new works were so far advanced towards completion that in 1240' the church was dedicated. Yet what exactly was accomplished in the thirteen years between 1227 and 1240 is not clear, especially as the 'work of the north transept may well lie between 1240 and 1255.' The remaining work is not dated; the new arcades in the nave are characterized as 'essentially Decorated,' a description that must therefore also apply to the south arm of the transept.[98] The alterations of the southeast wall and the vaulting of the south arm, accompanied by the enlargement of the south choir aisle, are positioned after its rebuilding, but Hope was not entirely clear as to whether this work was carried out in the late thirteenth or early fourteenth century. He did seem to believe that it was all accomplished by the time an altar to the Virgin was established in the south arm, an event he dated to circa 1322, and perhaps was even occasioned by the desire to create a Lady chapel there.[99]

Building Sequence: Archaeological and Stylistic Evidence

Habitual practice and a logical order of construction would lead us to expect an east to west building sequence, with the preparation of the extension – the presbytery and the minor transept east chapels – taking place outside the old apsidal (or straight) east end, before reaching the stage at which the demolition of the (original or rebuilt) eastern part of the presbytery and crypt would be necessary. The construction of the new minor transept could then have proceeded, allowing the continued use of the old (truncated?) presbytery and the choir in the crossing and nave, if not the use of the new presbytery. Once the new presbytery and minor transept were completed, the renovation of the old presbytery could begin; work on the side aisles could have been simultaneous with, or either before or after, the remodelling of the presbytery. Once the choir was complete, the monks' stalls could be moved from the crossing and nave – if they had not already been temporarily moved into the new presbytery while the old was being worked on. With the choir finished and usable, work could begin on the major transept. The dates of these phases of construction, however, are less easy to determine than the phases themselves.

Crypt, Presbytery, and Minor East Transept

It is quite clear that the entire crypt, presbytery, and minor transept formed one uniform campaign of construction, one that, however, may be divided into two major phases. The division is horizontal rather than vertical, and is attested by a slight change in the original design intentions. A double chamfer base course runs around all this section of work, and it is particularly characterized by a base for a re-entrant shaft at each angle of all the buttresses and turrets (fig. 52). Such shafts were not, however, ever put in place, for it is evident that when the work reached the level of the first string-course (marking the main interior floor level placed on the vaults of the crypt), the idea of angle-shafts had been given up: there was no provision made to accommodate the shafts; the string-course turns the corners in simple re-entrant right angles.[100]

Within the crypt (figs. 61, 62), the work appears remarkably consistent in its detailing, the only variation being the use of Purbeck for string-courses and the appearance of wall ribs in the eastern portion of the work (east arm and transept east chapels) and the absence of wall ribs in the western (transept end and west walls), along with the use of Bethersden for string-courses. Nevertheless, it is clear that the perimeter wall of the crypt was laid down to one uniform design, and the structure inside it was carried up with only this variation, which may or may not mean that it was constructed from west to east rather than east to west.[101]

At the upper level, there is no sign of any building breaks, *pace* Willis who identified a break at the junction of the north wall of the minor transept chapels and the east turret of the north arm; the coursing is continuous across the angles between the walls and buttresses or turrets at all levels.[102] Perhaps Willis thought there was a break here because the west jamb of the north window of the northeast chapel runs *west* of the exterior *east* face of the turret, which has been cut back to accommodate the outer order of the window. However, the window jambs have been completely restored, so now the only visible discontinuities in coursing are relatively minor, as they are in the area of the outer voussoirs and the small portion of the spandrel above, as might be expected.

Unfortunately, because every window on the exterior of the crypt, presbytery, and transept has been restored, except for parts of the jambs of four, any evidence of building sequence that might have been revealed by small changes in the profiles of the bases, capitals, or arches has been eliminated.

The interior of the presbytery and minor transept (figs. 63, 64, 65), which is less heavily restored in other of its details than the windows, presents a remarkably consistent appearance; it is quite uniform and regular in style and execution with regard to the basic details of base, capital, and rib profiles. One minor variation may be noted: the appearance of wall ribs in the vaults of the chapels (figs. 66, 67) – linking these vaults to those below – and their absence in the high vaults. This suggests that the use, or non-use, of wall ribs, is not a reliable indicator of relative date, 'progressiveness,' or order of work.

Another somewhat more obvious variation is found in the southern of the two northeast chapels. Restoration of its window revealed pairs of limestone jamb-shafts, with shaft rings, adjacent to the Purbeck vaulting shafts in the eastern corners of the chapel (fig. 66). They imply that in the original construction this chapel had two longer lancet windows with double jamb-shafts, rather than the shorter single lancet with single jamb-shafts that has been restored in this chapel, and the one adjoining, on the model of those in the presbytery and transept terminal walls.[103]

An indication of a possible change in intentions is evident higher up, also in the north arm (fig. 64). A narrow, horizontal, chamfer-like setback in the upper walls – on east and west, but not on the north – of the north transept suggests that there was a moment when vaults over that arm were in abeyance.[104] Nevertheless, the overall stylistic unity of the work and the lack of any obvious vertical building breaks does suggest that the east termination, whatever its form, was neatly amputated at the beginning of the work on the new east end. A temporary wall must have been erected at the east end of the solid side walls of the presbytery.

It may be appropriate at this point to ponder why the extension of the east end began where it does, rather than with the perimeter of the rectangular eastern arm – if such there was. More particularly, one can question why half of an apparently substantial rectilinear, straight-ended crypt (fig. 5) – whether of circa 1080 or circa 1115–24 or after 1137[105] – was completely demolished to its foundations rather than simply extended. There is no apparent reason why the minor transept and presbytery could not have been placed somewhat further east, thereby allowing for the retention of the entire aisled, straight-ended crypt, as well as of the full 'original' length of the presbytery above which, as a result of the Gothic rebuilding, was supposedly reduced by one-third. Alternatively, if such a placement lengthened the east end inordinately, there is no reason why the section of the arms of the minor transept extending beyond the line of the aisles could not have been supported by additions to the existing crypt. If an apsidal termination, dating from the late eleventh century, still existed a hundred years later, the present junction would make greater sense. So too would the encasing of the easternmost remaining piers of the Gundulfian crypt, as well as of the eastern ends of its aisle walls: the casing converted the beginnings of apsidal curves into flat surfaces directed towards the extension. Whatever its form, the destruction of the original termination was remarkably neat and complete, leaving absolutely no other sign of its existence above the floor level of the crypt.

Choir

The blind arcading, clerestory, and vaults of the choir offer only subtle differences in style from the minor transept and presbytery (fig. 70). As the adaptation and alteration of an existing structure, they would logically constitute a separate and distinct campaign, one which has the appearance, however, of following directly on the completion of the work to the east. Indeed, Willis noted a building break or joint towards the east end of each of the side walls of the choir (fig. 70): a vertical strip of wall, five feet eight inches (1.7272 m) wide and of slight projection, was identified by him as 'the end of the [minor] transept [west] wall'; a nook-shaft at the west side of each partially hides the vertical joint and the change in the levels of coursing.[106] The nature of the junction – the minor transept's west walls overlapping the ends of the solid presbytery walls – also suggests that it was an apsidal termination that was removed from the end of the presbytery, as well as in the case of each aisle, and that the solid walls extended as far east as they do now before the 1179 fire. In Hope's scheme (fig. 7), the west wall of the minor transept aligns with the middle pier of the four-bay arcade. Thus, when this middle pair of piers, and the pair to the west, had been cleared away, the new west piers of the crossing could – or would – have been built as one with the new stretch of wall replacing the two western arcade bays and linking the new crossing piers with the extant solid side walls. Furthermore, if they had intended to replace the solid walls with an arcade, it is likely that the eastern crossing piers would have been quite differently designed.

The stylistic differences between choir and presbytery are but slight. The two most obvious ones are the use of thinner wall-shafts, creating the impression of a somewhat more elegant design, and the appearance of foliage decoration, along with carved heads and animals as an enrichment of certain members, albeit in a most restrained manner. The appearance of these added decorative elements may be explained as much by the fact that it is the choir, as by any significant stylistic change. Some minor details are simpler: the arches of the blind arcade have a single large filleted roll instead of triple (filleted) rolls as in the presbytery, and the choir shaft capitals have only a single roll to the abacus, rather than the two of the presbytery capitals. The clerestory is very similar in its design and construction to that of the eastern arm. One difference is found in the choir clerestory: the shaft bases stand on high stone plinths placed on a ledge raised above the passage floor, whereas in the transept the (Purbeck) bases of the shafts rest directly on a similar ledge. Both clerestories use spanning lintels between the shaft capitals and the outer wall as supports for transverse pointed barrel vaults.

A second possible change in plan may be found at the east end of the choir walls (fig. 71). On the south side, there is a damaged and unutilized Purbeck base adjacent to (on the west of) the base of the Purbeck shaft that occupies the angle created by the junction of the end of the west wall of the minor transept and the solid side wall of the choir. It sits on four courses of ashlar of which the lower two, with the adjacent courses under the Purbeck shaft, give the appearance of two Romanesque nook-shafts. This base has been interpreted as evidence of an intention to replace the solid choir walls with an arcade.[107] Instead, a wide horizontal cavetto moulding at the level of the bases supports an increase in the thickness of the south choir wall. On the north side, where there is only one shaft and base, rising above two rounded stone courses that in turn rest on a rectangular course, there is no apparent addition to the thickness of the choir wall. The unused shaft on the south could be explained as an initial response to a slight misalignment of the new work with the inner faces of the choir walls. The second shaft was given up in the interest of symmetry and the wall face thickened, supported by the horizontal cavetto moulding. If the lowest limestone courses under the shafts are indeed *in situ* Romanesque masonry, they could be explained as the remains of responds belonging to the chord of an apse or to a narrow (barrel-vaulted) bay that preceded it.

Choir Aisles

The original appearance of the north aisle would not have been very different from that at present, although, with only the three lancet windows, rather darker (fig. 72). If a vault was constructed in the thirteenth century – and there is no evidence that it actually was – it would have been in four simple quadripartite bays.

The south aisle would seem to be in a very different form than that originally intended. It also may be doubted that those intentions were ever fully realized. Nonetheless, the intentions are reasonably clear, even if the processes or stages by which the aisle arrived at its present form are not. Despite these ambiguities, its intended form certainly did not duplicate the north aisle. Unlike the original late-eleventh-century arrangement, an entrance to the (enlarged) crypt was retained only on the south side.[108] It was therefore necessary to widen the eastern half of the aisle to allow for the placement of enlarged descending stairs, their increased width equal to one half of the length of the projection of the minor transept's south arm, and for a parallel set of ascending stairs, occupying the outer (southern) half of the length of the arm, leading to a landing at the level of the transept floor. Thus, entering from the major transept's south arm, after one long bay (equal to one-third of the length of the aisle), the normal narrow width of the aisle was doubled in order to accommodate the two parallel flights of stairs.

The vaulting shafts on the west face of the west wall of the south arm of the minor transept and the two large arches with jambs of two orders indicate that this west face of the transept never was an external wall.[109] These arches, along with a single shaft on the south face of the south choir wall (there is no corresponding shaft on the north face of the exterior wall), suggest that the space to its west, over the stairs, was intended to receive vaults in four oblong bays (figs. 75, 78). Such a vault would have required a central column. There is, however, no trace of its implacement that would have fallen on the stepped bench between the two flights of stairs (fig. 78). The vault, therefore, may not have been erected, although wall ribs for the vault do remain above the (later) wooden ceiling, against the south face of the south choir wall. They can be seen from the doorways opening into the roof space from the choir clerestory passageway: at the east, there are two wall ribs, the east one decorated with billet, the west one interrupted by the massive buttress later placed against the south choir wall; at the west, corresponding to the narrow section of the aisle, the lunette face can be seen but the wall rib has been ripped out (fig. 79).

Certain features of the south wall of the choir aisle, which is now such a tantalizing mess (fig. 75), reveal, or at least suggest, that when the aisle wall of the wider, eastern section (equal to two-thirds of the length of the aisle) was initially built, it incorporated an earlier wall as its lower half. They are the two adjacent segmental arches at its eastern end, next to the stairs leading up to the minor transept's north arm, and, on the exterior, evidence of a cloister roof in the form of corbels for the roof plate, below a plain string-course (fig. 56).[110] It is likely, then, that a wall of the twelfth century, probably initially associated with work in the cloister carried out under Bishop Ernulf (1115–24),[111] and rebuilt or repaired after the fire of 1137, existed here before the construction of the south arm of the early Gothic minor transept and the rebuilding and expansion of the south choir aisle. On the north face of this wall there were the three unmoulded arches already mentioned, of which the western one may have belonged to a portal. The austere details of the trefoiled arched recess now found in the wall at the foot of the stairs suggest that it is a later insertion: the arch is chamfered, not moulded, and the chamfered label lacks stops. A tomb recess with a steeply pointed but simply chamfered arch is also located in the east bay of the north aisle. Neither recess has been attributed to any personage, but both probably date to either the late twelfth or the early thirteenth century.[112]

Inside and out, the original (thirteenth-century) build of the upper eastern section of the south aisle wall ends just west of the long lancet window with paired limestone shafts to its jambs that clearly belongs to the new work at the east: the vertical joint is marked on the exterior by the change from ashlar (around the window) to rubble construction (fig. 56), and inside (where the wall is plastered) by the abrupt ending of the Purbeck string-course (fig. 75).

The south wall was eventually continued westwards, still over an earlier wall, judging from the remains of the semicircular arch (belonging to a former portal?) above the arch of the existing doorway in the south wall that gives access to the site of the cloisters (figs. 75, 76). At its west end, this wall abutted the northeast angle of the pre-existing structure forming the west range of the cloister,[113] now revealed as a line of (restored) quoins – with a continuous, vertical joint at the east – above the west jamb of the (later) cloister portal (fig. 76). It is the slope of the lean-to roof of this range that accounts for the shorter of the two additional lancet windows, placed at the west end of the extended (upper) section (fig. 57). What is not at all clear is why this section of wall (between the easternmost lancet window of the aisle and the line of quoins) is not of the same build and date as the east window and the other early features of the aisle. Later in the thirteenth century, it would seem, the portal with the pointed arch replaced the (hypothetical) twelfth-century one.

The final phase – although just where and how it fits in chronologically is difficult to discern – must have involved the demolition of the south wall of the narrow western section of the aisle (which was very likely still that of the late-eleventh-century fabric), and possibly of a wall at its east end returning to the south, in order to incorporate this area into the aisle, thereby producing a space uniform in its width from west to east. Whether this area had been the north end of the west range or a small open court between it and the aisle is not clear, as excavations have never taken place under its floor. If the latter was the case, the present south wall of this section would in part be the original north wall of the west range. At some later date, part of the north end of the west range was partitioned off in order to create a small room that may have served as a vestry to an altar in the adjoining south arm of the major transept; a small doorway between room and arm was opened in the east wall of the transept. The date of these alterations might be indicated by the two-bay arcade on the north face of the partition wall and the inserted portal. The large pier buttress projecting strongly from the middle of the north wall was probably constructed as a consequence of either the decision not to erect or the removal of an arch at the end of the narrow section of the south aisle, of which the north respond remains *in situ*.[114]

Despite the fact that both choir aisles have been greatly altered from their initial build, there remains some evidence to suggest that they formed a separate campaign from the choir and from work to the east, one possibly under the direction of a different (a second or third?) designer, although the major 'stylistic change' that is evident could just as well have been motivated by a need for economic restraint, even if it is one that has a significant aesthetic impact. Throughout the presbytery and minor transept, the design is characterized by the use of Purbeck for bases, shafts, and capitals.[115] This is also true of the choir. In the north aisle (fig. 72), however, the use of Purbeck for bases, shaft-rings, and abaci was gradually lessened in a somewhat asymmetrical fashion, as construction moved from east to west, until, in the west arch opening into the major transept (fig. 81), all the elements are of limestone – except for the shaft-rings on the south and the abaci of the capitals on both north and south. Thus, all the elements of the responds of the east arch opening to the minor north arm are of Purbeck, except the capitals and arches, as is the case throughout the minor transept. Thereafter, on the first pair of shafts, Purbeck is used for bases, shaft-rings, and abaci; on the second pair, only the base on the south and the abaci on north and south are of Purbeck; for the third pair, Purbeck is used for the base on the south and the abacus on the north; none of the aisle shafts is of Purbeck. In addition, the base mouldings of the shafts in the aisle are slightly different from work to the east – including the east arch respond shafts, as their profile is essentially reduced to an emphasis on a double roll as a scotia is eliminated (cf. figs. 11h and 11i),[116] although the profile of the shaft-rings remains unchanged from work to the east.

A similar turning away from the use of Purbeck is found in the south aisle (figs. 73, 74). In contrast to the use of Purbeck shafts at the east end of the aisle – for the arches to the minor transept, the north shaft for the unexecuted vault, and the southeast window – the north respond of the arch intended or formerly at the junction of the wide and narrow sections of the aisle employs only limestone. And the same is true for the responds of the arch between the aisle and the south arm of the major transept, where Purbeck was only used for the north and south abaci (fig. 84). Again, their base mouldings differ from those at the east (fig. 11j). In other words, it could be argued that, initially, the south aisle was constructed only as far west as was sufficient to encompass the ascending stairs to the minor transept arm and the southeast window above them, the west end of the Romanesque aisle being retained: shafts and wall ribs had been inserted into the choir wall in preparation for vaulting. Much of this work, employing Purbeck, may actually have preceded the north choir aisle. Work in the north aisle was probably simultaneous with the *west* end of the south aisle, as both are characterized by the reduced use of Purbeck.

The lancets as revealed in the north aisle, like the two western windows in the south aisle, apparently lacked any shafts: can this be taken as an indication of a further economy, along with the abandonment of ashlar for the upper part of the wall in the south aisle? Or does it reflect first a pause in construction and then, when work was resumed, the constraints of reduced means? This leads to a further question or problem: was either aisle actually vaulted at this time or were both left protected only by their wooden roofs? Evidence for a firm answer to this question is lacking, although the lack of a vaulting shaft in the south wall of the south aisle opposite that on the north wall suggests that the vault of this aisle at least was not attempted.[117]

The remaining problem concerning the chronology of events resulting in the present form of the south aisle focuses on the massive buttress erected in the middle of the north wall. It only makes sense as a consequence of the removal of the arch at the east end of the narrow western bay of the aisle *or* as a substitute for the failure to construct that arch. The dating of the buttress is problematic because the elements of the arch at the top of its south face could have been reused from earlier dismantled work. Certainly, however, the west bay of the aisle had been widened and the buttress erected by the time of the construction of the asymmetrical ceiling now in position over the entire space, a work that can be dated to the fourteenth century on the basis of the carvings of the bosses that decorate it.[118] However, the buttress can date no later than the late thirteenth century, as it appears that the tomb canopy attributed to Bishop John de Bradfield (1277–83) was constructed between it and the early-thirteenth-century respond to the west (fig. 77).[119]

Crossing

It would be expected that the responds at the west end of the choir walls, which effectively form the eastern 'piers' of the crossing, would relate to the remodelling of the choir, since the construction of the east crossing arch would seem to be necessary for the completion of the choir vaults; that arch in turn is dependent, to some extent structurally, to a great extent visually, upon the piers or, in this case, the responds from which it springs. And indeed, the bases and plinths of the responds against the west ends of the old solid presbytery walls, like those of the adjacent north and south aisle responds (fig. 11j), are of limestone.[120] So, too, as in the case of the arches at the west end of the choir aisles, the shafts of the west-facing responds of the east side of the crossing are made of limestone (which has been coated with a pale lilac-coloured plaster or cement), with a darker stone more like Purbeck used for shaft-rings, capitals, and abaci (fig. 81, at right; fig. 84, at left).[121]

Considering this uniform use of materials in the shafts of the choir responds and of the aisle arches, not surprisingly, the east crossing arch does match the choir vaults stylistically, for it has a large, even giant, dogtooth on its middle order; the other two major orders are each a large filleted roll. Yet it should be noted that the west ends of the diagonal ribs of the west bay of the choir vault spring from (Purbeck) corbels – not shafts – hence they are structurally independent of the east crossing arch and its responds. However, the capitals of the responds match those in the choir and, significantly, are different from those elsewhere in the transept arms.

The east-facing responds of both west crossing piers, like the west-facing responds on the east side of the crossing, also utilize limestone for their bases (profile, fig. 11 l) and plinths.[122] This is also true of the bases of the responds for the arch from the north arm of the transept into the nave aisle, that is, of its north respond and the opposing respond against the northwest crossing pier: all bases are of limestone. In addition, the shafts of this north nave aisle arch are of limestone in the case of both of its north and south responds (fig. 82). This use of limestone for the shafts suggests that this arch belongs to the same constructional phase that saw the erection of the choir aisle arches *and* preceded the construction of the east face of the northwest crossing pier above the level of the bases, since its shafts are of Purbeck once again.[123] The east face of the southwest crossing pier also saw the reappearance of the use of Purbeck for its shafts (fig. 80). The east faces of both west crossing piers therefore mark the return to the aesthetic of the east end (presbytery and minor east transept).

In contrast to the north nave aisle arch, that on the south forms a more confusing picture in the mixed use of limestone and Purbeck encountered there. On the aisle face of the southwest crossing pier, where the bases are all of limestone, a pairing of limestone and Purbeck occurs on either side of the axial element.[124] The two bases towards the transept of the south respond of the nave aisle arch are Purbeck, but the axial one and the four others facing into the aisle are limestone – a reversal of expectations considering the bases of the other piers and responds on the west side of the crossing.[125] The axial shaft of the respond and the two towards the transept are of Purbeck, while towards the aisle, where one shaft (Purbeck) is missing, they may have alternated, as the sequence thereafter is limestone, Purbeck (this shaft corresponds to the diagonal rib of the unexecuted aisle vault), and limestone (visible in fig. 89). Thus, the constructional sequence in terms of the methodical use of either limestone or Purbeck is unclear. However, the use of hollow chamfers on the angles between the shafts appears for the first time on the south respond only. Their appearance makes it evident, at least, that the south respond is the latest and was not started with the southwest crossing pier. The bases also feature triple rolls (fig. 11 m).

As the pier element corresponding to the middle order of the choir arch with the giant dogtooth is that part of the core of the pier that is shaped like a pilaster with chamfered sides,[126] it is clear that the middle element of the west-facing responds and the east faces of the west piers were intended to correspond to an arch order decorated with giant dogtooth, like that in the choir arch. Yet, in the event, both the north and south crossing arches lack the giant dogtooth and have, instead, a large filleted roll (like the western crossing arch).

The opposed faces of the west crossing piers are not symmetrical, although both are distinguished by the continued use of Purbeck for their shafts (figs. 80, 84, 86, 87); admittedly, it is a very dull Purbeck.[127] The *south* face of the northwest pier has a chamfered axial element, which means it was designed for a middle arch order of giant dogtooth (figs. 80, 87), but the *north* face of the southwest pier was not, for it has an axial shaft (figs. 84, 86). As built, the middle order of the west crossing arch is a large roll with a wide fillet (as is also true of the north and south arches).

The respond of the south face of the southwest pier was also designed for an aisle arch with a middle order of giant dogtooth, as is again demonstrated by the presence of the chamfered axial element, yet the opposed south aisle respond was not, for it has an axial shaft (on the north side of the arch, a foliage corbel supports the capital that corresponds to the filleted roll). The arch into the south nave aisle also eliminated the use of the giant dogtooth in favour of the large filleted roll.

Thus, it would seem that the west crossing piers were begun at the same time as the east responds, but that they were not carried up uniformly above the level of their shaft bases (which were of limestone). The aisle wall and pier responds of the north aisle arch were constructed first (the respond, with limestone shafts, carried up in advance of the rest of the pier that received Purbeck shafts), followed by the east faces of both west piers, the south face of the northwest pier (all with Purbeck shafts), and the south or aisle face of the southwest pier; lastly, the north (nave) face of the southwest pier and the aisle wall respond of the south aisle arch were carried up with a changed design to the middle order. That these piers were not carried up to their full height along with the east side of the crossing is witnessed by the fact that the first set of shaft-rings on both the west piers corresponds in design to those of the north arm,

not to those of the north and south choir aisles or to the east responds. Their capitals also match those of the vaulting shafts in the
north arm. Consequently, it is quite clear that the crossing was not
raised as a unit to provide abutment for the choir vaults, or to serve
a similar function successively for each transept arm. Rather, the
piers were raised in piecemeal fashion, and the north, west, and
south arches only constructed prior to the anticipated vaulting of
the north arm (which was delayed a century). This raises the possibility that the Romanesque crossing piers were retained, only to be
gradually recased as the work proceeded.[128]

Once completed, the crossing was not vaulted. Since the diagonal
faces of the piers are composed of five shafts, it is possible that,
initially, the axial shaft was intended to correspond to a diagonal
vault rib. In the final form, each of these shafts corresponds to a pair
of departing labels for the adjacent crossing arches. These labels
project far enough to suggest that a vault was not finally precluded,
although its rib pattern could not have had any visual coordination
with the shafts.

Inside the lowest stage of the tower – the present bell ringers'
chamber – certain constructional differences between its rough rubble walls suggest that the walls were built in two separate phases.
Each of the walls is pierced by a small doorway with a pointed arch
leading to the adjacent roof space. On the south and west walls,
above the doorways, there are big relieving arches with horizontal
bands of pure flint work above. The relieving arches and bands of
flint work are lacking on the east and north walls, indicating that
they may have been a separate build and the earliest erected.

Major East Transept

Because the internal elevations of the two transept arms are different (cf. figs. 80, 81, and 84), they evidently were not carried up at the
same time, as the documents do suggest. The lower part of the south
transept arm follows the general system established and adhered to
throughout all the work to the east in its continued use of the tall
arched recesses in the wall below the clerestory. By contrast, the
three nearly equal tiers of the north arm's elevation are a radical
departure from the 'Rochester system,' and it might seem more logical on these grounds that this north arm followed the south; furthermore, because the south arm was on the monastic side, it might

again be expected that work proceeded there first. However, the south arm has later features, notably the lower south windows in which tracery, in the form of a simple 'Y' pattern, makes its first appearance in the building. The windows in the north transept are all simple lancets in form. At the clerestory level, the interior screen on the southwest side was designed to correspond to the newer concept, also present in the outer windows, of a single window composed of two lancet-like lights with the spandrel between the sub- and superordinate arches pierced: a timid approach to true bar tracery that seems less advanced than that of the lower south windows, and that again has no parallel on the north side.

The bases and capitals used in the north major arm show a distinct change from those in the north choir aisle, and suggest a fourth campaign and certainly a second, possibly a fourth, designer. The bases are neither of the water-holding type nor the double roll: they now have three rolls (fig. 11k). The profile of the shaft-rings has changed as well, to a large split roll over a small necking roll from the bold undulating roll/hollow/roll of presbytery and choir. The capitals are squatter, with more, and more exaggerated, mouldings. As a whole, the design is characterized and given a distinctly different flavour by the use of large carved heads as label stops and corbels. Another distinguishing feature is the appearance in the clerestory arcade of a straight-sided pointed arch for the bay in the line of the window (south bay on east side; both bays on west side). Purbeck marble is used generally throughout the north arm for bases, shafts, capitals, and string-courses: an exception is the capitals of the second zone of windows. At floor level, the design of the north arm seems to anticipate two bays of quadripartite vaulting, instead of the unit of sexpartite vaulting actually built, the latter a vault pattern that constitutes a link with the earlier work to the east. The shafts for the intermediate transverse rib of each bay spring from corbels that themselves consist of a short shaft and a carved head.

The mural design of the south arm (fig. 84), which was inspired by that of the presbytery and minor transept, marks a return to tradition after the innovation of the north arm, initially appearing as the work of a more conservative designer – certainly the third, possibly the fifth. The use of Purbeck is continued for most elements, the four continuous vaulting shafts (rising from the floor), the bases, shaft-rings, and capitals of the south wall arcades (but not, apparently, those originally on the east and west), the clerestory arcade shafts and capitals, as well as the jamb-shafts of the windows (but not their capitals; on the west side, the window frames lack shafts). The appearance of several simple forms of tracery is a surprising innovation for this designer, unless it marks yet other hands coming to the fore. One might expect that the east wall of the clerestory preceded the western; if that were the case, one could speculate that its tracery was originally of the 'Y' type, as in the lower south windows; but even so, the west clerestory tracery would have to be considered as a regression from that type.[129] The appearance of 'Y' tracery in the south elevation of the south arm suggests a date for its construction some time around 1240/45 (figs. 59, 84).[130]

Perhaps not long after its completion, the east wall of the south arm was altered by the substitution of one large arch for the initial two, creating a shallow recess that mimicked the shallow chapel on the north arm (cf. figs. 84, 81).[131] The new east arch has limestone shafts and moulded bell capitals, but Purbeck bases, and a label with head stops.[132] The corbel inserted below the clerestory string in order to receive the vault shaft (of limestone below the string) also is carved in the form of a human head. It is unlikely, however, that the renewal or alteration of the tracery of the east windows was done at this time, as the forms – if Scott's restoration can be trusted – look to be from several decades later.[133]

Neither transept arm was completed by receiving its vaulting in this period, the transition from Early Gothic to the Geometric phase of the Decorated, although the presence of stone springers indicates the intention. The style of the vault bosses indicates their construction was nearly a century later.[134]

Nave

Work on the remodelling and restructuring of the eastern bays of the nave followed on the completion of the south transept clerestory (figs. 88, 89, 90). The nave arcade pier capitals are related to those of the clerestory because of the appearance of a roll moulding under the abacus. This moulding also links the clerestory capitals to the capitals of the southwest crossing pier and separates them from the arcade capitals of the lower transept wall, which relate to the capitals of the northwest crossing pier. A mannerism that distinguishes the nave arcade arches from the south aisle arch is the way the nave arcade mouldings rise from cones of masonry on top of the capitals, in contrast to the latter where the mouldings spring directly from the *flat* upper surface of the capitals (fig. 90). This a mannerism (congé) somewhat anticipated by the capitals of the two centre arcade shafts on the south wall of the south arm (fig. 84).

The nave piers are also the product of two separate campaigns. The east pair rise from plinths that anticipate the multi-lobed shape of the pier created by the attached shafts, while the west pair sit on octagonal plinths formed by partially adapting, remodelling, and extending the Romanesque ones (cf. figs. 91 and 92). There are also minor differences in the profile of the shaft bases: they both have two astragals above a roll; on the east ones these astragals have a slight ogee curvature, on the southwest pier they are more pronounced in scale (figs. 11n, 37), and on the northwest pier the hollow returns (fig. 11o). And, although the piers have the same design, the shafts of the pair at the west are of coursed limestone rather than the Purbeck of the eastern pair, an economy perhaps anticipating the cessation of work.

Summary of Constructional Sequence

The sequence of construction at the east end of the building is straightforward and as might be anticipated. The crypt, the presbytery, and the minor transept with its chapels can be assigned to one campaign, carried forward from season to season under the supervision of one master mason. Furthermore, it is a campaign that has the appearance of being swiftly carried out without any significant alterations in plan or changes in style. The remodelling of the choir probably followed directly upon the completion of the minor east transept. The stylistic differences between it and work to the east need not necessarily be taken as evidence of a new master mason. Work in the choir may have been accompanied by the beginning of the rebuilding of the aisles. The subsequent reduction in the use of Purbeck might be taken as a reflection of their subsidiary position, or of economy (allowing the more lavish decoration of the choir), or of a change in master mason that might otherwise be reflected not so much in general concept as in smaller details such as base profiles.

The order of construction in the area of the crossing and transept is less straightforward and more complicated.[135] The sequence that seems to emerge is the following:

(1) *a.* construction of the west-facing responds of the east crossing arch and of the responds and arches at the west end of the north and south choir aisles, all for their full height;

b. construction of the responds of the arch to the north nave aisle and the bases of the east-facing responds of the west crossing piers; all this work is characterized by the abandonment of Purbeck;

(2) construction of the north arm of the major transept and completion of the northwest crossing pier (evidence: design of string-courses and shaft-rings); return to Purbeck for the shafts; erection of the south arm of the major transept up to clerestory level;

(3) construction of the clerestory of the south arm of the major transept and the completion of the southwest crossing pier followed by the aisle respond of the arch to the south aisle;

(4) erection of the north, south, and west crossing arches (with filleted roll in place of dogtooth);

(5) reconstruction of the nave begun, with only two bays completed.

As has been seen, there is no reason to place the construction of the choir after either of the choir aisles – except to accommodate the documentary references to the entry into the choir in 1227 and the building of the choir by William of Hoo as sacrist, that is, by 1239. In addition, as has been seen, the stylistic evidence argues that the north transept was built before the south and *both* preceded the beginning of the nave. Finally, the vaulting of the transept arms did not belong to this period, but is more likely to be associated with the completion of the central tower by Bishop Hamo de Hethe (1319–52) in the second quarter of the fourteenth century.[136]

The Problem of Dating: A Hypothetical Chronology

It may be useful to recall the hitherto accepted chronology for the early Gothic work, which is basically that established by Hope in 1898. The conventional date usually accepted for the initiation of construction, which is not documented, is circa 1200.[137] The documentary date of 1227 for the entrance into the choir has been accepted for the completion of all work east of the main transept, with the presbytery apparently finished by 1214.[138] This work therefore would have followed hard upon the Chichester Cathedral presbytery (1187–99), being contemporary with the great transept at Lincoln

Cathedral (ca. 1200/5–20), the retrochoir of Winchester Cathedral (1202–ca. 1235), and the east arm retrochoir of Southwark Priory (ca. 1212?–30/5). By comparison with the last three, Rochester might appear at least quite sedate – if not very conservative. The completion of the choir was then followed by the construction of the major transept (after 1239), which was carried out in two campaigns, one for each arm, the north arm, completed circa 1255, apparently preceding the south one, which was begun some time after 1255.[139] The dates for the two arms of the transept, therefore, as inferred from the documentary evidence, have generally been cited as 1240–55 for the north arm, with a completion as late as circa 1280 for the south arm.[140] This would place the north arm in the years of the Ely Cathedral presbytery (1235–52), the north transept at Lichfield Cathedral (begun ca. 1240), or the Chapel of the Nine Altars at Durham Cathedral (1242–80), and the south arm with the beginnings of the Exeter Cathedral Lady chapel and retrochoir, circa 1275/80. These stylistic 'parallels' suggest that the traditional interpretation of the documentary references and the dates inferred from them cannot be correct, unless Rochester was some extraordinary manifestation of a revival of earlier forms or was executed by a peculiarly archaic workshop of exceptional longevity.

Thus, a consideration of the important aspect of style does not provide support for the traditional interpretation of the documentary evidence regarding dating. In this respect, then, the sources can be seen to be both somewhat unhelpful and misleading; in short, they must be considered as unreliable, if not slightly suspect. The sequence of construction as finally arrived at by Hope, however, is generally confirmed, as has been seen, by a stylistic analysis of the fabric.

At this point it may be appropriate to consider, or rather to search for, evidence of the possible impact of the Interdict of 1209–13, imposed by Pope Innocent III, and the events of the last years of the reign of King John,[141] on the constructional history and progress of the rebuilding of the eastern arm.[142] It will be recalled that the bishop, Gilbert Glanville, had been forced to flee his see in 1207 and probably did not return before his death in 1214, when he was reportedly buried on the north side of – it has been assumed – the presbytery.[143] In 1215, King John laid siege to Rochester, but there does not seem to have been any significant damage to the cathedral fabric.[144] There is no evidence in the presbytery or minor east transept or, indeed, in the choir (or in the remaining portion of the Romanesque nave) of any destruction and subsequent repairs or rebuilding at that time. If the conventional chronology is accepted, the Interdict should have had an impact on some part of the presbytery and minor transept, the parts generally considered to have been in construction between 1200 and 1214, but none is visible.

Except for the slight evidence suggestive of an intention to place a wooden roof over an unvaulted north arm, the construction of the presbytery and minor transept appears to have been quite seamless. So, too, there does not seem to have been a significant break between these parts and the choir. Although there may be small differences indicating changes in workshop or master mason between the presbytery and minor transept on the one hand and the choir on the other, or between those units and the choir aisles, it is in the south choir aisle alone that one sees considerable evidence of a disruption and discontinuity in intentions: here work appears to have been broken off and, when resumed, continued in a simpler way, with a radical alteration in plan.

An attempt to take into account the majority – if not necessarily all – of the many diverse features of this area (as described above), results in the following scenario for the constructional history of this troublesome space. Before the Interdict, work was already in progress at the east end of the south aisle with the intention of creating a large vaulted central-plan space, a double aisle accommodating the two parallel flights of stairs. This work was interrupted but perhaps not completely halted by the Interdict, for during this period it may have been hastily closed in with a necessary economy in the use of materials. The south wall, west of the easternmost lancet window, was continued westwards over the earlier wall to abut the east wall of the end of the west cloister range: this work was executed in rubble, the windows without shafts to the jambs. At the same time, in the north aisle, and possibly because that aisle still retained its Romanesque north wall, simple lancet windows were inserted in the west and east bays. Both aisles were closed by wooden roofs.

If the change in plan in the south choir aisle represents an interruption of work occasioned by the flight of the bishop (1207) and, subsequently, the Interdict (1209–13), then that means that the crypt, presbytery, and minor transept and the remodelling of the choir were all complete by 1207/9, with the erection of a new enlarged south choir aisle begun. All this suggests a date for the initiation of construction well before 1200, that is, soon after the fire of 1179. The completion of the south aisle to a simplified plan (the vault abandoned), and the economical work in the north aisle, could well date to the period between 1207/9 and 1213/15 or even 1217.

Therefore, it could be argued that the roof of which the leading was nearly finished by prior Ralph de Ros, some time between 1193 and 1203/8, could have been that for the new presbytery, minor transept, and choir, and possibly those over the aisles.[145] This process was initially interrupted by the Interdict, but was completed by prior Elias some time by 1214/18, that is, during the Interdict. If the building of the roofs preceded the construction of the vaults, the construction of the presbytery, minor transept, *and* choir vaults would have been accomplished under Ralph de Ros, rather than during the decade 1203/8–1214/18 under Elias or even his successor, between 1214/18 and 1227.[146] As a result, it is surprising that the entry into the new choir is not recorded for 1217: might the date 1227 have been 'chosen' by the chronicler to coincide with the majority of King Henry III?

After the termination of the Interdict, work was resumed in the choir aisles. Indeed, hypothetically, work on the choir aisles should have – of necessity – involved the arches of the choir aisles opening into the transept and the elevation above them, as well as the eastern crossing piers and arch between them. This actually seems to have been the case. As has been described, the use of Purbeck in both aisles was diminished as work moved westward, to the point of being nearly eliminated. In the south aisle, the arches at the east and west ends of the narrow western section, essentially the western part of the Romanesque aisle, were constructed, work paralleled stylistically by the insertion of the vaulting shafts in the north aisle and the construction of the arch at its west end. This work was also accompanied by work on the east responds of the crossing (the west ends of the solid side walls of the former presbytery) and the beginning of the crossing's western piers.

It might be expected that the crossing would have been completed before either arm of the transept was begun: the piers raised to their full height and the tower carried up at least one stage in order to receive the abutment of the choir and transept roofs, so as to allow the construction of the vaults (under the protection of a roof), unless the Romanesque tower had been retained for that purpose. This does not seem to have been the case, as the evidence suggests that the western Romanesque piers were gradually recased, with the three crossing arches erected only after work on the transept arms was nearing completion. It is also clear that before the remodelling of the crossing piers was carried to its full height, and the north, south, and west crossing arches erected, work had begun on the transept arms. Work on the major transept also proceeded despite the unfinished state of both choir aisles: the south, and very likely the north, aisle without its vaults.

The implication of the sources is that the major transept was not begun until circa 1239/40, about the time of the consecration, and that building proceeded rather slowly.[147] The lack of dates for Richard of Walden prevents one from knowing just how slowly this may have been and introduces a further uncertainty into any theoretical chronology. Equally ambiguous, owing to the absence of references, is the beginning of work on the nave, nor are the reasons for its abrupt cessation anywhere hinted at. Nevertheless, it is quite certain that the dates heretofore accepted for the construction of the great transept are much too late, and are quite implausible. Rather than being begun after 1240, it must have been nearing completion no later than the early 1240s.

The failure to complete the vaults of either arm in stone may be a reflection of financial difficulties. The priory was reported to be hopelessly in debt by 1255, a debt not due to building, but one that has been interpreted as the result of the general economic changes adversely affecting Benedictine monasticism at large, as well as being the consequence of the protracted legal battle to resecure some of the rights that had been taken away from the monks by Bishop Gilbert.[148] Necessary economic reforms were not effected at Rochester until after 1283, owing to the efforts of archbishops Peckam and Robert Winchelsey (1293–1313). By this time, however, the idea of reconstructing the nave certainly had been long abandoned. The fact that it was started perhaps indicates that its beginnings pre-dated the climax, after mid-century, of the intensifying economic crisis.

It was only later in the century that the large buttress in the south choir aisle was constructed, when it was decided to create a space of uniform width by removing the walls of the western third of the aisle. This work may have been carried out at the time the alterations were made in the west face of the east wall of the south arm of the major transept, work that seems stylistically similar to the buttress, at least in attitude, because of the possible reuse of earlier material.

This hypothetical sequence of events, however internally consistent or plausible, does raise an awkward question. If the choir was complete as early as 1207/9, or even 1215/17, why was it not 'entered' for another decade? One possible explanation is that the work of erecting the arches at the ends of the choir aisles, and the piers in the area of the crossing, had to be completed before the choir could actually be put into service; admittedly, however, ten years seems rather a long time for the amount of work involved. An alternative possibility is that the formal 'entry' was delayed until the choir could be furnished in an appropriately sumptuous way, that is, with new choir stalls and so forth, which William of Hoo paid for with funds that had accumulated from the pilgrims attracted to the tomb of William of Perth during the two decades since his murder in 1201.[149] Considering that date, it seems unlikely that the promotion of his cult could have yielded significant material reward in time to influence the design of the choir, let alone the presbytery and/or minor transept. By the time the crossing was reached, if it was as late as circa 1227, the pilgrimage to the shrine of William may have been yielding material rewards to the priory. In the work around the crossing, evidence of a slight change in style, one reversing that noted in the aisles, can be detected in the resumption of the use of Purbeck marble for the east-facing shafts of the west piers (figs. 80, 86). Whether this resumption of the use of coloured stone represents a more prosperous situation resulting from the increasing donations of pilgrims to the shrine of Saint William of Perth is a moot point.

On the other hand, if the choir had not been begun before the Interdict, the period 1215/17–27 might seem a very long one to complete the relatively modest amount of work required to accomplish the transformation of the choir, especially if the construction of the choir aisles had been simplified by giving up their vaulting. The conventional chronology also leaves unexplained the thirteen-year gap in continuing with work on the transept after the occupation of the choir in 1227, as well as the delay in its consecration until 1240. Although the 1240 consecration could be taken as marking the true completion of the choir, its significance, however, may have to do less with the history of the fabric than with the Council of 1237 held at St Paul's, London, and its decree concerning church consecrations: with no exceptions, all cathedrals and conventual or parish churches 'whose walls had been completed must be consecrated within two years of that time, even if the structure remained unfinished after the stipulated two years had elapsed.'[150] Nevertheless, the possibility should be entertained that the consecration in 1240 marked the completion of both arms of the major transept except for their vaults.

Liturgical Arrangements

The existing arrangement of the choir would appear to date from the completion of the new Gothic east end. That is, a choir raised for its full length well above the floor level of the main transept and nave, and approached, therefore, by a flight of steps occupying the east half of the crossing.[151] (The floor level of the western portion of the choir was determined by the height of the vaults of the Gundulfian bays of the crypt under its eastern part.) A screen was placed in the line of the east wall of the transept,[152] with the stalls against the solid side walls of the choir that stretched between the major and minor transepts.[153] The high altar occupied the second or third of the four half-bays of the two sexpartite vaults covering the sanctuary/presbytery; the matutinal altar was probably placed under the eastern crossing.[154]

The end result of the rebuilding was the accommodation of thirteen altars, in addition to the high altar, in discrete architectural compartments of varying sizes and degrees of separateness. The end wall of the presbytery section of the crypt was divided into three narrow bays, each with a window and two with a piscina. Each of the arms of the crypt under the minor transept provided for two larger, more self-contained chapels. Their form was repeated on the main level of the church in taller bays forming an aisle to the minor transept. In addition, there was an altar in each arm of the major transept, that in the north arm provided for by a shallow rectangular projecting chapel.[155] In contrast to these architecturally defined spaces, the north arm of the minor transept was adopted to house the shrine of Saint William. With the withdrawal of the monks' choir east of the crossing, thereby freeing all of the nave for use as the parish church, a stone screen appears to have been built with the remodelling of the west crossing piers.[156]

The liturgical day at Benedictine Rochester would have followed the conventional seven canonical hours. It began with matins – the longest service of the day – about 2:30 a.m., consisting of the Pater noster, Ave, and Credo, followed by the recitation of the fifteen gradual psalms (CXX–CXXXIV) and the reading of the lessons for the day (of which there could be as many as twelve), and finally lauds (Laudate Dominum). Prime followed at daybreak (hymn, psalms, and prayer), then terce, sext, none, vespers, and compline before the monks retired to bed. High mass was celebrated in mid-morning by the hebdomadarian or, on Sundays and feast days, by the prior or bishop, at which times there was a procession to asperge all the altars in the church.[157]

The monks would have entered the church through the door at the west end of the north walk, which led into the south aisle, and from there into the south arm of the major transept and thence up the steps in the crossing, proceeding into the choir through the choir screen. The crypt and its chapels were accessible only by the stairs in the south aisle. The chapels in the minor east transept and the presbytery would be reached from the south aisle by the flight of stairs (paralleling those descending into the crypt) leading up to the south arm of the minor transept. The privacy of the monks was partly achieved by the rood screen, which closed the nave off from the crossing, placed between the western crossing piers and by stone 'portal screens' later placed midway in the north aisle and at the entrance to the south choir aisle.[158]

The Place of Rochester in the Evolution of Early Gothic Architecture in England

In the history of Gothic architecture in England, the Gothic work at Rochester has been generally ignored, overshadowed by the cathedrals of Canterbury (1174–84) and Wells (begun circa 1175), then Lincoln (begun 1192) and Salisbury (begun 1220). Yet, it contains a number of features of unusual interest. The new extension was remarkable in three major respects: the extensive crypt; the aisleless presbytery; and the secondary eastern transept.

Although crypts were not unusual as part of a large Romanesque church, they are rather less common in the Early Gothic.[159] Indeed, Rochester's, along with those of the cathedrals of Canterbury, 1180–4, and Hereford, circa 1190/1200–20, are the major examples.[160] In the case of Rochester, it is of interest that the crypt extends under all of the new addition, which, primarily because of the minor transept, makes it a very large area indeed. The obvious inspiration for such an extensive crypt would be that of Canterbury, where the new east end begun by Ernulf circa 1096, when he was prior, and which replaced the short apsidal east arm of Lanfranc's building, begun circa 1070, included a matching crypt, a crypt that was further extended during the rebuilding begun after the fire of 1174 by William of Sens, and continued after 1179 by William the Englishman. The plan of Rochester, however, has nothing to do with that of Canterbury, as the latter's late-eleventh-century crypt included an ambulatory and radiating chapels, while in the later extension, an additional ambulatory led to the substructure of the circular Corona.[161] In short, Canterbury in either phase was not straight-ended. The crypt at Hereford was, in contrast, flat-ended, but, since it was confined to the area of the projecting, four-bay Lady chapel, it was much less extensive than that at Rochester.[162] It may properly be compared to the portion of the crypt at Rochester under the presbytery, for like it, the Hereford crypt is three-aisled, although significantly taller than Rochester's. Stylistically, the Rochester crypt seems to have anticipated the two-aisled undercroft of the chapel at Lambeth Palace, which therefore may date to 1193–1205 (Archbishop Hubert Walter), rather than to the later part of the episcopate of Stephen Langton, 1213–28, following the lifting of the Interdict.

The aisleless presbytery is a feature without any exact parallel among the larger abbeys and cathedrals, especially at this date. Eleventh-century York Minster (1080s–1100) had an aisleless presbytery (and an aisleless nave), ending apsidally, probably over a crypt; some time between 1100 and 1184 it was extended twenty feet to a flat east wall.[163] The church of the Cluniac priory of St Saviour, Bermondsey, from the late eleventh or early twelfth century, also seems to have had a long, aisleless presbytery ending, however, in triple apses and with flanking absidioles.[164] In the early thirteenth century, Premonstra-tensian St Radegund at Dover (Kent) had a long solid-walled, flat-ended presbytery, flanked by shorter aisles.[165] The lack of aisles gives the eastern extension at Rochester a visual analogy to the standard early Cistercian plan type of flat-ended presbytery with transept arms of two square chapels, but it does not follow Cistercian proportions. It is also notable that the chapels are fully open to each other and to the west bay of the presbytery in the manner not traditional with the Cistercians. It could be considered an exaggeration of the earlier standard Cistercian plan. A number of monastic churches, circa 1200, especially in the north of England and in Scotland, had aisleless presbyteries projecting two or three bays beyond aisled choirs, for instance, the abbeys (or priories) of

Arbroath (Angus), Jedburgh (Roxburgh), Tynemouth (Northumberland), and Lanercost (Cum-berland) and the cathedral of St Andrews (Fife),[166] although the custom was already passing out of use among Cistercian churches in the late twelfth century, as is demonstrated at Byland Abbey (Yorkshire) in the 1170s.[167]

As a church with double eastern transepts, Rochester was one of the first. The double eastern transept may have been initially introduced into England at Cluniac Lewes Priory (Sussex), begun between 1077 and 1091/98, certainly before 1142/7.[168] Lewes may have been preceded, at the turn of the century, by Canterbury, in the rebuilding of Lanfranc's choir, circa 1096–1130, where the idea of a secondary transept was approached, but not truly created because the nave elevation was continuous, therefore eliminating a transverse space and isolating the two arms – or wings – from each other.[169] In the rebuilding following the fire of 1174, William of Sens altered the Romanesque arrangement to introduce a true transept with a crossing.[170] Canterbury, therefore, may have provided the idea but not the form for Rochester, for, at Canterbury, the squarish wings with their pairs of apsidal chapels in the thickness of the wall were inherited from the Romanesque building. Rochester, however, may have preceded the east end of Lincoln, begun circa 1192, which, like Canterbury, had two apsidal chapels in each arm.[171] Unlike the chapels of Lincoln or Canterbury, the chapels at Rochester were formally eastern aisles, in this respect anticipating the minor east transept at Salisbury Cathedral where, indeed, the east chapels are truly aisle-like in form, as there are proper arcade piers rather than the heavy wall-like masses at Rochester.[172]

Also unlike either Canterbury or Lincoln, the arms of the minor transept at Rochester were equal to the nave in width, thereby resulting in a square crossing.[173] But, characteristic of the churches with double eastern transepts in England, there was no secondary crossing tower.[174] Despite the differences, the presence of the minor transept at Rochester is most likely to be attributed, rather more exclusively than in the case of the crypt, to the influence and model of Canterbury.

In other respects, the east end of Rochester displays some features worthy of remark. This is particularly true of the internal elevation of the presbytery. It might be thought that it would have some relationship to the upper level of the eastward extension of Hereford, circa 1200–25, where the four-bay, aisleless Lady chapel, raised over the earlier three-aisled crypt, is flanked by large transept-like spaces. However, the elevation of the Hereford Lady chapel is similar to that of the aisleless presbytery at Tynemouth (ca. 1200) or the elevations of aisleless naves such as Ripon Minster (Yorkshire, 1190s) or Nun Monkton (Yorkshire, ca. 1200). In all of these buildings, a dado, plane or decorated, is present below the windows;[175] none has the niche-like arcade of Rochester, which creates a sense of the separation of the arcade supporting the passageway from the wall in which both the upper and lower windows are located. This type of wall construction has a certain similarity to that of the Trinity chapel and Corona at Canterbury, a similarity that is more visual than structural because of the distinctive free-standing arcade there, as a consequence of the floor-level wall passage.

The presence of Purbeck shafting and mouldings at Rochester is not unexpected in the vicinity of Canterbury. What is unexpected is the methodical and consistent use of the shafts and the string-courses that cut across them. The shafts rise from floor to vault-springing, another distinctive characteristic – although they were similarly arranged in the earlier Corona at Canterbury, 1179–84, and the much later Chapel of the Nine Altars at Durham Cathedral, 1242–80, both of which also have smooth dadoes. Nonetheless, even if there are projecting continuous shafts in the elevations of these buildings, a niche-like arcade is not created in any of them, earlier or later. Floor to vault shafts also occur in the main arcades of other buildings during this period, such as in the western nave bays of Worcester Cathedral, circa 1175, the great transept at Lincoln, after circa 1200/5, as well as in the later presbytery at Southwark Priory (St Mary Overie, now cathedral), after 1212? to circa 1230/5. The elevation of the wooden-roofed choir of Ripon, circa 1175, might also be mentioned.

The clerestory design is of interest for its triparite pattern that features a very wide central arch flanked by extremely narrow ones almost of equal height, but with the outer jamb-shafts half the height of the inner free-standing shafts. Lopsided arches occur as early as the Canterbury choir, circa 1174, and at least as late as the Ely presbytery, circa 1235, in contrast to the 'normal' pattern, for instance, Worcester choir and presbytery, circa 1224–31, wherein the capitals of the shafts and jamb-shafts alike are at the same height.

It is notable that the vaults spring from a level well up in the clerestory, actually at the top of the passageway between the windows. Although their sexpartite form surely derives from Canterbury, and even repeats the pattern of the choir there exactly – two bays of sexpartite vaults plus one quadripartite bay at the west – the rational is quite different. While at Canterbury their appearance may be an ingenious solution to covering five bays of varying dimensions – some exceedingly oblong rectangles – necessitated by the decision to build on the Romanesque supports, at Rochester, where there were no constraints, the alternating rhythm was introduced deliberately, for its own sake, *de novo* in the earlier work at ground level, with the shafts – in groups of three or singly – attached to the pseudo-arcade piers. The two double bays could just as well have been designed as three bays, not excessively narrow for vaulting with a quadripartite system. Sexpartite vaults also appeared over the transept arms at Rochester – one unit per space – again as at Canterbury.[176]

The decorative details, the extensive use of billet and dogtooth in particular, are also partly reminiscent of Canterbury where, along with chevron, they are sometimes combined on the same arches. At Rochester, the billet and dogtooth always occur separately, and the chevron is not present at all.[177] More unexpected is the absence of crocket or stiff-leaf forms for capitals and the prevalence of the simpler moulded or 'bell' type.[178]

Rather less can be said about the decorative details of the exterior. The two features of particular interest both concern the buttresses: their shape and the intention, quickly given up, to provide them with angle shafts. Polygonal or chamfered buttresses occur in the late twelfth century in Saint Hugh's choir at Lincoln, where they are still to be seen in the eastern chapels and the south wall of the choir and are then continued into the major transept and the nave. In the next century, another major display occurs at York in the transept, where they are found in both arms on the east and west faces, circa 1220–44/50. Although polygonal buttresses are not found at Canterbury, the addition of shafts to the outer angles of buttresses is found in the work of William the Englishman, in the Trinity chapel and the Corona, 1180–4. The use continues well into the next century, as on the east end of Worcester, circa 1224–31, and in combination with chamfered forms on the east end of the priory church at Kirkham (Yorkshire), circa 1230.

Thus, while showing not unexpected influence (or awareness) of Canterbury, the eastern extension at Rochester is neither a reduced version of it nor without several original and individual characteristics: 'no scholar has yet suggested any satisfactory explanation for the highly individual character of this work, which is typical of contemporary practice neither in England nor, as far as we know, anywhere on the continent.'[179]

The rationale and purpose of the eastern extension at Rochester are far from clear. Whether begun – or planned – after the fire of 1179, or as late as circa 1200, an explanation based upon prominent relics attracting large numbers of pilgrims is not in order. The place of the relics of the early sainted bishops, Paulinus and Ithamar, in the new east end (as in the old) is unknown.[180] Their names are not included among the dedications of the crypt chapels known from a later period. Nor is the large crypt explained by the shrine of Saint William of Perth. His tomb shrine was placed in the north minor transept arm (not in one of its eastern chapels), where it was accessible, via the north choir aisle, to pilgrims presumably entering at the portal in the north wall of the north major arm. Exit more humble could have been made through a modest portal in the south bay of the west wall of the minor north arm into a space between that arm and the north tower.[181] Therefore, the size of the crypt and its seven chapels cannot be explained as a response to an existing need or situation: to allow the proper veneration of relics by providing for their better display to growing crowds controlled by an orderly circulation system.

At the upper level, the aisleless presbytery was not meant to serve as a Lady chapel and never appears to have served as such. At this date, as earlier, prominent eastern extensions were not necessarily Lady chapels. Nor were Lady chapels fixed in their position: they could be accommodated in choir (Canterbury, York) or nave aisles (Ely before 1320, Croyland Abbey), transepts (St Albans), or in special structures built at the west end (Glastonbury Abbey, Durham).[182] The location of an altar to the Virgin at Rochester is not known until the early fourteenth century, at which time it is thought to have been established in the south arm of the major transept. Part of the rationale for the extension may have been similar to that suggested for the extension of the Canterbury sanctuary in the late eleventh century: to remove the choir from the east end of the nave (and crossing), thus providing greater separation between the monks and the laity, who then had the complete nave at their disposal.[183]

Compared to the eastern extension, the major transept is altogether less remarkable. The most distinctive feature for the thirteenth century is the lack of an eastern aisle to serve as chapels. This lack, and the substitution of a shallow rectangular chapel (at least in the north arm), can be easily explained as a necessary accommodation to the unfortunate location of the late-eleventh-century free-standing tower on the north, and the proximity of claustral buildings on the east of the south arm.[184]

The differing elevations of the two arms have already been described. The three clearly defined storeys of the north arm form the more conventional solution for the period, and the only aspects of the design especially worthy of remark are the triangular or straight-sided 'arches' of the middle bays of the clerestory screen arcade and the ubiquitous use of head stops. The former are somewhat akin to the later arches of Hereford's north transept arm, particularly in the second stage, the work of Bishop Aquablanca, circa 1245–68, or later still, to the arches of the south clerestory arcade in the fourteenth-century (after 1349) nave bays of Worcester Cathedral.

Corbels or label stops carved in the form of human heads seem to have had a particular currency in the 1220s and 1230s. An early instance is their use as label stops in the nave arcade and triforum at Wells (ca. 1190–1239). Thereafter, they appear in the choir of Boxgrove Priory (Sussex), circa 1220, and at Salisbury soon after 1220, for the corbels of the vaulting shafts beginning right at the east end of the presbytery; they are used for the ends of the labels in the nave of Lincoln (before 1233), and as corbels in the south porch at Chichester (second quarter of the thirteenth century); and they appear in the choir at West-minster Abbey, circa 1245–60.[185] The tall arcades of the south arm are more unusual, although, in the context of Rochester, they represent an appropriate but conservative link with the earlier design.

The appearance of tracery in the south arm is remarkable in the context of Rochester, marking its first use there (fig. 84). Because the forms are so general and simple, it may appear that in the history of tracery in England they hold little or no significance, but they could well be among the earliest – and the oldest surviving – manifestations of this French development in Britain.[186] The simple patterns may seem a distant and later reflection of the complex forms introduced to England from France about that time, as they appear in the windows of the west front of Binham Priory (Norfolk), circa 1240, or in the east end of Westminster Abbey, circa 1245.[187] Nonetheless, 'Y' form tracery may have appeared slightly earlier, or at the same date, judging from its appearance in two of the lancet windows of the southwest chapel at Lincoln, which most probably also dates between 1240 and 1245.[188]

The pattern of the west clerestory windows (figs. 60, 85), which could be considered as a kind of plate tracery, or an intermediate between plate and true bar tracery, possibly had its antecedents in the design of the blind lancets in the east gable of the same southwest chapel at Lincoln mentioned above. Other possible antecedents can be found at Salisbury or in the clerestory windows of the choir of Hereford in the period 1220 to 1240. At Salisbury, the windows in the end and west walls of the minor and major transepts are compositions formed by two lancets with a quatrefoil above, essentially a kind of plate tracery.[189] A very similar pattern is found in the windows of the Hereford choir clerestory, with something closer to true 'Y' tracery used for the inner arcade.[190] Early in the reign of Henry III (1216–72), the Painted Chamber of Westminster Palace received several windows with similar simple early forms of tracery.[191] Two windows at the east end of the hall were in the form of a pair of lancets with an oculus piercing the tympanum above. At the west end of the hall, a pair of two-light windows with a slender central shaft had a diamond-shaped piercing filling most of the tympanum. In addition, a small window in the upper part of the east wall had simple 'Y' tracery. But a source of inspiration closer to home may have been the windows of the Archbishop's Palace at Canterbury, certainly finished before 1245, and possibly as early as 1205–20. The window tracery of one bay survives, consisting of pairs of twin lancets, with unmoulded frames, which were apparently placed under a superordinate arch, with the intervening tympanum pierced by an oculus, probably foiled.[192]

The vaults of both arms of the major transept are more deserving of comment, primarily because of their conservative character. Although the actual erection of the vaults belongs to a century later, their forms perhaps more appropriately should be dated to the initial design phase of the transepts, at which time the disposition of vaulting shafts and ribs was decided upon. The appearance of sexpartite vault forms in the north arm as late as the 1230s (if that is their date) is decidedly unusual. Vis-à-vis the sexpartite vaults of choir and presbytery, they reveal their later date only by the presence of a longitudinal ridge-rib, which could equally be due to the actual period of construction. The quadripartite vault units of the south arm (fig. 84), compared to the survival of sexpartite units in the north arm (fig. 80), are more typical of the period circa 1240, yet may also be regarded as conservative owing to the lack of any tierceron ribs. As in the north arm, the basic pattern is only modestly complicated by the addition of longitudinal and very thin transverse ridge-ribs, which also could just as well reflect their actual date of erection.

One of the most interesting aspects of the design for the rebuilding of the nave was the apparent intention to continue the axial shaft of the pier up in front of the spandrel into the second stage. At this period it was more usual for wall shafts, now frequently related to vaulting, to begin in the area of the spandrel rising from elaborate corbels, as in the nave of Lincoln, completed circa 1233, the south arm of the York transept, begun circa 1225/6 (to 1244), the Ely retrochoir, begun circa 1235 (to 1252), and the Lincoln retrochoir, begun circa 1260. A curious mannerism may also be emphasized. As described above, the mouldings of the arcades do not spring directly from the flat upper surface of the abaci but rather from a cone-like element. Similar parallels for this device can be found in prominent buildings of the same general period. At Salisbury, for example, on the arcade piers of the north and south arms of the major transept, the mouldings spring out of polygonal elements above the axial shaft of the pier. The same mannerism is found in the first pair of nave piers, but in this case the element is round. An additional and more exact parallel for this mannerism occurs in the presbytery of Westminster Abbey, in at least one of the piers of the north arcade.[193] These two parallels would seem to confirm a mid-century date for the two Gothic bays at Rochester, rather than one much later in the century as has been suggested.[194]

Conclusions

The Early Gothic work at Rochester, although modest in scale, exhibits idiosyncratic characteristics in almost all of its aspects: plan, elevation, and details. Together they produce an entity more curious and interesting than its relative neglect in the history of that style would suggest or merit. Considering that the early Romanesque church was probably dependent upon the metropolitan church for some aspects of its plan, the relative lack of correspondence between the early Gothic work at Rochester and that at Canterbury is the more remarkable. The lack of a close dependency on Canterbury is all the more surprising, not only because of its physical proximity, but because of the traditional relationship – even if not free of disputes – between the two sees.

The fire at Rochester occurred just four years after that at Canterbury, just at the time when William the Englishman took over from William of Sens. The exact extent of the devastation is no longer evident but, if it was severe, it must have primarily affected the eastern arm simply because of the lack of any evidence of damage or repairs to the nave dating to the late twelfth or early thirteenth centuries. That the fire provided the 'excuse' for the rebuilding of the east end on an enlarged scale seems more likely and plausible than that the damaged structure was patched up and then, a decade later, demolished *completely*, motivated perhaps by the murder of the baker from Perth (in 1201). As the shrine of the victim was established in what might appear to be a marginal position in the new structure, it is difficult to maintain that the rebuilding was focused on the potential of the pilgrimage to the would-be saint and its accommodation in an architectural context that would allow for a convenient access undisturbing to the monks and also for the shrine to be a distinct and visible focus. The location of the shrine of William of Perth strongly implies, contrary to the implication that has been derived from the documents, that construction of the new east end had been begun well before 1200 and was indeed probably nearing completion by the time of his murder in 1201. The funds resulting from the growing pilgrimage to his shrine, after it was situated in the north arm of the minor transept, were more likely later available to William of Hoo for the rebuilding of the major transept than for the refurbishment of the choir.

Is it significant that the shrine of Saint William was not located in the crypt? This seems to be a reflection of the fact that access to the crypt was arranged in a manner favouring the monastic community, rather than the lay population, since it was reached only from the south aisle, which seems to have been reserved to the monks. Perhaps the function of the crypt was not just to provide altars for relics but also, primarily, to accommodate the priestly population among the monks.

The presence of the crypt seems to reflect the continuity of tradition as an extension of Gundulf's crypt, and possibly influence from Canterbury. But Canterbury did not provide the formal model as a result of its allegiance to its own tradition of the curvilinear ambulatory, a form present in both of its phases, early (1096–1110) and late (1174–9), and reiterated in the ultimate form of the Trinity Chapel (1179–84). The simple round shafts of the column-like supports in the crypt at Rochester seem designed to harmonize with those of the remaining section of the early crypt (fig. 24). As similar floor levels and ceiling (vaults) heights were maintained, the effect is very much one of a continuation of the venerable core. Even the austerity of the detailing – the use of plain mouldings for bases, capitals, and string-courses, the simple ribs – contributes to the result, increasing the effect of harmonious continuity (figs. 61, 62).

The lack of curved forms, the absence of fanciful little towers, create an exterior massing in marked contrast to that of Canterbury: the more planar, rectilinear, and sober massing of the Rochester east end, marked by the massive posts of the salient turrets at its angles, is quite different in effect and spirit from Christ Church.

In a similar fashion, except for the extensive use of Purbeck, the interior elevation initially appears to reveal as little regard for Canterbury as did the plan, but the initial impression may be incorrect. The two-storey aisleless elevation of the presbytery might have been an inspired reduction of the Corona's more conventional three stages. In the case of the minor transept, the wall passage with its use of a continuous arcade could reflect the second stage of the northeast transept arm at Canterbury. Yet, here again the differences may be of greater significance and interest than the points held in common, which may be viewed as superficial, the result of a common vocabulary rather than of direct influence.

In any extensive rebuilding of the east end, it might have been expected that the opportunity would have been taken to replace the old-fashioned element of the solid side walls of the choir by open arcades. Their retention might be a reflection of the fact that the initial building campaign was limited to the extension, that is, presbytery and minor east transept (and crypt), and only after that much was accomplished was it considered desirable or possible to continue westwards with the choir and its aisles and then with the reconstruction of the main transept. At that time, it may have been considered 'easier' to remodel the choir than to demolish it in order to effect a complete rebuilding.

As a design and construction of the 1230s and 1240s, the main transept, in the context of other major buildings of the period, is unusual for its lack of an eastern aisle. As observed, its absence seems to be a reflection of the constraints imposed on the site by the presence of the north tower and, possibly, of the desire to reuse the Romanesque foundations, although it might have been possible to have included an aisle by moving the west wall of the transept westward. This, of course, would have involved shortening the nave, unless it was intended to eventually replace it and provide it with an additional bay to the west (which may not have been feasible). The tall wall arcades of the south transept arm seem to project the illusion of an aisled transept, or one in which the lower half takes its proportions and system from the presence of an eastern arcade.

With the beginning of work on the nave, the design of Rochester falls more fully into the contemporary mainstream either side of 1250. The multi-shafted piers – not quite true shaft-bundles in form – were not at all new but still very much in vogue, as witness the presbyteries of Ely (begun 1235) or of Lincoln (Angel Choir, ca. 1260).

As pointed out above, although the building sequence is relatively straightforward and moderately clear, it is difficult to attach any precise dates to sections of the work other than those roughly provided by stylistic comparison. Thus, the few and sometimes vague, confusing, or even contradictory documentary references occasionally seem at odds with the visible fabric, especially with regard to the completion of the choir and the erection of the major transept. The work accomplished by successive sacrists, especially, is unclear. Here it would seem necessary to give precedence to the fabric as the essential document rather than to the historical documents, which were, perhaps, composed with other values in mind than providing a coherent building chronology for later historians.

If a date in the early 1180s for the beginning of construction, as a consequence of the 1179 fire, is accepted, then the late date of 1227 for the entry into the choir is difficult to explain.[195] Forty-seven years seem an inordinately long time for the construction of the eastern arm, exclusive of the major transept at that, especially as the stylistic uniformity and lack of evidence for prolonged building breaks suggest that the work of crypt, presbytery, minor transept, and choir was carried forward rapidly and continuously. The south choir aisle may have been incomplete when and if the work stopped owing to the events before and during the Interdict. The decade 1207–17 might well have seen little accomplished except for the hasty closing in of the choir aisles. After the chaotic events of the end of John's reign, when work was resumed in the choir aisles, the scheme to vault the aisles, perhaps only 'temporarily' set aside in the case of the south aisle, was permanently abandoned. The choir aisles were 'completed' to a less ambitious program. Once again, ten years seem a long time to accomplish this work, even if it was accompanied by the remodelling of the crossing. Once more, it is difficult to reconcile the date of 1227 with the specifics of the building fabric, and therefore it is difficult to accept it authoratively.

As dates no later than the 1240s for the erection of the south arm of the major transept and the 1230s for the north arm of the major transept would seem to be conservatively plausible, the result is an unexplained gap of more than twenty years between the erection of the crypt, presbytery, minor transept, and choir, circa 1180/90 to circa 1207/9 (again, more than twenty-five years seems more than adequate time for the construction of these parts – even fifteen years seems sufficient) and the work of the major transept, a gap that is only partially explained by the interruption due to the Interdict and related events. With the resumption of construction after 1217, the work of terminating the choir aisles and remodelling the crossing area, by its nature, hardly seems extensive enough to have consumed ten to fifteen years. It is, consequently, difficult not to suggest that the north arm of the major transept was undertaken in the 1220s, with the south arm following in the 1230s: even then, the pace of construction would seem quite leisurely. The south arm may have been finished by 1240/5, and was followed by a brief aborted campaign in the nave. Work on the nave probably ceased by circa 1250, at which time the transept still lacked its vaults and the crossing its tower. It was to be nearly a century before the major transept was vaulted and a belfry stage added to the tower, allowing finally for the proper accommodation of the cathedral bells.

At a later date within the thirteenth century, the decision was made to extend the full width of the aisle to the major transept. The south wall of the narrow western section of the aisle was removed and the arch – if it had actually been built – that separated it from the wider east half was taken down, leaving only its north respond against the south face of the choir wall. With the removal of the south wall of the narrow section of the aisle, the west part of the aisle became equal in width to the east section. The construction of the strongly projecting buttress against the south face of the south choir wall that partially blocks access to the stairs descending to the crypt now took place. This final work in the south choir aisle may also have been accompanied by the creation of the wide but shallow arched altar recess in the east wall of the south arm of the major transept replacing the original design of two tall blind wall arches. With these changes, major campaigns of reconstruction within the cathedral came to a halt for over two centuries. During this period, alterations to the fabric were primarily limited to the creation of portals, the insertion of tracery, and the completion of the major transept and crossing tower.

SIX

Later Gothic Alterations and Additions

Historical Précis: Personages and Events

From the third quarter of the thirteenth century, the priors of Rochester were elected from within the house; only three priors were elevated to the bishopric: Thomas de Wouldham (prior from 1283) in 1292(–1317), Hamo de Hethe in 1319(–52); and John de Sheppey (prior from 1333) in 1352(–60).[1] Of these three, indeed, of any of the bishops since the early thirteenth century, Hamo de Hethe is the most significant for the building history of the cathedral church.[2] A man of independent wealth,[3] after he was appointed bishop, he is credited with restoring the shrines of saints Paulinus (634–44) and Ithamar (644–55), the third and fourth bishops, in marble and alabaster,[4] as well as having constructed the belfry of the central tower and placed four new bells in it. Yet, he too was accused by his monks of simony and other abuses in the archiepiscopal visitation of 1329.[5]

In addition to the recorded works mentioned above, it is very likely that it was under Bishop Hamo that the major transept received its vaults. He also appears to have carried out a major redecoration of the choir, as is suggested by the diaper pattern uncovered on its wall during the restoration carried out by Sir G.G. Scott (1811–78) in the 1870s.[6] A bishop's throne has also been attributed to him and this suggests that some of the ancient woodwork surviving in the choir stalls, usually attributed to the thirteenth century (ca. 1227), may have been part of Hamo's work.[7]

The Black Death raged in Rochester between 1349 and 1352. (Was the death of Hamo in 1352 the result of the plague?) The number of monks before the Black Death was around thirty-five to forty; afterwards, it was reduced to about twenty-three.[8] It may be recalled that when monks were introduced at Rochester, in place of secular clergy, by Archbishop Lanfranc (1070–89) and Bishop Gundulf (1076/7–1108), circa 1083, the initial community numbered twenty-two.[9] During Gundulf's episcopate, the number increased to sixty. It would seem that the twelfth century was the apogee of the monastic community.

The dissolution of the priory was effected gradually.[10] In June 1534, the prior, subprior, and eighteen monks took the oath of acknowledgment of the royal supremacy. Dr Richard Layton (ca. 1500–44), principal agent of Thomas Cromwell (ca. 1485–1540), visited the house in 1535. The prior resigned early in 1538. The final surrender occurred in April 1540. A document of 4 July 1540 proposed to establish a foundation consisting of a dean, six prebenders, one of whom was an archdeacon, six minor canons, an epistoler, and a gospeller. In addition, there were to be six lay singing men, a master of choristers, eight choristers, a schoolmaster, an undermaster (usher), twenty scholars, two sextons, and six poor serving men. This seems to have been carried out.

Alterations and Additions

During the later Middle Ages, there were numerous minor alterations to the cathedral fabric, primarily in the form of inserted portals and new larger traceried windows. Specifically, the minor work consists of the screen across the north choir aisle, midway in its length, and the one formerly at the west entrance to the south choir aisle; the portal in the south choir aisle leading to the cloister; the portal at the west end of the north nave aisle; and the portal, attributed to Bishop Hamo, now in the southeast bay of the south minor transept. In addition, there are four small portals: one in the west wall of the north arm of the minor transept, one in the west wall of the south minor arm, one at the west end of the south choir aisle, and one in the east wall of the south arm of the major transept. Other work included the sedilia in the presbytery, attributed to the episcopate of Thomas Brinton (1373–89); the 'near-Perpendicular' tracery formerly in the windows of the presbytery, and a nine-light Perpendicular window formerly in its east clerestory; the windows of the south nave aisle; the five eastern windows in the north nave aisle and, in its sixth bay, the portal and straight-headed window above.

Apart from these miscellaneous doorways, and the enlargement or renovation of windows to receive tracery in other parts of the building such as the presbytery, there are seven significant later Gothic remodellings or additions, six of which are yet extant. This work comprised the erection of the belfry stage of the central tower, the vaulting of both of the major transept's arms, the partial rebuilding or remodelling of the north choir aisle, the construction of the wooden ceiling in the south choir aisle, the replacement of the clerestory of the nave, the insertion of the huge west window, and the addition of a large structure (the so-called Lady chapel) west of the south arm of the major transept.

The Minor Work

Thirteenth-Century Work: Portals

A small doorway inserted in the south bay of the west wall of the north arm of the minor transept may be the earliest alteration to the newly built fabric. It was constructed in the rear wall of a recess and now only its north half is preserved (fig. 93). Of the jamb, a hollow chamfer preceded two quarter-round shafts with bell capitals. A label, the stop gone, paralleled two filleted rolls separated by three thin rolls. This portal may have served as an exit from this arm of the minor transept for pilgrims who had completed their homage at Saint William's shrine or it may have provided access to a service space formed between the transept arm and the north tower, perhaps to be identified as the sacrist's 'checker.'[11]

The next likely alteration was probably the erection of nearly identical screens in the form of portals that were placed midway in the north choir aisle (fig. 72) and (formerly) at the west end of the south choir aisle (fig. 73). That in the north aisle probably had as its primary purpose the control of pilgrims visiting the tomb of Saint William of Perth: the site of the tomb in the north arm of the minor transept was accessible only via the north choir aisle, which, in turn, was probably usually reached from the large north portal in the north arm of the major transept (figs. 54, 80). The primary purpose of that at the west end of the south choir aisle may have been the preservation of monastic privacy in the south aisle – especially after the establishment of a major altar to the Virgin in the major transept's south arm. The screen at the entrance to the aisle would also have blocked or controlled access to the crypt by the public.[12]

The profiles of both portals consist of a hollow chamfer at the jamb followed by a keeled moulding, a hollow, and a thin shaft supporting a roll with a thin fillet (figs. 94, 12a). The bases are composed of two tori with a scotia between (*not* water-holding) (fig. 11p). There are moulded bell capitals with a pronounced necking-ring and a flaring rim-ring and abaci with a profile formed by a torus over one or two fillets (fig. 11w). Distinctive features are the use of demi-pyramidal base stops to the jamb moulding, and heavy labels that terminate in head stops or curl up at the end (north aisle screen, north stop – curl, south stop – curl; south aisle screen, north stop – male head with tonsure? balding? [restored?], south stop – female head with wimple [restored?]).[13]

The profiles of the two screen portals are identical to those of a small (blocked) doorway in the west wall of the widened south aisle (figs. 74, 95). Portal and screens also share the same features of labels with head stops (portal, south stop – male head [defaced] wearing bishop's mitre, north stop – male head [defaced], with wavy hair framing face), shafts with bell capitals and non-water-holding bases, paralleled by continuous thin rolls with keels or thin fillets, and demi-pyramidal base stops instead of moulded bases for the jambs (fig. 12b). Because its sill is sixteen inches (40.64 cm) above the pavement, it has been suggested that the portal possibly once opened onto the platform of an altar in the transept's south arm. This is not unlikely, but the mouldings appear to be earlier in date than the earliest evidence for an altar (ca. 1305 or 1322).[14]

The portal exiting to the former north walk of the cloister from the south choir aisle probably replaced a taller, earlier portal that may have been retained from the twelfth century when the south aisle was widened by extending it to the north wall of the north cloister walk. Its details are similar to those of the aisle screens but are more elaborate (fig. 96). The sequence of mouldings consists of a hollow chamfer jamb and keeled moulding followed immediately by a large shaft and then two additional quarter-round mouldings separated by a re-entrant angle (fig. 12c). The pyramidal base stop is used again and the moulded capitals are close in profile to those of the screens. The bases of the shafts are, however, quite different, as the torus has been replaced by a narrow scotia. The prominent label, composed of a hollow and a keeled, filleted roll, includes a decorative motif absent from the other portals, a four-petal flower in the hollow. The label stop at the east – there was none at the west – is large and badly eroded: it seems the hollow moulding with its four-petal flowers curled up to form the stop. These details suggest a date in the late thirteenth century.[15]

The portal at the end of the north nave aisle (fig. 93), inserted in the west front, has been dated by W.H.St.J. Hope (1854–1919) to 1327, yet the source for that date which he quoted as evidence suggests that this northwest portal was already in existence, and that the new door, and a window, referred to in the medieval text were to be made in the north wall of the *aisle*: 'that the said religious shall make for the said parishioners an Oratory in the corner of the nave of the said church, *beside the north door*, with a *door and a window on the outer side of* the said church' [Hope's translation; emphasis added].[16] However, as the (blocked) portal with a straight-headed window over it now in the second bay from the west is clearly fifteenth century in date, it must have replaced the ensemble that was first inserted there in 1327. The profile of the northwest portal features two rolls with broad fillets flanked by hollows and a label that is also a filleted roll without stops (fig. 12d). The mouldings are continuous, for there are no capitals, and, equally distinctive, is the absence of any base mouldings.[17] The date of the portal more likely is late thirteenth century than early fourteenth. The northwest portal is linked to the north portal in the major transept by a common profile that features a filleted roll flanked by deep hollows.

Two other doorways within the cathedral share the features of the absence of capitals and bases, although with simpler profiles and of a smaller scale. One of them is a small portal inserted in the north bay of the west wall of the south arm of the minor transept.[18] Its arch and jamb are continuous and it also lacks bases. The simple profile consists of a quarter-round followed by a hollow and a roll (fig. 12e). These characteristics link it with the second, a small doorway inserted in the east bay of the south arm of the major transept that also has continuous mouldings, focusing on a hollow with a roll towards the jamb and a quarter-round to the outer margin; a triangular base stop is used rather than horizontal mouldings (fig. 12f).[19]

Fourteenth-Century Work: Tracery and 'Bishop Hamo's' Portal

The tracery currently in the east clerestory of the south major arm (figs. 58, 84), a re-creation due to Scott, no doubt replaced an earlier simpler pattern.[20] It now consists of two pointed lights, each with a pair of large cusps, supporting a pointed quatrefoil. The central mullion, without base or capital, and the mouldings are very thin, but an effect reminiscent of plate tracery is created by the large flat solid areas between the various arches, cusps, and foils. The original may have dated to circa 1300, late Geometric Decorated in character, prior to the acceptance of the ogee curve.

The Romanesque windows of the south nave aisle were all completely replaced by larger early Gothic ones. As a result of modern restoration, their tracery has disappeared and they now appear as simple lancets. They may have been two-light windows with a pair of cusps in each light and a quatrefoil above.[21]

The portal now in the south bay of the south arm of the minor transept (figs. 98, 99), replacing an original chapel window, is a complete contrast to the others discussed, for it is a sumptuous display piece that includes figured sculpture.[22] It has been attributed to Bishop Hamo and dated to 1342. Two miniature buttresses, with pinnacles linked horizontally at the top by a crested parapet, form a rectangular frame for an ogee arch decorated with oak and vine leaves. A broad, flattish order between two very thin shafts (base profile: fig. 11s) provides a field for two standing figures, identified as Ecclesia and Synagoga, that occupy the upper half of the jambs. In the arch, there are four seated figures at desks without any additional identifying attributes; in the apex, a soul is depicted between pairs of angels. Elaborate diapering fills the spandrels as well as the area below the jamb figures.

It may be questioned whether the portal is in its original location. The room behind it, now serving as the cathedral library, was thought to be formerly a vestry, then, following the Dissolution, the chapter house (fig. 56, at right). It has been heavily rebuilt; Hope thought it – and the room beneath it – may have dated to the fourteenth or even the late thirteenth century.[23] There is, however, no evidence in the fabric for such an early date. As to the portal's original purpose, Hope associated it with an entrance used by the monks into the church following the supposed construction of a bridge from the dorter across the west end of the chapter house, which was dated to the same period (fourteenth century).

The portal seems overly elaborate and pretentious to dignify such a routine function. That it may have been altered to fit its present location is suggested by the prominent horizontal joint that cuts across each jamb, below the consoles of the figures of Ecclesia and Synogoga, and that cuts through a quatrefoil and the lion's head within. A quatrefoil and a half may have been cut out here in order to reduce the height of the portal to fit its present location. Since the design is otherwise so finely considered, it is difficult to accept that the original workers would have sliced so crudely through one of the quatrefoils. The other two horizontal joints are neatly hidden by their placement at the top of the bases and, correspondingly, at the top of the capitals. While the jamb may not have been of one piece, an intermediate joint placed above a finished quatrefoil, perhaps accompanied by some mouldings, would have been less conspicuous. Since there is some evidence of work in this period at the southwest end of the chapter house (although not at the northwest end), it is difficult not to consider whether 'Hamo's' portal might originally have been the inner doorway of the chapter house first built by Bishop Ernulf (1115–24).[24]

The most elaborate tracery to remain in the building is found in the north arm of the minor transept, in the windows on either side of the portal of Bishop Hamo, that is, in the east window of the north chapel and the south window of the former south chapel (figs. 67, 56). The tracery is fully developed Decorated, the latter of three cusped, ogee-arched lights.[25] The mullions rise to the outer arch, thus creating taller side lights with three cusped compartments between the upper and lower arches, and a large central section with seven compartments of four different shapes, all cusped and employing ogee curves.[26]

Elsewhere in the building tracery patterns were rather simpler. Tracery of three steeply pointed and cusped lights, with encircled trefoils between them, has been inserted in the enlarged eastern windows of the two chapels under the north arm of the minor transept (fig. 51). The tracery in the lower windows of the side walls of the presbytery is of four different patterns, each of three lights (fig. 50); this work was accompanied by a slight widening of the window opening accomplished by removing the original inner order. The pattern of the eastern window is similar to the crypt windows but more elaborate, as each light has a pointed oval in its head 'supported' by cinquefoil cusping. The west window introduces ogee curves, with four mouchettes dominating the head, while the two middle ones, not identical, are Perpendicular with two or three hexagons in the heads. The lower-level east windows were also all filled with tracery, forming three lights. Apparently two different patterns employing the orgee curve were deployed in an aba sequence.[27] During Scott's restoration, these windows were restored to their supposed early-thirteenth-century form.[28]

The sedilia was inserted in the third bay from the east on the south side (a piscina is located in the easternmost bay on the north). It is of the usual three stalls separated by buttresses that are not rotated. Thin shafts with moulded capitals support semicircular arches with cusping and sub-cusping. Above each arch is a concave-sided gable with foliage snails and fleuron enclosing a quatrefoil framing a shield.[29] Panelling behind the gables consists of pairs of cusped arches within a rectangular frame. The crenellated cornice bears square flowers of three different patterns in the cavetto. The miniature vaults within are quadripartite with both transverse and longitudinal ridge ribs.

Fifteenth-Century Work: Tracery

The original windows of the north nave aisle were replaced in the fifteenth century by larger two-light windows, the lights with five cusps and a quatrefoil with ogee curves to its lobes (the bottom lobe the largest).[30] The portal in the penultimate bay and the flat-headed window above it belong to the same renovation (fig. 100), as the window's tracery matches that of the others to the east. Although the tracery seems very conservative for the date, the form of the portal, the arch placed in a rectangular frame, is typical of the fifteenth century. This ensemble probably replaced one dated circa 1327.[31]

At clerestory level in the east wall of the presbytery, a huge pointed arch was inserted that was filled with nine lights of tracery, the arched heads of the central seven forming the equivalent of a horizontal transom with the five middle lights rising above to fill the apex of the arch.[32]

The Vaults of the Major Transept

Vaults were eventually erected over the major transept arms, but they are not symmetrically designed. The north arm is covered by two broadly oblong sexpartite units (fig. 80), the south arm by three narrow oblong quadripartite units (fig. 84).[33] In both arms, wall ribs, which were not generally used in the work to the east (they occur only in the chapels under the presbytery in the crypt and in the minor transept east chapels), and longitudinal ridge ribs appear. The stone springers put in place in the thirteenth century determined the profile of the ribs, which consist of a filleted roll flanked by a hollow and a thin roll. While the general plan of the vault was determined by the springers, the ridge ribs – longitudinal in the north arm, longitudinal and transverse in the south – may have been introduced by the fourteenth-century builders, although ridge ribs would not have been impossible in the 1230s and 1240s. A stone vault was never constructed over the south arm, although the stone springers for the ribs are evidence of the intention to do so in the previous century. Rather, a wooden vault was put up.[34] The date of the erection of the vaults is revealed by the conspicuous bosses placed at the intersection of the major ribs. Their lumpy-surfaced, lobed foliage, generally still bearing a resemblance to oak leaves, or even particularized as such, reveals their place in the fourteenth rather than the thirteenth century.[35]

In the north arm, a large boss marks each intersection of the transverse or diagonal ribs with the ridge rib (figs. 101a–c). Reading from the crossing out, the subjects of the bosses are (1) two rather flat trilobed leaves; (2) a bovine head with branches of oak leaves and acorns coming out of its mouth; (3) a human face surrounded by oak leaves and acorns; (4) one large oak leaf in the centre surrounded by four smaller ones; and (5) foliage.

The south vault also received carved bosses (figs. 102a–e). These bosses arc similar in style and motifs to those in the stone vault of the north arm: they are plump roundels of oak-like foliage with, in all cases but two, human or animal heads or an animal at the centre. Reading from the crossing out, the subjects are (1) foliage; (2) a human face surrounded by leaves, branches coming out of its mouth; (3) four small human faces and leaves; (4) a dragon (on east half) and foliage; (5) bare branches forming a central square within a circle of foliage; and (6) a dog's head (on west half) and foliage.[36]

The wooden vault eventually constructed over the south arm should be seen in the context of the late thirteenth and fourteenth centuries, when wooden ribbed vaults appear to have 'suddenly' come into prominence or respectability, and even achieved a certain vogue. Wooden vaults were built over the royal chapel at Windsor in 1243,[37] inspired by those recently completed over the transept of Lichfield

Cathedral. Subsequently, wooden vaults were erected over the presbytery of St Albans Abbey in the late thirteenth century,[38] and the chapter house at York Minster by 1285.[39] The 'tradition' continued in the next century, notably with the nave vaults of York between 1346 and 1360.[40] In this context, the Rochester vault might appear less the result of economy than fashion were it not for the stone vault of the north arm.

The nature of the foliage of the bosses of both vaults suggests that they were not too far apart in time and could date from the 1340s. Their erection may have been the work of Bishop Hamo as a prelude to raising the central tower one stage above the abutting roofs. The foliage and grotesques of the bosses, although rather crude, may be compared with the foliage and lion-head masks that appear on the portal attributed to him as well as with the foliage and 'Green Men' on the tomb against the north wall of the north choir aisle, also attributed to him. The carving on these last two monuments, meant to be seen close up, is of great delicacy and refinement, but it is related to the transept vault bosses typologically and in its essential spirit. For example, the foliage snailing up the ogee arch of the portal is distinctly rendered as oak leaves, which recalls the appearance of oak leaves accompanied by acorns in the north transept arm bosses. As well, the foliage of the ogee gable of the tomb canopy is similar to some of the less particularized foliage of the bosses of the north transept arm.

The Central Tower

In 1343, Bishop Hamo de Hethe is recorded as having a belfry stage and spire added to the central tower: '18th year of the reign of Edward III [1343]. The bishop [Hamo] caused the new bell tower [steeple] of the church of Rochester to be raised [carried up] higher with stones and timbers and to be covered with lead; he also placed in it [the same] four new bells whose names are Dunstan, Paulinus, Ithamar and Lanfranc.'[41] This work no longer exists. The tower and spire were reportedly in bad condition in 1670 and by 1679 in alarming condition, but only modest repairs were carried out in 1680.[42] Further attempts to strengthen the spire in 1703 and the tower in 1711 followed.[43] In 1749, the spire was finally taken down and rebuilt to a design by Charles Sloane (1690–1764).[44] The south and east faces of the tower were refaced with brick and stone in 1790,[45] no doubt not much improving its appearance, which had been described by Henry Keene (1726–76) in 1760 as 'decay'd & moultered away ... bricks have been us'd for patching and stopping up the decay'd places; in other places the moultering stones have been plaistered over ... it has a most shabby appearance, with a motley face of brick, stone & plaister [the result of repairs in 1703 and 1711?].'[46] Sloane's spire was removed by L.N. Cottingham (1787–1847) during the restoration he carried out from 1825 to 1830, and the lower storey recased and a new upper stage built without a spire.[47] Cottingham's tower has since been replaced by one loosely based on the 'original.'[48]

The tower raised by Bishop Hamo was not elaborate; indeed, it appears to have been merely functional – a bell chamber. Above the stage abutted by the choir, transept, and nave roofs, which was decorated with tall trefoil-head blind bays of the thirteenth century, he added a rather low stage with pilaster buttresses at the angles and a single rather modestly-sized opening in each side; the parapet was straight, the spire probably octagonal. There was no architectural detailing except for a striped effect created by the use of stone and brick in alternating bands. The appearance of brick would be a notable early example of its use.[49]

Alterations and Rebuilding in the North Choir Aisle

The outer wall of the north choir aisle was altered by the insertion of new windows forming a kind of clerestory, for they are placed high up in the wall (fig. 81, at right). They replaced a series of irregularly spaced lancets whose ghostly outline is once again revealed on the interior of the wall. The new windows were in the form of one double- (at the east) and three three-light units with late Decorated tracery. At the same time, the aisle received a vault (fig. 72), possibly for the first time, as there is no evidence that a vault was actually constructed in the thirteenth century.[50] The wall shafts put in position at that earlier date were, however, (re)utilized, supplemented by corbels inserted at the east and west ends of the aisle, next to the capitals of the arches to the transepts, in order to receive the diagonal and wall ribs, as well as an additional rib. It was probably also at this time that the aisle wall was strengthened by refacing the exterior and adding a massive buttress in its middle (one towards its west end was removed). This may have been the consequence of the addition of the vault.

The new vault used transverse and longitudinal ridge ribs, with bosses. The bosses are all carved, and now, lacking paint, are very difficult to read in the dim light of the aisle. Reading from east to west, the subjects seem to be (1) bear? face; (2) foliage (four fleur-de-lis?); (3) large rose; (4) encircled face with open mouth; (5) feline face; (6) Green Man (fig. 103); (7) human? face, bearded?, hooded?; (8) two interlocked figures, seen from the back, arranged so that each one reads twice to create four; and (9) feline face.

It was perhaps at this time that two portals were opened in the exterior wall of the aisle. The larger one was inserted in the western bay.[51] Its jambs, which sit on the low bench of the aisle, and pointed arch are composed of seven large blocks and given a simple chamfer with a roll stop at the base. A second narrower portal, also with a pointed arch and simply chamfered jambs, was inserted in the second bay from the east, on the east side of the screen. It very clearly was built with the facing of the wall and the new buttress, for the lower part of the east face of the buttress forms the west jamb of the portal.[52] The purpose of both these doors was similar: to provide access to the space between the aisle and the north ('Gundulf's') tower; the west one led out to the ground level, while the east one opened onto a wooden stair leading up to a first-floor level and perhaps to the top of the tower and aisle roof.[53]

The Wooden Ceiling of the South Choir Aisle[54]

The curious wooden ribbed ceiling that now covers the south aisle should provide some clue as to when the aisle assumed its final form, for the intersections of the ribs are marked by bosses, fourteen all told (figs. 73, 74, 104).[55] The most conspicuous and bizarre boss is one that is dominated by a large head with its tongue stuck out (fig. 104i). Another prominent boss displays a winged dragon (fig. 104c). Aside from these two, however, the motifs of the other bosses are rather more conventional. Four of the bosses – those at either end, against the wall – are carved with the motif of the Green Man spouting and surrounded by foilage that varies in each case (figs. 104a, e, f, l). Four other bosses are based upon a central four-petal or wild (Tudor) rose-like flower with surrounding or radiating foliage (figs. 104b, d, g, j). Of the remaining ones, one has fleur-de-lis motifs arranged axially and diagonally; in another, a small head at the centre is surrounded by a mass of foliage (fig. 104k); and one has a winged head spouting foliage (fig. 104c).[56]

The rib profiles consist of an axial, filleted roll flanked by a hollow articulated by fillets and a half roll. The vault ribs spring from prominent corbels positioned along the north and south walls, each carved with a human figure. From east to west on the south wall they are a head, apparently with a high ruffled collar, with its forearms raised to either side; a head between its raised forearms, with the hands prominent; a head with a wimple and crown; a strongly projecting male head, with a curl at the level of each earlobe, the forearms and hands supporting it like a bracket; and a monk wearing a cowl, also strongly projecting, with the arms again prominent, the right one raised to the jaw. The series repeats itself, but from west to east, on the north side. In the southwest corner, a very large corbel appears to be the head and naked shoulders of a youth with long hair, while that at the northeast corner has a crowned head with the hair arranged in large curls at the level of the ears placed back to back with the head of a bishop (which faces east). This latter corbel appears to have been carved for a different position than it now occupies.

The quality of carving is much ruder and less detailed than in the south transept vault and the foliage is more generalized in type. None of the leaves, for instance, can be identified as oak. They are also more angular, sharp, and facetted than in the transept bosses. The prevalence of faces and the repeated use of the rose may be roughly paralleled by the wooden vault of the south walk of the cloister at Christ Church, Canterbury, of circa 1395.

The Nave Clerestory and West Window

During the fifteenth century, the Romanesque clerestory of the nave was replaced (figs. 34 and 80, at left). The new design eliminated the clerestory passageway, and hence any easy convenient access to the major transept's clerestory. However, the nave was increased in height, as the new clerestory is twenty-one feet high (6.4 m), only two feet (0.61 m) less than the Romanesque nave arcade (from the present floor to the string-course under the gallery arches).[57] It is unlikely that the Romanesque clerestory was as tall, although it is doubtful that the modest new windows were a significant increase in size over the old or that the amount of light they admitted was significantly greater.[58] The new windows were not centred on the axes of the nave arcades, no doubt because, at the east end, owing to the Gothic arches, closer spacing or narrower windows would have been required. Rather, it appears the entire length of the nave, starting as close to the crossing tower as structural stability permitted, was divided into equal units so as to provide equal spacing between all the windows. The low-pitched roof must have been introduced at this time.[59]

The great eight-light west window belongs to the same general period, but it is difficult to say if all this work represented one coherent campaign or a succession of renovations, which, in the latter case, might then have begun with the west window. On the other hand, the rebuilding of the clerestory would have necessitated the rebuilding of the roof, and that in turn suggests that the great west window could well have been part of the same campaign of construction.[60] The tracery pattern has two tiers, of nearly equal height, of eight lights that only in the head of the window are grouped into two units of four by sub-arches (figs. 34, 41).[61] Four rows of small arches fill the two heads and the intervening kite-shaped field. The pattern is a rather unusual one for a great Perpendicular window (east or west). An odd number of lights, especially nine, is more generally favoured than eight, the latter an arrangement that eliminates the possibility of a pair of strong vertical mullions enframing a central unit of one or three lights. Parallels seem to be few: the great east eight-light window of Great Malvern Priory (Worcestershire), circa 1430–60, where the resulting 'Y' mullion is strongly emphasized, or the great west six-light window of the tower of Croyland Abbey (Lincolnshire), circa 1460–9, in which the central mullion and major sub-arches are not pronounced.[62] In both of these, however, there are prominent staggered horizontals in the heads. There is also a passing resemblance to the main east six-light window of Maidstone Collegiate Church (Kent) of 1395–8.[63]

These renovations may have been instigated by the removal of the parish from the nave to a separate new church (St Nicholas, 1418–23) in 1423. In the mid-fifteenth century, two bishops willed money for the repair of the nave. Bishop John Langdon, in a will dated 2 March 1433/4, left £20 'to the reparation of the nave roof of our church at Rochester,' and former Bishop Thomas Brouns (1435–6), in a will dated 28 October 1445, also left £20 'to the fabric of the nave of the cathedral church of Rochester ... provided that work is made in such a way as to be a memorial with sculptures on it showing my arms and my name.'[64] If his money was used for this purpose, his stipulation was ignored, as neither his name nor arms are recorded as having been present in the nave.

The So-called Lady Chapel[65]

The last sizable addition to the building before the Dissolution was a large structure built against the three east bays of the south wall of the nave aisle, and opening off the south transept arm, which it equalled in width (fig. 1).[66] It is usually identified as a Lady chapel, but strictly speaking, it was the nave to a chapel that had been long established in the south transept arm.[67] The south arm of the transept was in fact the Lady chapel since at least the early fourteenth century, when it appears that an altar to the Virgin was first recorded there.[68] Hope, no doubt correctly, associated the 'western annex to the south transept' with a payment recorded in 1512–13 to one John Birch, carver, in the accounts of Prior William Fressell (1509–32).[69]

The new addition was three bays long by two bays wide, with tall windows of three lights, and a transom (figs. 105, 106).[70] Three large window-like arched openings were inserted in the aisle wall, but without tracery.[71] The extension (presumably) was meant to be fan vaulted in six compartments, perhaps involving two central supports; sadly, the vaulting was never carried out.[72] The wall responds consist of five thin shafts with filleted rolls between, shafts and rolls separated by articulated hollows. The bases are rather bulbous (elephant-foot) in character, while the small capitals are very elongated bells with double rolls at the top (fig. 11u).[73] The windows are each set in a tall recess formed and framed by a continuous moulded arch that rises from a bench running all around the walls. The tracery pattern in the window heads is particularly distinctive for its use of straight bars to create three horizontal lozenge-shaped compartments at the top.[74]

Certain features suggest that the existing structure may have replaced an earlier chapel that was slightly narrower. The axis of the existing chapel is not lined up with that of the large arch in the west wall of the transept, as is very evident from the west (fig. 107): the entrance arch is more or less centred on the space of the two arcades of the east face of the transept west wall that it replaced (fig. 85), but the corbel between the north and south wall ribs for the (unexecuted) vault is considerably to the south of the apex of the arch. Furthermore, the responds of the entrance arch do not course with the thin shafts forming the vault respond at either side of the chapel.

The style of the arch is completely different in its massive heavy forms from the details of the space into which it now opens (cf. figs. 106, 107, and 108).[75] The responds have a large axial shaft flanked by shallow hollows and a double ogee. These forms contrast with the order of the arch, which, lacking a roll, has hollow angle chamfers flanked by thin rolls that undulate smoothly into a large reverse curve. The base, which is circular, has a large torus over two elements that are successively ogee and concave in profile; the straight-sided polygonal plinth is divided into two sections by a hollow chamfer (fig. 11t). Above, the capitals have a necking ring then a squat flaring bell and two polygonal elements separated by fillets. Thus, in all respects, the profiles and sections of the entrance arch differ from the wall responds or wall vaulting shafts within (fig. 108).

The profile of the base and plinth of the entrance arch is very close to that of the nave aisle wall responds of Christ Church, Canterbury, of circa 1380, while the combination of a double-ogee moulding flanking a three-quarter attached shaft is close to the section of one face of the Canterbury nave arcade piers of circa 1390.[76] The wall system of the chapel has a general resemblance to that of the Christ Church Lady chapel, which dates circa 1450. In that structure, there are five thin shafts with small capitals for the wall responds (relating to a fan vault), and the windows are set in tall arcades that rise from the floor since there is no bench. The base profiles, however, are a variant of the type found in the Christ Church nave aisle responds and arcade piers and have no resemblance to those of the Rochester Lady chapel.[77] Nor is there any relationship between the tracery forms of the windows in the two chapels. The differences in the base profiles, capitals, and tracery patterns, especially in comparison with the mid-fifteenth-century works at Canterbury, may be evidence of the later date of the Rochester chapel.[78]

Just why the chapel was not finished is not apparent. If it was well under way by 1512/13, considering its relatively modest size, it would seem that it should have been completed with its vaults well before the period of the Dissolution, between 1534 and 1540.

Coda

These various major and minor alterations, some of which have disappeared, have nevertheless, and despite the several restorations of the nineteenth century in particular, produced the building that we see today. Little of the essential fabric of the cathedral church itself was lost at the Dissolution. The major loss consequent to that event was the almost total destruction of the monastic buildings and, perhaps more gradually, the disappearance of the medieval bishop's palace. The elimination of some of the late tracery inserted in earlier windows cannot be considered a significant loss; nor can the rebuilding of Hamo's belfry and steeple be considered to have robbed the building of a strongly positive feature. Most likely, the greatest alteration to the appearance of the cathedral, and therefore the greatest loss, was the destruction of much of the liturgical furniture and fittings as a consequence first of the Dissolution and then, probably more gravely, of the Great Rebellion in the following century (1642–60).

Epilogue

To any reader who has diligently or even casually read the foregoing chapters, it will be obvious that many aspects of the constructional history of Rochester Cathedral and the dating of its various phases remain unresolved. The interpretation offered here can be – and no doubt will be – challenged at many points. Some aspects of the building history can only be solved by careful excavation, although one has to admit that excavations may produce more problems than they solve or at best prove inconclusive.

Without further exploration and careful re-excavation, the date, form, and function of the apsidal structure hitherto identified as the Saxon cathedral must remain unresolved. So, too, must the location of the earliest cathedral, whether a single structure or a complex of several, remain unknown and the subject of mere speculation until further concrete discoveries are made.

In a similar fashion, the problems surrounding the form of the original east end of Gundulf's church must remain unresolved until a careful excavation can be carried out in the crypt. This also extends to the possible rebuildings or alterations to the east end between 1100 and 1200. It would, indeed, be particularly satisfying to discover if there had been some form of flat termination to the eastern arm within this period. The form of transept in the early Romanesque church can also only be solved by further excavation.

With regard to the standing early Gothic structure, the resolution of the questions concerning the dating of its several phases is more likely to be achieved by a closer attention to the actual fabric and a more detailed comparison with other better-documented early Gothic buildings than it has been possible to give here. In this respect,

Hope's reliance on the historical sources would seem to have produced a very distorted chronology that has appreciably lessened the significance of Rochester in the development of the new 'Gothic' style in England.

Excavations under the Lady chapel are also called for in order to confirm or refute its hypothetical building history.

Other problems of interpretation remain. Why did Rochester have a crypt in the first place? Was it in imitation of Lanfranc's Canterbury? More important, what motivated the extremely large Gothic crypt? Was it, again, a response to Canterbury, although formally quite different? What was the source for the aisleless presbytery – so unusual a solution in major churches of the period? It is hoped that others will be motivated to tackle these and related questions regarding Rochester, and that the primary function of this study will have been once again to focus attention on this cathedral, so as to occasion debate about its form and significance – a debate that has failed to materialize for much of the past century.[1]

Notes

PREFACE

1 DRc/Emf 77/1–134
2 Hope wrote three histories of the cathedral: 'Notes on the Architectural
   History of Rochester Cathedral Church,' *Transactions of St. Paul's
   Ecclesiological Society* 1 (1881–5), 217–30; 'Gundulf's Tower at Roches-
   ter, and the First Norman Cathedral Church There,' *Archaeologia* 49
   (1886), 322–34; (a brief summary, 'Rochester Cathedral Church,' *The
   Builder* 61/2539 [3 October 1891], 259–61); and 'The Architectural
   History of the Cathedral and Monastery of St. Andrew at Rochester,'
   Arch. Cant. 23 (1898), 194–328, and 24 (1900), 1–85, also published
   separately under the same title (London 1900).
   G.H. Palmer, in his volume for the Bell's Cathedral Series, *The
   Cathedral Church of Rochester: A Description of Its Fabric and a Brief
   History of the Episcopal See* (2nd ed., London 1899), so closely followed
   Hope's version of the history of the building fabric as to remove it, in
   that respect at least, from consideration as a separate study.
3 E. Fernie, *An Architectural History of Norwich Cathedral* (Oxford 1993)
4 See I. Lavin, 'The Crisis of "Art History,"' *AB* 78/1 (1996), 13–15, who
   further described the 'contextual approach' as the 'devisualization/
   hypercontextualization process.'
5 'Rochester Cathedral,' *Jnl BAA* 9 (1854), 271–85

CHAPTER 1 The Pre-Conquest Church

1 See M. Brett, 'The Church at Rochester, 604–1185,' in N. Yates, ed.,
   with P.A. Welsby, *Faith and Fabric: A History of Rochester Cathedral*,

604–1994 (Kent History Project, 4: Woodbridge 1996), in general, 1–10, and in particular, the following comments: 1, 'The smallest of the dioceses ... has a long history, but until the eleventh century it is also an obscure one'; 2, 'almost every other aspect of the early history of the church is dark'; 5, 'the narrative sources for the history of Rochester after Bede are slight'; 8, 'Remarkably little can be known of the character of the life of the cathedral clergy before the Norman conquest.'

2 According to Bede: B. Colgrave and R.A.B. Mynors, eds, *Bede's Ecclesiastical History of the English People* (Oxford Medieval Texts: Oxford 1969), ii, 3 (pp. 142/3): 'Anno dominicae incarnationis DCIIII Augustinus Brittaniarum archiepiscopus ordinauit duos episcopos, Mellitum uidelicet et Iustum.' Justus later succeeded Mellitus (619–24) as archbishop of Canterbury (624–7); upon their deaths, both were buried in the porticus of St Gregory on the north side of the nave of the abbey church, Sts Peter and Paul (later St Augustine's Abbey), built by King Aethelberht outside the city walls of Canterbury.

3 In addition to Brett, 'Church at Rochester,' 2–3, see N. Brooks, 'The Creation and Early Structure of the Kingdom of Kent,' in S. Bassett, ed., *The Origins of Anglo-Saxon Kingdoms* (Leicester 1989), 55–74, esp. 67–8 and 73. Pope Gregory I, the Great (590–604), may have intended that the archbishopric would be transferred to London from Canterbury; nonetheless, before the late seventh century, it was unusual for there to be two bishoprics in one kingdom. For Surrey, relinquished by the successors of Aethelberht, ca. 694/5, see K.P. Witney, *The Kingdom of Kent* (Chichester 1982), 116, 144, 146, 150, 160, and 163–4.

4 For further on the kingdom of Kent, see Witney, *Kingdom of Kent*, particularly 109–22 and 198–230; also D. Hill, *An Atlas of Anglo-Saxon England* (Oxford 1981), 30–1 and figs. 41–3.

5 With respect to the above, see T. Tatton–Brown, 'The Towns of Kent,' in J. Haslam, ed., *Anglo–Saxon Towns in Southern England* (Chichester 1984), 12–16, and 'The Anglo-Saxon Towns of Kent,' in D. Hooke, ed., *Anglo-Saxon Settlements* (Oxford 1988), 221–4; also S.C. Hawkes et al., 'A Seventh-Century Bronze Metalworker's Die from Rochester, Kent,' *Frühmittelalterliche Studien* 13 (1979), 382–92, esp. 384 and 386, for the Saxon cemeteries.

6 R.A.L. Smith, 'The Early Community of St. Andrew at Rochester, 604–c. 1080,' *English Historical Review* 60 (1945), 289–99; Brett, 'Church at Rochester,' 8

7 W. de G. Birch, ed., *Cartularium Saxonicum: A Collection of Charters Relating to Anglo-Saxon History*, 3 vols. (London 1885–93), vol. I, *A.D. 430–839* (1885), no. 312 (pp. 434–7)

8, Birch, ed., *Cartularium Saxonicum*, vol. II, *A.D. 840–947* (1887), no. 562 (pp. 201–3)

9 Colgrave and Mynors, eds, *Bede's Ecclesiastical History*, ii, 3 (pp. 142/3): 'Iustum uero in ipsa Cantia Augustinus episcopum ordinauit in ciuitate Dorubreui ... In qua rex Aedilberct ecclesiam beati Andreae apostoli fecit.'

10 Ibid., iii, 14 (pp. 254/6–255/7): 'Paulinus ... sepultusque est in secretario beati apostoli Andreae, quod rex Aedilberct a fundamentis in eadem Hrofi ciuitate construxit.' Colgrave and Mynors, 132 n. 1 (reference from 256 n. 1), observed that 'secretarium' in Medieval Latin usually means either a room in which bishops conducted their business or a sacristy, but that Bede seemed to use the word in the sense of a sanctuary. This interpretation was also accepted by D. Rollason, *Saints and Relics in Anglo-Saxon England* (Oxford 1989), 43.

11 G.M. Livett, 'Foundations of the Saxon Cathedral Church at Rochester,' *Arch. Cant.* 18 (1889), 263; W.H.St.J. Hope, 'Notes on the Architectural History of Rochester Cathedral Church,' *Transactions of St. Paul's Ecclesiological Society* 1 (1881–5; hereafter cited as Hope [1881–5]), 217; Hope, 'Gundulf's Tower at Rochester and the First Norman Cathedral Church There,' *Arch.* 49 (1886; hereafter cited as Hope [1886]), 323; and Hope, *The Architectural History of the Cathedral Church and Monastery of St. Andrew at Rochester* (London 1900 = *Arch. Cant.* 23 [1898], 194–328, and 24 [1900], 1–85; hereafter cited as Hope [1900]), 2

12 Rochester upon Medway Studies Centre, DRb/Ar2 (formerly Rochester, Dean and Chapter Library, then West Kent Archives Office [Maidstone], DRc/R3), 'Registrum Temporalium Ecclesie et Episcopatus Roffensis,' f. 4 (= J. Thorpe, ed., *Registrum Roffense: or A Collection of antient records, charters, and instruments of divers kinds, necessary for illustrating the ecclesiastical history and antiquities of the diocese and cathedral church of Rochester* [London 1769], 1): 'In hac ecclesia Roff. sanctus Justus episcopus sedit primus, et presbiteros, ad serviendum Deo in ea ordinavit, ad quorum victum presbyterorum, rex Ethelbertus unam porcionem terre dedit, quam vocavit Prestefelde, eo quod presbiteri Deo servientes jure perpetuo eam possiderent. Addidit eciam ecclesiam dotare cum Doddyngherne et cum terra que est a Medewaye usque ad orientalem portam Civitatis Roffe in australi parte et aliis terris extra muraum civitatis versus partem aquilonem.'

13 Thorpe, ed., *Registrum Roffense*, 13–14 (from the 'Textus Roffensis'); Birch, ed., *Cartularium Saxonicum*, I, no. 3 (pp. 7–8); A. Campbell, ed., *Charters of Rochester* (British Academy Anglo-Saxon Charters, 1: London 1973), 1, no. 1; Brett, 'Church at Rochester,' 6

14 Livett, 'Foundations,' 263; Hope (1900), 21; G.H. Palmer, *The Cathedral Church of Rochester: A Description of Its Fabric and a Brief History of the Episcopal See*, 2nd ed. (Bell's Cathedral Series: London 1899), 6; A.W. Clapham, *English Romanesque Architecture*, vol. I, *Before the Conquest* (Oxford 1930), 21

15 According to Bede: Colgrave and Mynors, eds, *Bede's Ecclesiastical History*, iv, 12 (pp. 368/9).

16 C. Plummer and J. Earle, eds, *Two Saxon Chronicles*, 2 vols. (Oxford 1892–9), I, 125 and 131–3; Palmer, *Cathedral Church*, 5–6; M.E. Simkins, 'Political History,' in *VCH: Kent*, III (London 1932), 275–7

17 Livett, 'Foundations,' 261–5 and 268; pl. II, sect. nos. 5 and 6, and sketch no. 3. The basic facts were repeated by Hope (1900), 19–20; Palmer, *Cathedral Church*, 4–5; Clapham, *English Romanesque Architecture*, I, 21 (not very accurately); and H.M. Taylor and J. Taylor, *Anglo-Saxon Architecture*, 2 vols. (Cambridge 1965), II, 518–19, and H.M. Taylor, *Anglo-Saxon Architecture*, vol. III (Cambridge, 1978), 753 and 992.

   The work at the west front was carried out under the direction of the architect, J.L. Pearson (1817–97).

18 G.M. Livett, 'Medieval Rochester,' *Arch. Cant.* 21 (1895), 18–19

19 The curve of the apse shown in Livett, 'Foundations,' pl. I, is parabolic ('hairpin'); Clapham, *English Romanesque Architecture*, I, 21, called it 'elliptical'; Taylor and Taylor, *Anglo-Saxon Architecture*, II, 519, described it as 'stilted,' which is not quite the same thing.

20 On the use of Kentish rag in the Roman and Saxon periods, see B.C. Worssam and T. Tatton-Brown, 'Kentish Rag and Other Kent Building Stones,' *Arch. Cant.* 112 (1993), 104–5. For tufa, and its use in the same periods, see G.M. Livett, 'Early-Norman Churches in and near the Medway Valley,' *Arch. Cant.* 20 (1893), 137–9. See also A. Clifton-Taylor, 'Building Materials,' in J. Newman, *BE: West Kent and the Weald*, 2nd ed. (1976), repr. & corr. (Harmondsworth 1980), 29–30, for both Kentish rag and tufa.

21 Livett, 'Foundations,' 262 and 265–7; only one grave (east of the north-west façade turret) was excavated with any care, but no finds were mentioned nor any date for it given.

22 C.R. Peers, 'On Saxon Churches of the St. Pancras Type,' *Arch. Jnl* 58 (1901), 418–19; Clapham, *English Romanesque Architecture*, I, 17–33; G. Webb, *Architecture in Britain: The Middle Ages* (Harmondsworth 1956), 1–3; H.M. Taylor, '[Summer Meeting at Canterbury:] The Special Role of Kentish Churches in the Development of pre-Norman (Anglo-

Saxon) Architecture,' *Arch. Jnl* 126 (1969), 192–8. All are now rather superseded by E. Fernie, *The Architecture of the Anglo-Saxons* (London 1983), 34–9.

23 For St Pancras, see Peers, 'On Saxon Churches,' 408–13; W.H.St.J. Hope, 'Excavations at St. Austin's Abbey, Canterbury, I. The Chapel of St. Pancras,' *Arch. Cant.* 25 (1902), 222–37; Clapham, *English Romanesque Architecture* , I, 19–20; Taylor and Taylor, *Anglo-Saxon Architecture,* I, 146–8, and Taylor, *Anglo-Saxon Architecture,* III, 980. Part of the fabric may belong to a pre-Augustinian Roman church: see C. Thomas, *Christianity in Roman Britain to AD 500* (London 1981), 172–4.

At the other early churches in Canterbury, Sts Peter and Paul and the chapel of St Mary at St Augustine's Abbey, the eastern terminations do not survive. The chancel of St Martin's, which is rectangular, may be a Roman structure: Thomas, 170–2; Fernie, *Architecture of the Anglo-Saxons,* 38–9.

24 For St Mary at Lyminge, see Peers, 'On Saxon Churches,' 419–20; Clapham, *English Romanesque Architecture,* I, 21–2; Taylor and Taylor, *Anglo-Saxon Architecture,* I, 408–9, and Taylor, *Anglo-Saxon Architecture* (III), 742 and 988; and Fernie, *Architecture of the Anglo-Saxons,* 39.

25 For St Mary at Reculver, see Clapham, *English Romanesque Architecture,* I, 22–3; Taylor and Taylor, *Anglo-Saxon Architecture,* II, 503–9, and Taylor, *Anglo-Saxon Architecture* (III), 990; and Fernie, *Architecture of the Anglo-Saxons,* 35–8.

26 Clapham, *English Romanesque Architecture,* I, 21; Taylor and Taylor, *Anglo-Saxon Architecture,* II, 519, fig. 252, but cf. Taylor, *Anglo-Saxon Architecture* (III), 742, 753, and 992

27 Hope (1900), 21; the suggested dimensions of the nave (42 ft by 28 ft 6 in. [12.8016 x 8.6868 m]) are close to those of St Pancras (42 ft 7 in. by 26 ft 7 in. [12.9794 x 8.1026 m] internally).

28 A. Ashpitel, 'Rochester Cathedral,' *Jnl BAA* 9 (1854), 273, pointed out that there is no mention in Domesday of *any* church at Rochester, but this is not surprising as it was not the purpose of the Domesday survey to be a record of church property or edifices. See W. de G. Birch, *Domesday Book. A Popular Account &c.,* 2nd rev. ed. (London 1908), 255–6; H.C. Darby and E.M.J. Campbell, eds, *The Domesday Geography of South-East England* (Cambridge 1962), 483–562, esp. 494–500, 544–5 (churches), and 550–2 (Rochester); P. Sawyer, 'Domesday Studies since 1886' and '1066–1086: A Tenurial Revolution,' in P.H. Sawyer, ed., *Domesday Book: A Reassessment* (London 1985), 1–4 and 71–85,

esp. 82. For the text of the Kent Domesday see *VCH: Kent*, III, 203–52, esp. 219–20 (Domesday Monachorum, 255–69, esp. 264–8) and introduction by N. Neilson, 177–200. There were two churches *outside* the city, St Mary the Virgin, referred to in a charter of 850, and St Margaret's, first heard of in the late eleventh century: see Hope (1900), 21.

29 See Hope (1900), 21–2 and pl. II; and Taylor and Taylor, *Anglo-Saxon Architecture*, II, 519, fig. 252.

30 Irvine's observations, mainly concerning the Romanesque fabric, made in the course of his restoration activities, are recorded in his papers that are part of the Dean and Chapter archives on deposit in the Rochester upon Medway Studies Centre, DRc/Emf 77/1–134: see particularly DRc/Emf 77/26 (plan) and 77/41 (section). It should be noted that there is a discrepancy in the location of the masonry between the plan, in which the fragments are located near the first and third buttresses west of the Lady chapel, and the section, in which they are east of the central axis of bays two and three, thus encompassing one bay rather than two.

31 See RMSC, DRc/Emf 77/76. It also should be noted that the extent of both walls is shown as being considerably greater in Hope's plan, (1900), pl. II, than in Irvine's drawing, DRc/Emf 77/26, and Hope gave a decidedly different curve to the east fragment than Irvine tentatively suggested.

32 See the plan, Hope (1900), pl. II.

33 A. Ward, 'Excavations at Rochester Cathedral 1990–1995' (Canterbury Archaeological Trust [unpublished archive report (no pagination)]: 1997), sect. 2 ('Previous Archaeological Work in the Cathedral Area') [pp. 2–6], considered the possible and various chronological relationships of these elements at some length, concluding that they could well represent a Roman structure. Of the five possible interpretations of the 'meagre' evidence that he ably put forward [p. 4] as the basis for further interpretive argument, I consider only points 1 and 3 to be valid.

34 E.F. Cobb, 'Explorations on the South Side of the Nave,' *Annales Amicorum Cathedralis Roffensis being the Third Annual Report of the Friends of Rochester Cathedral* ([February] 1938), 22–4; five more burials were found opposite the third bay from the west, with their heads at the west. Ward, 'Excavations,' sect. 2 [p. 3], suggested that the 1937 excavation failed to find the walls because it did not go deep enough.

35 It was tentatively accepted by F.H. Fairweather, 'Gundulf's Cathedral and Priory Church of St. Andrew, Rochester: Some Critical Remarks on the Hitherto Accepted Plan,' *Arch. Jnl* 86 (1929), 192, plan facing p. 187, and Taylor and Taylor, *Anglo–Saxon Architecture*, II, 518.

36 Colgrave and Mynors, eds, *Bede's Ecclesiastical History*, v, 23 (pp. 556/
7): 'Sepultus uero est in porticu sancti Pauli apostoli, quam intro
ecclesiam sancti Andreae sibi ipse in locum sepulchri fecerat.'

37 Hope (1886), 324 and 334, and (1900), 19

38 Hope (1881–5), 218 and n. 2. His translation of *porticus* as apse was
based on R. Willis, *The Architectural History of Canterbury Cathedral*
(London 1845), 39 n. *m*. For Lyminge, see above, n. 24. For Canterbury,
see Clapham, *English Romanesque Architecture*, I, 87 and 94, and F.
Woodman, *The Architectural History of Canterbury Cathedral* (London
1981), 13–22. Recent excavations at Canterbury have uncovered the
foundations of the west apse of the pre-Lanfranc building; the apse
appears to have been an addition of the early eleventh century to an
earlier structure: K. Blockley, M. Sparks, and T. Tatton-Brown, *Canterbury Cathedral Nave: Archaeology, History and Architecture* (The Archaeology of Canterbury, new ser., 1: Canterbury 1997), 106–11 and fig. 40.
   The small building under the north half of the west front did not
have a western apse: F.H. Duffield and H.T. Knight, with S.W.
Wheatley, *A Sketch of the History of the Diocese of Rochester with a
Short Account of the Cathedral and Precinct* (Chatham 1926), 42,
'Recent drainage excavations have practically proved that our Saxon
church had no western apse.'

39 See, for example, H.M. Taylor, '[Summer Meeting at Canterbury.
Proceedings:] Reculver Church,' *Arch. Jnl* 126 (1969), 226, fig. 15, and
esp. Fernie, *Architecture of the Anglo-Saxons*, 41–2 for altars, and, for
burials and *porticus*, 42–6.

40 Fernie, *Architecture of the Anglo-Saxons*, 37 and 39

41 See Livett, 'Foundations,' 266 and 267, esp. n. *, and pl. I: the number of
'bodies' was not specified nor were any dates cited.

42 This was *not* suggested by Livett, 'Foundations.'

43 Livett, 'Medieval Rochester,' 19, specifically reported: 'No signs of
aisles, quasi-transepts [porticus], or porch were revealed.'

44 Fernie (*Architecture of the Anglo-Saxons*, 39), was sceptical of the
Reculver-like plan restored for Rochester (and Lyminge); he also questioned whether the remains at Rochester date to the seventh century and if they were part of the cathedral: cf. Taylor, *Anglo-Saxon
Architecture* (III), 742 and 753. C.A.R. Radford, 'Rochester Cathedral: A
New Fragment of pre-Conquest Wall,' *Annales Amicorum Cathedralis
Roffensis being the Annual Report of the Friends of Rochester Cathedral* ([May] 1969), 13–14, also dismissed the little apsidal structure at
the west and the remains on the south side of the nave as too small to
have been the cathedral.

45 Livett, 'Foundations,' 264 n. *: no information about the nature of the burials was given, but (275 n. *) he made the surprising suggestion that in the 'interval between the building of the early and later [Romanesque west] fronts [i.e., between 1095/1100 and 1125] ... the little strip of ground between the west front (northern part) and the remains of the half demolished Saxon church was used as a burial-ground.'

46 At Canterbury, at the abbey church of Sts Peter and Paul, burials (of the archbishops) were accommodated in the nave as the result of a lack of space in the north porticus (of St Gregory) from the late seventh century; (saints) Theodore (668–90) and Berhtwald (693–731) were buried just outside (on either side of?) the door to the porticus in the middle of the north nave wall: see Fernie, *Architecture of the Anglo-Saxons*, 43 and fig. 15.

47 From Livett's account, 'Foundations,' esp. 265–7, it would seem that there were no finds that independently corroborated the identification of the apsidal structure as Aethelberht's church of ca. 604; nor did there seem to be any evidence for the date of the burials relative to the apsidal remains. Livett, 266 and 267, only commented on the absence of any weapons or personal ornaments that led him to conclude that the burials were Christian rather than pagan.

48 Radford, 'Rochester Cathedral,' 13–16

49 Apparently no photographs were taken; a plan (dated 28 August 1968), but no sections or elevations, was prepared by Carden, Godfrey & MacFadyen, Architects (Chancery Lane, London).

50 Radford, 'Rochester Cathedral,' 15; the chalk foundation was otherwise described as a 'sleeper wall of chalk blocks ... running east and west under the arch of the crossing' and identified as 'a type of foundation [that] belongs to the oldest Norman work dating from the late 11th and early 12th century.' According to the plan (fig. 4), which does not elucidate Radford's description of the relationship of the 'pre-Conquest' wall to the purported 'Norman sleeper' wall, only the north face of this wall, located 3 ft 4 in. (1.016 m) from the supposed north face of the wall on the east–west foundations, was uncovered for a length of 2 ft (0.6096 m).

51 The use of the terms 'transept' or 'crossing,' by Radford and others, without some kind of qualification, in a pre-Romanesque English context is misleading: no Anglo-Saxon building had the fully developed form in which the crossing is defined by four wide and tall arches, the result of the intersection of a nave and transept of equal height and similar width. For the developments in Anglo-Saxon architecture

tending towards the formulation of a true crossing see Fernie, *Anglo-Saxon Architecture*, 112–36 (chap. 8: 'Anglo-Saxon Romanesque: The Crossing'), wherein some of the north or south projecting chambers are referred to as porticus.

52 Ward, 'Excavations,' sect. 2 [p. 6], also pointed out the possible variant readings of these fragmentary foundations and the consequent contradictions of Radford's interpretation. He also suggested that the chalk foundation could be thirteenth century, and hence the L-shaped wall 'Norman rather than of pre-Conquest date.'

53 Radford, 'Rochester Cathedral,' 14

54 Fernie, *Architecture of the Anglo-Saxons*, 121–4

55 Ibid., 124–7

56 On the type in general see Fernie, *Architecture of the Anglo-Saxons*, 112, 121–9, 134 and 163.

57 See below, chap. 3, esp. pp. 27–8 and 44–7.

58 Fernie, *Architecture of the Anglo-Saxons*, 169–70; Hadstock is one of Fernie's six later examples which are 'not definitely pre-Conquest' (see 163). Cf. Taylor and Taylor, *Anglo-Saxon Architecture*, I, 272–5 and fig. 120 (plan), dated to period C, 950–1100.

59 See Taylor and Taylor, *Anglo-Saxon Architecture*, I, 214–17 and fig. 94 (plan); Fernie, *Architecture of the Anglo-Saxons*, 115 and fig. 61, who refers to the wings as porticus.

60 See Livett, 'Foundations,' 273 and 276; he does not specifically mention the colour of the mortar used in the walling that he identified with Bishop Gundulf's building, and dated ca. 1080–7. Only two of the four types of foundations uncovered elsewhere in the building in the 1870s and 1880s, those under the west front and those under the west end of the north nave aisle, utilized mortar, in both cases in association with 'red sandy mould.'

61 Hope (1886), 332, based on Irvine, RMSC, DRc/Emf 77/3. To complicate matters, a continuation of the north–south wall may have been encountered during the excavation for a 'chair store' outside the west side of the north arm of the (Gothic) transept: see A.C. Harrison, 'Investigations and Excavations during the Year, II. Reports from Local Societies and Groups: *Rochester*,' *Arch. Cant.* 87 (1972), 241.

62 Radford's identification of this masonry as the northwest angle of a north transept belonging to a 'later, larger Saxon cathedral' was accepted by Newman, *West Kent*, 473.

63 However, see below, chap. 3, esp. pp. 30 and 41, chap. 4, pp. 72–3, and chap. 5, n. 135.

64 As a parallel to the scanty architectural remains, only a very few fragments of pre-Conquest sculpture have been found in or around the
cathedral. See Livett, 'Foundations,' 267 n. *, and pl. II, sketches 9 and
10 (the latter fragment is now missing); M. Swanton, 'A Pre-Conquest
Sculptural Fragment from Rochester Cathedral,' *Arch. Cant.* 88 (1973),
201–3; M.J. Swanton, 'A Second Anglo-Saxon Sculptured Fragment from
Rochester,' *Arch. Cant.* 95 (1980), 34–5; and M. Covert, 'An Exciting
Find,' *Friends of Rochester Cathedral: Report for 1988* (1989), 10–11.

65 BL, Cotton MS Nero A.VIII ('Vita Gundulfi episcopi Roffensis'), f.
56[53]r: H. Wharton, ed., *Anglia Sacra*, 2 vols. (London 1691), II, 280; O.
Lehmann-Brockhaus, *Lateinischen Schriftquellen zur Kunst in England,
Wales und Schottland, vom Jahre 901 bis zum Jahre 1307*, 5 vols.
(Munich 1955–60), II, 391 (no. 3715)

66 BL, Cotton MS Nero D.II, f. 111[110]v (Wharton, *Anglia Sacra*, I, 343
[sub anno MCXXVIII], 'Transtulit corpus Ithamari Episcopi'). Ithamar is
not mentioned in the 'Vita Gundulfi' but, according to the author of the
'Miracula S. Ithamari Ep.' (Cambridge, Corpus Christi College, MS 161,
ff. 63v–68), which may date to the late 1130s or 1140s, Gundulf, the
second Norman bishop (1076/7–1108), had Ithamar's relics translated to
a 'testudo' on the north side of the church, and at a later date removed
them into the presbytery, where they were placed in a 'theca
inestimabilis thesauri,' in a position accessible to the faithful: see D.
Bethell, 'The Miracles of St Ithamar,' *Analecta Bollandiana* 89 (1971),
425 (the initial location is mistakenly identified as the west end of the
cathedral) and 429–30 ('Miracles,' c. ii); R. Sharpe, 'The Setting of St
Augustine's Translation,' in R. Eales and R. Sharpe, *Canterbury and the
Norman Conquest: Churches, Saints and Scholars, 1066–1109* (London
and Rio Grande [Ohio] 1995), 9–10; neither author mentions the 1128
translation, indeed, both seem quite unaware of it. The claims of the
author of the 'Miracles' are probably apocryphal.

67 The cult of Saint Paulinus had developed by the end of the eighth
century; for the *Life* of Paulinus, see C. Horstman, ed. (Wynkyn de
Worde, ed.), *Nova Legenda Angliae [1516]*, 2 vols. (Oxford 1901), II,
312–16. Ithamar was the first native English bishop; his cult did not
develop until the late eleventh century: see Bethell, 'Miracles,' 421–7,
esp. 424; for the text of the 'Miracula S. Ithamari Ep.' (Cambridge,
Corpus Christi College, MS 161), see Horstman, ed., *Nova Legenda*, II,
83–6, or Bethell, 'Miracles,' 427–37 (complete Latin text). Paulinus is
the only saint cited for the Rochester diocese in pre-Conquest lists:

D.W. Rollason, 'Lists of Saints' Resting Places in Anglo-Saxon England,' *Anglo-Saxon England* 7 (1978), 65, 67, and 88.

68 See below, chap. 4, nn. 3 and 77.

69 In 1874, when a tunnel was excavated under the floor of the present choir, in order to install the wind trunk for the bellows of the organ, Irvine reported that no trace of any building earlier than Gundulf's was found: see RMSC, DRc/Emf 77/2 (letter from Irvine, probably to Scott, 8 December 1874), p. 1; DRc/Emf 77/133, 'An Account of the Church of St. Andrew at Rochester, otherwise the Cathedral of the Castle of the Kentishmen,' Notebook no. 2, pp. 9–10 (see also DRc/Emf 135 [a typed transcript prepared by Livett], p. 7); and DRc/Emf 77/85 (lengthy response from Irvine to various questions posed by Hope, November 1882), pp. 7–8.

CHAPTER 2 **The Free-Standing Tower**

1 For a more detailed consideration of the problems surrounding the free-standing tower than can be presented here see J.P. McAleer, 'The So-called Gundulf's Tower at Rochester Cathedral: A Reconsideration of Its History, Date and Function,' *Ant. Jnl* 78 (1998), 111–76.

2 W.H.St.J. Hope, 'Gundulf's Tower at Rochester and the First Norman Cathedral Church There,' *Arch.* 49 (1886; hereafter cited as Hope [1886]), 325–7 and 334; repeated in Hope, *The Architectural History of the Cathedral Church and Monastery of St. Andrew at Rochester* (London 1900 = *Arch. Cant.* 23 [1898], 194–328, and 24 [1900], 1–85; hereafter cited as Hope [1900]), 8–10; and G.H. Palmer, *The Cathedral Church of Rochester: A Description of Its Fabric and a Brief History of the Episcopal See*, 2nd ed. (Bell's Cathedral Series: London 1899), 52 and 54–5

3 The distance is approximately 8 ft (2.50 m): the south wall of the tower is not parallel to the aisle wall. W.H.St.J. Hope, 'Notes on the Architectural History of Rochester Cathedral Church,' *Transactions of St. Paul's Ecclesiological Society* 1 (1881–5; hereafter Hope [1881–5]), 219 n. 3, stated that 'its plane agreed with that of Gundulf's church,' and showed it thus in his restored plan of Gundulf's church, between 224 and 225 (and *The Builder*, 61/2539 [3 October 1891], 259), but this statement is not repeated in Hope (1886), 326, nor in Hope (1900), 8, and is evidently not the case from his later plan, (1900), pl. I; see also F.H. Fairweather, 'Gundulf's Cathedral and Priory Church of St.

Andrew, Rochester: Some Critical Remarks on the Hitherto Accepted Plan,' *Arch. Jnl* 86 (1929), plan facing 187.

4 The earliest identification of the tower with Gundulf may be that of B. Willis, *An History of the Mitred Parliamentary Abbies and Conventual Cathedral Churches*, 2 vols. (London 1718–19), I, 286. Later in the century, the anonymous authors (S. Denne and W. Shrubsole) of *The History and Antiquities of Rochester and Its Environs* (London 1772), 73, commented that the tower was 'generally allowed to have been raised by Gundulph.' A view of it, dated 1781 and captioned 'Gundulph's Tower, Rochester,' was published in F. Grose, *The Antiquities of England and Wales*, 6 vols. (London 1773–87), V (Supplement, I, 1777). See also E. Hasted, *The History and Topographical Survey of the County of Kent*, 4 vols. (Canterbury 1778–99), II (1782), 29; H. Boswell, *Complete Historical Descriptions of a New and Elegant Collection of Picturesque Views and Representations of the Antiquities of England and Wales* (London 1786), sect. no. 6; and S. Denne, 'Memorials of the Cathedral Church of Rochester,' in J. Thorpe, ed., *Custumale Roffense, from the Original Manuscript in the Archives of the Dean and Chapter of Rochester* (London 1788), 173 ('traditional notion') and 182.

5 A lease (quoted by Hope [1886], 327) granted by the Dean and Chapter in 1545 (RMSC, DRc/Elb 1A [formerly A.4.15.], 'Primum Registrum Ecclesie Cathedralis Roffensis [1541–7],' f. 84v) seems to refer to it as the 'three-bell steeple'; the anonymous authors of *History and Antiquities of Rochester*, 73, stated: 'In after times it was called the five bell tower.'

6 Its restoration, paid for by the Freemasons of Kent, is recorded in a plaque in the base of the tower: work was completed in 1925. Photographs (glass negatives) in the Guildhall Museum at Rochester record much of the interior before its restoration: nos. AF 54–70 and AG 70–75, 77, and 79–80. A quarter of a century earlier, C. Hodgson Fowler (1840–1910), surveyor to the fabric (1898–1910), in a letter of 4 June 1898 (RMSC, DRc/Emf 144) to the Dean and Chapter (concerning a new crossing tower), had recommended (p. 5) roofing 'Gundulf's' tower to preserve the walls from frost and suggested it might be put to some purpose, such as housing the bellows for the organ.

7 F.H. Duffield and H.T. Knight, with S.W. Wheatley, *A Sketch of the History of the Diocese of Rochester with a Short Account of the Cathedral & Precinct* (Chatham 1926), 44: 'Recently the tower has been repaired in the most conservative spirit, with every ancient stone

and feature preserved, while within it has been supported and strengthened with the blunt honesty of sound brickwork, an honesty not
appreciated by all.'

8 The tower is about 35 ft (10.668 m) square on the exterior, with an
internal space of 19 sq. ft (5.7912 m²): T. Tatton-Brown, '"Gundulf's"
Tower,' *Friends of Rochester Cathedral: Report for 1990/91* (1991),
9.

9 For Kentish rag, a hard sandy limestone, see A. Clifton-Taylor, 'Building Materials,' in J. Newman, *BE: West Kent and the Weald*, 2nd ed.
(1976), repr. & corr. (Harmondsworth 1980), 29–30; B.C. Worssam and
T. Tatton-Brown, 'Kentish Rag and Other Kent Building Stones,' *Arch.
Cant.* 112 (1993), 93–125; in the late eleventh century, for example, it
was used for the rubble walling of the White Tower of the Tower of
London; it was also used in the Roman and Anglo-Saxon periods (see pp.
104–6). According to B.C. Worssam, 'A Guide to the Building Stones of
Rochester Cathedral,' *Friends of Rochester Cathedral: Report for 1994/5*
(1995), 25, the stone used for the quoins is tufa, which was much used
in northern Kent in the early Norman period: in this respect he accepts
the findings of G.M. Livett, 'Early-Norman Churches in and near the
Medway Valley,' *Arch. Cant.* 20 (1893), 137–54, esp. 139–40; also
Clifton-Taylor, 30.

10 Hope (1900), 8, dated the buttresses to the thirteenth century (Hope
[1886], 326: 'early-English') and identified the stone of the plinth as
Purbeck marble, confirmed for me by T. Tatton-Brown; as a result of
weathering, the chamfer of the plinth visible at the northwest angle
today looks like freestone. Recently, part of the plinth at the southeast
angle was uncovered: see T. Tatton-Brown, 'Observations Made in the
Sacrist's Checker Area beside "Gundulf's" Tower at Rochester Cathedral – July 1989,' *Arch. Cant.* 107 (1989), 390–4. Tatton-Brown, 393,
dated the buttresses to the 'later thirteenth or early fourteenth century';
in '"Gundulf's" Tower,' 9, he dated them ca. 1343. See also Worssam,
'Guide to the Building Stones,' 25, who accepted Tatton-Brown's
fourteenth-century date for the buttress, and identified the stone used
for the quoins as sandstone from beds near either Hastings or
Tonbridge.

11 Hope (1886), 326, and (1900), 8, stated that it was 'formed by knocking
out the back of an original recess there': if 'there' means inside the
tower, there is no sign of any such 'original recess' today. But in Hope's
favour, it must be pointed out that J.T. Irvine (1825–1900), in five
sketch plans of the tower, RMSC, DRc/Emf 77/35 and 134, ca. 1876,

drew a square recess half the thickness of the wall at this location. The date of the linking tunnel is rather a mystery: it first appears in the first complete plan, Hope (1886), pl. I. Yet, although he did not show it in his sketch plans, in DRc/Emf 77/129 [no pagination], a draft of a projected history of the cathedral, Irvine wrote (at a later but unascertained date): 'With the older City wall Tower he [Gundulf] had erected he neither made any attempt to connect his new building nor did he regard the lines of its walls which thus are at skew with those of his Cathedral. Its present connecting passage with Church being a work executed long afterwards the very materials of the same being in part provided by the destruction of his work, its side walls shewing the reuse of his Tufa quoins and other mouldings [p. 6].'

12 This is the doorway that Denne, 'Memorials,' in Thorpe, ed., *Custumale Roffense*, 173, claimed that Grose, *Antiquities*, V, had found: in the caption to his plate, 'Gundulph's Tower,' Grose mentioned 'one [entrance] on the north side at the base of the tower.' Only the north entrance (with splayed jambs) appears in the plan in Thorpe, pl. XL, and in J. Caley, H. Ellis, and B. Bandinel, eds, *Monasticon Anglicanum*, I (London 1817), pl. before 153; neither entrance appears on the plan in *Winkles's Cathedral Churches of England and Wales*, I (London 1838), pl. between 106 and 107, or in A. Ashpitel, 'Rochester Cathedral,' *Jnl BAA* 9 (1854), pl. 31. Irvine, in three of his sketch plans, RMSC, DRc/Emf 77/35 and 134, showed only the north 'entrance,' and in all five none at the south (as mentioned above, n. 11), a square recess was shown instead; in three of the plans, he also seems to suggest an original entrance at the *north* rather than the south end of the west wall; see also DRc/Emf 129 [p. 3], where Irvine mentions but does not describe this 'original' entrance.

13 In a letter to Irvine of 23 September 1882 (RMSC, DRc/Emf 77/83), Hope commented: 'They have cobbled up the entrance, to G's tower from the outside. It is plain work and unpretentious but fortunately undeniably 19th Cent: – It was a necessity [unfortunately, he did not say why].'

14 A number of Anglo-Saxon graves were discovered under the southwest corner of the tower in 1960 when a heating system was being installed: D. Wilson and D.G. Hurst, 'Medieval Britain in 1960,' *Medieval Archaeology* 5 (1961), 309.

15 It and the lower part of the east wall disappeared behind a series of lavatory compartments installed in 1989/90: see Tatton-Brown, 'Observations,' 390–3.

16 Grose, *Antiquities*, V, pl. 'Gundulph's Tower, Rochester'; dated 1783, it is noted, 'This view was drawn anno 1781.'

17 Palmer, *Cathedral Church*, 54, thought the 'machicolation-like supports' were added to allow the addition of a wooden storey forming a bell chamber.

18 The corbelled arches were removed in the early nineteenth century, probably between 1804 and 1817. They still appear in a pencil drawing of 1804 by J. Buckler (1770–1851), BL, Add. MS 36.368, 'Buckler Architectural Drawings,' XIII, ff. 81v–82r, published in 1810 as a large engraving titled 'North West View of Rochester Cathedral,' and in other engavings published in 1804 (Wm. Byrne after T. Hearne: T. Hearne and W. Byrne, *Antiquities of Great Britain Illustrated in Views of Monasteries, Castles and Churches*, 2 vols. in 1 [London 1786–1806], vol. II, no. XXVIII [view taken in 1781] or 1806 (A. Warren after [J.] Schnebbelie: D. Hughson [D. Pugh], *London: Being an Accurate History and Description of the British Metropolis and Its Neighborhood to Thirty Miles Extant from an Actual Perambulation*, 6 vols. [London 1805–9], V [1808], 193). In the second edition of *History and Antiquities of Rochester* (Rochester 1817), 66, it is noted that 'a part of this antique tower has lately been taken down, to supply materials for the repairs of the church.' The tower's demolition was first recommended by Henry Keene (1726–76) in his rcport, RMSC, DRc/Emf 34, 'A Survey of the State and Condition of the Buildings of the Cathedral Church of Rochester, 10 October 1760.' At that time, he still referred to it as the 'Five Bell Tower.'

19 Certainly the inserted doorway of the mid-thirteenth century (as it is stylistically related to the northeast buttresses of the tower – which some date to the fourteenth century), which opened into this space from the west end of the aisle, and a smaller one towards the east end of the aisle, inserted in the mid-fourteenth century, indicate that during those centuries the space was not filled with the rubble debris. See J.P McAleer, 'Rochester Cathedral: The North Choir Aisle and the Space between It and "Gundulf's" Tower,' *Arch. Cant.* 112 (1993), 127–65, esp. 147, 155, and 160–4 (where I dated both portals to the fourteenth century).

20 RMSC, DRc/Emf 144/1, p. 2: 'Ranges of holes in the East and West walls show that the First stage was 23 feet [7.01 m] above the present Ground floor. The timbers were 10" to 11" [25.4–27.94 cm] in depth from 8" to 9" [20.32–22.86 cm] in width and about 2'-4" [0.7112 m] apart. They were laid upon a 9" x 5" [22.86 x 12.7 cm] plate and had bearings extending as much as 4'-6" [1.3716 m] into the wall.'

21 [Denne and Shrubsole,] *History and Antiquities of Rochester*, 73–4, noted the 'appearances' of two floors, one 20 feet (6.0926 m) above ground, the second 25 feet (7.62 m) above the first; they thought that the walls rose about another 20 feet. Hope (1886), 325–6, initially thought that the tower was originally twice its present height of 40 feet (12.192 m); later, in (1900), 8, he reduced it to 'at least half as high again as now.'

22 The passageway is 67.5 cm (26¹/₂ in) wide and approximately 197 cm (77¹/₂ in.) high.

23 The general consensus of eighteenth-century writers was that it was built as a place of security, primarily for records and the church treasury: Willis, *History of ... Cathedral Churches*, I, 286; Grose, *Antiquities*, V, text to Rochester pl.; Hasted, *History and Topographical Survey*, II, 29; E. King, 'Sequel to the Observations on Ancient Castles,' *Arch.* 6 (1782), 296*. Only Denne, 'Memorials,' in Thorpe, ed., *Custumale Roffense*, 173–4, disagreed. C. Spence, *A Walk through Rochester Cathedral* (London 1840), 19, noting that the tower was 'generally attributed to Gundulph, but present[ed] nothing in any of its architectural details to warrant such a supposition,' thought 'the more probable hypothesis was that it was originally a bell-tower,' offering later examples such as those at Chichester and Salisbury cathedrals as justification. Hope (1881–5), 219, and Palmer, *Cathedral Church*, 54, thought it likely its original purpose was defensive, as have many twentieth-century authorities: e.g., Fairweather, 'Gundulf's Church,' 194 ('a small keep'); Newman, *West Kent*, 55–6 ('defensible tower'); and C. Platt, *The Architecture of Medieval Britain: A Social History* (New Haven and London 1990), 9 ('square defense work').

24 Hope (1886), 326–7, and (1900), 8–10; he believed it functioned as a bell tower or a 'campanile' from an early date (mid-twelfth century), identifying it as the 'major turris' mentioned in several texts, *because* he thought 'there was no central or other tower until the middle of the fourteenth century.'

25 Tatton-Brown, '"Gundulf's" Tower,' 7–8, and 9 and 10 for date; see also Tatton-Brown, 'Observations,' 394. He has restated Hope's thesis that it was a campanile while forgetting Hope's reasons for identifying it as such in the mid-twelfth century. If *built* as a campanile, ca. 1150, as Tatton-Brown claims, is it not odd that the upper level should have had, *at most*, only *two* small windows (north and east? walls)?

26 See RMSC, DRc/Emf 77/84, letter from Hope to Irvine, 6 November 1882. Of the buildings mentioned by Hope, only in the case of the

abbey at West Malling is there a documented association with Gundulf, who was its founder ca. 1090: BL, Cotton MS Nero A.VIII ('Vita Gundulfi episcopi Roffensis'), f. 72[69]r and 74[71]v (H. Wharton, ed., *Anglia Sacra*, 2 vols. [1691], II, 287 and 288; *The Life of the Venerable Man, Gundulf, Bishop of Rochester*, trans. the nuns of Malling Abbey [Malling Abbey 1968], 54 and 57; R. Thomson, ed., *The Life of Gundulf Bishop of Rochester* [Toronto 1977], 58 [cap. 34] and 60 [cap. 36]).

27 It is still a valid question despite its dismissal by Tatton-Brown, '"Gundulf's" Tower,' 7, who also seems to have forgotten that the north choir aisle of the Romanesque church underlies the Gothic one, as well as the likelihood that the earlier structure had a transept! See below, n. 29.

28 Fairweather, 'Gundulf's Cathedral,' 212, noted certain reused fragments set in the south face, in particular a fragment of 'honeysuckle' ornament that he dated ca. 1130. It is the only reused piece I can locate; it comes from the west front. Despite Fairweather's claim that it was set with the oldest type of mortar, its position is superficial, and it cannot be taken as evidence (as does also Tatton-Brown, 'Observations,' 394) for a late construction date, especially as the tower was repointed ca. 1898: see RMSC, DRc/Emf 148 (specifications of Fowler).

29 Although the existing fabric of the north choir aisle wall and the east wall of the north arm of the major transept is Gothic, there is evidence – unequivocable for the former – that they are on the line of the corresponding parts of the early Romanesque building. See below, chap. 3, pp. 40–1, and nn. 67–8, 81, and 86–7.

30 The north arm of the Gothic transept has only a very slightly projecting shallow rectangular chapel; there is no evidence that either arm of the Romanesque transept had any projecting chapels, which would be normal for the period. The absence of a projecting apsidal chapel could be explained by the presence of the tower. Of course, one could then wonder why the transept was not planned further west in order to allow for an east chapel.

31 See J. Taylor and H.M. Taylor, 'Herringbone Masonry as a Criterion of Date,' *Jnl BAA*, 3rd ser., 27 (1964), 6–13.

32 See RMSC, DRc/Emf 77/41–2; also J.P. McAleer, 'Some Observations on the Building Sequence of the Nave of Rochester Cathedral,' *Arch. Cant.* 102 (1985), 156 n. 25; and below, chap. 3, n. 35, p. 42, and figs. 15, 16.

33 See above, n. 26. For the abbey church, see F.H. Fairweather, 'The Abbey of St. Mary, Malling, Kent,' *Arch. Jnl* 88 (1931), 175–92, esp. 185–8; and F.C. Elliston-Erwood, 'The Plan of the Abbey Church of the

Benedictine Nunnery of Saint Mary, West Malling, Kent,' *Ant. Jnl* 34 (1954), 55–63, esp. 61–3.

34 Newman, *West Kent*, 254

35 G.M. Livett, 'The Medieval Church of St. Mary the Virgin, West Malling,' in A.W. Lawson and G.W. Stockley, *A History of the Parish Church of St. Mary the Virgin, West Malling, Kent* (West Malling 1904), 1, fig. on p. 2; Newman, *West Kent*, 600–1

36 Newman, *West Kent*, 255–6

37 E.g., Livett, 'Medieval Rochester,' 23. For St Leonard's Tower see G.T. Clark, 'St. Leonard's Tower, West Malling,' *The Builder* 39 (1880), 640–2 (641: 'The work is roughly but decidedly coursed, with a slight tendency to the herring-bone pattern'); Newman, *West Kent*, 55 ('clearly built for defense') and 605 ('Yet this is no church tower, but a free-standing keep tower'). It has also been associated stylistically with the part of the north circuit wall of Rochester castle attributed to Gundulf: Livett, 24.

38 In his recent study, Tatton-Brown ('"Gundulf's" Tower,' 9 and fig. on 10) located a newel-stair in the northeast corner, but photographs taken before the 1925 restoration reveal no evidence of a stair in that location. See Guildhall Museum, Rochester, AF 69 (fig. 23).

39 RMSC, DRc/R1 ('Textus Roffensis'), cap. 201, f. 210v: T. Hearne, ed., *Textus Roffensis* (London 1720), 212; P. Sawyer, ed., *Textus Roffensis: Rochester Cathedral Library Manuscript A.3.5.* (Early English Manuscripts in Facsimile, VI [Part I] and XI [Part II]: Copenhagen 1957 and 1962), XI. For the tower, see RCHM, *London*, vol. V, *East London* (London 1930), 86–92; R.A. Brown and H.M. Colvin, 'The Royal Castles 1066–1485,' in R.A. Brown, H.M. Colvin, and A.J. Taylor, *The Middle Ages* (H.M Colvin, gen. ed., *The History of the King's Works*), 2 vols. (London 1963), II, 706–29, esp. 706–8; D. Renn, *Norman Castles in Britain*, 2nd ed. (London 1973), 34, 326, and 330; R.A. Brown, *English Castles*, 3rd ed. (London 1976), 65–6; and D.J.C. King, *Castellarium Anglicanum: An Index and Bibliography of the Castles in England, Wales and the Islands*, 2 vols. (London 1983), I, 270.

40 For Colchester, see RCHM, *Essex*, vol. III, *North-East* (1922), 50–4, esp. 51; D.W. Clark, *Colchester Castle, A Brief Guide*, 3rd ed. (Colchester 1954), esp. 6; Renn, *Norman Castles*, 34 and 151–4; and Brown, *English Castles*, 66. For Rochester see Brown and Colvin, 'Royal Castles,' II, 806–14, esp. 806–7; Renn, 41 and 299–303; Brown, 67 and 69 ('The entrance, as usual, is at first-floor level'; but cf. D.T.D. Clark, *Colchester Castle: A History, Description and Guide* [Colchester 1966],

19, 20–1); King, *Castellarium Anglicanum*, I, 232–3; and R.A. Brown, *Rochester Castle, Kent*, 2nd ed. (London 1986), 9–11 and 32–45.

This system had already appeared in the earliest castles of northwestern France, Doué-la Fontaine (Maine-et-Loire), ca. 950, and Langeais (Indre-et-Loire), of 994 (or ca. 1017?): see F. Lesueur, 'Le château de Langeais,' *Cong. arch.* 106: *Tours* (1948), 378–85, esp. 384 and 385; Brown, *English Castles*, 24; D.F. Renn, 'The Anglo-Norman Keep, 1066–1138,' *Jnl BAA* 23 (1960), 1.

41 Some church west towers also have a defensive appearance, e.g., that added ca. 1100 to the Saxon church at Leeds: S.E. Rigold, '(Summer Meeting at Canterbury: Proceedings.) Leeds Church,' *Arch. Jnl* 126 (1969), 256: a 'massive "keep-like" W tower of which Kent has several'; Newman, *West Kent*, 369. According to Newman, 56 (and BE: *North-East and East Kent* [Harmondsworth 1969], 423–4), the very late-twelfth-century tower of St Radegund's Abbey (Kent) may 'have been designed partly for purposes of defence.'

42 Only one (late) Anglo-Saxon or Saxo-Norman tower, that at Great Hale (Lincolnshire), perhaps 1050–1100, had a newel-stair in the thickness of the wall; five others, all after 950, if not 1000, had attached stair-turrets: Brigstock (added, stairs of wood) and Brixworth (added) in Northamptonshire, Broughton (added?) and Hough-on-the-Hill in Lincolnshire, and North Elmham in Norfolk. See H.M. Taylor, *Anglo-Saxon Architecture*, vol. III (Cambridge 1978), 887–8, and respective entries in H.M. Taylor and J. Taylor, *Anglo-Saxon Architecture*, 2 vols. (Cambridge 1965), I.

43 Newman, *West Kent*, 473, 'belongs ... to the earliest Norman period' (cf. 605, ca. 1100, the date he also assigned to the tower at Malling); N. Pevsner and P. Metcalf, *The Cathedrals of England: Southern England* (Harmondsworth 1985), 235–6, added (235): '(Contemporary with the White Tower of London, where Gundulf supervised building).'

44 Tatton-Brown, 'Observations,' 394; '"Gundulf's" Tower,' 9 and 10, ca. 1150

45 There is no evidence that the Romanesque fabric ever rose much higher than it does now; however, there is no sign in Grose's engraved view of a horizontal seam that would demarcate early work from a later addition constituting the third, windowless, stage as here identified. The traces of an upper floor observed in the eighteenth century (see above, n. 21) may have been of the original roof beams or the result of the thirteenth-century additions, when an additional floor might have been inserted in place of the original roof.

46 See below, chap. 6, n. 41.

CHAPTER 3 **The Late-Eleventh-Century Romanesque Building**

1 M. Brett, 'The Church at Rochester, 604–1185,' in N. Yates, ed., with
   P.A. Welsby, *Faith and Fabric: A History of Rochester Cathedral, 604–
   1994* (Kent History Project, 4: Woodbridge 1996), 11–22

2 See the life of Gundulf, the 'Vita Gundulfi episcopi Roffensis,' BL,
   Cotton MS Nero A.VIII, ff. 39–81: H. Wharton, ed., *Anglia Sacra*, 2
   vols. (London 1691), II, 273–92; *The Life of the Venerable Man,
   Gundulf, Bishop of Rochester*, trans. the nuns of Malling Abbey
   (Malling Abbey 1968); and R. Thomson, ed., *The Life of Gundulf,
   Bishop of Rochester* (Toronto Medieval Texts: Toronto 1977). In
   addition, on Gundulf, also see R.A.L. Smith, 'The Place of Gundulf in
   the Anglo-Norman Church,' *English Historical Review* 58 (1943), 257–
   72 (*Collected Papers* [London 1947], 83–102); M. Ruud, 'Monks in the
   World: The Case of Gundulf of Rochester,' *Anglo-Norman Studies* 11:
   Proceedings of the Battle Conference 1988 (1989), 245–60; and M.
   Brett, 'Gundulf and the Cathedral Communities of Canterbury and
   Rochester,' in R. Eales and R. Sharpe, *Canterbury and the Norman
   Conquest: Churches, Saints and Scholars, 1066–1109* (London and Rio
   Grande [Ohio] 1995), 15–26.

3 RMSC, DRc/R1 ('Textus Roffensis'), cap. 88, f. 173v, 'in opere caemen-
   tarii plurimum sciens et efficax erat': T. Hearne, ed., *Textus Roffensis*
   (Oxford 1720), 146; P. Sawyer, ed., *Textus Roffensis: Rochester
   Cathedral Library Manuscript A.3.5.* (*Early English Manuscripts in
   Facsimile*, VI [Part I] and XI [Part II]: Copenhagen 1957 and 1962), XI.

4 RMSC, DRc/R1, cap. 201, f. 210v: Hearne, ed., *Textus Roffensis*, 212;
   Sawyer, ed., *Textus Roffensis*, XI. For the Tower of London see RCHM,
   London, vol. V, *East London* (London 1930), 86–92; R.A. Brown and
   H.M. Colvin, 'The Royal Castles 1066–1485,' in R.A. Brown, H.M.
   Colvin, and A.J. Taylor, eds, *The Middle Ages*, 2 vols. (H.M. Colvin,
   gen. ed., *The History of the King's Works*), 2 (London 1963), II, 706–29
   (no. 85), esp. 706–8; D. Renn, *Norman Castles in Britain* (London
   1973), 34, 326, and 330; R.A. Brown, *English Castles*, 3rd ed. (London
   1976), 65–6; D.J.C. King, *Castellarium Anglicanum: An Index and
   Bibliography of the Castles in England, Wales and the Islands*, 2 vols.
   (London 1983), I, 270

5 RMSC, DRc/R1, cap. 88, ff. 173r–4v: Hearne, ed., *Textus Roffensis*,
   145–8; Sawyer, *Textus Roffensis*, XI; Hope (1900), 7/8 n. ‡. It reportedly cost £66. In return, William Rufus gave the manor of Haddenham
   to Gundulf for the support of his monks.

6 H.M. Colvin, 'The Castles of the Conquest' ('The Norman Kings
   1066–1154,' pt. I), in Brown, Colvin, and Taylor, *The Middle Ages*, I,
   31; Colvin thought 'it would be going too far to describe him [Gundulf]
   as the architect of the White Tower.' Cf. Renn, *Norman Castles*, 34:
   'principal overseer and surveyor.'

7 See R.A. Brown, *Rochester Castle, Kent*, 1st ed. (MPBW/DoE Official
   Guidebook: London 1969), 8–9; 2nd ed. (EH: London 1986), 6–7.

8 E.A. Armitage, *The Early Norman Castles of the British Isles* (London
   1912), 195–201; and Brown, *English Castles*, 65

9 See Brett, 'Gundulf,' 17; for the problems this later created see A.
   Oakley, 'Rochester Priory,' in Yates, ed., *Faith and Fabric*, 29.

10 Bishop William of St Calais (1081–96) replaced the clerks at Durham
   in 1083. See W.M. Aird, 'An Absent Friend: The Career of Bishop
   William of St Calais,' in D. Rollason, M. Harvey, and M. Prestwich,
   eds, *Anglo-Norman Durham, 1093–1193* (Woodbridge 1994), 283–97,
   esp. 283 and 292–3, where it is suggested that it may have been due to
   the influence of Lanfranc.

11 D. Knowles, *The Monastic Constitutions of Lanfranc* (V.H. Galbraith
   and R.A.B. Mynors, gen. eds, Medieval Classics: London 1951), or
   Knowles, *Decreta Lanfranci Monachis Cantuariensibus Transmissa*
   (K. Hallinger, gen. ed., *Corpus consuetudinum monasticarum*, 3:
   Siegburg 1967)

12 D. Knowles, C.N.L. Brooke, and V. London, eds, *The Heads of Religious Houses: England and Wales, 940–1216* (Cambridge 1972), 63

13 D. Bates, 'The Character and Career of Odo, Bishop of Bayeux, 1049/
   50–1097,' *Speculum* 50 (1975), 1–20, esp. 18. Brett, 'Church at Rochester,' 8 n. 24, points out that Odo was remembered at Rochester as a
   benefactor rather than as a 'predator': J. Thorpe, ed., *Custumale
   Roffense, from the Original Manuscript in the Archives of the Dean
   and Chapter of Rochester* (London 1788), 37; RMSC, DRc/R1 ('Textus
   Roffensis'), cap. 203, f. 211v (Hearne, ed., *Textus Roffensis*, 214;
   Sawyer, ed., *Textus Roffensis*, XI).

14 H.W.C. Davis, et al., ed., *Regesta Regnum Anglo-Normannorum 1066–
   1154*, 3 vols. (Oxford 1913–68), vol. I, *1066–1100* (1913), 78–9, nos.
   301 and 302; Ruud, 'Monks in the World,' 251 and 252. According to
   A.M. Oakley, 'The Cathedral Priory of St. Andrew, Rochester,' *Arch.
   Cant.* 91 (1975), 54, '[t]he monks lost a good deal in the battle of 1088.
   Much of their house was destroyed.'

15 N.E.S.A. Hamilton, ed., *Willelmi Malmesbiriensis monachi de gestis
   pontificum Anglorum libri quinque* (RS, 52: London 1870), 136:

'derelicta ecclesia miserabili et vacua, omnium rerum indigentia intus
et extra.'

According to BL, Cotton MS Nero A.VIII ('Vita Gundulfi'), ff.
55[52]r–v (Wharton, *Anglia Sacra*, II, 280; Nuns of Malling, trans., *Life*,
25; *Thomson*, ed., *Life of Gundulf*, 40 (cap. 17); and excerpt in O.
Lehmann-Brockhaus, *Lateinischen Schriftquellen zur Kunst in
England, Wales und Schottland, vom Jahre 901 bis zum Jahre 1307*, 5
vols. [Munich 1955–60], II [1956], 390, no. 3710), the old church had
been destroyed.

16 RMSC, DRc/R1 ('Textus Roffensis'), cap. 86, f. 172r (Hearne, ed.,
Textus Roffensis, 143; Sawyer, ed., *Textus Roffensis*, XI): 'ecclesiam
Sancti Andreae, pene vetustate dirutam, novam ex integro, ut hodie
apparet, aedificavit.' See also R.W. Southern, '(Presidential Address:)
Aspects of the European Tradition of Historical Writing: 4. The Sense
of the Past,' *Transactions of the Royal Historical Society*, 5th ser., 13
(1973), (243–63) 253. According to a number of sources, Lanfranc was
generous in his support of the new construction: BL, Cotton MS Nero
A.VIII ['Vita Gundulfi'], ff. 55[52]r–v (see above, n. 15); M. Rule, ed.,
Eadmeri Historia novorum in Anglia [auct. Eadmero] (RS, 81: London
1884), 15 [bk. i]; and *Gervasii monachi Cantuariensis [actus pontificum Cantuariensis ecclesiae]* in Wm. Stubbs, ed., *The Historical
Works of Gervase of Canterbury*, 2 vols. (RS, 73: London 1879 and
1880), II, 368 (Lehmann-Brockhaus, *Lateinischen Schriftquellen*, II,
390, no. 3712). In the 'Mortilogium Ecclesiae Christi Cantuariae'
(Lambeth Palace, MS 20; ca. 1520), f. 190 (cited by Hope [1900], 7, n.†),
the construction of the new cathedral is credited entirely to Lanfranc.

17 W.H.St.J. Hope, 'Gundulf's Tower at Rochester and the First Norman
Cathedral Church There,' *Arch.* 49 (1886; hereafter cited as Hope
[1886]), 324–5; and *The Architectural History of the Cathedral Church
and Monastery of St. Andrew at Rochester* (London 1900 = *Arch.
Cant.* 23 [1898], 194–328, and 24 [1900], 1–85; hereafter cited as Hope
[1900]), 5. Cf. R. Gem, 'The Origins of the Early Romanesque Architecture of England,' PhD dissertation, Cambridge University 1973, 545:
church begun shortly after 1077; advanced far enough by 1083 to
receive the monks. It should be noted that the translation of the relics
of Bishop Paulinus (625–44), who, according to Bede, was buried in the
'secretarium' of the Saxon cathedral (see above, chap. 1, p. 10 and n.
10), did not take place until ca. 1088: BL, Cotton MS Nero A.VIII ['Vita
Gundulfi'], f. 56[53]r (Wharton, ed., *Anglia Sacra*, II, 280; Lehmann-
Brockhaus, *Lateinischen Schriftquellen*, 391, no. 3715), and BL, Cotton

MS Vespasian A.XXII, ff. 85v–86r[87vr–88r] (J. Thorpe, ed., *Registrum Roffense: or A Collection of antient records, charters, and instruments of divers kinds, necessary for illustrating the ecclesiastical history and antiquities of the diocese and cathedral church of Rochester* [London 1769], 120; Lehmann-Brockhaus, 390, no. 3713): if the presbytery was complete in 1083, one would expect that the translation would have been about the same date, even earlier if the relics had been placed in the crypt.

18 The number cited in modern accounts is sometimes given as twenty: Hope (1886), 325 (20); Hope (1900), 138; G.H. Palmer, *The Cathedral Church of Rochester: A Description of Its Fabric and a Brief History of the Episcopal See,* 2nd ed. (Bell's Cathedral Series: London 1899), 6 (20); R.C. Fowler, '(Religious Houses:) Cathedral Priory of St. Andrew, Rochester,' in *VCH: Kent,* II (London 1926), 121; Smith, 'The Place of Gundulf,' 265; and Oakley, 'Cathedral Priory,' 48. For the pre-Lanfranc secular history of Rochester see R.A.L. Smith, 'The Early Community of St. Andrew at Rochester,' *English Historical Review* 60 (1945), 289–99.

19 Hope (1886), 325, and (1900), 7 and n. ‡. For a summary of the financial history between 1066 and 1083 see Oakley, 'Cathedral Priory,' 48–50, and also Brett, 'Church at Rochester,'12–15.

20 W.H.St.J. Hope, 'Notes on the Architectural History of Rochester Cathedral Church,' *Transactions of St. Paul's Ecclesiological Society* 1 (1881–5; hereafter Hope [1881–5]), 219–20; (1896), 329–31; and (1900), 12–14

21 The bases are mentioned by S.E. Rigold, 'Romanesque Bases in and South-east of the Limestone Belt,' in M.R. Apted, R. Gilyard-Beer, and A.D. Saunders, eds, *Ancient Monuments and Their Interpretation: Essays Presented to A.J. Taylor* (London 1977), 113 (Class A [Non-Attic forms found in archaic contexts], VII [Weighted double-convex forms], and fig. 3, no. 37); described as having a 'weakly defined upper roll,' the lower roll does not quite fit this category as it is more 'oblate' than 'bulbous or campaniform' (see 106 and fig. 1). In any case, the profile of the Rochester crypt bases is unlike any other illustrated.

22 A. Ashpitel, 'Rochester Cathedral,' *Jnl BAA* 9 (1854), 275, described them as 'heavy cushion-like capitals'; Hope (1886), 330, as a 'rude square cushion'; Palmer, *Cathedral Church,* 116, as 'rough, convex, cushion capitals, with the lower corners chamfered'; Gem, 'Origins of Early Romanesque,' 546, as a 'chamfered cubic form'; and J. Newman, *BE: West Kent and the Weald,* 2nd ed. (1976), repr. & corr.

(Harmondsworth, 1980), 40, as 'capitals of the type with keeled corners that came before the invention of the block capital.'

23 Hope (1886), 330; F.H. Fairweather, 'Gundulf's Cathedral and Priory Church of St. Andrew, Rochester: Some Critical Remarks on the Hitherto Accepted Plan,' *Arch. Jnl* 86 (1929), 200–1, claimed that 'firestone' (Reigate stone) was present as well. However, according to T.W.T. Tatton-Brown, 'Building Stone in Canterbury c. 1070–1525,' in D. Parsons, *Stone: Quarring and Building in England, AD 43–1525* (Chichester 1990), 73, the 'columns, capitals and bases' are actually Marquise rather than Barnack limestone; see also B.C. Worssam, 'A Guide to the Building Stones of Rochester Cathedral,' *Friends of Rochester Cathedral: Report for 1994/5* (1995), 29. For Reigate stone, see G.M. Livett, 'Early-Norman Churches in and near the Medway Valley,' *Arch. Cant.* 20 (1893), 137–54 (use of firestone, 153–4; of tufa, 139–40); T. Tatton-Brown, 'Medieval Building Stone at the Tower of London,' *London Archaeologist* 6/13 (1991), 363; and B.C. Worssam and T. Tatton-Brown, 'Kentish Rag and Other Kent Building Stones,' *Arch. Cant.* 112 (1993), 94.

24 The north aisle of the crypt is now occupied by the bellows mechanism for the organ. Both windows were reduced in size at a later date: the absence of diagonal tooling on the remade jambs – which are best preserved in the western window – suggests this was done in the Early Gothic period. Towards the exterior, where the windows are reduced to near slits, the rectangular window frames are rebated for shutters.

25 Ashpitel, 'Rochester Cathedral,' 275

26 Hope: (1881–5), 219–20; (1886), 329; and (1900), 11

27 Hope: (1881–5), 220; (1886), 331–2 and pl. I (plan and section); and (1900), 15 (where the measurements are slightly different); based on Irvine's sketch sections, RMSC, DRc/Emf 77/3 and 77/4 (two sections), dated 2 January 1875, and his description in a letter of November 1882 to Hope, DRc/Emf 77/85, pp. 7–8. A lengthy account is given in a draft dating from 1876 of Irvine's projected history of the cathedral, 'An Account of the Church of St. Andrew at Rochester otherwise the Cathedral of the Castle of the Kentishmen,' DRc/Emf 77/133, Notebook no. 2, pp. 6–12 (or see DRc/Emf 135 [a typed transcript prepared by G.M. Livett (1859–1951)], pp. 5–8). Irvine's observations, mainly concerning the Romanesque fabric, made in the course of his restoration activities under the direction of Sir G.G. Scott (1811–78) in 1871–8, are recorded in his papers that are part of the Dean and Chapter archives on deposit in the Rochester upon Medway Studies Centre, DRc/Emf 77/1–134.

28 Irvine thought flights of steps at each side could have led from the lower to the upper level: see RMSC, DRc/Emf 77/85, a letter of November 1882, from Irvine to Hope, pp. 7–8.

29 Hope (1886), 330–1 and (1900), 14: see Irvine's description in RMSC, DRc/Emf 77/133, Notebook no. 2, pp. 6–7 (DRc/Emf 135, p. 5).

30 C.A.R. Radford, 'Rochester Cathedral: A New Fragment of Pre-Conquest Wall,' *Annales Amicorum Cathedralis Roffensis being the Annual Report of the Friends of Rochester Cathedral* ([May] 1969), 14 and 15

31 This wall was used by Radford, 'Rochester Cathedral,' 15, as the basis for reconstructing a large cruciform-plan church on the site: see the discussion in chap. 1, pp. 14–16.

32 RMSC, DRc/Emf 77/8, 77/16, 77/36 (bottom half), 77/39, and 77/46 (and 77/2, letter to G.G. Scott) document the north aisle wall; DRc/Emf 77/36 (top half), 77/41, and 77/42 the south aisle wall. Other relevant sketches, including one of the west bay of the south aisle wall, are contained in DRc/Emf 77/134, a miscellany of sketches assembled without order and unfortunately glued together or onto larger sheets. See also Irvine's later narrative account contained in DRc/Emf 77/133, Notebook no. 2, pp. 12–15, 17, and 18 (DRc/Emf 135, pp. 9–13), as well as my earlier discussion, J.P. McAleer, 'Some Observations on the Building Sequence of the Nave of Rochester Cathedral,' *Arch. Cant.* 102 (1985), 155–6 and 169–70.

33 G.M. Livett, 'Foundations of the Saxon Cathedral Church at Roches-ter,' *Arch. Cant.* 18 (1889), 271–3 and pl. II, sections no. 1, 2, and 4: he identified two campaigns, 'Gundulf' and 'Early-Norman,' although the latter encompassed three distinct phases distinguished by three different – albeit similar – types of foundations.

34 Livett, 'Foundations,' 271–2 and pl. II, sections nos. 1 and 4. See A. Clifton-Taylor, 'Building Materials,' in Newman, *West Kent*, 30 for chalk and flint, 29–30 for Kentish rag; for the latter also see Worssam and Tatton-Brown, 'Kentish Rag,' 93–125, esp. 105–6; Kentish rag was used earlier in the so-called Gundulf's Tower and, later, in the castle keep (after 1127).

35 Livett, 'Foundations,' 272, n. *: 'These [two courses of stone founda-tions, 11 in. deep] have disappeared from the south aisle wall (exte-rior).' RMSC, DRc/Emf 77/42 (fig. 15) shows one row of rough blocks, labelled 'Foundation courses of Gundulph's wall' (but under two-thirds of its length there is an unexplained eight-inch 'gap' between it and a layer of 'small chalk'), in the bay immediately west of the Lady chapel, but a corresponding row is missing in the next two western bays,

which are recorded in DRc/Emf 77/41 (fig. 13) and 77/42 (section); in the second bay west of the Lady chapel the layer of chalk seems to be present but in the third bay it disappears and Gundulf's foundations are evident only in the layer of gravel; chalk is again indicated in DRc/Emf 134 under the westernmost buttress, here over a layer identified as 'dry flints.'

36 RMSC, DRc/Emf 77/16 (elevation) and 77/36 (section), and three sketches in DRc/Emf 77/134. On one of the sketches in DRc/Emf 77/134, Irvine indicated that the footing projected 9¹/₂ in. (24.13 cm) beyond the face of the walls (or 3¹/₂ in. [8.89 cm] beyond the face of the buttresses) rather than 1 ft 2 in. (0.3538 m) – indicated on DRc/Emf 77/16 and 77/36 as '1/2.'

37 Excavation outside these bays in 1990, to underpin the storage area ('chair store') built in 1970, uncovered about sixty-three burials, of which twenty-five were medieval, six of those possibly Anglo-Saxon, but no other archaeological evidence for the Anglo-Saxon period: A. Ward and T. Anderson, 'Excavation at Rochester Cathedral,' *Arch. Cant.* 108 (1990), 91–151, esp. 91–8; also A. Ward, 'Excavations at Rochester Cathedral,' *Friends of Rochester Cathedral: Report for 1990/91* (1991), 13–15.

38 RMSC, DRc/Emf 77/8, dated 7 October 1875

39 RMSC, DRc/Emf 47/1, 'Report on the State and Condition of the North Wall of the West Nave of the Cathedral,' 9 September 1802

40 Irvine, RMSC, DRc/Emf 77/134; Livett, 'Foundations,' 272 and pl. II, sect. no. 4

41 Ibid., 272 and pl. II, sect. no. 2

42 As recorded by Irvine in his aborted history of the cathedral, RMSC, DRc/Emf 77/133, Notebook no. 2, p. 12 (DRc/Emf 135, p. 9). Similar foundations had been found in the fifth bay from the east: see above, n. 38.

43 Livett, 'Foundations,' 271 and 275

44 Ibid., 272 and 274–5, and pl. II, sect. nos. 3 and 5. Tracings from the notebook of John Thompson of Peterborough, the contractor for the work, were later made by Irvine: see RMSC, DRc/Emf 77/90–1.

45 Ashpitel, 'Rochester Cathedral,' 276 and pls. 29 and 30

46 Hope: (1881–5), 220; (1886), 331; and (1900), 15 and 16, and pl. I; he stated a length of six bays but his plan shows six buttresses to the north aisle wall, so seven is really more accurate, especially as the length of the solid wall is equal to three of the (four) arcade bays. In his earliest plans (1881–5, between 224/5) and 'Rochester Cathedral

Church,' *The Builder* 61/2539 (3 October 1891), 259, the solid walls extended for the entire length of the choir and presbytery, with small doors to the aisle in the middle of their length; the latter plan also includes small doorways in the eastern bay.

47 See above, n. 17. Palmer, *Cathedral Church*, 7, called Hope's chapel a 'small recess.'

48 Fairweather, 'Gundulf's Cathedral,' esp. 201–5

49 Ibid., esp. 207 and pl. I

50 Fairweather's arguments were accepted by A.W. Clapham (*English Romanesque Architecture*, vol. II, *After the Conquest* [Oxford 1934], 24 and 66), who, however, suggested the *entire* crypt dated to the time of Bishop Ernulf; they were reviewed and rejected by Gem, 'Origins of Early Romanesque,' 547–8.

51 Fairweather, 'Gundulf's Cathedral,' 210. One of his major arguments, a later change in axis between the rebuilt east end and the nave, could be read in reverse and dated earlier: the nave laid out on a slightly different alignment from the eleventh-century east end as Gem, 'Origins of Early Romanesque,' 547–8, has observed.

52 Ashpitel, 'Rochester Cathedral,' 276 and pl. 29; he reported traces of a 'large circular arch on its north [*sic*; he must have meant the south] face – the side adjoining the church' as evidence that the lower part of 'Gundulph's' tower had opened into the nave as a transept; he, of course, had the (later) arrangement at Exeter Cathedral (see M. Thurlby, 'The Romanesque Cathedral, *circa* 1144–1200,' in M. Swanton, ed., *Exeter Cathedral – A Celebration* [Exeter 1991], 37–41) in mind. No traces of any such large arch are now visible on either face of the south wall of the tower; Fairweather, 'Gundulf's Cathedral,' 212, also mentioned that it was 'not now traceable.'

53 Hope: (1881–5), 220; (1886), 325, 332, and 333; and (1900), 10 and 17–18, and pl. I (plan)

54 Cf. Ashpitel, 'Rochester Cathedral,' 276. Hope (1881–5), 220 n. 4, gave the 'entire credit of identifying' the south tower to Irvine.

55 Fairweather, 'Gundulf's Cathedral,' 191–9

56 Hope: (1881–5), 220–1; (1886), 328 and 333–4; and (1900), 11, 23, and 24. Before the 'Saxon' apse was found, he had placed the early church in the area occupied by the western half of the north aisle (Hope [1881–5], 221).

57 Fairweather, 'Gundulf's Cathedral,' 207–8

58 Ashpitel, 'Rochester Cathedral,' 275, claimed he probed the ground on the line where he thought an apse should be but found nothing.

According to Hope (1886), 329, he 'had a trench cut down the central line,' but he did not say where at the west he started (or ended) it. Fairweather, 'Gundulf's Cathedral,' 201, remarked that 'no exploration has ever been carried out where the proofs of a normal church would be found,' but he placed the line of 'his' apse, which swung around the western bay of the existing crypt (which he believed to be post-Gundulf), much further west than any earlier explorations.

59 Hope (1886), 329: 'I sunk a number of holes in various places ... My labours were fully repaid by the finding of the foundations of sundry walls.'

60 It is a letter of 20 October 1881, RMSC, DRc/Emf 77/81, the only contemporary document thus far known to me. In a subsequent letter of 8 November 1881, DRc/Emf 77/82, Hope sent Irvine a tracing of his find in the crypt asking for it back, but it does not seem to have been preserved.

61 Hope (1900), 18

62 See Livett, 'Foundations,' 271–2.

63 As far back as 1990, T. Tatton-Brown surmised that 'Hope's central chapel could have been part of an eastern apse with its curved north and south sides cut away by the massive foundations for the large internal piers of the later crypt,' and concluded that '[o]nly a careful modern excavation would provide the answer': 'Archaeology and Rochester Cathedral,' draft copy, p. 8 = 'Archaeology and Rochester Cathedral,' in T. Tatton-Brown and J. Munby, eds, *The Archaeology of Cathedrals* (Oxford University Committee for Archaeology, Monograph no. 42: Oxford 1996), 109.

64 T. Tatton-Brown, 'Rochester Cathedral – Eastern Crypt: Trial Excavation, 17th–18th October 1994' (draft typescript: unpublished archive report), pp. 4–6: 'No trace, however, was found of the extreme east end of the foundation of St John Hope's putative chapel of St Paulinus. The area of excavation was ... restricted.' The trench ('A+B') was immediately east and north of the southern Gothic pier at the entrance to the eastern arm of the crypt. Also see A. Ward, 'Excavations at Rochester Cathedral 1990–1995' (Canterbury Archaeological Trust [unpublished archive report (no pagination)]: 1997), sect. 5 ('The Cathedral Crypt Trenches 1994–5: The Cathedral Crypt 1994') [pp. 17–18] and figs. 10 and 11 (trenches 6 and 7 = Tatton-Brown's trenches A, B, and C).

65 Fairweather, 'Gundulf's Cathedral,' 199–205

66 Gem, 'Origins of Early Romanesque,' 548; G. Zarnecki, ed., *Canterbury, Romanesque Work* (P. Lasko, gen. ed., *Courtauld Institute*

Illustration Archives, Archive I, *Cathedral and Monastic Buildings in the British Isles*, pt. 8: London 1978), 1/8/2–1/8/4; Newman, *West Kent*, 40–1

67 Hope: (1886), 332; (1900), 17–18. Irvine's record of what he found during the underpinning of the south façade of the transept is found in RMSC, DRc/Emf 71/7 (plan and elevation dated 17 August 1874), and later descriptions contained in DRc/Emf 77/85, a letter of November 1882 from Irvine to Hope, p. 4, and DRc/Emf 77/133, Notebook no. 2, pp. 1–6 (DRc/Emf 135, pp. 1–5). Except for the 'quoins,' nothing he described is visible today. And what exactly was found under the east wall of the transept arm remained unrecorded (see below, n. 81).

68 Hope (1881–5), 222, associated the quoins with a rebuilding of the transept by an architect from Canterbury after the fire in 1179; at that time, 'its previous narrow width was not increased.' Fairweather, 'Gundulf's Cathedral,' 195–7, thought Hope's straight joint of tufa quoin stones (some of which are actually of Caen) marking the supposed west angle of the hypothetical narrow transept's south face was 'a dovetail repair joint caused probably by the tear-away of a pilaster buttress.'

69 Of course, both Irvine and Hope (also Palmer, *Cathedral Church*, 56, and Fairweather, 'Gundulf's Cathedral,' 192) assumed that the monastic cloister (of wood?) of Gundulf's time was next to the nave, not in the area east of the transept arm and south of the presbytery.

70 The east wall of the cellarer's range was only excavated in 1938: W.A. Forsyth, 'Rochester Cathedral. Restoration of the Norman Cloister,' *Annales Amicorum Cathedralis Roffensis being the Fourth Annual Report of the Friends of Rochester Cathedral* (1939), 20–2. A 'rescue' excavation took place outside the south choir door in 1983: D. Bacchus, '(Researches and Discoveries in Kent) Rochester Cathedral. South Door Porch Excavations,' *Arch. Cant.* 102 (1985), 257–61; a section of the wall foundation to the 'cellarer's building' was uncovered, extending south from the east wall of the 'vestry' (see fig. 1). For a separate study of the west range, which forms the basis for the following observations, see J.P. McAleer, 'Rochester Cathedral: The West Range of the Cloister,' *Friends of Rochester Cathedral: Report for 1992/93* (1993), 13–25. The date of the ribbed-vaulted room has not been firmly established: the multi-scallop capitals do not preclude its belonging to Bishop Ernulf's documented building of the cloister sometime between 1115 and 1124 (see below, chap. 4, nn. 3 and 77), although, as C. Flight and A.C. Harrison, 'The Southern Defenses of

Medieval Rochester,' *Arch. Cant.* 103 (1986), 17–18, pointed out, the west range is not credited to him; they drew the inference that the cellarer's range was built of wood, and was only replaced by a stone structure after Ernulf's time, some time before the end of the century. However, if not by Ernulf, it must have been built before mid-century.

71 RMSC, DRc/Esp 1/2, ff. 54–5. In a notebook ('De Conventu Roffensi') compiled by S.A. Hankey in 1843, now in the Guildhall Museum, Rochester, the east–west building (no. 11) is identified as 'Heath's Parlour,' and the north–south building (no. 12) as the 'former Residence of the four[th] Prebend.' The latter was probably replaced by the house positioned diagonally across the southwest corner of the cloister, the plan of which appears in Livett, 'Medieval Rochester,' folding map, and Hope (1900), pl. V. It was demolished in 1937; a photograph of it appears in *13 Centuries of Goodwill: Friends of Rochester Cathedral, 604–1935* (1982), 16.

72 Hope (1900), pl. VII, shows the west range ('Cellarer's lodging') as a structure much narrower (less than 30 ft [9.144 m] wide) than the south (frater: 40 ft [12.192 m]) or east (dorter: about 50 ft [15.24 m]) ranges, and, rather than continuing the line and width of the south transept arm, he located it east of the transept so as to overlap the transept only slightly at its southeast corner. This was probably based on Irvine's identification of a wall running south from the south-east angle of the transept as an old wall of the monastic buildings (RMSC, DRc/Emf 77/85, p. 4). Later, Irvine, DRc/Emf 77/133, Notebook no. 2, p. 4 (DRc/Emf 135, p. 3), identified it more specifically as the west wall of a 'Hall' that rose 'to a height greater than the triforum passage inside'; he thought another wall, parallel to the south face of the transept, was the north wall of Gundulf's purported chapter house.

73 BL, K. Top. XVII/8.1–2, 'A drawn Plan of the Precinct of Rochester Cathedral, by Daniel [Asher] Alexander, with References &c by (Dr) Thos Dampier [dean, 1782–1802], 1801' (McAleer, 'West Range,' fig. 7; Yates, ed., *Faith and Fabric*, pl. 6), where its occupant is identified as a 'Mr. Foote.' Robert Foote was the canon, 1798–1804, holding the fourth prebend: J. LeNeve, *Fasti Ecclesiae Anglicanae, 1541–1857*, vol. III, comp. J.M. Horn, *Canterbury, Rochester and Winchester Dioceses* (London 1974), 66. Alexander, an engineer, was surveyor to the London Dock Company and to the Rochester Bridge Wardens: see P. Eden, ed., *Dictionary of Land Surveyors and Local Cartographers of Great Britain and Ireland, 1550–1850*, Part I (Folkestone [Kent] 1975), 20;

A.W. Skempton, *British Civil Engineering, 1640–1840: A Bibliography of Contemporary Printed Reports, Plans and Books* (London & New York 1987), 2–3; H. Colvin, *A Biographical Dictionary of British Architects 1660–1840* (London 1978), 64–5.

74 It appears as a separate L-shaped range in an earlier map, 'A Plan of the City of Rochester from the Bridge to the Victualling Office' (F. Baker, Surveyor), in [S. Denne and W. Shrubsole,] *The History and Antiquities of Rochester and Its Environs* (London 1772), frontispiece; McAleer, 'West Range,' fig. 6.

75 BM, Add. MS 15.966, f. 'd': McAleer, 'West Range,' fig. 8; the drawing is neither signed nor dated. Written on its back in pencil: 'Rochester Cathedral before the old houses were taken down. Anno about 1798 – W.A. –.' William Alexander was born and died in Maidstone; he was the first Keeper of Prints (1808–16) at the British Museum.

76 By 1816, only this bay remained, with a trace of two arches (the window head and the larger superordinate arch): see J. Storer, *History and Antiquities of the Cathedral Churches of Great Britain*, 4 vols. (London 1814–19), IV, pl. 6 ('SE view of Rochester Cathedral'). These arches seem to be referred to by Irvine, RMSC, DRc/Emf 77/133, Notebook no. 2, p. 5 (DRc/Emf 135, p. 4): 'In the heart of the wall an impost moulding of an arch or part of a string was discovered. It unfortunately could not be left open but was carefully left intact.'

77 This bay is the site of the former vestry (Hope [1900], pl. II; Palmer, *Cathedral Church*, 52 and 72), which itself occupies the southern half of the site of Hope's supposed south tower; the vestry is now used as the storeroom for the cathedral's gift shop. Of it, Irvine, in RMSC, DRc/Emf 77/133, Notebook no. 2, p. 5 (DRc/Emf 135, p. 4) rather unclearly stated: 'This wall it will be seen was of extraordinary thickness so far as the south side went with a very incommensurate depth of foundation (as will be seen [never explained]). On the stump of this the small building in the angle then a coal and lumber store and now a vestry had been formed by cutting away the outer face of the Norman wall and on the inside by setting back on it. Of this wall of Gundulph the inside was found to have been plastered: this still remains under the new wooden floor.'

78 Irvine in RMSC, DRc/Emf 133, Notebook no. 2, p. 6 (DRc/Emf 135, p. 4) mentioned that 'during the underpinning of the wall of St. Edmund's chapel [the south choir aisle] when that point was reached where the wall unites at the door jamb with Gundulph's, his chalk

foundation constructed as usual was exposed'; see also DRc/Emf 77/ 59, an ink sketch of the excavations. These foundations could represent the wall of a cloister walk built by Gundulf.

79 Scott's (and Irvine's) treatment of this bay in such an apparently cavalier fashion can only be understood if even the bit of the Romanesque window remaining ca. 1816 (see above, n. 76) had subsequently totally disappeared. Indeed, Scott, RIBA, ScGGS[159]31, f. 1r, noted, 'E chapel against transept projection against E side of transept seems modern.'

80 Fairweather, 'Gundulf's Cathedral,' plan facing 187

81 Yet excavations ('removal of earth') inside the 'vestry' room by Irvine 'discovered only that the E wall of the transept had been rebuilt': i.e., it would seem no trace of the east wall of the (early?) Romanesque transept was actually found: RMSC, DRc/Emf 77/133, Notebook no. 2, p. 6 (DRc/Emf 135, p. 4); cf. above, n. 67.

82 Fairweather, 'Gundulf's Cathedral,' 195–6

83 Ibid., 196

84 Gem, 'Origins of Early Romanesque,' 550–1

85 It is not shown in the section of the tunnel for the organ bellows in Hope (1886), pl. I (facing 326), but see Irvine's drawings, RMSC, DRc/ Emf 77/55 and 77/63–5, and Hope (1900), 35–6 and 38–9, and figs. 11 and 12 (elevation and section), who dated it 'after one of the fires'; it is no longer visible owing to the pulpitum.

86 Fairweather, 'Gundulf's Cathedral,' 199. Hope had ignored its implications, as well as that of a sleeper wall found by Irvine (Hope [1886], pl. I), as was pointed out by Gem, 'Origins of Early Romanesque,' 549–50, who also found a normal square crossing more probable.

87 Radford, 'Rochester Cathedral,' 14, claimed that the crossing of the '12th century church' was 4 ft (1.2192 m) narrower in the north–south direction than east–west, but his reasons for making that statement are not clear (except to establish his hypothesis regarding a late-tenth-century church); Hope's plan (1900), pl. II, shows a square crossing. Nor did Radford seem to take into account the evidence of the Romanesque bay system as preserved in the three east bays of the north aisle wall (and the five west bays of the nave arcade): see Hope (1900), pl. I. In addition, according to A. Brodie, 'Rochester Cathedral: The Chronology of the East End,' MA thesis, University of London (Courtauld Institute of Art) 1984, 6–7, the Romanesque nave bays measure 15 ft (4.572 m) centre to centre; two more replacing the two

Gothic bays would fall on the line of the west crossing piers and west wall of the major transept. It is more than likely that the Gothic crossing reflects the Romanesque one: see Gem, 'Significance,' fig. 5.

88 Cf. Radford, 'Rochester Cathedral,' 14–15, with Livett, 'Foundations,' 271–2 and 273. Livett described the chalk used as 'small lumps, such as could be dug with an ordinary garden spade.'

89 What exactly was found was so poorly recorded that speculation about its significance is futile. Radford's remarks, 'Rochester Cathedral,' 14 and 15, suggest a reasonable quantity of masonry, but the plan (fig. 3) prepared by Carden Godfrey & MacFadyen, Architects (Chancery Lane, London), dated 20 August 1968, records or suggests much less.

90 Radford, 'Rochester Cathedral,' 15; see above, n. 31. A continuation of the north–south segment may have been encounted in 1970 during excavations for a chair store outside the west wall of the north arm of the transept: see A.C. Harrison, 'Investigations and Excavations during the Year,' Arch. Cant. 87 (1972), 241.

91 See Hope (1900), 15: based on the floor levels found under the existing choir and choir steps, for which see Irvine, RMSC, DRc/Emf 77/133, Notebook no 2., pp. 7 and 10 (DRc/Emf 135, pp. 5 and 7).

92 Radford, 'Rochester Cathedral,' 15; cf. Livett, 'Foundations,' 273 and 276. Unfortunately, Radford did not describe the composition of the foundation to this wall so it cannot be compared to any of the four types of foundations described by Livett, 271–2, and identified as 'Gundulfian' or 'Early Norman,' although the use of mortar (colour not described) occurred in the foundations of the first west front (flint set in alternate layers of mortar and 'red mould') and the west bay of the north aisle (four thin layers of mortar separated by layers of flints and 'mould').

93 Indeed, only the three east bays of the north aisle and the west bay of the south aisle are Romanesque: the three east bays of the south aisle disappeared as a result of the construction, ca. 1500, of the large structure now known as the Lady chapel (see below, chapter 6, pp. 161–2); the remaining four bays were, at least, refaced in the 1660s; bays four to six (and part of seven) of the north wall were also rebuilt in the 1660s; and the westmost bay was rebuilt ca. 1892–4. See below, chap. 4, nn. 10 and 11, and p. 60.

94 See Irving's drawing, RMSC, DRc/Emf 77/20; also Livett, 'Foundations,' 273 and 'Medieval Rochester,' pl. I, no. 2.

95 Irvine, RMSC, DRc/Emf 77/41–2, and 77/134; see above, nn. 32, 35.

96 See above, nn. 32, 36, 38, and 39.

97 Hope (1900), 11 and 26, 'The inner orders are plain and square-edged, but while those of Gundulf's work on the south side are faced with tufa, those on the north are of Caen stone.' This was first stated by Hope (1881–5), 220 ('with the outer order on the nave side altered'), and again (1886), 328 ('now with later Norman outer order substituted on the nave side') and 334 ('Gundulf's arcades consisted of semi-circular arches of two plain square-edged orders'), without giving any reasons. It was also stated by Livett, 'Foundations,' 275–6, where the discovery was attributed to Irvine; again no reasons were given, although it was remarked that '[t]he lower orders of the arches, and the upper orders also on the aisle side, are all of tufa, now plastered over.'

98 Initially, Irvine thought these orders were of *plaster*, as he reported in a letter (of which there are – curiously – four near identical versions) with sketch (of one bay) of 30 March 1876 to Scott: RMSC, DRc/Emf 77/16, 77/17, 77/19, and 77/134 ('To day I found what had escaped me. That all the lower orders of the Norman arches on South Side of Nave were of plaster and not of stone ... It is also remarkable that unlike their north sides the outer order towards south aisle is also of plaster ... on side to nave this order is stone' [for full text and variants see McAleer, 'Some Observations,' 167–8]). In his most 'complete' sketch of the six west bays of the south arcade, DRc/Emf 77/18, dated 31 March (partially duplicated in DRc/Emf 77/39), which even then is detailed only for the two west bays, tufa is only shown in the spandrels and some of the rear pilasters of the aisle side. It is only in DRc/Emf 77/133, Notebook no. 2, pp. 15–17 (DRc/Emf 135, p. 11), that he recorded some of the orders were of tufa: 'those on the south were seemingly plastered but on a more careful search were found to be Tufa.' For tufa, see Livett, 'Early-Norman Churches,' 139–40, and Clifton-Taylor, 'Building Materials,' 30.

99 Livett, 'Foundations,' 276

100 Ibid., 261; see also Livett, 'Medieval Rochester,' 39–40.

101 Fairweather, 'Gundulf's Cathedral,' 197 and 200–1 (he claimed Hope had 'pointed out that the tufa [in the crypt] may have been re-used'; his incomplete reference – simply to '*Archaeologia*, xlix' – seems to be to p. 334; if so, he misquoted Hope, who there wondered if the *Barnack* stone [as he supposed] of crypt shafts, bases, and capitals was reused 'from the earlier church,' i.e., the Saxon church).

102 In his sketch, RMSC, DRc/Emf 77/18 (see McAleer, 'Some Observations,' 168 and above, n. 98), Irvine specifically noted only that the

spandrel of the penultimate bay and the western pilaster were of tufa; the penultimate pilaster was all Caen and the third from the west partly Caen and partly tufa; the distribution of materials in the remaining bays was not noted.

103 As I have argued in McAleer, 'Some Observations,' 161 n. 32; also see Gem, 'Origins of Early Romanesque,' 552. Hope (1881–5), 221, thought that 'Gundulph's' arcade of 'two plain, square-edged orders ... rested on square piers with re-entering angles, having a semi-circular vaulting shaft on the nave side, and a flat pilaster one to the aisle.'

104 No evidence of a cloister came to light during the excavation of the triangular area from the southwest stair-turret to the west wall of the Lady chapel in 1937: see E.F. Cobb, 'Explorations on the South Side of the Nave,' *Annales Amicorum Cathedralis Roffensis being the Third Annual Report of the Friends of Rochester Cathedral* ([February] 1938), 23 (plan) and 24. Although, Livett, 'Foundations,' 270, Hope (1881–5), 221 and 222, (1886), 333, and (1900), 19, and Fairweather, 'Gundulf's Cathedral,' 192, all assumed Gundulf built his cloister next to the nave, none advanced any reasons why Ernulf built a new complex further to the east. Fairweather, 197 and 205, merely noted that Gundulf's cloister was 'removed' or 'destroyed' by Ernulf. For a review of the topography of the cathedral close see T. Tatton-Brown, 'Three Great Benedictine Houses in Kent: Their Buildings and Topography,' *Arch. Cant.* 100 (1984), 186–7 and fig. 6; he only remarked that 'early in the twelfth century a decision was clearly taken to move the cloister eastwards,' but did not offer any explanation for the 'shift.'

The only other cloister of the Romanesque period placed alongside a choir, rather than next to the nave, is that built by Bishop Roger (1107–39) at Old Sarum Cathedral (which was not monastic), where it is on the north. In the next century, a similar location of the cloister is found again at Lincoln Cathedral, also non-monastic; the cloister dates from circa 1290, but already a chapter house had been erected north and east of the north arm of the minor transept, perhaps starting as early as circa 1220: see N. Pevsner, *BE: Lincolnshire* (Harmondsworth 1964), 122–5. The late Gothic cloister (ca. 1400) of Chichester Cathedral, also secular, was constructed south of the transept and choir: I. Nairn and N. Pevsner, *BE: Sussex* (Harmondsworth 1965), 161–2. It should be noted that secular chapter houses were often placed on the north, e.g., at Wells, Lichfield, and York cathedrals and Beverley Minster: see G. Webb, *Architecture in Britain: The Middle Ages* (Harmondsworth 1956), 62.

105   At a later date, the bishop's palace was further up this slope: see Livett, 'Medieval Rochester,' 42–7 (but see below, this note); Palmer, *Cathedral Church*, 58–9 (like the other authorities, he also accepted the location of Gundulf's cloister as south of the nave). Gundulf apparently lived with his monks as bishop and abbot: a separate household for the bishop may not have been established until after the fire of 1137 by Bishop John II of Séez (1139–42): see Oakley, 'Cathedral Priory,' 49, 50, and 53. For remains of a twelfth-century (pre-1150) structure (39 ft 9 in. x 18 ft [12.1158 x 5.4864 m]) that might have been part of the northeast range of a palace (a staircase leading to a first-floor hall?), see A.C. Harrison and D. Williams, 'Excavations at Prior's Gate House, Rochester, 1976–77,' *Arch. Cant.* 95 (1979), 19–36. The remaining wing of the palace (just outside the line of the Roman wall) may be fifteenth century; any residence erected by Gundulf (or by Bishop de Glanville [1185–1214]) may have been inside the wall: see A.C. Harrison and C. Flight, 'The Roman and Medieval Defences of Rochester in the Light of Recent Excavations,' *Arch. Cant.* 83 (1968), 77–8, and C. Flight and A.C. Harrison, 'The Southern Defenses of Medieval Rochester,' *Arch. Cant.* 103 (1986), 18–19 (in both of these papers some of the conclusions of Livett [and Hope] are discarded).

106   The first Norman (pre-Gundulf) castle (of motte and bailey type) was thought to have been on Boley Hill: S.W. Wheatley, 'Boley Hill, Rochester,' *Arch. Cant.* 39 (1927), 159–64 and 'Boley Hill, Rochester, after the Roman Period,' *Arch. Cant.* 41 (1929), 127–41, esp. 130–1; Brown and Colvin, 'The Royal Castles, 1066–1485,' 806–7. But recent excavations have produced 'slight indications' that the motte was partly under the later keep: C. Flight and A.C. Harrison, 'Rochester Castle, 1976,' *Arch. Cant.* 94 (1978), 27–60, esp. 38; for the earthworks erected soon after 1066, see 30–2.

107   Although in the 'Vita Gundulf' (see above, n. 15) it is stated that the old church was destroyed before the new one was begun, the late translation of the relics of Paulinus in 1088 (see above, n. 17) suggests otherwise. See Hope (1886), 333, and (1900), 33. No record of the translation of Tobias (693–726), the ninth bishop, who was also reputedly buried in a porticus of the church (see above, chap. 1, pp. 13, 14, and 17 and n. 36), exists; the relics of Ithamar (644–55), the fourth bishop, were translated to some part of the new church in 1128, but it is not known where he was buried originally: see above, chap. 1, p. 17 and n. 66.

108   See above, nn. 17 and 107.

109 Hope (1881–5), 220, and (1900), 16, placed Paulinus's tomb in the (his) square niche in the middle of the east wall of the presbytery, behind the high altar. See also A. Arnold, 'The Shrine of St. Paulinus at Rochester,' *Friends of Rochester Cathedral: Report for 1988* (1989), 16–21. According to BL, Cotton MS Vespasian A.XII, fol. 87v (Thorpe, *Registrum Roffense*, 120), the relics of Paulinus were translated at Lanfranc's expense; they were placed in a silver shrine along with relics of other benefactors. For the attitude of the Normans towards Anglo-Saxon saints, especially of Lanfranc and Gundulf, see D. Rollason, *Saints and Relics in Anglo-Saxon England* (Oxford 1989), 215–39, esp. 223–4, 230, and 234–5; and R. Sharpe, 'The Setting of St Augustine's Translation, 1091,' in Eales and Sharpe, *Canterbury and the Norman Conquest*, 1–13, esp. 9–10.

110 See Gem, 'Significance,' 1; even if this is an exaggeration, it seems likely that at least the east end was ready for use by 1077/8.

111 See R. Gem, 'Bishop Wulfstan II and the Romanesque Cathedral Church of Worcester,' in G. Popper, ed., *Medieval Art and Architecture at Worcester Cathedral* (BAACT, I [for the year 1975]: [London] 1978), 16–19.

112 Thorpe, ed., *Registrum Roffense*, 6

113 Livett, 'Foundations,' 270

114 See above, nn. 33 and 40–1.

115 Livett, 'Foundations,' 273

116 See above, cf. n. 41 and 42.

117 Hope (1900), 18, n.†

118 Hope (1881–5), 221, and (1900), 19 and 22–4. Despite his conclusion that the foundations of the west end of the nave were indicative of work carried out by the parishioners ca. 1095–1100, Livett, 'Foundations,' 276 (cf. 270), appears to have been partially swayed by Hope's view and left it as an open question whether the 'Early Normans did after all quite finish their church ... Perhaps ... they were content for a time with some temporary structure on the north side to support a temporary roof.'

119 Regarding his concern for the poor and sick, see, e.g., BL, Cotton MS Nero A.VIII, 'Vita Gundulfi,' ff. 64[61]v–66[63]r and 76[73]v–77[74]v: Wharton, ed., *Anglia Sacra*, II, 284 and 289; nuns of Malling, *Life*, 42–4 and 61–2; and Thomson, ed., *Life*, 51–2 (cap. 29–30) and 62–3 (cap. 39). The reference to his tears are innumerable, but see, e.g., ff. 45[42]v–46[43]r: Wharton, 275; nuns of Malling, 7; and Thomson, 29 (cap. 7). Despite his being swayed by Hope's view (see above, n. 118),

Livett's ('Foundations,' 270 n. *) mildly stated surmise that 'it is possible that [Gundulf] may have originally meant to build the whole church at once, and that he stopped for want of funds' represents his true view – one more in keeping with Gundulf's character.

120 Despite the fact the inside of the first façade was plastered right down to its footing, Livett, 'Foundations, 276, and after him Hope (1881–5), 221, and (1900), 18 and 23–4, maintained that the first church was never completed by Gundulf because, in the first bay of the north aisle, the 'Early-Norman' walling, of which two *unplastered* courses remained, were succeeded by 'at least an inch of mould' before a Later-Norman course (of tufa) took its place. It seems unlikely that an inch of organic soil ('mould') could have accumulated on the unfinished wall before the Late-Norman builders completed it and equally unlikely – if it had – that they would have resumed construction *without* cleaning the surface off. As already mentioned, 'mould' was used systematically in the 'Early-Norman' foundations of both the west front and the west bay of the north aisle (Livett, 272). This 'hiatus,' however the 'mould' is explained, can just as well be interpreted as evidence that the later Norman builders demolished 'Gundulf's' aisle walls down to the higher level of the new floor of their nave.

121 See RMSC, DRc/Emf 77/3 (included in Hope [1886], pl. I) and his later account, DRc/Emf 77/133, Notebook no. 2, pp. 8–9 (DRC/Emf 135, p. 6). Irvine's section seems to imply that the remains were at a higher level, but in his writing he definitely associated them with Gundulf's building.

122 Hope (1881–5), 220 and plan facing 224

123 Hope (1900), 15

124 See above, n. 27, and Hope (1900), 15 (cf. Hope [1886], 332).

125 See RMSC, DRc/Emf 77/85, a letter from Irvine in response to one from Hope (DRc/Emf 77/84, 6 November 1882), November 1882, p. 7 (with sketch).

126 Since Hope's reconstruction of the plan did not include a regular crossing, the space he allocated to the monks' stalls – three 'nave' bays – is equal to a crossing and one nave bay. For the liturgical layout of Christ Church, Canterbury, see A. Klukas, 'The Architectural Implications of the *Decreta Lanfranci*,' *Anglo-Norman Studies* 6: *Proceedings of the Battle Conference 1983* (1984), 148–9 and fig. 3; and K. Blockley, M. Sparks, and T. Tatton-Brown, *Canterbury Cathedral Nave: Archaeology, History and Architecture* (Archaeology of Canterbury, new ser., 1: Canterbury 1997), 123 and figs. 46 and 53.

127 B.L. Cotton MS Nero A.VIII, f. 83[80]r: Wharton, *Anglia Sacra* II, 291;
nuns of Malling, *Life*, 71; Thomson, ed., *Life*, 68 (cap. 46, ll. 38–42).
Lanfranc was buried in a similar position at Canterbury.

128 Clapham, *English Romanesque Architecture*, II, 64–6

129 There is no direct evidence for an ambulatory at St Paul's, and the
existence of a crypt is only inferred: see R. Gem, 'The Romanesque
Architecture of Old St Paul's Cathedral and Its Late Eleventh-Century
Context,' in L. Grant, ed., *Medieval Art, Architecture and Archaeology in London* (BAACT, X [for the year 1984]: [London] 1990),
53–5.

130 The exception may have been the crypt or crypts at Evesham, known
only from textual sources and never excavated. Recently, again based
on textual evidence, it has been suggested that the Romanesque choir
of Evesham did not have an ambulatory: D.C. Cox, 'The Building,
Destruction, and Excavation of Evesham Abbey: A Documentary
History,' *Transactions of the Worcestershire Archaeological Society*,
3rd ser., 12 (1990), 126.

131 Other early but small crypts exist at Lastingham Abbey (Yorkshire),
ca. 1078–88, and Christchurch Priory (Hampshire), begun before 1099:
Clapham, *English Romanesque Architecture*, II, 67.

132 See F. Woodman, *The Architectural History of Canterbury Cathedral*
(London, Boston, and Henley 1981), 45–76, esp. 51–6. During the
twelfth century, with the exception of York Minster, crypts were
confined to minor churches, although some were sizeable, e.g., St Peter
in the East, Oxford, ca. 1140–50: see Clapham, *English Romanesque
Architecture*, II, 64–7. The large aisled crypt at York begun by Archbishop Roger Pont L'Évêque (1154–81) was straight-ended: see E.A.
Gee, 'Architectural History until 1290,' in G.E. Aylmer and R. Cant,
eds, *A History of York Minster* (Oxford 1977), 121–5.

133 For Rouen, see G. Lanfry, 'La crypte romane de l'onzième siècle de la
cathédrale de Rouen,' *Bull. mon.* 95 (1936), 181–201; and J. Verrier,
'Fouilles et découvertes,' *Les monuments historiques de la France*, II
(1956), 93–100; the crypt was associated with an ambulatory and
radiating chapel plan. For Bayeux, see J. Vallery-Radot, *La cathédrale
de Bayeux* (Petites monographies des grands édifices de la France: Paris
[1922]), 67–9; the remains consist of six bays of a central section of
three aisles; the plan of the east end is unknown. For La Trinité, see
M. Baylé, *La Trinité de Caen* (Bibliothèque de la Société française
d'archéologie, 10: Geneva 1979), 41–3 and 59. The groin vaults of the
crypts at Bayeux and La Trinité, like Rochester's, also lacked transverse arches.

134 Gem, 'Significance,' 3; H.J.A. Strik, 'Remains of the Lanfranc Building in the Great Central Tower and the Northwest Choir/Transept Area,' in Coldstream and Draper, eds, *Medieval Art and Architecture at Canterbury*, 25 and figs. 2, 3, and 5; cf. Woodman, *Architectural History*, 30–2 and fig. 13, who had accepted a plan with a longer choir of three bays plus apse. Also see Blockley, Sparks, and Tatton-Brown, *Canterbury Cathedral Nave*, 114 and fig. 48. The crypt, entered by steps descending from the middle of the crossing, was divided into three aisles, the rectangular section probably composed of twelve bays of vaulting.

135 See Clapham, *English Romanesque Architecture*, II, 20–4 and 27, figs. 4, 5, and 7; and M.F. Hearn, 'The Rectangular Ambulatory in English Medieval Architecture,' *Jnl SAH* 30/3 (1971), 188 and n. 3. Bishop Roger's choir at Old Sarum (after 1110?) has been put forward as another possibility: Hearn, 190–1. However, recently R. Gem, 'The First Romanesque Cathedral of Old Salisbury,' in E. Fernie and P. Crossley, eds, *Medieval Architecture and Its Intellectual Context: Studies in Honour of Peter Kidson* (London and Ronceverte 1990), 10 and 16, has pointed out that the evidence is too slight to support Clapham's conclusion that there were solid choir walls in the first church (the choir in any case was very short, scarcely more than equal to one [nave] bay).

136 Half the original length of the solid side walls at St Albans is thought to survive: C.R. Peers, '[City of St. Albans:] Abbey Church and Buildings,' in RCHM, *Hertfordshire*, II (London 1908), 490–1.

137 Baylé, *La Trinité de Caen*, 39, 43, and 57

138 See A. Rhein, 'L'église abbatiale de Cerisy-la-Forêt,' *Cong. arch.* 75: *Caen*, 2 vols. (1908), II, 565–6; P. Héliot, 'Les dates de construction des abbatiales de Bernay, Cerisy-la-Forêt et Lessay,' *Bulletin de la Société des Antiquaries de France* (1959), 199.

139 The Romanesque choir of Saint-Étienne at Caen very likely also had solid side walls: E.G. Carlson, 'Excavations at Sainte-Étienne [*sic*], Caen (1969),' *Gesta* 10/1 (1971), 23–30 (esp. 26) (also 'Fouilles de Saint-Étienne de Caen, 1969,' *Archéologie médiévale* 2 [1972], 89–102).

140 E.g., in his discussion of the early-twelfth-century choir of Bishop Roger at Old Sarum, Hearn ('Rectangular Ambulatory,' 191) remarked that 'it would be inconsistent with all known English structures to suppose that a large choir designed after 1110 could be closed in on the ground story by a solid wall.'

141 Fairweather, 'Gundulf's Cathedral,' 189–91; Smith, 'The Place of Gundulf,' 264–6. Despite the close relationship of Lanfranc and Gundulf, the subsequent relationship between their sees was often difficult and contentious: see Fowler, 'Cathedral Priory,' 122, and Oakley, 'Cathedral Priory,' 57.

142 See Hearn, 'Rectangular Ambulatory,' 187–208. He accepted Rochester as possibly the earliest example; but, while he regarded Hope's reconstruction as plausible, he preferred Clapham's date of 1115–25 (thus, assigning it to Bishop Ernulf), rather than Hope's, and considered it not improbable for the type (201). See also M.F. Hearn, 'Ripon Minster: The Beginning of the Gothic Style in Northern England,' *Transactions of the American Philosophical Society* 73/6 (1983), 82–4.

143 The first two are cited by Hearn, 'Rectangular Ambulatory,' 202 (along with Jervaulx Abbey and, for some reason, York Minster, where the existing east end, which replaced Bishop Roger's straight-ended ambulatory-type plan of ca. 1160–74, dates from 1361–1420); also see Bond, *Introduction*, 84, I, 150. P. Fergusson, *Architecture of Solitude: Cistercian Abbeys in Twelfth-Century England* (Princeton 1984), 84 n. 55, drew attention to the late-twelfth-century examples (including Roger's York) that were not mentioned by Hearn.

144 For these buildings see E. Fernie, *The Architecture of the Anglo-Saxons* (London 1983), 39 and fig. 20; 47–56 and figs. 22, 23, 24, and 26; 113 and fig. 60; 145–9 and fig. 85; 124–7 and fig. 70.

   The reappearance of the rectangular form has been interpreted as a re-emergence of Saxon custom: E.S. Prior, *A History of Gothic Art in England* (London 1900), 70–1 (Prior, 65 and 71, also accepted the precociousness of Rochester), and Hearn, 'Rectangular Ambulatory,' 203 and 208.

145 For the early churches, see above, chap. 1, nn. 22–5, and Fernie, *Architecture of the Anglo-Saxons*, 32–9. Of the twenty-five possible examples of later (after 950) Anglo-Saxon churches (many actually more likely 'Saxo-Norman' overlap) cited by Taylor and Taylor, *Anglo-Saxon Architecture*, II, 727 and 730, the chancel or evidence for the termination of the chancel survives at few: Aldington (Saxo-Norman overlap), Kingsdown (Saxo-Norman), Kingston (?Saxo-Norman), Paddleworth (probably post-Conquest), Shorne, Whitfield, and Wouldham probably had flat-ended chancels. It is worthy of note that the largest remaining church, St Mary-in-Castro, Dover (ca. 1000?), had a rectangular sanctuary; an apsidal termination has been proposed only for the

basilica at Lydd, possibly of Romano-British date: see Fernie, 115 and
72, respectively.

146 The type appears after the Conquest, most notably at the extraordinary
little church at Brook, attributed to Ernulf when prior of Canterbury
(1096–1107): S.E. Rigold, '[Summer Meeting at Canterbury. Proceedings:] The Demesne of Christ Church at Brook,' *Arch. Jnl* 126 (1969),
270–1. The parish church of St Margaret at Darenth, sometimes
associated with Gunfulf, is another example worthy of note, not only
because the chancel was flat-ended but also because it was groin-
vaulted with a room above it: see above, chap. 2, p. 22 and n. 34. But it
is doubtful that small parish churches would influence large-scale
monastic and cathedral buildings, although they might reflect them.

147 See F.C. Elliston-Erwood, 'The Plan of the Abbey Church of the
Benedictine Nunnery of Saint Mary, West Malling, Kent,' *Ant. Jnl* 34
(1954), 57–60 and pl. X.

148 Despite the emphatic statement made by D.M. Wilson and D.G.
Hurst, 'Medieval Britain in 1961,' *Medieval Archaeology* 6–7 (1962–3),
316, and Newman, *West Kent*, 40 and 602, the results of these excavations were not, not surprisingly, any more conclusive: see Gem,
'Origins of Early Romanesque,' 569 n. 45, wherein he cited M. Biddle
who had informed him that no trace of an apse had been found where
it should have been if it existed, but that a straight terminal wall was
not actually uncovered; the flat-ended chapel was taken to be contemporary with the earliest work. (To date, Biddle's 1961 excavations have
not been published.)

149 Recent excavations at St Gregory's Priory, a foundation of Lanfranc,
revealed a small aisleless presbytery of ca. 1085 that probably was flat-
ended since no evidence of an apse – or projecting chapel – was found
(the chancel was later lengthened, before ca. 1145): M. and A. Hicks,
'St. Gregory's Priory,' *Canterbury's Archaeology, 1989–1990: 14th
Annual Report* (Canterbury Archaeological Trust, 1991), 1–5. It would
fit into the same group of small Kentish churches with flat sanctuaries
as did West Malling.

150 Hearn, 'Rectangular Ambulatory,' 202, pointed out the similarity
('closest precedent') of the Rochester plan – for which he accepted a
date in the episcopate of Ernulf (1115–24) – to Saint-Bertin and
Gournay. Gem, 'Origins of Early Romanesque,' 555, had found the
closest parallels to be Saint-Bertin and, because of its small east
chapels, Nesle.

151 For these buildings, see P. Héliot, 'Le chevet roman de Saint-Bertin à Saint-Omer et l'architecture franco-lotharingienne,' *Revue belge d'archéologie et d'histoire de l'art* 22 (1953), 73–96, esp. 73–8; and Héliot, 'Le chevet de la collégiale de Nesle, l'architecture scaldienne et les influences allemandes en Picardie,' *Revue belge d'archéologie et d'histoire de l'art* 20 (1951), 273–94, esp. 276–84, 286, and 287.

152 For Gournay, dated by Hearn, 'Rectangular Ambulatory,' 202, ca. 1110, see L. Régnier, 'Gournay-en-Bray,' *Cong. Arch.* 76: *Beauvais* (1905), 74–9, esp. 75.

153 Gem, 'Origins of Early Romanesque,' 548

154 See J. Bilson, 'Plan of the First Cathedral at Lincoln,' *Arch.* 62 (1911), 549 and 559–60; the chapels were possibly 13 feet (3.9624 m) deep by 20 feet (6.096 m) wide.

155 See Bilson, 'Plan,' 547–8 and 558, and pl. LXXVII; also P. Kidson, 'Architectural History,' in D. Owen, ed., *A History of Lincoln Minster* (Cambridge 1994), 16–18.

156 F.H. Fairweather, 'The Abbey of St. Mary, Malling, Kent,' *Arch. Jnl* 88 (1931), plan between 174/5; Elliston-Erwood, 'Plan,' plan (pl. X) between 56/7

157 Clapham, *English Romanesque Architecture*, II, 24

158 Hope (1886), 329, reported that a box containing bones was discovered in his excavation of the eastern chapel. It lay just below the surface of the then earthen floor; the box was 'nearly demolished' by the workman who came on it; the bones were reburied when the trench was filled in. Hope speculated that the bones may have been the relics of one of the saints – Paulinus, Ithamar, or William – rescued at the time of the Dissolution. This seems highly unlikely.

159 St Albans Abbey begun after 1077, and Ely Abbey (later cathedral), begun after 1081, also had presbyteries of four bays; both, with Rochester, anticipating Durham Cathedral, begun in 1093: Clapham, *English Romanesque Architecture*, II, 22–5; Webb, *Architecture in Britain*, 28.

CHAPTER 4 **Alterations and Rebuilding in the Twelfth Century**

1 For Ernulf, see J. Le Neve, *Fasti Ecclesiae Anglicanae, 1066–1300*, vol. II, comp. D.E. Greenway, *Monastic Cathedrals (Northern and Southern Provinces)* (London 1971), 75–6.

2 M. Brett, 'The Church at Rochester, 604–1185,' in N. Yates, ed., with
P.A. Welsby, *Faith and Fabric: A History of Rochester Cathedral,
604–1994* (Kent History Project, 4: Woodbridge 1996), 26 and, for this
paragraph, 22–7.

3 J. Thorpe, ed., *Registrum Roffense: or A Collection of antient records,
charters, and instruments of divers kinds, necessary for illustrating
the ecclesiastical history and antiquities of the diocese and cathedral
church of Rochester* (London 1769), 120; N. Adams and C. Donahue,
Jr, eds, *Select Cases from the Ecclesiastical Courts of the Province of
Canterbury c. 1200–1301* (Selden Society, 95 [for 1978–9]: London
1981), 43; H.R. Luard, ed., *Flores Historiarum*, 3 vols. (RS, 95: London
1890), II, 45 (= BL, Cotton MS Nero D.II [which is dependent upon
Cotton MS Vespasian A.XXII], f. 110[109]v, 'Fecit etiam Dormitorium,
Capitulum, Refectorium': H. Wharton, ed., *Anglia Sacra*, 2 vols.
[London 1691], I *[Annales ecclesiae Roffensis ex historia ecclesiastica
Edmundi de Hadenham monachi Roffensis, 341–55]*, 342)

4 For this period in Kent, see R. Eales, 'Local Loyalties in Norman
England: Kent in Stephen's Reign,' *Anglo-Norman Studies, 8: Proceedings of the Battle Conference 1985* (1986), 88–108.

5 Brett, 'Church at Rochester,' 25; for William of Ypres, see Eales, 'Local
Loyalties,' 91, 93, and 99–101.

6 William of Ypres left England in 1155; his revenues from Kent were
cancelled by King Henry II (1154–89) in 1157: presumably Rochester's
debt to William was also thereby cancelled.

7 By F.H. Fairweather, 'Gundulf's Cathedral and Priory Church of St.
Andrew, Rochester: Some Critical Remarks on the Hitherto Accepted
Plan,' *Arch. Jnl* 86 (1929), 205. Also see above, chap. 3, p. 33 and nn.
50–1.

8 Lewis Nockalls Cottingham (1787–1847) was appointed by the Chapter
in December of 1824 (RMSC, DRc/Acz 1); Sir George Gilbert Scott
(1811–78) prepared his survey for the chapter in June 1867 (DRc/Emf
136); John Loughborough Pearson (1817–97), submitted his report
regarding the condition of the west front in March 1888 (DRc/Emf
142). Cottingham was succeeded as architect by Lewis Vulliamy
(1791–1871) in 1844; Pearson was replaced by the appointment of
Charles Hodgson Fowler (1840–1910) in 1898.

9 W.H.St.J. Hope, *The Architectural History of the Cathedral Church
and Monastery of St. Andrew at Rochester* (London 1900 = *Arch.
Cant.* 23 [1898], 194–328, and 24 [1900], 1–85; hereafter cited as Hope
[1900]), 89, confirmed by a stone embedded in the wall under the

remaining easternmost window bearing the letters 'C/IG' under the date '1664.' Also see D. Holbrook, 'Repair and Restoration of the Fabric since 1540,' in Yates, ed., *Faith and Fabric*, 186 (RMSC, DRc/Arb 2). According to B.C. Worssam, 'A Guide to the Building Stones of Rochester Cathedral,' *Friends of Rochester Cathedral: Report for 1994/5* (1995), 25, it was refaced in the nineteenth century 'with Kentish rag rubble and much reused Caen stone' (see below, n. 12); he attributed the lancets of Portland stone to D.A. Alexander (see below, n. 10).

10 Hope (1900), 89, gave 1670 for the rebuilding of the north aisle wall. According to S. Denne ('Memorials of the Cathedral Church of Rochester,' in J. Thorpe, ed., *Custumale Roffense, from the Original Manuscript in the Archives of the Dean and Chapter of Rochester* [London 1788], 182), in 1670, a Robert Cable was to take down 40 ft (12.192 m) of the north wall and rebuild it; see now in addition, RMSC, DRc/Ac 2/4 and Arb 3, as well as an earlier survey of 1667 by Captain Richard Rider and Joseph Warner, DRc/Emf 7/127, who estimated a cost of £90 for the demolition and rebuilding of the north aisle wall (Holbrook, 'Repair and Restoration,' 186 and 187). DRc/Emf 5/2, 'A Survey of Bricklayers and Masons and Plasterers Worke of necessary renovations of Cathedral church,' 14 August 1660, from Thomas Fflight and John Nellis, includes references to the 'repairing' of both the north and south aisles without specifying the extent of the work required.

The rebuilding of the north wall in the 1660s was not done very well, as in 1760 this wall is described by Henry Keene (1726–76), in DRc/Emf 34, 'A Survey of the State and Condition of the Buildings of the Cathedral Church of Rochester,' 11 October 1760, as considerably bulged or thrust out in the middle. Forty years later, Daniel Asher Alexander (1768–1846), in DRc/Emf 38, 'Report on a General Survey of Rochester Cathedral,' November 1799, noted that the north aisle wall was in a bad state, and in a subsequent survey, DRc/Emf 47/1, 'Report on the State and Condition of the North Wall of the West Nave of the Cathedral,' 9 September 1802, he described the whole wall as leaning outwards, 11 inches (27.94 cm) at the west end and 3 inches (7.62 cm) at the east.

11 The remnants of the buttresses were probably restored by Scott. They had been preserved, despite the seventeenth-century refacing of the wall above them, because the ground level around the cathedral was not lowered to near its original level until the early nineteenth century: see the report of (Sir) Robert Smirke (1780–1867), RMSC,

DRc/Emf 52/1, 'Remarks on the State of Rochester Cathedral at a Survey made on March 11, 1825,' pp. 1–2. During the post-Dissolution period, until ca. 1800, a house for the fifth prebend had occupied the area outside the south aisle wall; a stair from it led into a window of the 'Lady chapel': see BL, K. Top. XVII/8.2 (key to the plan of Alexander by Thomas Dampier [dean, 1782–1802]) and the plan in the 1843 notebook of S.A. Hankey (Guildhall Museum, Rochester); also see above, chap. 3, nn. 73 and 71, respectively.

12 In 1801 and 1802, first the south, then the north aisle walls were completely repointed with the use of small stone gallets (it was specifically mentioned that the brick patches of the south aisle were to be cut out and replaced with Kentish rag); both parapets were to be rebuilt without any cornice; the northwest buttress was to be taken down and rebuilt with a stronger projection: RMSC, DRc/Emf 40, 'Specification of Repairs to be made at the Cathedral, Rochester,' March 1801, and DRc/Emf 42, 'Specification of Sundry Work to be done to Rochester Cathedral,' May 1802. Both aisle roofs had been releaded, which work involved some alterations and strengthening of timbers, in the early eighteenth century, the south one in 1717 and the north one about ten years later: Holbrook, 'Repair and Restoration,' 189 and 190. In 1845, Cottingham's successor, Vulliamy, restored the aisle roofs and constructed false ceilings: Holbrook, 206 (RMSC, DRc/Ac 12).

13 G.H. Palmer, *The Cathedral Church of Rochester: A Description of Its Fabric and A Brief History of the Episcopal See*, 2nd ed. (Bell's Cathedral Series: London 1899), 26, 30, and 36–7. Documents relating to the restoration under the direction of Pearson are found in RMSC, DRc/Emf 65/9–30, 34, 42, 43, 45, and 48, of which perhaps the most interesting are 9, 16, 17, and 48. See my account, J.P. McAleer, 'The Significance of the West Front of Rochester Cathedral,' *Arch. Cant.* 99 (1983), 145 and 147; 'The West Front of Rochester Cathedral: The Interior Design,' *Arch. Cant.* 103 (1986), 28 n. 4; and 'The Cathedral West Front: Form, Function, and Fashion,' *Friends of Rochester Cathedral: Report for 1990/91* (1991), 26 and 28. Now also see Holbrook, 'Repair and Restoration,' 193–4 (the rebuilding of the northwest stair-tower was completed by 1769) and 209–10.

The small vignette of the cathedral in the (lower left) margin of the large engraving, 'View of the City of Rochester' (T. Badeslade, Delin., J. Harris, sculpt.) from J. Harris, *The History of Kent* (London 1719), between 250/1, depicts the west front before the modern alterations.

14 Actually, only the south stair-tower retains its vice, for the north one, as a result of the two successive rebuildings (1763–9 and 1892–4), is now solid up to the level of a passageway across the west front (a small vice now begins at that level); presumably it originally also contained a vice rising from ground level. They and the two smaller vices at the ends of the nave arcade are mentioned in D. Parsons, 'Barrel-vaulted Staircases in England and on the Continent with Special Reference to Brixworth Church, Northamptonshire' *Zeitschrift für Archäologie des Mittelalters* 6 (1978), 144. All three vices have been rebuilt or restored in their upper parts, but, for example, the first eighteen steps of the southwest stair-tower are mostly original.

15 See RMSC, DRc/Emf 32, 'Report of Repairs Absolutely wanting to be Done,' 15 July 1760, in which a George Younger (unidentified) noted that the northwest stair-tower was in a 'very bad and rotten state' and recommended that it be taken down to the gallery level and covered with a temporary roof. It had already been strengthened with iron ties in 1728: Holbrook, 'Repair and Restoration,' 190 (RMSC, DRc/FTv 70). In his survey of 11 October 1760 (DRc/Emf 34), Keene reported that the northwest tower was 'impossible to repair and must be taken down and rebuilt, carrying it up to a height equal to the square part of the south-west tower from which the octagonal stage should be removed.' Keene also recommended that the octagonal top of the north 'middle tower' be removed and replaced with a copy of the south 'middle tower.' According to Denne, 'Memorials,' in Thorpe, ed., *Custumale Roffense*, 183, the northwest tower was taken down in 1763 and rebuilt, probably with money left for the repair of the fabric in the will of Dean John Newcombe (d. 1765). By June 1769, the rebuilding of the northwest stair-tower was nearing completion: DRc/ Emf 35/2–3, estimates from plumbers and carpenters for roofing the 'New tower,' 30 June 1769. Now see, in addition, DRc/FTv 117 and 124, and DRc/Ac 8/25.

Two engravings of 1772 show the result of the rebuilding of the north angle stair-tower: *Gentleman's Magazine*, 42 (December 1772), pl. facing 576 ('The West End of Rochester Cathedral': B. Cole, Sculp.); and [S. Denne and W. Shrubsole?] *The History and Antiquities of Rochester and Its Environs* (London 1772), pl. facing p. 57 ('The West End of Rochester Cathedral': F. Baker del.). Crenellations were added to the stair-tower and the aisle end walls at the same time. A number of views show the west front after all the eighteenth-century alterations: an engraving by J.C. Schnebbelie (d. 1792) in Thorpe, ed.,

Custumale Roffense, pl. XXXV ('N.W. View of Rochester Cathedral'),
between 154/5; a drawing of 1804 by J. Buckler (BL, Add. MS 36.368,
'Buckler Architectural Drawings,' XIII, ff. 81v–82r, published as a large
engraving in 1810); an engraving dated 1818 from J.C. Buckler, *Views
of the Cathedral Churches of England and Wales with Descriptions*
(London 1822); and one by John Coney, dated 1821, in J. Caley, H.
Ellis, and B. Bandinel, eds, W. Dugdale, *Monasticon Anglicanum*, I
(London 1817), pl. between 152/3. Also see two drawings by
Cottingham, 'West Front and Tower of Rochester Cathedral as it
appeared previous to the repairs in 1825,' and 'Restoration of the West
Front of Rochester Cathedral with the Ashlering of &c to the Tower
when finished' (RDCL: missing? [NMR, neg. nos. BB65/3736 & 3737]):
the latter shows the façade according to Cottingham's proposed
restorations, which were not carried out.

16 The rebuilding of the north angle stair-tower occasioned great debate,
with the participation of the wrong-headed Society for the Protection
of Ancient Buildings: Holbrook, 'Repair and Restoration,' 210.

17 As noted above, n. 15, its rebuilding to match the original south one
had been suggested as early as 1760, by Keene.

18 The crenellated parapets were added only in 1769/70: see above, n. 15.

19 The west front was originally built out of Caen stone; Cottingham
rebuilt the west window in Bath stone, while Pearson used Weldon
stone from Lincolnshire in his restoration: see Worssam, 'Guide to
Building Stones,' 25.

20 The nave roof was completely replaced in 1804 according to the
recommendations and specifications of Alexander: see Holbrook,
'Repair and Restoration,' 200–1 (RMSC, DRc/Emf 43, 45, 46, 47, and
48/1; DRc/Ac 9/34; DRc/FTv 134, 135, 161, and 167).

21 See Worssam, 'Guide to Building Stones,' 23.

22 See above, nn. 14 and 15.

23 D. Kahn, 'Romanesque Architectural Sculpture in Kent,' PhD dissertation, University of London (Courtauld Institute of Art) 1982, 117 and
fig. 71b, related this motif to a similar subject on a capital in St Gab-
riel's Chapel in the crypt at Canterbury (east face of no. 4). For the date
of the crypt capitals as ca. 1100 rather than ca. 1120 see G. Zarnecki,
'The Romanesque Capitals in the South Transept of Worcester Cathedral,' in G. Popper, ed., *Medieval Art and Architecture at Worcester
Cathedral* (BAACT, I [for the year 1975]: [London] 1978), 39.

24 The number of lobes to each leaf is usually three or five, sometimes
rounded, at other times pointed. The enclosing C-shaped arc is not

organic – the ends curl up into round knobs. The motif is pre-Roman-esque: a series of individual upright five-(pointed)lobed leaves under C-shaped arcs with knobby volutes at the ends is found, as one of a number of florid motifs, carved on a segment of a cornice from Anicia Juliana's church of St Polyeuktos (524–7) in Constantinople: see M. Harrison, *A Temple for Byzantium: The Discovery and Excavation of Anicia Juliana's Palace Church in Istanbul* (Austin 1989), 90 and figs. 100 and 103; unfortunately, he did not comment on the history of this particular motif.

25 The diaper pattern is similar to one on the north wall of the north passage to the crypt at Canterbury, while the dogtooth occurs in contemporary work such as the Water Tower, ca. 1150–5: Kahn, 'Romanesque Architectural Sculpture,' 117.

26 The patterned stones were removed during the restoration of the window by Cottingham, ca. 1825, who recorded the details in his notebook, Columbia University, Avery Memorial Architectural Library, AA430/R5/M46 ('A Sketch Book by an Unknown Architect' [1825], first attributed to Cottingham by M.R. Covert), pp. 1 and 4–6. A diaper pattern of circles and lozenges surrounds the head of the west window as it appears in the engraving of D. King in R. Dodsworth and W. Dugdale, *Monasticon Anglicanum* (London 1655), pl. facing 24. The view by Jacob Schnebbelie in Thorpe, ed., *Custumale Roffense*, pl. XXXV, between 154/5, gives a more impressionist rendering of random-ly arranged stones with X's or O's on them, with a large square stone bearing a face to either side of the arch. An anonymous (framed) water-colour (5 x 8⁷/₈ in. [12.7 x 22.5 cm]) in the Guildhall Museum, Roches-ter (acc. no. unavailable), of the central section of the façade, shows individual stones bearing one of three different patterns (woven, lattice, circles) placed at regular intervals in the spandrels and in the narrow zone above the lowest register of arcading.

C. Miele presented a paper on the spandrel stones (somewhat misleadingly titled 'The Romanesque Façade of Rochester Cathedral: A Reconstruction Made with the Help of Cottingham's Studies for the 1825 Restoration') at the annual meeting of the Society of Architec-tural Historians held in Cincinnati in 1991. This has been published as 'The West Front of Rochester Cathedral in 1825: Antiquarianism, Historicism and the Restoration of Medieval Buildings,' *Arch. Jnl* 151 (1994), 400–19.

The whereabouts of most of the stones removed from the façade by Cottingham, which were either once stored in the cathedral crypt (where they were seen by Hope) or formed part of Cottingham's personal collection sold after his death in 1847 to his son Nockalls Johnson Cottingham (d. 1854), are not known (Miele, 415–18). Only a few (one? – one of the roundels) are in the recently created lapidarium in the upper room over the chapels of the north arm of the minor transept.

27 For a reconstruction of the west window spandrels based on the Cottingham drawings, see Miele, 'West Front,' illus. 8 (p. 415); his speculations as to their place of origin are on p. 414.

28 According to T.W.T. Tatton-Brown, 'Building Stone in Canterbury c. 1070–1525,' in D. Parsons, ed., *Stone: Quarring and Building in England, AD 43–1525* (Chichester 1990), 74, 75, the material of the outer shaft on the north is onyx marble – a rare use of this material that appears slightly earlier on the cloister façade of the dorter undercroft (for which see Worssam, 'Guide to the Building Stones,' 27 and n. 20) and that was also used in contemporary work of Prior Wibert at Canterbury such as the vestiarium, ca. 1155–60, and the later infirmary cloister, ca. 1174, as dated by D. Kahn, *Canterbury Cathedral and Its Romanesque Sculpture* (London and Austin 1991), 107, 111, 135, and 179.

29 This may be the 'simple *acanthus*' capital compared by D. Kahn ('The West Doorway at Rochester Cathedral,' in N. Stratford, ed., *Romanesque and Gothic: Essays for George Zarnecki*, 2 vols. [Woodbridge 1987], 131) to the south tower at Chartres Cathedral.

30 Probably the capital with confronted birds in foliage compared by Kahn, 'West Doorway,' 131, to one at Sens Cathedral.

31 Compared by Kahn, 'West Doorway,' 131 (cf. pls. 3 and 4), with capitals at Saint-Denis (I fail to see the *stylistic* similarity).

32 This capital was compared by Kahn, 'West Doorway,' 131, to two capitals of the north portal at Bourges Cathedral.

33 The north half (voussoirs 4–22) of this outer order is a result of the 1888 restoration. Drawings of the portal by George Sharf (1820–95), carried out in June 1850, now in the Society of Antiquaries of London, show the carving completely gone or existing only as the merest traces: see Kahn, 'West Doorway,' 130 and pl. 2.

34 Compared by Kahn, 'West Doorway,' 131, to the similar motif on the round west façade window of Saint-Denis (cf. pls. 7 [a very poor photograph] and 8).

The 'harpy' (more properly identified as a siren?) compared by Kahn, 131, with some on a capital at Saint-Denis (cf. pl. 3 with pl. 5

[mislabelled 'Saint-Ours, Loches,' it is of Rochester; pl. 6, mislabelled 'Rochester,' is of Saint-Ours]) is in this row, left of centre.

35 The nave, like the later west front, is built of Caen stone: Worssam, 'Guide to the Building Stones,' 30. As measured between the faces of the westernmost pair of piers, the nave is 27 ft. 9 in. (8.4582 m) wide, and each aisle is 13 ft. 9 in. (4.1910 m); the piers are 5 ft. (1.524 m) thick in their north/south axis, and 6 ft. 4 in. (1.9304 m) in their east/ west axis, the westernost bay being 10 ft. 3 in. (3.1242 m) between pier face and respond shaft; the gallery piers, minus responds, are 4 ft. (1.2192 m) wide (east/west); the abaci of the piers are at 14 ft. 8^1/$_2$ in. (4.4831 m), the string-course below the false gallery is at a height of 23 ft. (7.0104 m), the gallery abaci at 28 ft. 7 in. (8.7122 m), and the string above the gallery arches at 35 ft. (10.668 m): Carden & Godfrey Architects, Rochester Cathedral, sheet 130/3 (23 December 1953).

36 The western of the two Gothic piers at the east end of the south arcade apparently belongs to two periods. The east half, similar in form to the eastern pier, is of the mid-thirteenth century. Initially, the west half of the pier (fig. 37), consisting of a large half-shaft against a rectangular core (without trace of a similar shaft having been on the aisle or nave faces) appears Romanesque as its form is similar to that of the following pier, the easternmost remaining Romanesque one. However, the capital of the half-shaft has oak-leaf-type foliage characteristic of the fourteenth century and the tooling of the finely jointed stonework is nearly invisible, quite unlike the conspicuous diagonal tooling – and thick joints – of the twelfth-century piers. In addition, the individual courses are different in height from those of the other arcade piers. This pier also has a more elaborate base (fig. 11r), consisting of two thin rolls above a narrow quarter-hollow, than the other Romanesque piers. The plinth has been remodelled to an octagonal form, as in the case of the three other Gothic piers. Taken together, all these details suggest that, for some reason not at all obvious, the west half of the pier was rebuilt in the mid?-fourteenth century, possibly in imitation of the original Romanesque form of this pier, which may not have been completely rebuilt in the mid-thirteenth century.

37 R. Gem, 'The Origins of the Early Romanesque Architecture of England,' PhD dissertation, Cambridge University 1973, 552, suggested this easternmost remaining pair represents an early type: he described them as simpler and less bulky; he thought they could 'hardly be recasings' and that 'it [was] possible that this pair of piers *reproduced* the design of the eleventh-century ones' [emphasis added]. His plan

(R. Gem, 'The Significance of the 11th-century Rebuilding of Christ Church and St. Augustine's, Canterbury in the Development of Romanesque Architecture,' in N. Coldstream and P. Draper, eds, *Medieval Art and Architecture at Canterbury before 1200* [BAACT, V (for the year 1979): (London) 1982], 12 fig. 5) shows them as part of Gundulf's work. Yet these piers stand on simple, large, square, chamfered bases like all the others. The nature of their coursing also corresponds to that of the other piers to the west: the coursing on all the piers is somewhat variable and not uniformly consistent in height.

38 The second pair were compared by B. Cherry, 'Romanesque Architecture in Eastern England,' *Jnl BAA* 131 (1978), 23, to Great Paxton (Huntingdonshire/Cambridgeshire) and accepted by E. Fernie ('The Romanesque Church at Waltham Abbey,' *Jnl BAA* 108 [1985], 72) 'as an example of the revival of interest in Anglo-Saxon architectural forms in Anglo-Norman England' (along with a miniature version in bays 3–6 of the south clerestory at Waltham). The Rochester piers are distinctly different from the more conventional Romanesque solution, in which there is a round core with four attached half-shafts, as seen for example, ca. 1160, in the crypt of Archbishop Roger Pont l'Évêque (1154–81) at York Minster: see J. Browne, *History of the Metropolitan Church of St. Peter, York*, 2 vols. (York 1847), II, pls. XVII–XIX.

39 These piers are somewhat larger than the others: their increased size has been taken as an indication of an intention to construct two west towers. See below, n. 73.

40 The plans of the piers and west respond were recorded in Thorpe, ed., *Custumale Roffense*, pl. XXXIV.
    M.J. Swanton, 'A Mural Palimpsest from Rochester Cathedral,' *Arch. Jnl* 136 (1979), 125–35, and 'The Decoration of Ernulf's Nave,' *Friends of Rochester Cathedral: Report for 1989/90* (1990), 11–18, has detected incised graffiti on the nave piers that he has interpreted as various religious figures and scenes. Whatever they represent, it is most unlikely that the Romanesque piers, because of their varying shapes, were originally frescoed and covered by a figurative programme as he suggests (134/17).

41 The base mouldings and plinths, as well as the bases of the north aisle responds, have all been varnished. This led me to identify them as Purbeck marble, or a related stone, in J.P. McAleer, 'Some Observations on the Building Sequence of the Nave of Rochester Cathedral,' *Arch. Cant.* 102 (1985), 158; T. Tatton-Brown has kindly set me straight on this matter. Others have also been deceived: N. Pevsner

and P. Metcalf, *The Cathedrals of England: Southern England* (Harmondsworth 1985), 238: 'Some of the pier bases are of brown local marble' (why it was said 'some' rather than 'all' is not clear, as all the bases were treated in the same manner); see also Newman, *West Kent*, 685, who described them as being of 'black marble'; about these bases, Worssam, 'Guide to the Building Stones,' 33 n. 36, noted only that he was not able to confirm 'Newman's report.' All are of the same stone, and that stone is Caen limestone. Just when this deception was perpetrated is not known; there are no references to it in the papers of J.T. Irvine (1825–1900), the notes he made during the restoration of 1871–8, under the direction of Scott (which are in the Dean and Chapter archives now on deposit in the Rochester upon Medway Studies Centre), for instance, nor any mention of it by Hope in any of his histories of the cathedral. F.H. Duffield and H.T. Knight, with S.W. Wheatley, *A Sketch of the History of the Diocese of Rochester with a Short Account of the Cathedral and Precinct* (Chatham 1926), 53, mentioned that 'the walls of the nave also show signs of decay, due probably to leaking leadwork, which must be renewed soon.' Could the varnishing of the bases have occurred in a restoration of the nave after 1926?

42 Mary R. Covert brought to my attention a small griffe on the base of the shaft at the southwest angle of the third pier from the west in the south arcade. Beak-shaped spurs occur on the bases of the shafts to the chapter house doorway, ca. 1140, a work roughly contemporary with the nave.

S.E. Rigold, 'Romanesque Bases in and South-east of the Limestone Belt,' in M.R. Apted, R. Gilyard-Beer, and A.D. Saunders, eds, *Ancient Monuments and Their Interpretation: Essays Presented to A.J. Taylor* (London 1977), 106, only commented that spurs or griffes were rare in England (and 'little explored' in his paper).

43 The decorative patterns of the nave greatly interested the late-eighteenth-century antiquarian and restorer James Essex (1722–84). He recorded them – string-courses, pier plans, tympana, diapers, etc. – in a notebook, now BL, Add. MS 6758C, ff. 92–9, 108, and 109. Elevations of the inside and outside of the west front are also included on ff. 100 and 102.

44 Twelve diaper patterns and nine medallions were reproduced in Thorpe, ed., *Custumale Roffense*, pl. XXXIV.

45 Palmer, *Cathedral Church*, 15 and 69, thought part of this tympanum, executed partly in green sandstone (i.e., Upper Greensand = Reigate,

also known as 'firestone'), was 'reproduced' ca. 1320 when (as he thought) the plan for rebuilding the nave was finally given up and the juncture between the new and old work was finished off. But the use of greensand is more extensive than just in the southeast tympanum: on both north and south in this bay, it is used for some of the shafts, subarches, tympana, and superordinate arches. For Reigate stone see T. Tatton-Brown, 'Medieval Building Stone at the Tower of London,' *London Archaeologist* 6/13 (1991), 363; and B.C. Worssam and T. Tatton-Brown, 'Kentish Rag and Other Kent Building Stones,' *Arch. Cant.* 112 (1993), 94. Tatton-Brown (letter of 22 January 1995) informs me that Upper Greensand or Reigate was in use in north Kent from the mid-twelfth century: e.g., the west portal of the parish church at Luddenham.

46 For a full discussion see McAleer, 'West Front,' 27–43.

47 Hope (1900), 30, specified 'an arcade of seven Norman arches alternately blind and open.'

48 Hope (1900), 30: 'large circular or other window, or pair of windows.' For fuller particulars, see McAleer, 'West Front,' 35 and nn. 18 and 19.

49 As pointed out above, n. 14, the base of the northwest angle stair-tower is solid up to this level, presumably as a result of its rebuilding, first in the 1760s (see above, n. 15) and again in 1890s (see above, n. 16); there is no evidence as to whether it originally had a newel-stair from the ground up.

50 The passages were blocked up ca. 1875, during the restoration directed by Scott, at which time iron tie rods were inserted: see RMSC, DRc/ Emf 65/3.

51 See McAleer, 'West Front,' 27–31, for a full description of the circulation system.

52 There are two sources: B. Thorpe, ed., *The Anglo-Saxon Chronicle*, 2 vols. (RS, 23: London 1861), I, 380, and II, 227; and BL, Harleian MS 636, f. 99 (Hope [1900], 34 n. *).

53 See above, n. 3.

54 E.g., Norwich Cathedral, completed ca. 1145, seems not to have been consecrated until 1278!: N. Pevsner, *BE: North-East Norfolk and Norwich* (Harmondsworth 1962), 210. Indeed, the dedication in 1130 of the so-called Glorious Choir of Christ Church, Canterbury, took place 'long after the completion of the fabric,' if not of the decoration, ca. 1110: F. Woodman, *The Architectural History of Canterbury Cathedral* (London 1981), 76. For other examples of 'delayed' consecrations, see R. Morris, 'Early Gothic Architecture at Tewkesbury,' in

T.A. Heslop and V.A. Sekules, eds, *Medieval Art and Architecture at Gloucester and Tewkesbury* (BAACT, VII [for the year 1981]: [London] 1985), 97: about five dedications carried out in 1239, Morris remarked, '[T]here is a suspicion that the bishop of Worcester was catching up on business of this kind that was long overdue.'

55 R. Gem, 'Bishop Wulfstan II and the Romanesque Cathedral Church of Worcester,' in G. Popper, ed., *Medieval Art and Architecture at Worcester Cathedral* (BAACT, I [for the year 1975]: [London] 1978), 19 (in the case of Worcester)

56 BL, Cotton MS Nero D.II, f. 111[110]v (Wharton, ed., *Anglia Sacra*, I, 343): 'Transtulit corpus Ythamari episcopi.' As Palmer, *Cathedral Church*, 10, remarked: 'It seems peculiar that this relic was not moved to the new church at the same time as the remains of St. Paulinus [in 1088].' According to D. Bethell, 'The Miracles of St Ithamar,' *Analecta Bollandiana*, 89 (1971), 424, there is no evidence of the cult of Ithamar before the late eleventh century. In addition, according to the text of the 'Miracula S. Ithamari Ep.,' Gundulf had moved Ithamar's bones to a position at the north side of the cathedral, and then, after a Rochester monk had experienced a vision, Gundulf had the relics moved into the chancel: see Bethell, 425 (where he mistakenly identifies the first site of the resting place of the relics in the cathedral as the *west end*) and, for the Latin text, 429–30 (see also below, n. 106). The relics were moved yet again to a new and better shrine by Bishop John 'of Escures' after he was cured of a 'sickness of the eyes': Bethell, 425 (who suggested that this may have been at the time of the 1130 consecration; he made no reference to the event and date – which would fall within the early years of the episcopate of John – chronicled in Cotton MS Nero D.II) and, for the Latin text, 431–2. Also see R. Sharpe, 'The Setting of St Augustine's Translation, 1091,' in R. Eales and R. Sharpe, eds, *Canterbury and the Norman Conquest: Churches, Saints and Scholars, 1066–1109* (London and Rio Grande [Ohio] 1995), 9–10, who suggested that the author of the account, which he dated to the 1130s, may have backdated the moving of the relics; Sharpe also made no reference to the translation in 1128.

57 W. Stubbs, ed., *The Historical Works of Gervase of Canterbury*, 2 vols. (RS, 73: London 1879–80), I, 100: 'Tertio nonas Junii combusta est ecclesia Sancti Andreae Roffensis et tota civitas cum officinis episcopi et monachorum.' Also BL, Cotton MS Vespasian A.XXII, f. 29[28]v. BL, Cotton MS Nero D.II, f. 112[111]v gives the date as 1138: Wharton, ed., *Anglia Sacra*, I, 343. The damage to the monastic buildings

constructed by Ernulf (see above, n. 3) was great enough to make it necessary for the monks to seek temporary refuge elsewhere: R.C. Fowler, '[Religious Houses:] Cathedral Priory of St. Andrew, Rochester,' in *VCH: Kent*, II (London 1926), 122.

Another earlier fire on 7 May 1130, when the king was in Rochester, presumably for the consecration of the cathedral the next day, and which supposedly nearly destroyed the city, is mentioned in the 'Anglo-Saxon Chronicle' (Thorpe, ed., *Chronicle*, I, 380/II, 227 [*sub anno* 1130]; no month or day is given) and also by Florence of Worcester (B. Thorpe, ed., *Florentii Wigorniensis monachi chronicon ex chronicis*, 2 vols. [English Historical Society: London 1848–9], II, 92; or see T. Forester, ed., *The Chronicle of Florence of Worcester with the Two Continuations* [London 1854], 247). Also see Palmer, *Cathedral Church*, 10.

58 G.M. Livett, 'Foundations of the Saxon Cathedral Church at Rochester,' *Arch. Cant.* 18 (1889), 276: 'the Later-Norman front was the closing work of what was practically a rebuilding of the first Norman church.' Later, Livett, 'Early-Norman Churches in and near the Medway Valley,' *Arch. Cant.* 20 (1893), 39, preferred to date the rebuilding to Bishop John I (1125–37), who 'practically rebuilt the early-Norman cathedral in the more advanced style of his period, at the same time as Archbishop William [of Corbeil, 1123–36] was engaged in building the keep of the castle.'

59 See above, chap. 3, pp. 45–6.

60 W.H.St.J. Hope, 'Notes on the Architectural History of Rochester Cathedral Church,' *Transactions of St. Paul's Ecclesiological Society* 1 (1881–5; hereafter cited as Hope [1881–5]), 221, and (1900), 22–23 and 28; and, even earlier, A. Ashpitel, 'Rochester Cathedral,' *Jnl BAA* 9 (1854), 274.

61 It was one of four floor levels found by Irvine in 1872: Hope (1886), (331–2, first floor) section in pl. I (facing 326), based on Irvine's 1875 sketch, RMSC, DRc/Emf 77/3, and Hope (1900), (15, for first floor) 25 (for second-floor level). Hope said 2 feet (0.6096 m) above the lowest level of Gundulf's floor, but Irvine's sketch indicates only about 13 inches (33.02 cm). This floor was close to the level of the present nave paving, which according to Livett, 'Foundations,' 278, is 7 inches (17.78 cm) above the plaster floor of the 'Later-Norman' nave at the west end.

62 Fairweather, 'Gundulf's Cathedral,' 205; A.W. Clapham, *English Romanesque Architecture*, vol. II, *After the Conquest* (Oxford 1934),

24 ('a later extension, perhaps the work of Bishop Ernulf'); also see above, n. 7, and chap. 3, p. 37

63 Short lengths of two walls meeting at an oblique angle (embedded in a so-called sleeper wall of chalk blocks) were uncovered east of the northwest crossing pier in 1968; they were apparently at a level that could be associated with a twelfth-century (or later?) rebuilding: see below, pp. 72–3.

64 These are spelled out in detail in McAleer, 'Some Observations,' 158–66.

65 Also noted by Gem, 'Origins of Early Romanesque,' 552–3, but attributed to the earlier building (Gundulf's), in the form of groin vaults, although he observed the evidence is stronger in the *north* aisle, which no one else except Ashpitel, 'Rochester Cathedral,' 274, has suggested is of Gundulf's period.

66 Cherry, 'Romanesque Architecture,' 8 n. 21

67 Clapham, *English Romanesque Architecture*, II, 55 n. 2, dated the removal of the aisle vault to 1137 – following the fire – when 'a triforum passage [was] contrived in the thickness of the main wall, between the triforum openings.' Regardless of date, this is incorrect, as the passageway was definitely *built* with the arcade and was not cut through at a later date.

Hope (1881–5), 221, and (1900), 27, stressed that the arches of the wall 'passage' throughout are *pointed*, not round. This, too, is incorrect, as many arches are either semicircular or ambiguous in shape; there is no sequence to their varied forms.

68 For Romsey, see M.F. Hearn, 'A Note on the Chronology of Romsey Abbey,' *Jnl BAA*, 3rd ser., 32 (1969), esp. 35–8 for the east bay of the nave arcade (ca. 1140/45–50).

69 Hope (1881–5), 221, and (1900), 27

70 Its foundations were partly uncovered in 1888: see Livett, 'Foundations, 277 and pl. II, sect. no. 5. They were described as being of the 'same character as that of their predecessors, but less compact and serviceable.'

71 The west bays of the nave arcades and the west front had been identified as a separate build, one attributed to Ernulf, by Ashpitel, 'Rochester Cathedral,' 274.

72 J. Newman, *BE: West Kent and the Weald*, 2nd ed. (1976), repr. & corr. (Harmondsworth 1980), 43 n. *, explained the lack of a gallery floor as 'due to rebuilding in the C17,' but this is evidently not the case.

73 Livett, 'Foundations,' 278; Hope (1881–5), 221, and (1900), 28: unfortunately, no precise plan (or description) of these blocks was given. Irvine's papers include only one tiny sketch, RMSC, DRc/Emf 77/39, which shows the location of these blocks; see also a brief reference in DRc/Emf 77/77 (undated letter from Irvine, probably to Hope).

74 It will be recalled that the foundations of the east chapel as described by Hope did not conform to the foundations in the nave attributed to Gundulf but rather, because of the absence of gravel and the use of some mortar, had some resemblance to foundations of the first west front. See above chap. 3, pp. 30–2 and pp. 36–7.

75 Hope (1881–5), 221–2, and (1900), 24 and 25

76 G. Zarnecki, ed., *Canterbury, Romanesque Work* (P. Lasko, gen. ed., *Courtauld Institute Illustration Archives*, Archive I, *Cathedral and Monastic Buildings in the British Isles*, pt. 8: London 1978), 1/8/10–11; Kahn, *Canterbury Cathedral*, 117

77 See Kahn, 'Romanesque Architectural Sculpture,' 58 (late 1140s). That it was much later than the time of Ernulf was first pointed out by J. Zarnecki, 'Regional Schools of English Sculpture in the Twelfth Century. The Southern School and the Herefordshire School,' PhD dissertation, University of London (Courtauld Institute of Art) 1950, 189–90; in addition, Zarnecki, *English Romanesque Sculpture, 1066–1140* (London 1951), 18 and 37, and pl. 70 (ca. 1140). Nonetheless, Newman, *West Kent*, 41 n. *, 49, and 487–8, continued to attribute the chapter house diapering to the original building of Ernulf while considering the doorway an insertion of ca. 1140. For further on the east range, see T. Tatton-Brown, 'The East Range of the Cloisters,' *Friends of Rochester Cathedral: Report for 1988* (1989), 4–8, and 'The Chapter House and Dormitory Façade at Rochester Cathedral Priory,' *Friends of Rochester Cathedral: Report for 1993/94* (1994), 20–8.

78 For the 'Glorious Choir' of Canterbury, begun in 1096 when Saint Anselm was archbishop (1093–1109), and completed by Prior Conrad (1108–26), see Woodman, '*Architectural History*,' 45–76.

79 C.A.R. Radford, 'Rochester Cathedral: A New Fragment of pre-Conquest Wall,' *Annales Amicorum Cathedralis Roffensis being the Annual Report of the Friends of Rochester Cathedral* ([May] 1969), 14–15; also see above, chap. 1, pp. 14–16, and chap. 3, p. 41.

80 See above, chap. 3, n. 91.

81 Livett, 'Foundations,' 276; 'Later-Norman' was his term for the work of the present nave and west front, which, in this paper, he attributed to bishops Ernulf and John of Canterbury, with a completion date of

1130. The main distinction between early (late eleventh century, viz., the church built by Gundulf) and late (mid-twelfth century, viz., the existing nave and west front) Romanesque work seems to be the later use of Caen stone replacing the earlier more limited use of tufa for elements such as quoins: ibid., 272 and 278; also A. Clifton-Taylor, 'Building Materials,' in Newman, *West Kent*, 30 and 31. Unfortunately, neither material seems to have been present in any of the walls uncovered in 1968.

82 Livett, 'Foundations,' 277 and pl. II, sect. no. 3, was not very specific about the nature of the 'Later-Norman' foundations of the existing west front uncovered in 1888; he described them as consisting of 'material of the same character as that of their predecessors, but less compact and serviceable.' Since mortar was used in the 'Early-Norman' (by which he meant work at the west end of the nave carried out during Gundulf's lifetime, ca. 1095–1100, by the parishioners) foundations (see p. 272), it presumably was present in the 'Later-Norman' work; and since the 'Early-Norman' foundations at the west front abandoned the use of 'chalk in small lumps' that had characterized the foundations he narrowly associated with 'Gundulf's' (unfinished) building, presumably the 'Later-Norman' work also did not use chalk.

83 A possible continuation of the north–south line of the L-plan segment was reportedly encountered outside the west wall of the north transept arm in 1970 when excavations for a chair store were being conducted: A.C. Harrison, 'Investigations and Excavations during the Year,' *Arch. Cant.* 87 (1972), 241.

84 In McAleer, 'Some Observations,' esp. 165–6, I argued for a date of the 1140s and 1150s for the nave. But the mistaken attribution to Ernulf continues: see Swanton, 'A Mural Palimpsest' or 'Decoration of Ernulf's Nave.'

85 Hope (1881–5), 222 and (1900), 28 and 33

86 E.g., Clapham, *English Romanesque Architecture*, II, 143 and pl. 28, 1160–70 (on the basis of the west portal sculpture); G. Webb, *Architecture in Britain: The Middle Ages* (Harmondsworth 1956), 49 and pl. 43, mid-twelfth

87 Clapham, *English Romanesque Architecture*, II, pl. 22

88 Kahn, 'West Doorway,' 130

89 The roll chevron of the inner order, while it softens the angle, is not of the 'opposed' type that could be more firmly dated after 1140: Fernie, 'Waltham Abbey,' 59–61 and n. 33.

90 See Cherry, 'Romanesque Architecture,' esp. 8–19 and 24–5. Ornamental variety also is a theme of the period after ca. 1160: see M. Thurlby and Y. Kusaba, 'The Nave of Saint Andrew at Steyning: A Study of Variety in Design in Twelfth-Century Architecture in Britain,' *Gesta*, 30/2 (1991), 163–75.

91 L. Hoey, 'Pier Alternation in Early English Gothic Architecture,' *Jnl BAA* 119 (1986), 45–67, esp. 46–7 and 54. In another paper ('Pier Form and Vertical Wall Articulation in English Romanesque,' *Jnl SAH* 48/3 [1989], 279 n. 113), Hoey remarked: 'Rochester is only the most spectacular surviving example of a late Romanesque tendency to invent pier forms for the sake of innovation.' The phenomena of asymmetrical arcade designs within this period, of which the choir of the parish church at New Shoreham (1180s) is a well-known example, should be noted: see S. Woodcock, 'The Building History of St. Mary de Haura, New Shoreham,' *Jnl BAA* 145 (1992), 89–103, esp. n. 57.

92 R.A. Brown, *Rochester Castle, Kent*, 1st ed. (MPBW Official Guidebook: London 1969), 10, 30, and 41–4

93 For chevron (sunk) roundels see G. Zarnecki, 'The Carved Stones from Newark Castle,' *Transactions of the Thornton Society of Nottinghamshire*, 60 (1956), 23.

94 For the numerous projects of Prior Wibert at Canterbury, see Woodman, *Architectural History*, 76–86; and Kahn, *Canterbury Cathedral*, 95–137.

95 Trilobe leaf spurs are also found on the alternating piers of St Margaret at St Margaret's at Cliffe (Kent); see Newman, *West Kent*, 43, ca. 1150–75, and *BE: North East and East Kent*, 3rd ed. (Harmondsworth 1983), 435–7, ca. 1140; and Kahn, 'Romanesque Architectural Sculpture,' 116.

96 Kahn, 'Romanesque Architectural Sculpture,' 116 and *Canterbury Cathedral*, 136, compared the 'trumpet leaves' of some of the shaft capitals at the west end of the nave to the leaves of the central pier of Wibert's Water Tower at Canterbury that she dated ('Romanesque Architectural Sculpture,' 73) ca. 1150–5 or (*Canterbury Cathedral*, 102) ca. 1155; the corbel heads of another tympanum were compared to examples in the nave of St Margaret at St Margaret's at Cliffe, which she dated (114) after ca. 1165/70.

97 See above, n. 77.

98 Melbourne has usually been dated to the period between the late 1130s and the late 1150s (1136–57): R.J. Barman, *History and Guide to the Parish Church of Melbourne* (1960). But more recently, a beginning

date of ca. 1120, under royal patronage (Henry I), has been proposed:
R. Gem, 'Melbourne, Church of St. Michael and St. Mary,' *Arch. Jnl*
146 (1989), *Supplement* (N.H. Cooper, ed., *The Nottingham Area*),
24–30. For the York crypt, see Browne, *History of the Metropolitan
Church*, II, pls. XXIII–XXIV; and E.A. Gee, 'Architectural History until
1290,' in G.E. Aylmer and R. Cant, eds, *A History of York Minster*
(Oxford 1977), 123.

99 Kahn, 'Romanesque Architectural Sculpture,' 63 and 117, and *Canterbury Cathedral*, 120; its absence in the Rochester monastic buildings
confirmed for her that they pre-dated 1150. Of course, the fret motif
appeared earlier in Normandy, in the latest work at La Trinité and
Saint-Étienne, Caen, and appeared at Old Sarum Cathedral (ca. 1130)
and the central west portal of Lincoln Cathedral (ca. 1145–50:
G. Zarnecki, *Romanesque Sculpture at Lincoln Cathedral* [Lincoln
Minster Pamphlets, 2nd ser., no. 2: Lincoln 1963], 16 and figs. 26 and
27; Zarnecki, *Romanesque Lincoln: The Sculpture of the Cathedral*
[Lincoln 1988], 22; and Kahn, 'Romanesque Architectural Sculpture,'
83).

100 BL, Cotton MS Vespasian A.XXII, f. 83[85]r (Thorpe, ed., *Registrum
Roffense*, 118): 'Reginaldus prior fecit duas campanas et posuit eas in
majori turri.'

101 A. Vallance, *Greater English Church Screens* (London 1947), 46–7; cf.
Irvine, RMSC, DRc/Emf 77/51. There is not actually any evidence of a
rood screen having been located between this pair of piers – the
easternmost surviving ones of the twelfth-century nave.

102 A.W. Klukas, 'The Architectural Implications of the *Decreta
Lanfranci*,' in H.A. Brown, ed., *Anglo-Norman Studies*, 6: *Proceedings
of the Battle Conference 1983* (1984), 155 and fig. 5; Klukas's plan is
based upon Gem, 'Significance,' fig. 5, but introduces certain features
for which there is no evidence, such as doorways in the end walls of
the transept and at the east end of the south aisle, and terminates the
nave with the plan of the later twelfth-century west front (including
the north portal, which is a later insertion) instead of the first front as
recovered by excavation.

103 See above, chap. 3, p. 30 and esp. n. 27; Irvine's findings were accepted
and described by Hope (1900), 15 (cf. Hope [1886], 332 and section in
pl. I [facing 326]).

104 See above, n. 61.

105 Irvine thought the floor very similar to Gundulf's in construction:
RMSC, DRc/Emf 77/133, 'An Account of the Church of St. Andrew at

Rochester otherwise the Cathedral of the Castle of the Kentishmen,'
Notebook no. 2, pp. 11–12 (or see DRc/Emf 135 [a typed transcript
prepared by G.M. Livett], p. 8). See also Irvine's account in DRc/Emf
77/129 [no pagination], [sheet 8], wherein he did not clearly distinguish
between the two levels, and appears to have associated the second
with Gundulf. Yet in DRc/Emf 77/3, Irvine identified it as the 'floor of
choir previous to Death of S. Will.'), and in 77/133, Notebook no. 2, p.
10 (DRc/Emf 135, p. 7), he described it as the 'floor of Bishop
Glanville's church prior to the death of St. William in 1201.'

106 Cambridge, Corpus Christi College, MS 161 ('Miracula S. Ithamari
Ep[iscopi].'), sect. xiiii: see Bethell, 'Miracles,' 427–37 for complete
Latin text (436: 'Veniebam, et ecce coram altari assistens prospexi
personas quatuor honoris et decoris eximii, sanctos videlicet, ut meo
animo suggerebatur, Petrum et Andream, Paulinum atque Ithamarum,
stantes super trabem que imminet crucem et capsas reliquiarum
gestans'). Bethell, 425, suggested that the 'Miracula' dated to the
period of Stephen's queen Matilda, i.e., 1135–52, but were no later
than the 1150s; the rood described might therefore be one that was in
place *before* the fire of 1137, that is, in Gundulf's building, even if not
necessarily of his time (the result of Bishop John's removal of the
relics to a new and better shrine in 1128?: see above, n. 56).

107 See Sharpe, 'St Augustine's Translation,' esp. 8–11; M. Ruud, 'Monks
in the World: The Case of Gundulf of Rochester,' *Anglo-Norman
Studies* XI, *Proceedings of the Battle Conference 1988* (1989), 245–60,
esp. 245–7.

108 Bethell, 'Miracles,' 429–30: 'Tempore igitur venerabilis et Deo dilecti
patris nostri Gundulfi episcopi, innovata Rofensi ecclesia et augustiori-
bus edificiis extructa, beatus Ythamarus eiusdem quondam loci episcopus de loco ubi prius sepultus fuerat in excelsam quandam testudinem
ad aquilonem transpositus est ... Audiens hec episcopus, illo in primis
suadente, preciosas sancti reliquias in presbiterium referri et in loco
decentiori tecam inestimabilis thesauri ubi cunctis esset accessibilis
locari precepit.'

109 Irvine, RMSC, DRc/Emf 77/3 (identified as 'choir floor after rebuilding
of Eastern end but before rebuilding present side walls of Chancel');
Hope (1886), section in pl. I, and (1900), 36

110 See above, chap. 3, pp. 29–30, 32–3, 37–8, 49–52.

111 See above, chap. 3, n. 64.

112 The following remarks should be considered in conjunction with the
discussion of certain features of the nave in support of a date for it
after the fire of 1137: see above, pp. 73–5.

113 On this aspect now see Hoey, 'Pier Form,' 258–83.

114 A more obvious alternation between round and compound had occurred in the transept, notably in the south arm (ca. 1084–93): see Hoey, 'Pier Form,' 270–80, for this significant type.

115 Ibid., 269–70

116 Zarnecki, ed., *Canterbury*, 1/8/2–4. The later crypt, begun by Ernulf when prior (1096–1107) under Archbishop Anselm (1093–1109), also included pairs of variously decorated shafts alternating with plain ones (1/8/12–13): see E. Fernie, 'St Anselm's Crypt,' in Coldstream and Draper, eds, *Medieval Art and Architecture at Canterbury*, 27–38.

117 One not always appreciated: Newman, *West Kent*, 43, 'it is a rather tired performance ... The piers in each bay have a different plan, but nothing is made of this hectic variety.'

118 L. Hoey, 'Piers versus Vault Shafts in Early English Gothic Architecture,' *Jnl SAH* 46 (1987), 244

119 See McAleer, 'Some Observations,' 164 n. 41, for other examples.

120 A survey carried out over thirty years ago, which I believe still has some validity, produced a list of over thirty certain examples for each type during the period 1066–1175/80; for definition of the types and lists, see J.P. McAleer, *The Romanesque Church Facade in Britain*, PhD dissertation, University of London (Courtauld Institute of Art) 1963; New York & London 1984, 350–65 (Appendix IV, Sectional Facades), and 321–38 (Appendix I, Twin-Tower Facades).

121 See McAleer, 'Significance,' 149 n. 17, and 'Some Observations,' 151 n. 6; and Kahn, *Canterbury Cathedral*, 130.

122 For these façades see, for Hereford, now destroyed, B. Willis, *A Survey of the Cathedrals of York, etc.* (London 1727), pl. facing 499, and G.G. Scott, 'Hereford Cathedral,' *Arch. Jnl* 34 (1877), pl. facing 329; for Castle Acre, E. Preston Willins, *Castle Acre Priory, Norfolk* (London [ca. 1880]), or F.J.E. Raby and P.K. Baillie Reynolds, *Castle Acre Priory, Norfolk* (MPW Official Guide: London 1936 and later); for Colchester, Croyland, and Malmesbury, J.P. McAleer, 'Particularly English? Screen Façades of the Type of Salisbury and Wells Cathedrals,' *Jnl BAA* 141 (1988), 131 and fig. 6, 133, and 137–40, respectively.

123 One cannot really agree with Newman, *West Kent*, 476 (Pevsner and Metcalf, *Cathedrals of England*, 238): 'The taste for this sort of façade treatment must have been learnt by English masons from West France and Poitou.' Rather the taste seems a manifestation of the *Zeitgeist*, showing up in different places at one time. It cannot be conclusively shown that the Poitevin church façades are significantly earlier than

the appearance of the fashion in England. See McAleer, 'Significance,' 135–6.

124 See McAleer, 'Significance,' 147–50, and the bibliography there cited, to which should be added Kahn, 'Romanesque Architectural Sculpture,' 120–39, and 'West Doorway,' 129–34.

125 The column figures have been variously identified, and varied stylistic comparisons have been made, resulting in a number of dates. E.S. Prior, *A History of Gothic Art in England* (London 1900), 131, identified them as King Henry II and his queen, Matilda (apparently the 'traditional' identification); see C. Spence, *A Walk through Rochester Cathedral* [London 1840], 4, who saw stylistic connections with sculptures at Vézelay (Yonne) and Fontevrault (Maine-et-Loire) so strong that if the sculptures were 'not themselves imported, one must believe that their chiseller learned his skill at small remove from the Cluniac ateliers of central France.' E.S. Prior and A. Gardner, *An Account of Medieval Figure Sculpture in England* (Cambridge 1912), 194 and 201–2, accepted the nave as a work of Ernulf, but thought the decorative sculpture was added to the façade after the 1137 fire, with the column figures (along with the tympanum and archivolts) much later insertions, ca. 1180. A. Gardner, *A Handbook of English Medieval Sculpture* (Cambridge 1935), 9, 93, and 95, identified the Rochester figures as Solomon and the Queen of Sheba (this identification of the figures was first proposed by W.R. Lethaby in W.H.St.J. Hope, 'The Imagery and Sculptures on the West Front of Wells Cathedral with Suggestions as to the Identification of Some of the Images [by W.R. Lethaby],' *Arch.* 59 [1905], 182; he considered the portal sculpture an offshoot of the Chartres school, via Le Mans or Angers); finding them similar to the figures at Chartres and Le Mans, although the draperies looked a little more 'primitive,' Gardner dated them a little later than 1140, but not as late as 1180 (repeated in A. Gardner, *English Medieval Sculpture* [Cambridge 1951], 82). T.S.R. Boase, *English Art, 1100–1216* (Oxford History of English Art: Oxford 1953), 206, accepted the figures as insertions and likened them to those at Saint-Denis or Chartres. G. Zarnecki, *Later English Romanesque Sculpture, 1140–1210* (London 1953), 39, also considered the column figures to be insertions, but dated them to ca. 1175; he speculated that they may have been carved by one of the Frenchmen working on the rebuilding of the Canterbury choir. L. Stone, *Sculpture in Britain: The Middle Ages* (Harmondsworth 1955), 85, like others before him, considered the column figures, which were 'evidently copied from those at St. Denis – and the earliest

series on the Portail Royal at Chartres of *c.* 1145–1150,' as insertions, carried out after 1150, but not later than 1160; he regarded them as stylistically different from the tympanum above. Later, Zarnecki, in 'The Transition from Romanesque to Gothic in English Sculpture,' in *Studies in Western Art*, I, *Romanesque and Gothic Art* (Princeton 1963), 155, accepted the column figures as original but retained a date of ca. 1175; this date was eventually revised by him to ca. 1160, on the basis of a comparison with a fragment from a lintel at Dover Priory (dedicated in 1160): 'A 12th Century Column Figure of the Standing Virgin and Child from Minster-in-Sheppey, Kent,' in A. Rosenauer and G. Weber, eds, *Kunsthistorische Forschungen Otto Pächt zu seinen (Ehren) 70 Geburtstag* (Salzburg 1972), 212, nn. 20 and 21. Kahn, 'West Doorway,' 131 n. 24, thought the female figure at Rochester was so close to that on the south jamb of the central portal at Chartres as to be 'a direct copy or a derivative example.' Finally, S. Bliss, 'A Question of Identity? The Column Figures on the West Portal of Rochester Cathedral,' *Arch. Cant.* 112 (1993), 167–91, favoured their identification as Solomon and Sheba, and considered them stylistically dependent upon the column figures (before 1152) from the destroyed collegiate church of Notre-Dame at Corbeil (Essonne), rather than those of Chartres. Actually, compared to the French examples, be they those at Chartres, Corbeil, or Le Mans, the Rochester figures are stylistically very distinctive: the French examples are characterized by numerous vertical folds to their garments and a near straight exterior silhouette. In contrast to this vertical rigidity, the Rochester figures are characterized by the appearance of gently undulating curves to their drapery and outline. There is a similarity to certain figures at Saint-Denis in the way the drapery, by means of tiered U-shaped folds flanking centred vertical folds, emphasize the separateness of the legs. For the Saint-Denis figures, see W. Sauerländer and M. Hirmer, *Gothic Sculpture in France 1140–1270* (London and New York 1972), 380–1 and ill. 1–3.

126 For Lincoln, see Zarnecki, *Romanesque Sculpture at Lincoln*, 18–19 and fig. 28a, or *Romanesque Lincoln*, 32–4 (ca. 1145–55).

127 For Minster-in-Sheppey, see Zarnecki, 'A 12th Century Column Figure,' 208–14; and Kahn, 'Romanesque Architectural Sculpture,' 139–40.

128 And for Colchester, see A.J. Sprague, '(Proceedings of the Committee:) Arch at Colchester,' *Jnl BAA* 1 [1846], 143; Gardner, *English Medieval Sculpture*, 81, n. 1; and G. Zarnecki, 'The Sculptures of the Old Moot

Hall, Colchester,' in P. Crummy, ed., *Aspects of Anglo-Saxon and Norman Colchester* (Colchester Archaeological Report, 1 [Council for British Archaeology, Research Report, 39]: London 1981), 63–7. Newman, *West Kent*, 45, with reference to the Rochester column figures, mentioned a shaft, reused in a sedilia at Bobbing (Kent), with two figures (Saint Martial and a deacon) only ten inches (25.4 cm) high (ca. 1190); but it really relates to a different tradition, for the figures are carved on two flat surfaces at right angles: see Newman, *North East and East Kent*, 147 and pl. 23.

129 Prior, *History of Gothic Art*, 133: 'the style at Rochester was but a small remove from the arrangement and style common to the Angevin dominion of the English crown.' Prior and Gardner, *An Account*, 198–9, compared the figure of Christ to the seated figures of the façade of Notre-Dame-la-Grande, Poitiers, which they dated ca. 1180; therefore, they considered the tympanum at Rochester to have been inserted after the 1177 (*sic*) fire; they further noted that the use of portal tympana was not a west French characteristic and consequently drew a parallel with the *composition* of the south portal at Le Mans. The same parallels were repeated by Gardner, *Handbook*, 91, and *English Medieval Sculpture*, 81. Boase, *English Art*, 205, continued the tradition that the tympanum was inserted after 1177, although he pointed out there was no sign of fire damage to the west front. Stone, *Sculpture in Britain*, 85, advanced the date for the insertion of the tympanum (as with the column figures) to ca. 1150 (erected on earlier jamb orders of the 1130s); because he detected Burgundian influence in the drapery style, he considered the tympanum to be stylistically distinct from the column figures. Zarnecki, *Later English Romanesque*, 39, also accepted the tympanum (as he did the column figures), as an insertion of ca. 1175; he, however (in contrast to Stone), saw the tympanum stylistically close to the Île-de-France but the *iconography* Burgundian; in a later paper, 'English 12th-Century Sculpture and Its Resistance to St. Denis,' in F. Emmison and R. Stephens, eds, *Tribute to an Antiquary: Essays Presented to Marc Fitch by Some of His Friends* (London 1976), 87, he hinted at a slightly different source: 'likely the portal was not derived from St. Denis but rather modelled on one of its derivatives in or near Beauvais.' Curiously, Kahn, 'West Doorway,' 131, felt compelled to insist that Prior and Gardner's comparison (*An Account*, 198) of the style of the tympanum Christ (and the lintel) to sculpture at Notre-Dame-la-Grande, Poitiers, had no validity, although that appraisal had long been dismissed by both Stone

and Zarnecki. For the most recent assessment, see Kahn, *Canterbury Cathedral*, 135: the *Majestas* tympanum and the column figures were probably derived from north French examples reflecting the developments in the Île-de-France.

130 Prior and Gardner, *An Account*, 198, first compared the voussoirs (and tympanum) to the sculpture of the Poitou, noting especially the same ornamental and foliage types at Notre-Dame-la-Grande, Poitiers, possibly due to the hand of 'some Continental sculptor.' Gardner, *Handbook*, 91 and *English Medieval Sculpture*, 81, noted especially that the ornament of the inner archivolt, consisting of half-leaf/half-bird motifs, was common in the Poitou and Charente, yet again singling out Notre-Dame-la-Grande. Boase, *English Art*, 206, pointed to the 'curious pattern of birds bending back their heads,' a motif common in the Aquitaine, yet again referring to Notre-Dame-la-Grande (which he dated to the mid-12th century). Zarnecki, *Later English Romanesque*, 39, specifically accepted the Poitevin character of the voussoirs as first recognized by Prior and Gardner, 195–201, but he re-dated them to ca. 1160 since a date of 1180 for Notre-Dame-la-Grande was no longer accepted, it having been re-dated to ca. 1130; he separated the voussoirs from the tympanum, as he did not accept a Poitevin style for the latter; instead, he linked it stylistically to the Île-de-France, and dated it to ca. 1175); 1160 represented 'the approximate date of the completion of the nave [of Rochester].' Zarnecki re-emphasized the Poitevin character in 'Transition,' 154 ('pure Pointevin [sic] tradition') and in 'Sculptures of the Old Moot Hall,' 63 ('south-west of France'). Stone, *Sculpture in Britain*, 85, also mentioned the distinctive birds with bent-back necks and upturned tail feathers 'as at Poitiers.' Zarnecki, 'English 12th-century Sculpture,' 87, first remarked that the voussoirs were in a 'pre-Saint-Denis tradition' (Zarnecki, *Romanesque Art* [New York 1971], 82 and pl. 91 [caption]), and then attributed the non-radiating arrangement of voussoir motifs at Saint-Denis and following Early Gothic portals to the introduction of what might be called the 'circumferential' mode in western France (Poitou, Saintonge), ca. 1130–5. Kahn, 'West Doorway,' 130 and 132, argued that the similarity of the sculpture of the west front (by which she meant the portal voussoirs) to that of western France had been exaggerated; she pointed out that the radial arrangement of motifs on voussoirs had gone out of fashion in the Poitou, ca. 1135 (following Zarnecki, *Romanesque Art*, 82); while admitting radiating voussoirs rarely appeared in the Early Gothic of the Île-de-France – noting only

their sporadic use in the Vexin and Beauvaisis, she placed emphasis on their appearance on the portal at Saint-Ours, Loches, ca. 1165. Loches is in Touraine, directly north of the Poitou, so it would seem the latter region accounts for the appearance of the radiating voussoirs at Saint-Ours; as Kahn, ibid., n. 34, pointed out, A. Henwood-Reverdot (*L'église Saint-Étienne de Beauvais* [Beauvais 1982], 146), had made a 'convincing case' for the relationship of the archivolts of Saint-Étienne's north portal (only the outer order is radiating) to Ruffec (Charente). Stylistically, Kahn made a limited number of comparisons of a few motifs at Rochester (as pointed out above, nn. 29–34), to Saint-Denis, Bruyères, and Loches (pls. 3–8 and 12–14): the motifs are similar, but I fail to see any stylistic similarity. In Kahn, *Canterbury Cathedral*, 135, the connection of some Rochester capitals with the Sens region or north France and Flanders (Villiers-Saint-Paul and Cambrai) is stressed.

131 Kahn, 'West Doorway,' 130 and n. 21, quite unfairly, I think, dismisses my paper ('Significance'), which was primarily concerned with the *architectural* form of the façade, on the grounds that it 'reiterates old misapprehensions concerning the carving.' This judgment was based on *two sentences* in my paper in which I made reference to the west French character of the voussoirs, citing Prior and Gardner, *An Account*, 198, who had first made this connection, because it had been subsequently accepted without qualification by Zarnecki – who had fully acknowledged them on more than one occasion. Thus, at the time my paper was in preparation (1982) and published (1983), I was following the most respected authority, G. Zarnecki. Therefore, my and Zarnecki's 'misapprehensions' about the sources of the voussoirs remained to be corrected by the research of Kahn herself, only published in 1987. However, I think her insistence on the non-Poitevin, Île-de-France influences in the portal voussoirs (and capitals) is overstated and not the final solution of this complex group of sculpture.

132 Zarnecki, *Later English Romanesque*, 39, seems to be the only authority to have mentioned the small tympana: he pointed to their use over blind niches at Parthenay-le-Vieux. Kahn, 'West Doorway,' 130–2, in her attempt to discount west French influence on the 'west front,' made no mention of them (but cf. her, 'Romanesque Architectural Sculpture,' 123 and 125).

133 See McAleer, 'Significance,' 157–8 and pls. IVA and B.

134 Stone, *Sculpture in Britain*, 84, dated the shafts to the 1130s on the basis of the 'East Anglian binding knots,' and the interlace and scroll capitals.

135 Prior and Gardner, *An Account*, 195, are perhaps the only ones until
     recently to have remarked upon the style of the capitals (and corbels,
     etc.). They found the nearest analogy in the Poitou and Charente,
     especially in the west fronts of Angoulême Cathedral (Charente) and
     the Abbaye-aux-Dames at Saintes (Charente-Maritime), the cloister
     capitals of Saint-Aubin, Angers (Maine-et-Loire), and, finally, the west
     front of Notre-Dame-la-Grande in Poitiers. Kahn, 'West Doorway,'
     131, while not commenting specifically on this attribution of Prior and
     Gardner (having attacked them previously over the tympanum Christ),
     compared four of the capitals (as noted above, nn. 29–32) to individual
     examples at Saint-Denis, and the cathedrals of Chartres, Sens, and
     Bourges.

136 The curious construction of the lintel, a flat arch with interlocking
     vertical joints, was noted by S. Smirke, 'Observations on the Mode
     Adopted by Masons at Various and Distant Periods in Forming a
     Straight Head over an Aperture,' *Arch.* 27 (1838), 384 and pl. XXVII,
     no. 4. A lintel, possibly from a portal of the priory church of St
     Martin at Dover, was constructed exactly the same way: see C.R.
     Haines, *Dover Priory* (Cambridge 1930), 159 and pl. XVIc; Kahn,
     'Romanesque Architectural Sculpture,' 135 and 'West Doorway,' 133
     and pl. 20.

137 From the above presentation it can be seen that there is no published
     account that presents a thorough analysis of the style, iconography,
     and *composition* of *all* the sculpture of the west front (*pace* McAleer,
     'Significance,' 149).

     Despite the numerous (and varied) foreign parallels for the type and
     style of some of the sculpture, several authors have insisted upon their
     overriding English character: e.g., Prior and Gardner, *An Account*, 201
     and 202; Stone, *Sculpture in Britain*, 85. On the other hand, F. Saxl
     omitted the Rochester portal sculpture from his *English Sculptures of
     the Twelfth Century*, H. Swarzenski, ed. (London 1954), 'as he felt
     they were merely imitations of French work' (p. 15).

138 For the architecture of the west front see McAleer, *Romanesque
     Church Facade*, 296–304; 'Significance,' 139–58; and 'West Front,'
     23–36.

139 G. Fleury, *La cathédrale du Mans* (Petites monographies des grands
     édifices de la France: [1908?]), 78–82; F. Salet, 'La cathédrale du Mans,'
     Cong. arch. 119: *Maine* (1961), 34–7; McAleer, 'Significance,' 152. *Pace*
     Kahn, 'West Doorway,' 131 n. 21, this comparison of the *architectural*
     form of the west front to the west front of Le Mans Cathedral was *not*
     first made by Prior and Gardner, *An Account*, 194–202.

140 The façade of the aisleless church at the Benedictine nunnery founded by Gundulf, ca. 1090, in Malling probably dates from 1160–80. It is a design derived from the cathedral façade: possibly a central portal (the existing portal is 'late'; there is no trace of a Romanesque portal), possibly flanked by niches (the entire central section was thickened ca. 1740–69), with false stair-towers at the angles bearing registers of arcading. The details of the last-mentioned feature provide evidence of the late date. See McAleer, *Romanesque Church Facade*, 743–8; and Newman, *West Kent*, 602, ca. 1190 (but he dated the lowest two tiers as 'clearly late C11').

141 For the development of the 'Salisbury type' screen façade, see McAleer, *Romanesque Church Facade*, 291–311 (chap. 5: 'The Screen Facade') and 'Particularly English?' 128–37.

142 Pamela Z. Blum, 'Liturgical Influences on the Design of the West Fronts at Wells and Salisbury,' *Gesta* 25/1 (1986), 145–50

143 There is a similar passageway in the twin-tower west front of Lichfield Cathedral (Staffordshire). It is enclosed like that at Wells, and opens to the exterior through small slit windows effectively hidden by the (restored) sculpture in the low arcade between central portal and west window: see J.P. McAleer, 'The West Front of Lichfield Cathedral: A Hidden Liturgical Function?' *Friends of Lichfield Cathedral: Fifty-Second Annual Report* (1989), 26–9.

   Scott, when he was restoring Lichfield, apparently observed this passageway and its similarity to the ones at Salisbury and Wells; he was, however, puzzled as to their purpose: see J.T. Irvine, 'Peterborough Cathedral: An Attempt to Recover the First Design of the West Front of the Abbey Church Dedicated to St. Peter, now the Cathedral,' *Jnl BAA* 49 (1893), 149 n. 1 ('There exists a curious passage in the thickness of the [west] wall [at Peterborough], which in the opinion of the late Sir Gilbert Scott, practically corresponded, though in a different position, to those singular ones found through the west walls of Wells, Salisbury, and Lichfield Cathedrals, presenting no openings from such passage into the naves. Sir Gilbert was at a loss to discover their object').

144 For Lindisfarne, see J.P. McAleer, 'A Note about the Reconstruction of the West Portal-Porch of Lindisfarne Priory,' *Durham Archaeological Journal* 3 (1987), 9–13.

145 For Colchester, see McAleer, 'Particularly English?' 137–40.

146 To recapitulate, the aisled crypt and choir, ending in a straight eastern wall with a small projecting chapel, was accepted as late eleventh

century by (in addition to Hope) Prior, *History of Gothic Art*, 63 and
fig. 35 (p. 74); F. Bond, *An Introduction to English Church Architecture*, 2 vols. (London 1913), I, 134 and *Gothic Architecture in England*
(London 1905), 652; and Gem, 'Origins of Early Romanesque,' 548. It
was assigned to the early twelfth century (Ernulf) by Clapham, *English
Romanesque Architecture*, II, 24 and 66; Boase, *English Art*, 60; and
M.F. Hearn, 'The Rectangular Ambulatory in English Medieval Architecture,' *Jnl SAH* 30/3 (1971), 201. Most eccentrically, it was identified
as (mostly) post-1137 work by Fairweather, 'Gundulf's Cathedral,' 205
(who also dated the west bays of the crypt, clearly late eleventh century, to the period of Ernulf). Webb, *Architecture in Britain*, 79, was
more cautious: 'the evidence for the earlier form of the eastern part of
the church is ambiguous, though it is clear that some extension was
built in the course of the 12th century.'

147 Ernulf, if he had indeed made an alteration to the east end, might
more logically have been expected, on the basis of his association not
only with Canterbury, but also with Saint-Lucien, Beauvais, where he
had been a monk, to have introduced an ambulatory plan, possibly
with an axial (tower) chapel. For Saint-Lucien see M. Aubert, 'A propos
de l'église abbatiale de Saint-Lucien de Beauvais,' in M. Kühl and
L. Grodecki, eds, *Gedenkschift Ernst Gall* (Berlin and Munich 1965),
51–8 and figs. 28 and 29. For the 'Glorious Choir' at Canterbury,
which he initiated, see above, n. 78.

148 This alternative is similar to the proposal of Fairweather, 'Gundulf's
Cathedral,' 205, except for the important factor of his attribution of
the existing west bays of the crypt to Ernulf, as well as a good deal of
the solid side walls of the present choir.

149 Stubbs, ed., *Historical Works of Gervase*, I, 292; 'Quarto idus Aprilis,
feria scilicet tertia post octavas Paschae, eidem Rofensi ecclesiae triste
accidit incommodum. Nam ipsa ecclesia Sancti Andreae cum officinis
suis, cum ipsa civitate, igne consumpta est et in cinerem redacta.'

150 It seems almost *de rigeur* for chronicles of fires to claim sweeping
destruction as their consequence. At Worcester in 1147, 'the whole
town together with the church were burnt' (R.R. Darlington, ed., *The
Vita Wulfstani of William of Malmesbury* [Camden Society, 40: 1928],
106: 'Tota ciuitas simul et ecclesia conflagrauit'). Or again, Matthew
Paris reported that the fire of 1187 in Chichester, 'consumed the
Mother Church and the whole town' (F. Madden, ed., *Matthaei
Parisiensis, monachi sancti Albani Historia Anglorum, sive, ut vulgo
dicitur, Historia minor. item, ejusdem abbreviatio chronicorum*

Angliae, 3 vols. [RS, 44: London 1866–9], I, *A.D. 1067–1189*, 443: 'Mater ecclesia Cicestrensis cum tota civitate').

151 BL, Cotton MS Vespasian A.XXII, ff. 30[29]v–31[30]r: 'mclxxix. Roffensis ecclesia cum omnibus officinis et tota urbe infra et extra muros secundo combusta est. iii. Id. Aprilis.' BL, Cotton MS Nero D.II, f. 118[117]r, gives the year as 1177: Wharton, ed., *Anglia Sacra*, I, 345.

152 *Pace* Hope (1900), 35, who reported: 'The lower parts of the Norman piers in the nave, and of the west end, shew plainly by their scorched and reddened surfaces the action of the burning roof that had fallen to the floor.' However, I have not been able to detect any scorched and reddened surfaces on the nave piers or west front.

153 Hope (1881–5), 222 and (1900), 35 and figs. 8, 9, and 10 (on 36). (According to Hope [1881–5], 222, when the transept was rebuilt by the 'Canterbury' architect, 'its previous narrow width was not increased,' as was evidenced by 'the straight joint of the angle quoins in the south wall.' For this line of quoins, see above, chap. 3, pp. 38–9, and fig. 59).

154 Thorpe, ed., *Registrum Roffense*, 633, 'fecit claustrum nostrum perfici lapideum.'

155 In RMSC, DRc/Emf 77/27, 'January 1876: Rochester Cathedral – Excavation for laying of gas pipes.'

156 During the decade my research on Rochester has been in progress, Tatton-Brown has several times made brief comments to this effect in print: see *The Great Cathedrals of Britain* (London 1989), 84; 'Observations Made in the Sacrist's Checker Area beside "Gundulf's" Tower at Rochester Cathedral – July 1989,' *Arch. Cant.* 107 (1989), 392; and recently, at slightly greater length, in 'The Eastern Crypt of Rochester Cathedral,' *Friends of Rochester Cathedral: Report 1996/7* (1997), 19–20; echoed by Worssam, 'Guide to the Building Stones,' 29 (crypt dates from the 1190s). We have, however, arrived at this possibility independently.

CHAPTER 5 **The Early Gothic Rebuilding**

1 In general, for much but not all of what follows, see A. Oakley, 'Rochester Priory, 1185–1540,' in N. Yates, ed., with P.A. Welsby, *Faith and Fabric: A History of Rochester Cathedral, 604–1994* (Woodbridge 1996), 30– 4.

2 See L. Stephen, ed., *Dictionary of National Biography*, XXI (London 1890), 411.

3 A. Oakley, 'The Cathedral Priory of St. Andrew, Rochester,' *Arch. Cant.* 91 (1975), 50–3; M. Brett, 'The Church at Rochester, 604–1185,' in Yates, ed., *Faith and Fabric*, 27

4 C.R. Cheney, 'King John's Reaction to the Interdict in England,' *Transactions of the Royal Historical Society*, 4th ser., 31 (1949), 129–50, esp. 141

5 It is often said that the cathedral was plundered so thoroughly that not even the host was left on the altar: e.g., A. Ashpitel, 'Rochester Cathedral,' *Jnl BAA* 9 (1854), 279; R.C. Fowler, '[Religious Houses:] Cathedral Priory of St. Andrew, Rochester,' in *VCH: Kent*, II (London 1926), 122. The modern repetitions are based on H. Wharton, ed., *Anglia Sacra*, 2 vols. (London 1691), I, 347 ('[sub anno 1215] ... & depraedata *est* Roffensis Ecclesia, [et tota civitas,] adeo ut nec *pixis* [busta] cum corpore *Christi* [domini] super [magnam] altare [monachorum] remaneret'), but it should be noted that this phrase is not found in Wharton's chief source, BL, Cotton MS Nero D.II ('Annales ecclesiae Roffensis ex historia ecclesiastica Edmundi de Hadenham monachi Roffensis'), f. 129[128]r, but rather in a marginal note to Cotton MS Vespasian A.XXII, f. 32v[31b], with slightly varied wording (as cited above, italicized words omitted, words in brackets added: see W.H.St.J. Hope, *The Architectural History of the Cathedral and Monastery of St. Andrew at Rochester* (London 1900 = *Arch. Cant.* 23 [1898], 194–328, and 24 [1900], 1–85; hereafter Hope [1900]), 116 n. *. See also I.W. Rowlands, 'King John, Stephen Langton and Rochester Castle 1213–15,' in C. Harper-Bill, C. Holdsworth, and J.L. Nelson, eds, *Studies in Medieval History Presented to R. Allen Brown* (Woodbridge 1989), 267–79.

6 I.J. Churchill, 'The See of Rochester in Relation to the See of Canterbury during the Middle Ages,' *Annales Amicorum Cathedralis Roffensis being the Third Annual Report of the Friends of Rochester Cathedral* (1938), 31–7 (repr. *Friends of Rochester Cathedral: Report for 1991/2* [1992], 24–7); Brett, 'The Church at Rochester,' 20–2; Oakley, 'Rochester Priory', 36

7 For the above, see Oakley, 'Rochester Priory,' 45.

8 R.A.L. Smith, 'The Financial System of Rochester Cathedral Priory,' *EHR* 56 (1941), 586–95 (*Collected Papers* [New York and Toronto 1947], 42–53); his conclusions have been qualified by A. Brown, 'The Financial System of Rochester Priory: A Reconsideration,' *Bulletin of the Institute of Historical Research* 51 (1977), 115–20, especially with regard to the severity of the financial crises reported in 1255

(H.R. Luard, ed., *Flores Historiarum*, 3 vols. [RS, 95: London 1890], II, 410: 'Similiter et Rofensis prioratus, inaestimabilibus debitis illaqueatus, se in manus praedicti Johannis et aliorum creditorum obligavit'), which she regarded as temporary.

9 Luard, ed., *Flores Historiarum*, II, 9, sub anno 1201: 'In illo tempore Sanctus Willelmus du Pert martirizatur extra civitatem Roffensem; et in ecclesia cathedrali Roffensi sepelitur, miraculis choruscando.' For his legend see C. Horstman, ed. (Wynken de Worde, ed.), *Nova Legenda* [1516], 2 vols. (Oxford 1901), II, 457–9. Also J.S. Richardson, 'Saint William of Perth and His Memorials in England,' *Transactions of the Scottish Ecclesiological Society* 2/pt. 1 (1906–7), 122–6.

10 BL, Cotton MS Vespasian A.XXII, f. 91[92]v (see below n. 90). Oakley, 'Rochester Priory,' 40: 'The income from the shrine of William of Perth had been absorbed in the vast building programmes of the early years of the century and in acquiring new estates.'

11 The claim that Bishop Lawrence of St Martin secured the canonization of William in 1256 while in Rome is not supported by any existing papal bull: Oakley, 'Rochester Priory,' 38.

12 See P. Draper, 'The Retrochoir of Winchester Cathedral,' *Architectural History* 21 (1978), 13–14.

13 See above, chap. 4, pp. 60–7. More than a century and a half ago, C. Spence, *A Walk through Rochester Cathedral* (London 1840), 10, commented that 'it is well known to the readers of monkish Chronicles that the terms, "igne combusta," "totaliter igne consumpta," and similar phrases were almost invariably applied, however trifling the mischief caused by the fiery element.'

14 The west wall of the east range dates to the rebuilding after the fire of 1137; there is no evidence of rebuilding in the fragments at the north and south ends of the west range. The north walk has completely disappeared: whether damaged by the fire or not, it most probably was rebuilt in response to the changed plan of the church.

15 J. Thorpe, ed., *Registrum Roffense: or A Collection of antient records, charters, and instruments of divers kinds, necessary for illustrating the ecclesiatical history and antiquities of the diocese and cathedral church of Rochester* (London 1769), 633: 'Fecit claustrum nostrum perfici lapideum.' As a specific building is not mentioned, there is always the possibility that he constructed the cloister arcades of which not a trace survive.

16 This part of the cathedral was subject to two major rounds of restoration in the nineteenth century. The first, by Louis Nockalls Cotting-

ham (1787–1847), in two phases: 1825–30, affecting primarily the south arm of the minor transept, the eastern roofs, and the crossing tower, and 1839–40, the interior, especially the choir. It is not well documented: see M.R. Covert, 'The Cottingham Years at Rochester,' *Friends of Rochester Cathedral: Report for 1991/2* (1992), 6–14. The second, between 1871 and 1878, was even more extensive and is more extensively documented. It was carried out under the direction of Sir George Gilbert Scott (1811–78), with James Thomas Irvine (1825–1900) serving as clerk of the works. Brief notices of the progress of the restoration appeared in several architectural journals of the day. *The Builder*: 28/1429 (25 June 1870), 503; 29/1484 and 1492 (15 July and 9 September 1871), 553 and 714; 32/1637 and 1650 (20 June and 19 September 1874), 533 and 797; 36/1855 (26 August 1878), 884 and 886 (organ case). *The Architect*: 6 (22 July 1871), 47 (restoration to begin with nave clerestory windows); 11 (3 January 1874), 14; 12 (26 September 1874), 157 (work in progress in choir and exterior of southwest transept); 18 (8 September 1877), 135 (final accounting: Scott paid £711.16s 6p; Mr White of Vauxhall Bridge Road, London, contractor, paid £5238; Farme & Brindley, sculptors, paid £2833.5s). *Building News*: 21 (1871), 36 and 165; 26 (2 January 1874), 24 (exterior complete; interior of choir still progressing); 28 (18 June 1875), 705 (restoration of choir complete). And by Scott himself: *Personal and Professional Recollections by the late Sir George Gilbert Scott, R.A.* (London 1879), 349–52, for Rochester. In addition, and of greater use and significance, there is Scott's descriptive assessment of the cathedral, before work began, in the RIBA library, ScGGS[159]31, and especially the papers of Irvine, already so frequently referred to in the analysis of the Romanesque work, RMSC, DRc/Emf 77/1–134.

17 Before the restoration by Scott, the east clerestory–level window was a nine-light 'Perpendicular' one; the gable was pierced by a single quatrefoil. The appearance of the east façade was recorded in a watercolour of 1805 by John Buckler (1770–1851): RDCL, Portfolio 15 (NMR, neg. no. AA78/465); see also a pencil drawing of 1804 in the BL, Add. MS 36.368 ('Buckler Architectural Drawings,' vol. XIII, Kent[E-W]-Lancaster), f. 83r. However, ca. 1788, the east gable had been taken down and rebuilt, and the chancel window removed and a new 'Gothic' window inserted: D. Holbrook, 'Repair and Restoration of the Fabric since 1540,' in Yates, *Faith and Fabric*, 196. That window was in turn replaced 'with entirely new work, with the exception of some tracery' in the 1820s during the restoration directed by Cottingham: Holbrook, 204.

The majority of Scott's drawings for the restoration of the presbytery and minor transept, formerly in the RDCL, are now in the RMSC (at the time of writing, they are not catalogued). Most of the drawings are numbered (nos. 1–4, 7–8, and 13, although two without numbers are preserved [nine other drawings – one of three sheets – relate to the reorganization of the choir and its furnishings]) and signed by the contractor, G.P. White. The drawings listed as items nos. 1–5 and 6 in G. Fisher, G. Stamp, et al., *Catalogue of the Drawings Collection of the Royal Institute of British Architects: The Scott Family*, ed. J. Heseltine (Amersham [Bucks] 1981), entry 112, 65, col. 3 (1–5, Contract and working drawings for restoration, ca. 1872; 6–7, Working drawings for restoration) have never been in the RIBA collection. Six of them were photographed by the NMR when they were still in the possession of the cathedral (RMSC, no. 1, east front: NMR, neg. no. BB68/3739 = RIBA, cat no. 112–1).

18 See B.C. Worssam, 'A Guide to the Building Stones of Rochester Cathedral,' *Friends of Rochester Cathedral: Report for 1994/5* (1994), 28. According to Worssam, there is some reused tufa, and the 'dressings' are primarily Chilmark stone, a stone favoured by Scott in his restoration work. Also B.C. Worssam and T. Tatton Brown, 'Kentish Rag and Other Kent Building Stones,' *Arch. Cant.* 112 (1993), 93–125.

19 According to J. Newman, *BE: West Kent and the Weald*, 2nd ed. (1976), repr. & corr. (Harmondsworth 1980), 477, the upper two strings were added by Scott, 'giving the elevation a coherence it may not originally have had.' There is no sign of them in Buckler's 1805 watercolour of the east front (see above, n. 17): Buckler shows only the lower two crossing over the angle stair turrets. There is no corresponding view of the side elevation to indicate whether or not the upper string-courses crossed the stair-turrets and midwall buttress.

20 W.H.St.J. Hope, 'Notes on the Architectural History of Rochester Cathedral Church,' *Transactions of St. Paul's Ecclesiological Society*, 1 (1881–5); hereafter Hope (1881–5), 224, as is still very evident. Scott's drawing of the presbytery north elevation, RMSC, no. 3, also includes the east face of the north minor transept arm.

21 See G.H. Palmer, *The Cathedral Church of Rochester: A Description of Its Fabric and a Brief History of the Episcopal See*, 2nd ed. (Bell's Cathedral Series: London 1899), 97–8, and J. Blair, 'The Limoges Enamel Tomb of Bishop Walter de Merton,' *Friends of Rochester Cathedral: Report for 1993/4* (1994), 28–33.

22 For Scott's drawings of the north arm of the minor transept, RMSC, no number, chapel gable and no. 4, north front, see NMR, neg. nos. BB68/

3742 (= RIBA, cat. no. 112–6) and BB68/3741 (= RIBA, cat. no. 112–3) respectively.

23 Hope (1900), 92 and 167; Palmer, *Cathedral Church*, 32; Covert, 'The Cottingham Years,' 10; Holbrook, 'Repair and Restoration,' 205. Its stability had long been a problem. For the attempts to deal with the structural problems presented by the south arm in the eighteenth century, see S. Denne, 'Memorials of the Cathedral Church of Rochester,' in J. Thorpe, ed., *Custumale Roffense, from the Original Manuscript in the Archives of the Dean and Chapter of Rochester* (London 1788), 169, and Holbrook, 'Repair and Restoration,' 192 and 195: two massive brick buttresses were added in the early 1750s on the advice of Charles Sloane (1690–1764); and, in 1776–8, under the direction of Robert Mylne (1733–1811), the front was further strengthened by bricking up the arches in the east side and in the crypt below. The condition of the façade before Cottingham's work is recorded by engravings in Thorpe, pl. XXXIII, fig. 1 (opp. 151), curiously without the buttresses of 1751; and J. Storer, *History and Antiquities of the Cathedral Churches of Great Britain*, 4 vols. (London 1814–19), IV, [Rochester] pl. 5 ('S. Eastern Trancept [sic] Rochester Cathedral'), with the buttresses. Scott's drawing: RMSC, no number (not signed by G.P. White).

24 An anonymous print (see Hope [1900], fig. 34; J. Myles, *L.N. Cottingham 1787–1847: Architect of the Gothic Revival* [London 1996], 79, fig. 19) shows a doorway with a flat lintel in the east bay (it is not visible in either of the prints mentioned above in n. 23: Thorpe, ed., *Custumale Roffense*, pl. XXXIII, fig. 1 and Storer, *History and Antiquities*, IV, [Rochester] pl. 5) – and only one buttress. The Gothic Revival architect John Loughborough Pearson (1817–97), who directed the restoration of the west front between 1888 and 1894, is said to have re-exposed the old work, which 'Cottingham had covered on the exterior with a copy,' and converted it into a window. Hope seemed to regard the doorway as original: (1900), 167 n. †, and fig. 34 (p. 91).

25 According to Hope (1900), 167, this Decorated window was replaced by Cottingham and later 'beautified' by Pearson, who apparently replicated the original pattern (based on Storer, *History and Antiquities*, IV [1819], [Rochester] pl. 5).

26 In order to reduce the load on the leaning south wall, the gable was taken down in 1768: RMSC, FTv 126 (Holbrook, 'Repair and Restoration,' 194 and n. 69). Its removal had been recommended in RMSC, DRc/Emf 32, an unsigned 'Report of Repairs Absolutely Wanting to be done, 15 July 1760.' It, like all the other gables, was rebuilt to a high

pitch by Scott, who hoped the original roof pitch would be restored over each vessel, but the roofs have never been raised: Hope (1900), 91 and 92. For Scott drawings relating to the roofs of presbytery, 'chancel,' and [minor] transept see RMSC, no. 13 and RIBA, cat. no. 112–7.

27 See plan, Hope (1900), pl. II, and F.H. Fairweather, 'Gundulf's Cathedral and Priory Church of St. Andrew, Rochester: Some Critical Remarks on the Hitherto Accepted Plan,' *Arch. Jnl* 86 (1929), fig. 1 ('B' for later buttress; 'C' for ripped-out buttress) and 208.

28 Under Cottingham, there was a general repair of the transept and choir roofs necessitated by dry rot between 1825 and 1829: see RDCL, (Dean) Robert Stevens (1820–70), 'Repairs to Rochester Cathedral, 1825–26: Mr. Cottingham Architect,' and typescript, 733.3 COT (also RMSC, DRc/Emf 135), 1, 3, 8, 9, and 18.

29 See above, chap. 3, pp. 38–40.

30 According to Hope (1900), 64, almost all of the external ashlar was renewed by Scott who, at the same time, restored the high pitch of the roof and the gable based on evidence from early views: R. Dodsworth and W. Dugdale, *Monasticon Anglicanum* (London 1655), pl. facing 28; an engraving of J. Harris, 'The North Prospect of the Cathedral Church of Rochester,' from the early eighteenth century; a pencil drawing of 1804 (BL, Add. MS 36.368 ['Buckler Architectural Drawings,' vol. XIII], ff. 81v–82r) by J. Buckler for his large engraved views of 1807 and 1810 (see large presentation volume, 'Views of the Cathedral, Abbey and Collegiate Churches of England' [1846], ff. 17 and 18, in the collection of the Society of Antiquaries, London); J.C. Buckler (1793–1894), *Views of the Cathedral Churches of England and Wales with Descriptions* (London 1822), unnumbered pl., 'Rochester Cathedral, N.W.,' dated 1818; and the view by J. Coney, dated 1821, in J. Caley, H. Ellis, and B. Bandinel, eds, W. Dugdale, *Monasticon Anglicanum*, I (London 1817), pl. between 152/3. Scott also gratuitously added the pinnacles that did not appear in any earlier views before the roof was lowered (on the evidence of engravings, between 1807/10 [Buckler] and 1821 [Coney]). See also Palmer, *Cathedral Church*, 51. According to T. Tatton-Brown, Scott used much Chilmark stone for the external repairs and Kilkenny marble for the renewed shafts: see Worssam, 'Guide to Building Stones,' 29.

31 The existing gable was built by Scott, and is his design. According to Palmer, *Cathedral Church*, 51, the original gable was taken down about 1800 and replaced by a 'low, commonplace one.' Holbrook, 'Repair and Restoration,' 195, presents evidence (RMSC, DRc/FTv 132)

that its removal (and rebuilding) dated to 1776. Both these statements appear to be in conflict with the evidence provided by [J.] Buckler's view of the cathedral from the northwest, published in 1810, but based on a drawing done in 1804 (see above, n. 30), in which a high gable, corresponding to a high pitched roof, is depicted, its area filled by three large thinly framed oculi that are tangent to each other, and which appears again in [J.C.] Buckler, *Views*, unnumbered plate. Oculi do appear in the engraving by D. King for Dodsworth and Dugale, *Monasticon Anglicanum*, I, pl. facing 28, and the small engraving that may be based on it by Harris. Both Storer, *History and Antiquities*, IV, pl. 4 (1816), and Coney, in Caley, Ellis, and Bandinel, *Monasticon Anglicanum*, I, pl. between 152/3 (1821), show a lowered roof and altered gable with a small slit window with an ogee label above.

32 Scott's drawing for the west elevation: RMSC, no. 7 (NMR, neg. no. BB68/3743 = RIBA, cat. no. 112–4). For its appearance before Scott's restoration, see the 1804 view of the cathedral from the northwest by [J.] Buckler for his engraving of 1807/10 (see above, n. 30); also [J.C.] Buckler, *Views* (1818) and Coney for Caley, Ellis, and Bandinel, eds, *Monasticon Anglicanum*, I (1817), pl. between 152/3 (1821).

33 Scott's drawing: RMSC, no. 8 (NMR, neg. no. BB68/3744 = RIBA, cat. no. 112–5).

34 The gable on this façade was removed some time in the early nineteenth century, before ca. 1816: Storer, *History and Antiquities*, IV (1819), [Rochester] pl. 6. Hope (1900), 71: 'The old gable was taken down in the early part of the century and replaced by a lower one of debased classical character, flanked by pedestals on the tops of the buttresses.' That in turn was removed by Scott, who based the design of the existing one on the old design as depicted in Thorpe, ed., *Custumale Roffense*, pl. XXXIX (facing 165); Hope (1900), 70–1. The original gable had been reported as 'secure,' and the roof still of a steep pitch, by Daniel Asher Alexander (1768–1846) in November 1799: RMSC, DRc/Emf 38, 'Report on a General Survey of Rochester Cathedral,' sect. 6.

35 Probably the most accurate and informative view is that by [J.] Buckler published in 1810 (cf. [J.C.] Buckler, *Views*, unnumbered plate, 'Rochester Cathedral, N. W.,' dated 1818). The 1821 view by Coney (for Caley, Ellis, and Bandinel, eds, *Monasticon Anglicanum*, I (1817), pl. between 152/3) is less complete and precise. For Cottingham's rebuilding see Covert, 'Cottingham Years,' 7–8 and 10. For the rebuilding in 1904, see F.F. Smith, *A History of Rochester* (London 1928),

289–91, and also pls. 29, 30, and 31; Charles Hodgson Fowler was the surveyor to the cathedral from 1898 to his death in 1910.

36 According to G.M. Livett, 'Early-Norman Churches in and near the Medway Valley,' *Arch. Cant.* 20 (1893), 153–4, 'the Early English choir and transepts' are (predominantly) built of 'firestone' from quarries at Godstone near Reigate (cf. Livett, 'Medieval Rochester,' *Arch. Cant.* 21 [1895], 30–1). This is indeed true, as the distinctive greenish cast of Reigate makes evident; its use continues into the beginning of the reconstruction of the nave arcade. According to T.W.T. Tatton-Brown, ('Building Stone in Canterbury c. 1070–1525,' in D. Parsons, ed., *Stone: Quarring and Building in England, AD 43–1525* [Chichester 1990], 76–7), the use of Reigate or Merstham stone began about 1200 in Canterbury; see above, chap. 4, n. 44 (its use began earlier in north Kent). However, Caen stone was also used: the mixture of the two is especially evident in the south arm of the major transept. See also Worssam, 'Guide to the Building Stones,' 30.

37 These two piers partly occupy the site – as identified by Hope (1900), pl. III – of his purported projecting east chapel of the earlier crypt: see above, chap. 3, pp. 33 and 36–7, and esp. nn. 63 and 64.

38 According to the evidence presented by Hope (1900), 132–3, five of the altars in the crypt were dedicated to Saints Katherine, Mary Magdalene, Michael, Edmund, and Denis, and one to the Holy Trinity.

39 See L. Hoey, 'Pier Alternation in Early English Gothic Architecture,' *Jnl BAA* 119 (1986), 52.

40 Four of the shafts have been replaced with granite ones, and two shafts and nine capitals are of Portland stone: they are all due to the restoration in the 1830s. The bases, shafts, and capitals of three columns in the presbytery section are of Kentish rag and may be a late medieval replacement. For a detailed study of the types of stone originally used in the crypt, and present as a result of restoration, see B.C. Worssam, 'The Building Stones of Rochester Cathedral Crypt,' forthcoming.

41 The mixture of Caen and Reigate stone characteristic of the entire east end begins in the crypt: see Worssam, 'Guide to Building Stones,' 29–30.

42 The points of change are not absolutely symmetrical: they are located near the windows of the north or south end walls of the transept chapels and on the north and west faces of the northeast major pier. In contrast to the latter, only the northeast corner of the string-course of the southeast major pier is Purbeck.

43 Bethersden is also known as Petworth, Sussex, or Wealden marble: geologically it is a large 'paludina' limestone. See A. Clifton-Taylor, 'Building Materials,' in Newman, *West Kent*, 31; Worssam, 'Guide to Building Stones,' 29–30 and esp. 33 n. 32. It is also used in place of Purbeck for some bases, string-courses, etc., in the main level above the crypt. For the Purbeck industry see J. Blair, 'Purbeck Marble,' in J. Blair and N. Ramsay, eds, *English Medieval Industries* (London 1991), 41–56, esp. 47–9, and R. Leach, *An Investigation into the Use of Purbeck Marble in Medieval England*, 2nd ed. (Crediton 1978), 13.

44 Newman, *West Kent*, 52, 'structurally Rochester, with its thick walls and vast clasping buttresses, reverts to Norman traditions.' The presbytery is 28 ft 5 in. (8.6614 m) wide between the wall faces behind the major vaulting shafts; the first string-course is at 10 ft 8 in. (3.2512 m), the abaci of the recess capitals at 19 ft 6 in. (5.9436 m), the clerestory floor at 28 ft 3 in. (8.6106 m), and the top of the capital from which the ribs spring is at 33 ft 11 in. (10.3378 m): Carden & Godfrey Architects, Rochester Cathedral, sheet 130/4 (7 January 1954).

45 Hope (1900), 50, suggested the presbytery wall recesses may have been intended for tombs; three are now so occupied: north side, second bay, Purbeck tomb attributed to Bishop St Martin (d. 1274; buried 'juxta magnum altare a parte boreali' [Wharton, ed., *Anglia Sacra*, I, 351]; Thorpe, ed., *Custumale Roffense*, pl. XLIII, between 192/3); third bay, Purbeck tomb attributed to Bishop Gilbert Glanville (d. 1214; buried 'a parte boreali predicte basilice' [Wharton, I, 347]; Thorpe, pl. XLII, facing 189; Newman, *West Kent*, 482, 'Still Romanesque in feeling'); south side, second bay, Purbeck effigy attributed to Bishop Ingoldsthorpe (d. 1291; buried 'juxta magnum altare ex parte australi' [Wharton, I, 353]; Thorpe, pl. XLIII, between 192/3).

46 The three upper windows are Scott's design, in place of the nine-light 'Perpendicular' window: for Scott's drawing of the east wall, see RMSC, no. 2 (NMR, neg. no. BB68/3740 = RIBA, cat no. 112–2); for the exterior see above, n. 17. There are a number of views of the interior before Scott: a small pencil drawing by G. Gunning, ca. 1840, RDCL (missing; NMR, neg. no. AA77/2448; Palmer, *Cathedral Church*, 87); an unattributed and undated early ?photograph, RDCL (missing; NMR, neg. no. BB68/3499); and an anonymous watercolour, RDCL, Portfolio 15 (NMR, neg. no. AA77/2442).

47 L. Grant ('The Choir of St.-Étienne at Caen,' in E. Fernie and P. Crossley, eds, *Medieval Architecture and Its Intellectual Context: Studies in*

Honour of Peter Kidson [London and Ronceverte 1990], 122) noted the use of a small buttressing strut between the capital and back wall of the passage in the 'west transept' (however, the minor *east* transept – and choir – must have been meant) at Rochester. She advanced such parallels as the east wall of the Chichester retrochoir (begun ca. 1186/7) and Saint Hugh's choir at Lincoln (begun ca. 1192), the source being found in the west wall of the minor transept at Canterbury (1179).

48 The main space of the transept is slightly wider than the presbytery, being 29 ft 4 in. (8.9408 m); the levels of string-courses, abaci, clerestory floor, and vault springing are the same as in the presbytery (see above, n. 44).

49 The room on the south was mostly rebuilt by Cottingham as a result of the extensive work necessary to stabilize the south wall of the minor transept in 1825–30 (see above, n. 16). There is evidence of there having been a pitched roof, as exists over the north room since Scott's restoration, against its west and northern walls. These rooms are sometimes referred to as the 'Treasury' (north) and the 'Indulgence Chamber': e.g., see Palmer, *Cathedral Church*, 87, and Ashpitel, 'Rochester Cathedral,' 282. Spence, *A Walk through*, 18, claimed that the indulgence room was 'where penitents or invalids not wholly worthy or fit to be admitted among the congregation were yet permitted to be auditors of the sacred service.' The north one has recently been converted into a 'lapidarium': see A. Arnold, 'The Lapidarium,' *Friends of Rochester Cathedral: Report for 1990/91* (1990), 21–2.

50 Ashpitel, 'Rochester Cathedral,' 19 and 282, identified this room (on what authority?) as 'the dreaded penance chamber,' describing it as 'a small, groined cell, perfectly dark, and receiving air from above by a small sort of flue; it is approached from the church by a stair in the thickness of the wall.'

51 The ascending staircase was filled up by brickwork by Mylne during his attempt to further stabilize the south front in 1776–8: Holbrook, 'Repair and Restoration,' 195 (RMSC, DRc/FTv 136, 138, and 140).

52 Both stair-vices are constructed in the Romanesque manner, i.e., the steps are supported on barrel vaults rather than being integral with the newel. The same conservative construction has been noted at Canterbury: see D. Parsons, 'Barrel-Vaulted Staircases in England and on the Continent with Special Reference to Brixworth Church, Northamptonshire,' *Zeitschrift für Archäologie des Mittelalters* 6 (1978), 145 and 'The Romanesque Vices at Canterbury,' in N. Coldstream and P. Draper, eds, *Medieval Art and Architecture at Canterbury before 1220*

(BAACT, V [for the year 1979]: [London] 1982), 39–45, esp. 40 and 45. The wooden door to the northeast vice may be reused from some place in the Romanesque building: see J. Geddes, 'Some Doors in Rochester Cathedral,' *Friends of Rochester Cathedral: Report for 1993/4* (1994), 19–22.

53 The choir is 29 ft 1 in. (8.8646 m) wide between the wall faces; the wall shafts begin at a height of 12 ft 2 in. (3.7084 m), the clerestory floor is at 29 ft 9 in. (9.0678 m) and the springing of the vaults at 35 ft 5 in. (10.7950 m): Carden & Godfrey Architects, sheet 130/4.

54 See above, chap. 3, pp. 29, 32–3 and 49. The eleventh-century date of the walls has never actually been ascertained by an examination of the core masonry. There are, however, no known examples of solid choir walls constructed during either the late twelfth or early thirteenth centuries, in the Early English phase of Gothic, so an early date for the full extent of the walls seems quite appropriate. Fairweather, 'Gundulf's Cathedral,' 202–3 and 210, proposed that they were *extended* in the course of the rebuilding that he postulated (205) followed the 1137 fire; according to him, the south wall was actually mostly rebuilt at that time; he provided no archaeological evidence, however, and his suggestion seems most unlikely.

55 The area of the dado between the top of the stalls and the string-course below the arcading is covered by a fourteenth-century painted diaper pattern restored by Scott in 1867: Hope (1900), 111; Smith, *History*, 286. Traces of an earlier thirteenth-century scheme were also found.

56 Hope (1900), 75, accepted the observation of G.M. Livett (1859–1951) that, because of the outward settlement of the south front, 'the entire reconstruction of [the transept's] vault and of parts of the upper works as well' was necessary 'not much more than a century after its building.' However, I could see no stylistic evidence of any such rebuilding, which, if done, was remarkably unsuccessful, as the continued outward lean of the transept front led to its encasement in the early nineteenth century by Cottingham (see above, nn. 16 and 23).

57 According to C.J.P. Cave, *Roof Bosses in Medieval Churches: An Aspect of Gothic Sculpture* (Cambridge 1948), 207, the bosses in the choir are modern, 'except perhaps the eastern one,' but T. Tatton-Brown assures me that both choir bosses, seen at close hand during the recent cleaning of the choir, are original.

58 S. Gardner, *English Gothic Foliage Sculpture* (Cambridge 1927), pl. 89 (the corbel at the east end of the south wall, dated ca. 1220)

59 R. Gem, 'The Origins of the Early Romanesque Architecture of England,' PhD dissertation, Cambridge University 1973, 546, and n. 39 (568) identified the aisle faces of the 'inner' (choir) walls as original, stating that the thirteenth-century shafts simply had been inserted and, in the north aisle, the wall surface cut back to accommodate the thirteenth-century vault wall rib. The latter wall is really only cut back at the east and west ends (more at the east than at the west) where the *fourteenth*-century corbels were inserted in order to support the ribs of the new vault.

60 These traces were uncovered when the aisle was refurbished by Fowler in 1910: RMSC, DRc/Emf 148 and 71/8. According to Hope (1900), 35, 59–60, and 85, the thirteenth-century rebuilding of the exterior aisle wall preserved part of a wall post-dating the fire of 1137 that in turn had been built on top of the wall of Gundulf's aisle, but on a slightly different axis (fig. 25). He claimed it differed in plane and thickness, and that traces of two round-headed windows (which he associated with Bishop Ernulf [1115–24]) in each bay were visible on the exterior; however, I have not been able to detect them: see RMSC, DRc/Emf 77/78 (horizontal section through crypt window by Hope) and 77/83, letter of 23 September 1882 from Hope to Irvine, p. 2 (sketch elevation).

61 For these alterations, see below, chap. 6, pp. 157–8. For the area between the choir north aisle wall and 'Gundulf's' Tower see Fairweather, 'Gundulf's Cathedral,' 208–10, fig. 1, and pl. II; and also J.P. McAleer, 'Rochester Cathedral: The North Choir Aisle and the Space between It and "Gundulf's" Tower,' *Arch. Cant.* 112 (1993), 127–65, esp. 134–44 and 152. Neither Hope nor Fairweather recognized the extent of the fourteenth-century work.

62 The south choir aisle has a width of 25 ft 6 in. (7.7724 m) between the wall faces; the cornice of the ceiling is at a height of 27 ft (8.2296 m) on the north side and 26 ft (7.9248 m) on the south. The north aisle has a 'normal' width of 12 ft (3.6576 m) between the wall faces; the shaft-rings are at a level of 15 ft 10 in. (4.8260 m), and the vault springs at 25 ft 9 in. (7.8486 m): Carden & Godfrey Architects, sheet 130/4.

63 This tall arch may originally have been open and was perhaps later blocked up because of structural problems resulting from the instability of this arm of the minor transept (see above, n. 23). The small doorway now inserted in the arch was formerly in the archway to the aisle from the major south arm: see [H. and B. Winkles,] *Winkles's*

Architectural and Picturesque Illustrations of the Cathedral Churches of England and Wales, 3 vols. (London 1838–42), I (1838), pl. 42, facing 120. It was moved to its present location by Cottingham, ca. 1825: Palmer, *Cathedral Church*, 115; Hope (1900), 75 and 92. See below, chap. 6, pp. 149–50.

64 Hope (1900), 54, considered it part of the original construction, to buttress the thrust of the choir walls. But this is not the case, as it overlies the wall rib of the northwest compartment of the unexecuted vault of the wide section of the aisle.

65 Each of the two eastern arches has a span of 81 inches (205.74 cm), separated by 9 inches (22.86 cm). The west arch is slightly narrower, being approximately 74 inches (187.98 cm) in width.

66 Two areas of wall in the south choir aisle retain vestiges of medieval wall decoration imitating ashlar work. One is high up on the west wall, south of the arch opening into the transept, where there are the remains of six courses of blocks created by single lines executed in reddish pigment with a fleur-de-lis motif in the centre of some. The other area is between the aisle respond and the later buttress on the north wall, above the tomb of Bishop John de Bradfield (1277–83); again, the ashlar blocks are created by a single reddish (or reddish brown) line, but there is no evidence of a central motif. The latter pattern could be said to be centred between its flanking architectural elements and therefore could post-date the tomb.

67 According to Hope (1900), 71–2, the south tower, which – following Irvine (see above, chap. 3, pp. 33–4 and 40) – he theorized Gundulf had built as a pendant to the tower on the north, was torn down ca. 1322. The quoins were considered as the only remnant of the south tower, marking the 'section' of its east side: Hope (1886), 332 and (1900), 17. They were uncovered by Irvine: see RMSC, DRc/Emf 77/133, Notebook no. 2, p. 5 (DRc/Emf 135, p. 4), where he reveals that the 'old quoins as far as could be done were preserved and *some others placed so as to preserve this curious bit of historical information*' (italics added). Irvine thought the 'south' tower had been removed 'at a period prior to the erection of Glanville's stone cloister,' that is, before ca. 1185/1214.

68 The inside of this room is not described in the literature. It must have been created by blocking off the end bay of the west range. See above, chap. 3, p. 39, and esp. n. 77. It was completely restored on the exterior by Scott: see RMSC, DRc/Emf 65/3 and 4, a report from Scott to the Dean and Chapter, 24 November 1875, of work done ('The small

building abutting on the eastern side of this [southwestern] transept has been restored externally and internally fitted up in an inexpensive manner for use as a vestry'). The shafts and bases have been painted in imitation of Purbeck. All of the east wall has been restored; it is mostly filled by two windows with widely splayed jambs. The east wall arch is also restored; its west springing and the west arch are original. The north wall is mostly covered by plaster, except at the bottom where rubble containing flints is visible.

69 As Fairweather, 'Gundulf's Cathedral,' 209, has pointed out, the exterior jambs of this window are still visible.

70 A piscina is located at the south end of the east wall of the chapel: bases, shafts, and moulded capitals of Purbeck support a stone arch; its back wall, with a projecting ledge of Purbeck at the level of the capitals, seems to be a Purbeck slab incised to imitate small ashlar blocks.

The shallow chapel may have been an imitation of a Romanesque predecessor, as there probably was not a strongly projecting eastern chapel in the transept arm of the earlier building for the same inhibiting reason. Such shallow chapels were rare in England: at Horton Kirby, there are two shallow non-projecting chapel-niches in each east wall, and a piscina on the adjoining north or south end wall, with the wall pierced by a lancet: see J.R. Larkby, 'Some Churches in the Darant Valley, I. St. Mary's, Horton Kirby, Kent,' *The Reliquary and Illustrated Archaeologist*, new ser., 11 (1905), 166–9; and Newman, *West Kent*, 335–6 (dated to ca. 1190). Also for French examples see E. Lefèvre-Pontalis, 'Les niches d'autel du XIIe siècle dans le Soissonnais,' *Cong. arch.* 78: *Reims*, 2 vols. (1911), II, 138–45, esp. 140 for examples in transepts. In France, non-projecting ones are also found at Saint-Germer-de-Fly (Oise) (J. Henriet, 'Un édifice de la première génération gothique: L'abbatiale de Saint-Germer-de-Fly,' *B. mon.* 143 [1985], 131–2) and La Trinité, Fécamp (Seine-Maritime) (J. Vallery-Radot, L'église de la Trinité de Fécamp [Petites monographies des grands édifices de la France: Paris 1928], 34).

71 Newman, *West Kent*, 54, noted that foliage capitals 'petered out' in Kent after the 1180s, and that stiff-leaf proper was rare.

72 See chap. 2, pp. 20–1.

73 Yet both arms have the same basic dimensions: each arm is 30 ft 2 in. (9.1948 m) wide between the wall faces behind the major vaulting shafts, the clerestory floors are at 34 ft 3 in. (10.4394 m) and the top of the abaci from which the ribs spring at 39 ft 6 in. (12.0396 m): Carden & Godfrey Architects, sheet 130/3 (23 December 1953).

74 The 'Y' tracery appears in pre-restoration engravings: Storer, *History and Antiquities*, IV (1819), [Rochester] pls. 1 ('Rochester Cathedral from the Canons Gate') and 6 ('S. East View of Rochester Cathedral').

75 Hope (1900), 72 and n.†, considered the tracery to belong to the opening up of the two south windows *after* the demolition of Gundulf's south tower, ca. 1322. But this tower, if it ever existed, must have been demolished to make way for the construction of the west range of the cloister, if not by Bishop Ernulf, then certainly before 1150: see above, chap. 3, n. 70. According to Hope, the tracery was all restored by Scott, 'copied from the remains of the old.' One wonders what could have remained: a view of the church from the southeast, by William Alexander (1767–1816), ca. 1801 (BL, MS Add. 15.966), and a later engraving in Storer, *History and Antiquities*, IV (1819), [Rochester] pl. 6, show the north window was blocked up, the middle one had a dividing vertical mullion only and no tracery, and the third was walled up and pierced by a narrow lancet. Scott, RIBA, ScGGS[159]31, f. 3v, described its condition thus: 'S transept. Interior (later than north) much of it in a good state. Clerestory wids much altered though two sides different the east ones have had tracery one only retains it intelligibly & that is blocked. The other side is intelligible.' Whatever tracery was found was clearly the product of a later alteration.

76 Willis (CUL, Add. MS 5128, f. 7), drew a small rough sketch of the west clerestory and part of the south wall, which appears to confirm that the patterns pre-date Scott's restoration. Scott, RIBA, ScGGS[159]31, f. 3v, referred to its condition as 'intelligible' (see above, n. 75).

77 The present crossing roof, which replaced an eighteenth-century wooden vault (see below, n. 127), was built by Cottingham in 1826, and enriched by him with the addition of plaster bosses in 1840 when he rebuilt the central tower: Palmer, *Cathedral Church*, 29, 33, and 73; Covert, 'Cottingham Years,' 14 n. 20; Holbrook, 'Repair and Restoration,' 205.

78 For the vaults, see below, chap. 6, pp. 154–6.

79 See above, chap. 4, nn. 25–6. There are no *in situ* examples of the small lattice pattern, which dates ca. 1140–50, elsewhere in the building. The date of this buttress is also a puzzle. The Gothic details suggest a date no earlier than the second quarter of the thirteenth century. Why would Romanesque material bearing scorch marks (due to the fire of 1179?) still be available for reuse? Was the material from a Romanesque choir screen only then (ca. 1220/40?) being dismantled?

Or have these blocks been inserted into the buttressing wall at some much more recent period? Hope (1881–5), 225, dismissed the possible function of this infill as a buttress and suggested that it had contained the staircase to the rood-loft.

80 Hope (1900), 67, described these piers as 'essentially decorated.' He attributed them to a new architect, his fifth, who was responsible for the south transept, which he thought followed after the (aborted) work in the nave.

81 The Purbeck shafts, particularly in their lower portion, have been repaired by patching with an orange-toned substance; the upper parts of the shafts are dull and lifeless. The core at some time has been given a coat of greyish plaster or cement, somewhat like the shafts of the east crossing responds.

82 L. Hoey, 'Piers versus Vault Shafts in Early English Gothic Architecture,' *Jnl SAH* 46/3 (1987), 263 n. 106, pointed out that the inclusion of a shaft apparently meant to rise to the nave vaults from the floor was consistent with the attitude towards vertical articulation shown in the eastern parts of the building, even if it was rare at the time.

83 On this pair of piers, shafts and cores have at one time been given a thin coat of greyish 'cement,' which is best preserved on the upper portions, particularly on the north pier. For the southwest Gothic pier, see above, chap. 4, n. 36.

84 BL, Cotton MS Nero D.II, f. 134[133]r, 'Introitus in novum chorum Roffensem': Wharton, ed., *Anglia Sacra* I, 347; O. Lehmann-Brockhaus, *Lateinischen Schriftquellen zur Kunst in England, Wales und Schottland, vom Jahre 901 bis zum Jahre 1307*, 5 vols. (Munich 1955–60), II (1956), 398, no. 3755.

85 BL, Cotton MS Nero D.II, f. 142[141]v, 'Eodem anno dedicata est ecclesia Roffensis a domino R. episcopo ejusdem loci et episcopo de Bangor Nonis Novembris': Wharton, ed., *Anglia Sacra*, I, 349; Lehmann-Brockhaus, *Lateinischen Schriftquellen*, II (1956), 398, no. 3756

86 J. Le Neve, *Fasti Ecclesiae Anglicanae, 1066–1300*, vol. II, comp. D.E. Greenway, *Monastic Cathedrals (Northern and Southern Provinces)*, (London 1971), 79

87 Le Neve, *Fasti*, 79–80; Elias was prior no later than 1218.

88 BL, Cotton MS Vespasian A.XXII, ff. 87v[89v] and 89r[90r], 'Radulfus prior ... fecit magnam ecclesiam tegere, et plurimam partem plumbare. Helyas prior fecit plumbare magnam': Thorpe, ed., *Registrum Roffense*,

122; Lehmann-Brockhaus, *Lateinischen Schriftquellen*, II (1956), 396, no. 3747, and 397, no. 3752

89 BL, Cotton MS Nero D.II, f. 128[127]v, 'Sepultus a parte boreali predicte basilice inter fundatores confundator sieut Saul inter prophetas': Wharton, ed., *Anglia Sacra*, I, 347. His tomb is identified as that now in the third recess on the north side of the presbytery (see above, n. 45 and Hope [1900], fig. 36, and below, n. 112). Hope (1900), 50 and 120, assumed the present location was the original site of burial, but the burial could have been moved, and the attribution of the existing tomb chest to him is based on a stylistic comparison with that of Archbishop Hubert Walter (1193–1205) at Canterbury.

90 Quoted by Willis in Hope (1900), 47, from BL, Cotton MS Vespasian A.XXII, f. 91[92]v, 'Richardus de Eastgate monachus, et sacrista Roffensis, incepit alam borialem novi operis versus portam beati Willelmi, quam frater Thomas de Mepeham fere consummavit. Richardus de Waledene monachus et sacrista, alam australem versus curiam. Willelmus de Hoo sacrista fecit totum chorum a predictis alis de oblationibus sancti Willelmi': Thorpe, ed., *Registrum Roffense*, 125; Lehmann-Brockhaus, *Lateinischen Schriftquellen*, II (1956), 398, nos. 3757 and 3758, and 389, no. 3753.

91 Le Neve, *Fasti*, II, 80

92 Thorpe, ed., *Registrum Roffense*, 99

93 Ibid., 64

94 Ashpitel, 'Rochester Cathedral,' 280–1

95 Hope (1881–5), 223–5

96 Hope (1900), 49: pp. 40–9 present Willis's account of the history; it was derived from a transcript of the (lost) notes made by D.J. Stewart and made available to Hope by him.

97 Hope (1900): (1) 55, 56, and 60; (2) 56; (3) 61, 62, and 66; (4) 66–7; (5) 67; (6) 67 and 69, also 60 and 66; (7) 68; (8) 71; (9) 71–2; (10) 72; (11) 83 and 85

98 Earlier, it will be recalled, Hope (1881–5), 225, had been more specific ('towards the end of the thirteenth century'); Fairweather, 'Gundulf's Cathedral,' 198, produced a date of ca. 1280 for 'the great rebuild' of the south arm.

99 Hope (1900), 71 n. †, and 100–5; an altar to the Virgin may have been one of two altars in this arm before the remodelling of the east wall.

100 In 1995, during work to clear a Victorian drain in the crypt, the top of the foundations was revealed in five trenches along the exterior of the

east and north walls of the presbytery. The most interesting observation (made by the author) is perhaps that the foundation projected about a foot (ca. 0.3048 m) beyond the face of the wall in the trench east of the polygonal buttress [trench 9], and almost 2 feet (ca. 0.6096 m) in the trench west of it [trench 8], in contrast to the face of the foundation being flush with the plane of the wall along the west face of the northeast turret [trench 9] and the east wall [trench 10], as also seemed to be the case under the east wall of the north chapels [trench 8]. Now see A. Ward, 'Excavations at Rochester Cathedral 1990–1995' (Canterbury Archaeological Trust [unpublished archive report – no pagination]: 1997), sect. 5 ('The Cathedral Crypt Trenches. The Cathedral Crypt 1995: The External Trenches'), trenches 8–12 [pp. 19–21], and figs. 10 and 11, and sect. 6 ('Discussion of the Crypt Trenches') [pp. 24–5].

101 Willis, in Hope (1900), 45 (CUL, Add. MS 5128, f. 41), was of the opinion that the part of the crypt underlying the minor transept (which he termed the 'vestibule') was built first, followed by the east chapels and the section under the presbytery – because of the use of wall ribs in these latter parts. Tatton-Brown, 'Eastern Crypt,' 20, accepted Willis's interpretation, which he felt was buttressed by the use of Purbeck in the eastern part of the crypt replacing Bethersden (Wealden) in the cross arm, while noting that it 'was only a constructional change in a continuous sequence of building.'

102 Willis in Hope (1900), 44–5 (CUL, Add. MS 5128, f. 41)

103 According to Scott's memoirs, *Personal and Professional Recollections*, 350, '[t]here is a confusion of design in the windows of this transept, owing to my having left the jambs of some later windows which had been inserted there.' While there is no record of what exactly was replaced, the window of the corresponding chapel in the north arm had been replaced in the fourteenth century by a two-light window with curvilinear tracery and pairs of jamb-shafts. The jamb shafts left by Scott, however, are clearly thirteenth century, not fourteenth, therefore not later insertions, but evidence that the chapels initially had pairs of lancets. Newman, *West Kent*, 479, mistook the presence of limestone, rather than Purbeck, shafts as evidence that 'a revised scheme was toyed with here and abandoned'; but limestone was characteristically originally used for window jamb shafts, Purbeck for vaulting shafts.

104 On the other hand, it may be completely meaningless. Hope (1881–5), 223, however, did initially identify it as evidence of a wooden *ceiling*

('when William de Hoo's building was sufficiently completed to receive a wooden ceiling – of which traces are visible in the north-east transept'). Later, Hope (1900), 50, seemed to associate this with the shrine: 'There are differences of treatment in the upper parts of the walls of this transept, which may indicate that the place of the tomb was covered in before the other parts.'

105 It will be recalled from the discussion in chap. 3, pp. 32–3 and 35–8, that Hope reconstructed such a plan as part of the church begun by Bishop Gundulf (1076/7–1107). Fairweather rejected Hope's dating and suggested that the long flat-ended choir over a crypt was begun by Bishop Ernulf but was not completed until after the fire of 1137. Clapham also rejected Hope's dating; however, he accepted the plan as the result of rebuilding by Ernulf.

106 In Hope (1900), 46 (CUL, Add. MS 5128, f. 44)

107 Hope (1881–5), 224; Palmer, *Cathedral Church*, 12; Hope (1900), 52; Newman, *West Kent*, 479 (N. Pevsner and P. Metcalf, *The Cathedrals of England: Southern England* [Harmondsworth 1985], 240)

108 W.H.St.J. Hope, 'Gundulf's Tower at Rochester, and the First Norman Cathedral Church There,' *Archaeologia* 49 (1886) (hereafter, Hope [1886]), 331 (and Hope [1900], 14), claimed no trace of an eleventh-century south entrance was found when the 'present top step' was taken up: 'had the doorway been there it must have been seen.' Why is not clear, as the upper half of the doorway could have been destroyed in the process of making the new stairs (in the west bay of the crypt aisle). A more thorough, deeper excavation would be needed to come to any firm conclusion.

109 According to Hope (1900), 75, the vaulting shaft in the middle of the west face, conspicuously *not* in Purbeck marble, was a result of later repairs to this arm necessitated by its sinking. This seems to be true because, although the bases (Purbeck) and capitals (limestone with Purbeck abaci) match those of the adjacent arches, the shaft ring has a decidedly different profile.

110 Hope (1900), 167, claimed that the lower part of the *exterior* of the wall showed traces of two large blocked openings with depressed pointed heads: I could not confirm this. Rather rashly, he suggested these blocked arches were formerly 'sunk recesses with trefoil heads like the recess within' and that there were a series of ten, measuring 12 feet (3.6576 m) centre to centre, running the length of the wall east of the early-fourteenth-century (his date) doorway to the cloister. Scott, RMSC, DRc/Emf 77/65/3 (or 4), remarked only: 'The south wall

of the South aisle of the Choir or St. Edmund's chapel, has been also restored. This wall contains externally interesting evidence of the arches of the ancient cloister and internally evidence of arched recesses before invisible.'

111 Ernulf is credited with building the chapter house, dormitory, and refectory; his work underlies the existing remains of the east and south ranges of the cloister: see above, chap. 4, nn. 3, 57, and 77. Bishop Gilbert is credited with having made the cloister of stone (see above, n. 15); this unspecified work might have been the construction of the cloister arcades, although Hope (1900), 106, appeared to think that these two arches belonged to Gilbert's work. The wall in question would have been a screen wall linking the east and west ranges of the cloister, separating the space of the garth from the south choir aisle wall of the Romanesque church. The function of the two nearly contiguous segmental arches in the context of this wall is obscure.

112 Hope (1900), 106, suggested that the arch in the south aisle – along with the two semicircular ones – may have formed part of the 'stone cloister' built by Bishop Gilbert. It is tempting to identify this tomb recess (69 inches / 175.26 cm wide) with the burial of Gilbert were it not for the fact that he is recorded as having been being buried on the north side of the church: perhaps the tomb recess (99 inches / 251.46 cm wide) in the dark north aisle may be associated with his burial. This location would seem to be more in keeping with the negative comments made by the chronicler regarding him than a location in the presbytery (see BL, Cotton MS Nero D.II, f. 128v[127b]: Hope [1900], 120 n.‡): there is no evidence that the remains of the sarcophagus (85.5 inches / 217.17 cm long at base) associated with him now on the north side of the presbytery (see fig. 63, in the west bay) is either *in situ* or actually Gilbert's (see above, nn. 45 and 89).

113 For the west range see above, chap. 3, pp. 38–40 and nn. 69–81.

114 C. Wilson in Newman, *West Kent*, 480 n. * (Pevsner and Metcalf, *English Cathedrals*, 242), offered a different reading: he suggested that a double aisle was originally intended, but that 'the blocking of the E arches and the compromise roof were expedients employed *when the solid choir walls were built*' (emphasis added). Even disregarding the fact that it is difficult to accept the solid choir walls as originating in the early thirteenth century, there is no doubt that the 'compromise roof' dates to the fourteenth; thus Wilson's interpretation has to be rejected because it fails to recognize these features as the work of three different periods.

115 Denne, 'Memorials,' in Thorpe, ed., *Custumale Roffense*, 168, identi-
fied the stone in the new work as 'Petworth' (cf. [S. Denne and W.
Shrubsole,] *The History and Antiquities of Rochester and Its Vicinity*
[Rochester 1772], 66), the stone also known as Bethersden, Sussex, or
Wealden marble (see above, n. 43); however, Purbeck dominates.

116 Also see Hope (1900), 60 fig. 21.

117 Hope (1900), 60, also doubted that the north aisle was vaulted in the
thirteenth century.

118 See below, chap. 6, pp. 158–9.

119 See below, n. 186.

120 See Hope (1900), 56 and figs. 18 (plan of northeast pier), 19, and 20
(profiles of base). The bases of the north respond of the north aisle
arch and some of the bases of the east crossing responds, on both the
north and south, have been patched and/or painted in imitation of
Purbeck.

121 They have been coated with a pale lilac-coloured plaster or cement.
Where this coating has fallen away on the lower parts of the shafts,
the true nature of their material is revealed. It is difficult to tell, even
with the aid of opera glasses, if the material of the shaft-rings is
Purbeck or not.

122 Here again the bases of the four north shafts and the six south shafts
have been painted to resemble Purbeck. The paint is well preserved,
but where the bases are chipped, their material is revealed to be
limestone.

123 As the lower part of these shafts can be inspected at eye-level, there is
no doubt they are of Purbeck.

124 The arrangement is not symmetrical, as the sequence is (from transept
into aisle): L, P, L (which may be a modern replacement), P.

125 Hope (1900), 60, attributed the western bases of the north and south
arches of the projected central tower (and perhaps those of its western
arch), together with those of the north and south responds of the arch
into the north aisle of the nave and the north respond of that into the
south aisle, to the architect of the north choir aisle.

126 The chamfered axial element of the east crossing arch responds can be
seen from inside the choir screen. This is done more easily on the
south side, but a glimpse of the north one can also be obtained.

127 The shafts of the west crossing piers facing the nave are very abused.
Some look as if they are indeed Purbeck patched with the same orangy
substance used on some of the shafts of the first pair of Gothic piers in
the nave (see above, n. 81). Others may be replacements.

Just when this rather deceptive work on the shafts and bases of the crossing piers was carried out is not known. As Hope (1900), 60, mentioned that the pier bases were painted in imitation of Purbeck, it presumably was done during one of the nineteenth-century restorations. James Savage (1779–1852), in his report on the condition of the central tower, in March 1826, RMSC, DRc/Emf 53 (typescripts: DRc/Emf 135 and RDCL, 733.3 COT, p. 14), described the crossing piers as being faced with Caen stone, the small 'columns' thereon of 'Caen-stone, Firestone, Purbeck,' with repairs of Portland stone. Alexander, in RMSC, DRc/Emf 38, 'Report on a General Survey of Rochester Cathedral' (November 1799), noted, not at all approvingly, that the four main piers of the tower were painted marble: 'real marble itself would perhaps not be the best coloured stone for this purpose – the resemblance is still worse.' This work might have been done when the crossing was redecorated in 1730/31. At that time, the bell ringers' gallery was finally removed and a new ceiling designed in the classical style by the London architect John James (ca. 1672–1746) was placed under the crossing (Alexander thought that 'the central ornament round the bell hole ... made in the grecian stile of Architecture' was 'particularly disgusting'): see Holbrook, 'Repair and Restoration,' 190–1 (DRc/Emf 19 and 20/2 and 3). This work was removed by Cottingham in 1826: see above, n. 77.

According to Palmer, *Cathedral Church*, 33, it is to Cottingham that we owe 'a final cleaning from whitewash of the Purbeck marble shafts throughout the building.' According to the anonymous authors of the *History and Antiquities of Rochester*, 63, n. †, 'The church was white-washed in 1743–4, when the choir was repaired and beautified.' Cottingham worked in the area twice, first when he inserted a new ceiling under the tower, ca. 1826, and secondly when he rebuilt the upper stages of the tower, ca. 1840. It may be that it was on one of those occasions that the Purbeck shafts were 'restored.' During a recent visit to Christ Church, Canterbury, the Surveyor to the Fabric, John Burton, pointed out to me that all the shafts in the choir and presbytery have been given a coating of a purplish 'plastic' substance, some time in the mid-nineteenth century he thought.

I am indebted to T. Tatton-Brown for looking at the shafts in the crossing with me and pointing out what had happened to them to give them such a peculiar colour.

128 In his report about the condition of the central tower, Savage, in March 1826 (RMSC, DRc/Emf 53, and typescript, DRc/Emf 135 and

RDCL, 733.3 COT, p. 14), observed that the core of the piers, which had been cut into in two places, was composed of flint and mortar of an extraordinary quality. The foundation of the southwest pier was found to be of the same construction and described as 'hard as rock itself.' He compared this with work in the Castle that he thought to be Gundulf's and that he found also to be 'as firm as if cut out of rock.' Can these observations be taken to confirm that the core of the piers is indeed Romanesque – close to the period (1127–36) of Archbishop William of Corbeil's work in the castle?

129 According to Newman, *West Kent*, 478 (Pevsner and Metcalf, *Cathedrals of England*, 239), the tracery in the *west* clerestory was of the 'Y' type 'before Scott's restoration.' This statement is in conflict with the evidence provided by the Willis sketch (see above, n. 76).

130 The date of and parallels for the tracery are discussed below, pp. 139–40.

131 Hope (1900), 69, 72, and n. †, considered that the altar niche (and the east clerestory tracery design, for it was about this time, he thought, that the hypothetical south tower he attributed to Gundulf was finally pulled down, thus allowing the east clerestory to be glazed) to be of ca. 1322, about which time certain sources suggested to him that a chapel of the Virgin Mary had been newly constructed. On the other hand, in Newman, *West Kent*, 481 n. * (Pevsner and Metcalf, *Cathedrals of England*, 242), it is noted that Pevsner (NP) thought 'the blocked doorway in the choir aisle ... together with the partly preserved lancet [in the S aisle wall], can only mean that the large arch in the [S] transept was built as part of a plan not carried on with and so left filled in against a future knocking out.'

132 Hope (1900), 71, claimed that the material of the voussoirs and shafts was reused from the two original arches.

133 Newman, *West Kent*, 478 (Pevsner and Metcalf, *Cathedrals of England*, 239), dated the *east* clerestory tracery to 'the last decade or two of the C13.'

134 See below, chap. 6, pp. 154–6.

135 Omitted from this discussion is the 'sleeper wall of chalk blocks' uncovered east of the northwest crossing pier in 1968 (see fig. 4), and identified by C.A.R. Radford, 'Rochester Cathedral: A New Fragment of Pre-Conquest Wall,' *Annales Amicorum Cathedralis Roffensis being the Annual Report of the Friends of Rochester Cathedral* ([May] 1969), 14–15, as dating ca. 1100. As pointed out in earlier discussions of this and an apparently somewhat earlier wall in which it was imbedded (see above, chap. 1, pp. 14–16, chap. 3, p. 41, and chap. 4, pp.

72–3), the reported levels (see chap. 1, p. 16 and n. 61; chap. 3, p. 41 and n. 91; chap. 4, n. 63) suggest that these walls should be asso-ciated with the twelfth and thirteenth centuries respectively, but their fabric as reported cannot be paralleled by any other dated foundations thus far uncovered elsewhere in the building. Therefore, until further excavation, the date and function of these walls would seem of necessity to remain a mystery, outside the realm of constructive speculation.

136 See below, chap. 6, pp. 156–7.

137 F. Bond, *An Introduction to English Church Architecture from the Eleventh to the Sixteenth Century*, 2 vols. (London 1913), I, 155, and *Gothic Architecture in England* (London 1913), 113 and 652; E.S. Prior, *A History of Gothic Art in England* (London 1900), 32; J. Harvey, *The English Cathedrals*, 2nd ed. (London 1956), 167; G. Webb, *Architecture in Britain: The Middle Ages* (Harmondsworth 1956), 79; T.S.R. Boase, *English Art, 1100–1216* (Oxford History of English Art: Oxford 1953), 256, ca. 1210.

138 By those authorities cited above, n. 137.

139 Because of these dates, Hope (1900), 66, dated the north transept arm *after* the consecration of 1240 (1240–55), leaving an unexplained thirteen-year gap in the building history (1227–40).

140 Bond, *Gothic Architecture*, 122 and 652; Harvey, *English Cathedrals*, 167

141 C.W. Previté-Orton, *The Shorter Cambridge Medieval History*, 2 vols. (Cambridge 1960), II, 654–5; W.H. Bliss, ed., *Calendar of Entries in the Papal Registers Relating to Great Britain and Ireland: Papal Letters*, vol. I, *A.D. 1198–1304* (London 1893), 38–40

142 A. Brodie, 'Rochester Cathedral: The Chronology of the East End,' M.A. report, University of London (Courtauld Institute of Art) 1982, 27–8, came to the conclusion that there was no visible caesura at Rochester that could be attributed to the period of the Interdict. He pointed out that none was visible in work at Lincoln, in the Ely west porch, or in the Winchester retrochoir; only perhaps at Wells was work interrupted. He, however, placed the minor transept and presbytery *after* (1217–27) the erection of the choir vaults and aisles (1179 to ca. 1200).

143 See above, nn. 45, 89, and 112.

144 See above, n. 5.

145 Hope (1900), 37, associated these entries with repairs following the fire of 1179. However, if the repairs took over twenty years to complete, they must have been extraordinarily extensive. Moreover, if they

extended into the early thirteenth century, they were either followed hard on by the enlargement of the east arm or (more likely) overlapped its inception. If the 'great church' referred to was the nave, it hardly seems likely it was twenty years before its roof was replaced after damage in the fire of 1179. Willis (Hope [1900], 48–9, and CUL, Add. MS 5128, f. 22) associated these entries with the new work at the east end on the basis of Thorpe, ed., *Registrum Roffense*, 122–3: 'Ad novum opus ecclesiae nunquam minus quam XX. libras sterlingorum, quam diu fuit sacrista in unoquoque anno ministravit & officias ad ecclesiam pertinentes bene servavit illesas.'

146 One William was prior at least from 1218 to 1222; Richard de Darente was elected prior in 1225 and served until at least 1238: Le Neve, *Fasti*, 80.

147 Hope (1900), 47 n. *, disagreed with Willis's conclusion that the major transept was built between 1227 and 1240: 'there is every possibility that the dedication in 1240 did not include the transepts [*sic*].'

148 See above, n. 8. Brown, 'Financial System,' 115–17, considered the crisis of 1255 as only temporary (cf. Smith, 'Financial System,' 589), since it was caused by the 'enormous bill as a result of the final battle to re-establish some of the rights granted away by Bishop Gilbert between 1197 and 1205.'

149 For the surviving remains of the choir stalls and screen that have been dated to the 1227 entry into the choir, see below, nn. 152 and 153.

150 Matthew Paris: H.R. Luard, ed., *Chronica majora*, 7 vols. (RS, 57: London 1872–83), III (1876), 421–2

151 In the process of tunnelling under the present choir floor in 1872 in order to install a bellows machine for the organ, Irvine reported encountering a plaster floor level close under the modern concrete one: see RMSC, DRc/Emf 77/133, 'An Account of the Church of St. Andrew at Rochester, otherwise the Cathedral of the Castle of the Kentishmen,' Notebook no. 2 (1876), p. 8 (= DRc/Emf 135 [typescript prepared by G.M. Livett], p. 6); and Hope (1886), 331 and section in pl. I (not shown in DRc/Emf 77/3). According to Hope (1900), 77, the existing steps date to the seventeenth century; he surmised that the medieval ones may have been broader, rather more like those surviving at Canterbury.

152 The present stone screen is of the fourteenth century, but the sculptural decoration of its west face is the design of Pearson: see Palmer, *Cathedral Church*, 83; Hope (1900), 76. On the east side of the stone screen, part of a wooden pulpitum survives: above a tall dado of

painted boards, there is an (formerly) open arcade of (six) trefoil arches with a double-decker arrangement of quatrefoil shafts (the upper short tier occupies the spandrels between the arches). A small fragment of carved drapery adjacent to the south entrance post can hardly be *in situ*. For measured drawings by J.T. Micklethwaite see *The Spring Gardens Sketch Book*, II (1867–8), pl. XLVI, and C.R.B. King, 'Choir Fittings in Rochester Cathedral,' *Spring Gardens Note-Book* (1874), 74–6 (notes for pl. XLVI). Also C. Tracy and C. Hewett, 'The Early Thirteenth-Century Choir Stalls and Associated Furniture at Rochester Cathedral, with Drawings and Carpentry Notes,' *Friends of Rochester Cathedral: Report for 1994/5* (1995), fig. 1 and pl. VI. On the basis of the 1227 entry into the choir, it has been considered to be of the same date (Hope; Tracy and Hewett, 10). Tracy, in Tracy and Hewett, 16, noted a feature in the pulpitum unusual for the early thirteenth century, that is, the mini-shaft bisecting the spandrel: he suggested that it was inspired by the linkage found in the triforia of French High Gothic buildings such as the nave of Amiens Cathedral. The comparison with Amiens, where the triforium is most likely after ca. 1240, implies that 1227 is too early a date for the Rochester pulpitum. Indeed, the profiles of the bases (torus over a very bulbous torus) and capitals (of an elongated cyma-like curve), and double abaci (lower, straight face over a cyma; upper, straight face over a hollow chamfer) suggest a date well after 1227, perhaps one in the fourteenth century.

153 The rear choir stalls (heavily restored by Scott), of which only one column actually survives, and the desk fronts in front of them have been considered, along with those of Salisbury Cathedral, the earliest remaining in England and as such are briefly mentioned in F. Bond, *Screens and Galleries in English Churches* (London 1908), 160 and 167, and *Wood Carvings in English Churches*, 2 vols., I, *Stalls and Tabernacle Work* (London 1910), 30–1; F.E. Howard and F.H. Crossley, *English Church Woodwork: A Study in Craftmanship during the Medieval Period, 1250–1550* (London 1917 [2nd ed., 1927]), 13 and 149.

Now see C. Tracy, *English Gothic Choir-Stalls, 1200–1400* (Woodbridge 1987), 1–8, esp. 1 and 4–5, and pls. 2, 5, 7, 8, 10, and 11; cf. Hope (1900), 108–11; Palmer, *Cathedral Church*, 89–90; and Tracy and Hewett, 'Early Thirteenth-Century Choir-Stalls,' 10–17 and 20–1, and pls. IV, VII, and VIII, and fig. 2. Tracy noted (14) that the cantilevering of the choir stalls (the seat standards are supported on brackets tenoned into a seat rail) is most unusual: it is probably to be explained

by the existence of the solid side walls of the choir, which allowed
this method of support otherwise impossible with arcades.

Tracy, *English Gothic Choir-Stalls*, 5 (and 'Early Thirteenth-Century
Choir-Stalls,' 10), like others before him, esp. Hope (1900), 76 and 108,
dated the stalls and desk supports according to the supposed 1227
entry into the choir, although noting the unusual feature of octagonal
rather than round shafts for that date; he admitted ('Early Thirteenth-
Century Choir-Stalls,' 16) that '[i]t is difficult to find anything stylistically comparable to this furniture.' This is indeed true, as the bases,
shafts, and capitals of the desk supports have the same profile as the
parallel elements on the pulpitum (see above, n. 152); their forms
contrast with the semicircular trefoil arches of the arcade, which are
cut out of a single plank of wood; the peculiar painted spandrel
decoration of circles and inverted U's (see a full-scale pencil and wash
drawing by Scott, 'Decoration on ancient desk fronts,' RMSC, unnumbered; Tracy and Hewett, 17), which has been interpreted as imitating
plate tracery, is sloppy and imprecise in execution. It may be questioned if these diverse elements really belong together. At Salisbury,
most of the tiny shafts that support each arm rest have polygonal
shafts and bases; the base profile consists of a thin torus above a larger
spreading one; the capitals are either stiff-leaf or plain bell-shaped, not
polygonal: all details *look* thirteenth century. On the other hand, the
crown posts of domestic timber roofs in Kent during the fourteenth
and fifteenth centuries are frequently polygonal, and some have
double-decker capitals: see S. Pearson, *The Medieval Houses of Kent:
An Historical Analysis* (London 1994), figs. 25a, 44a–c, 54, 72b, 84a–h,
and 96, and, for capitals, figs. 151c and 152f, m, and n. Some of these
elements could date from the period of Bishop Hamo; Hope (1900),
110, suggested that he set up the bishop's throne. The low height of
the desks, already noted by Hope, and the lack of parallels for them
again suggests that they may have been adapted from some earlier and
different function.

The choir furnishings have suffered so often from at times drastic
sounding restoration, especially in the eighteenth century, that there
is reason to question if the present arrangement has any authority.
Their rearrangement and reordering began in 1541, when 'the forms
were enclosed by new desks, the linenfold panel of which are still
exant' (Tracy and Hewett, 10).

In 1741 new seats were to be installed along the walls from the
prebendaries' stalls to the pulpit, with the wall above wainscotted (in

addition, 'a collonade of Ionick columns and arched Intablature' was to be added to the new fronts and seats of the prebendaries' stalls, while the choir was to be paved with Portland and Bremen stone: Holbrook, 191 [DRc/Emf 26 and 27]).

Again, in 1792 the old floors and joists of the choir stalls were replaced and new stalls were fitted; they were painted with burnt umber and stone ochre; the old stalls were demolished and a new organ was installed (Holbrook, 196 [FTv 145 and 146]; according to Spence, *A Walk through*, 11, the organ case, screen, and prebendal stalls were designed by a Rev. Mr Olive).

In 1825–6, the eighteenth-century refurbishment was removed by Cottingham and new stalls and canopies by Edward Blore (1787–1879) were erected (Tracy and Hewett, 10). In 1844, the fronts of the pews, which were 'of stained deal, and quite plain,' were removed and replaced by carved Gothic panelling; four new pews were erected (utilizing mid-sixteenth century panelling?: see Tracy and Hewett, pl. III).

The existing arrangement is the result of the 1871–4 restoration directed by Scott. According to King, 'Choir Fittings,' 74–6, 'Upon removal of the wooden pews, the lower part of the ancient stallwork on the north and south sides of the choir were found to be tolerably complete, and the whole design and detail of the upper part, with the exception of the capping, could be made out from fragments which were discovered ... The desks were nearly perfect, they have merely been repaired, and have had two or three missing shafts supplied [actually more than this number were replaced] ... The decoration found on the desk fronts remains untouched, as does a considerable portion of the lower part of the wall painting.' (The wooden enclosure built over the vault of the crypt aisle in the south choir aisle [see fig. 78] has likewise been dated to the early thirteenth century: Tracy and Hewett, 17, 20, 21, pl. X, and fig. 3, despite the fact that they accept a date of 1300 for the door into the enclosure, now used as a vestry; one might note that the south arm of the minor transept was not 'completely reconstructed' at that date as they remark]. Here again the architectural forms – a polygonal corner post with three knobs of foliage stuck on its capital with a profile differing from those of the choir stalls and screen – would fit more comfortably into the fourteenth century. The piers and responds of the three bay arcade of the large, early-fourteenth-century, south chapel at Bishop's Cleeve Church, Gloucestershire, provide a parallel in full-scale architecture.)

154 The footings for the high altar were uncovered during the restoration
of the presbytery under Scott in July 1873: see Society of Antiquaries,
Photographic Collection, Kent: Cathedral, nos. BB90/6406 and 6426,
and Hope (1900), 115–16. The remains of the platform uncovered in
1873 occupied the full depth of the second bay from the east (west half
of eastern sexpartite vault) and appear to have extended well into the
third bay from the east (eastern half of the western sexpartite vault);
the western limit was not established. Hope suggested that the altar
was on the west side of the platform, i.e., in the third bay, and therefore 'it would stand immediately over the early-English supports built
in the crypt below to carry its weight'; this is not quite true, as the
altar would actually have been positioned only over the western half
of these thin piers – of uncertain date – that extended east and west of
the second pair of columns from the east (i.e., they were positioned in
the middle of the length of this section of the crypt). (These piers were
removed in 1963–4: Holbrook, 'Repair and Restoration,' 215.) The
actual altar could have been located on the eastern part of the platform, that is, under the western half of the eastern sexpartite bay; the
fourteenth-century sedilia is in the third bay from the east (east half of
west sexpartite bay). (Scott placed the actual altar table on the east
edge of his platform, which is contained within the second [half] bay
from the east.) If the added piers in the crypt were for the support of
the high altar, they would place the high altar platform between the
two sexpartite bays. Tatton-Brown, 'Eastern Crypt,' 21, suggested that
the piers dated to 1344, rather than to the thirteenth century as Hope
assumed, when Bishop Hamo is known to have renewed the shrines of
saints Paulinus and Ithamar, and therefore may have rebuilt the high
altar and its platform. Whether or not Tatton-Brown is correct, a
thirteenth-century date for the piers seems unlikely.

155 See Hope (1900), plan pl. II; he also indicated an altar (St Ursula: see
96–9) against the pier between the north aisle and the north transept
chapel and one (St James: 93–4) at the east end of the south nave aisle;
he did not find any evidence of a screen or altar at the end of the north
nave aisle (94). With regard to the south choir aisle, which is called the
Chapel of St Edmund (= St Edmund of Canterbury?; there was a chapel
of St Edmund in the crypt: see above, n. 38), Hope (1881–5), 228,
observed that he could not find any 'authority' for this custom.

156 Hope (1900), 77 and 80

157 Oakley, 'Rochester Priory,' 43–4

158 Hope (1900), 75–7; and see below, chap. 6, pp. 149–50.

159 The aisled, straight-ended crypt (1154–60/66) of Archbishop Roger of Pont l'Évêque (1154–81) at York was the immediate chronological, if not typological, predecessor to Rochester's new crypt: see E.A. Gee, 'Architectual History until 1290,' in G.E. Aylmer and R. Cant, *A History of York Minster* (Oxford 1977), 121–5.

160 The only other large crypt of the thirteenth century is the vast one under the east end of Glasgow Cathedral, begun ca. 1240. There the crypt may be partially explained by the steep slope of the site; Canterbury, Rochester, and Hereford were all built on level ground. For Glasgow, see R. Fawcett, *Glasgow Cathedral* (HBM: Edinburgh 1985).

At St Paul's, London, a possible early crypt may have been extended eight bays at the time of the rebuilding of the choir, ca. 1258: see G.H. Cook, *Old St. Paul's Cathedral* (London 1955), 28–9, 35–7; R.K. Morris, 'The New Work at Old St Paul's Cathedral and Its Place in English Thirteenth-Century Architecture,' in L. Grant, ed., *Medieval Art, Architecture and Archaeology in London* (BAACT, X [for the year 1984]: [London] 1990), 77–9.

161 F. Woodman, *The Architectural History of Canterbury Cathedral* (London 1981), 115–16 and fig. 81, suggested that William of Sens may have intended a flat end (rectangular ambulatory). This proposal was rejected by P. Draper, 'William of Sens and the Original Design of the Choir Termination of Canterbury Cathedral 1175–1179,' *Jnl SAH* 42/3 (1983), 240–1 and 245–6. Now see also P. Kidson, 'Gervase, Becket, and William of Sens,' *Speculum* 68/4 (1993), 981–8, who suggests an ambulatory termination based on an ennaegon, and M.F. Hearn, 'Canterbury Cathedral and the Cult of Becket,' *Art Bulletin* 76/1 (1994), 19–52, whose various hypotheses may be treated with some scepticism, for which see P. Draper, 'Interpretations of the Rebuilding of Canterbury Cathedral, 1174–1186: Archaeological and Historical Evidence,' *Jnl SAH* 56/2 (1997), 184–203. The late-eleventh-/early-twelfth-century (Saint Anselm's) choir and crypt (1096–1110) may have had a rectangular axial chapel: see E. Fernie, 'St Anselm's Crypt,' in Coldstream and Draper, *Medieval Art and Architecture at Canterbury*, 30 and fig. 1; Woodman, 47 and fig. 26; Hearn, 'Canterbury Cathedral,' figs. 3 and 32.

162 The crypt under the Lady chapel at Hereford, of ca. 1200–20, was perhaps the next to last of the cathedral crypts: G. Marshall, *Hereford Cathedral: Its Evolution and Growth* (Worcester 1951), 52–64. Hereford, like Rochester, possessed no relics of significance when the crypt was begun.

163 D. Phillips, *The Cathedral of Archbishop Thomas of Bayeux: Excavations at York Minster*, II (London 1985), 91–5, 137–40, and 160–4

164 W.F. Grimes, *The Excavation of Roman and Medieval London* (London 1968), 210–17; R. Gem, 'The Romanesque Architecture of Old St Paul's Cathedral and Its Late Eleventh-century Context,' in Grant, ed., *Medieval Art, Architecture and Archaeology*, 48–50

165 Wm.H.St.J. Hope, 'On the Premonstratensian Abbey of St. Radegund, Bradsole in Polton, near Dover,' *Arch. Cant.* 14 (1882), 140–52

166 See Webb, *Architecture in Britain*, 84.

167 See P. Fergusson, *Architecture of Solitude: Cistercian Abbeys in Twelfth-Century England* (Princeton 1984), 73–82.

168 For Lewes, see A.W. Clapham, *English Romanesque Architecture*, vol. II, *After the Conquest* (Oxford 1934), 71–3; the secondary transept most likely dated from the second quarter of the twelfth century. Another possible example was York, ca. 1170–80: see Gee, 'Architectural History,' 123.

169 Woodman, *Architectural History*, 49

170 Ibid., 90

171 The Lincoln chapels are larger than the Canterbury ones and are fully expressed on the exterior: see, e.g., Webb, *Architecture in Britain*, fig. 46; P. Kidson, ed., *Lincoln: Gothic West Front, Nave and Chapter House* (P. Lasko, gen. ed., *Courtauld Institute Illustration Archives*, Archive I, *Cathedrals and Monastic Buildings in the British Isles*, pt. 5: London 1978), 1/5/2–6.

172 Other later examples are Worcester, begun ca. 1224, where the minor east transept lacks chapels, and Beverley Minster, ca. 1225.

173 J. Bony, *French Gothic Architecture of the 12th & 13th Centuries* (Berkeley, Los Angeles, London 1983), 507, n. 31, noted: 'The east transept of Rochester, freely repeated from Canterbury ... is much less narrow than in the Lincoln derived series.'

174 As there was at Cluny III, which, with respect to the secondary transept, was followed only by the Cluniac priory of Saint-Mayeul, Souvigny (Allier), in France: J. Evans, *The Romanesque Architecture of the Order of Cluny* (Cambridge 1938), 75 (there is *not* a secondary transept at Saint-Benoît-sur-Loire).

175 L. Hoey, 'Piers versus Vault Shafts in Early English Gothic Architecture,' *Jnl SAH* 46/3 (1987), 263

176 Tatton-Brown, 'Eastern Crypt,' 20 n. 8, noted that the profile of the 'ribs of the high vaults are very similar to those in the Canterbury eastern arm.' The ribs of the Rochester presbytery and minor transept

high vaults do belong to the same generic type – a roll flanked by a hollow and a thinner roll – but are thinner and lack the dogtooth decoration in the hollows. In the diagonal ribs of the choir vault, the axial rolls become more dominant while the transverse ribs basically have a new design consisting of a dogtooth between two equally sized rolls flanked by a thin hollow and roll.

177 The use of billet and dogtooth on separate mouldings calls to mind two of the (now lost) fragments recovered by Irvine from the south transept in 1872 (Hope [1900], 35 and 36, and figs. 8 and 9): but the moulding profiles, especially that with the dogtooth, are different. In the east end, the large dogtooth is found immediately adjacent to a big roll or, as in the choir ribs, flanked by large rolls.

178 T. Tatton-Brown, *Great Cathedrals of Britain* (London 1989), 84, saw such a close connection between elements such as the vertical shafting, the windows, and the vaults and the work of William the Englishman at Canterbury in the early 1180s as to suggest that the Rochester masons came from William's team. A.E. Sheckler, 'The Architectural Influence of Canterbury Cathedral on Rochester Cathedral,' MA thesis, Tufts University 1979 (copy: RDCL, 733.1 SHE), attempted an architectural comparison of the two cathedrals (chap. 4, 39–58). Her comparison of the details, to my mind, revealed rather the lack of dependence of Rochester on Canterbury than the opposite.

179 Webb, *Architecture in Britain*, 80

180 Their shrines were remade in marble and alabaster by Bishop Hamo in the 1340s: BL, Cotton MS Faustina B.V, f. 90[89]v (Wharton, ed., *Anglia Sacra*, I, 375: 'Episcopus circa festum Sancti Michaelis feretra sanctorum Paulini et Ythamari de marmore et alabaustro fecit renovare; pro qua quidem renovacione ducentas marcas dedit.') Hope (1900), 117, suggested these shrines may have stood on a low platform behind the high altar, but there is no real evidence of their location. Tatton-Brown, 'Eastern Crypt,' 21 n. 16, suggested that they may have been placed slightly *west* of the altar, to either side of it, and were supported by the piers (removed in 1963–4; see above, n. 154) later added to the columns of the crypt. But as the thin, elongated piers were added east and west of the second pair of columns from the east, that is, under the middle of the presbytery, if their purpose was to support the shrines, the shrines would have blocked the visibility and accessibility of the altar, being equidistant from each other and the side walls of the presbytery. It might be expected that, if supports for the two shrines were added in the crypt, the piers would have been placed in

the 'aisles' of the east arm of the crypt, rather than in the east–west line of the columns; and if to support the high altar, that the piers would have extended in a north–south rather than an east–west direction.

181 This area was later closed by an L-shaped wall constructed between the northwest angle turret of the arm and the north tower. Judging from the small window in its east face, now badly weathered, consisting of a twin light with a horizontal transom and trilobe heads, and a trilobe above, it dates to the fourteenth century.

182 P. Draper, '"Seeing that It Was Done in All the Noble Churches in England,"' in Fernie and Crossley, eds, *Studies in Honour of Peter Kidson*, 138–40

183 Fernie, 'St Anselm's Crypt,' 27

184 Although perhaps the result of necessity, and possibly based on the precedent of the Romanesque transept, rectangular chapels might have seemed less of a compromise because of their manifestation at other buildings long after their appearance at Lincoln, ca. 1072/3. For instance, ca. 1190, at Kirkwall Cathedral, in the place of small apsidal ones, and at Chichester Cathedral following the fire of 1187. See R. Fawcett, 'Kirkwall Cathedral: An Architectural Analysis,' and R. Cant, 'Norwegian Influences in the Design of the Transitional and Gothic Cathedral,' in B.E. Crawford, ed., *Saint Magnus Cathedral and Orkney's Twelfth Century Renaissance* (Aberdeen 1988), 97–9 and 132, respectively.

185 P. Brieger, *English Art, 1216–1307* (Oxford History of English Art: Oxford 1957), 129

186 See above, nn. 74, 76, and 129. In addition to the Archbishop's palace at Canterbury (by 1220?), plate tracery remains in Kent only at Stone parish church (nave), and in a secular building, Squerryes Lodge, Westerham (first-floor hall): Newman, *West Kent*, 53 n. * and, for Stone, 524–7. At Stone, a quatrefoil pierces the typanum above each pair of sub-lancets, which are moulded and shafted on the interior face (*The Builder*, 54/2356 [31 March 1888], 230 and pl. after 238). The forms in the transept contrast with the fully developed elaborate patterns used on the tomb of Bishop John de Bradfield (d. 1283), perhaps the earliest English example of 'Kentish' tracery: J. Bony, *The English Decorated Style: Gothic Architecture Transformed, 1250–1350* (Oxford 1979), 26.

187 Webb, *Architecture in Britain*, 112. On Binham, see M. Thurlby, 'The West Front of Binham Priory, Norfolk, and the Beginnings of Bar Tracery in England,' in W.M. Ormrod, ed., *England in the Thirteenth*

Century. Proceedings of the 1989 Harlaxton Symposium (Harlaxton Medieval Studies, 1: Stamford 1991), 155–65.

188 For Lincoln see Kidson, ed., *Lincoln*, iii and 1/5/2–6, and, specifically, G. Russell, 'The Thirteenth-Century West Window of Lincoln Cathedral,' in T.A. Heslop and V.A. Sekules, eds, *Medieval Art and Architecture at Lincoln Cathedral* (BAACT, VIII [for the year 1982]): [London] 1986), 85 and 89 n. 6. She described the gable tracery as plate; the central shafts lack capitals, and the spandrels are solid and decorated. See also Kidson, 'Architectural History,' in D. Owen, ed., *A History of Lincoln Minster* (Cambridge 1994), 38, where he remarked that, if the Consistory court tracery is original, it is not remarkable, as it is unlikely that it was the first time tracery was used in England; he proposes that the great west window had overlapping 'Y' tracery before or by 1240.

189 N. Pevsner, *BE: Wiltshire*, 2nd ed. (B. Cherry, rev.) (Harmondsworth 1974), 394: 'The windows appear with and without tracery, the tracery being of the plate variety.'

190 N. Pevsner, *BE: Herefordshire* (Harmondsworth 1963), 150 and 158; it was probably remodelled about the time the Lady chapel was finished, i.e., ca. 1220–40.

191 See a small pen-and-wash drawing of the interior in 1788, and a pen-and-ink and watercolour drawing of the exterior, ca. 1790, both by John Carter (1746–1817) (Westminster City Archives) and a watercolour view of 1799 by William Capon (1757–1827) (Society of Antiquaries).

192 Woodman, *Architectural History*, 133–5, and figs. 101 and 102; he described it as 'a mixture of plate and quasi-bar tracery,' and likened it to an 'exploded version of the Chartres clerestory'; he further suggested that 'English masons were experimenting with the possibilities of "bar" tracery at much the same time as the French.'

193 The fourth pier from east: see Webb, *Architecture in Britain*, pl. 102; and esp. V. Jansen, 'Dying Mouldings, Unarticulated Springer Blocks, and Hollow Chamfers in Thirteenth-Century Architecture,' *Jnl BAA* 135 (1982), pl. XXA (cited, 41, as a mid-thirteenth-century example of *congé*).

194 According to Newman, *West Kent*, 481 (Pevsner and Metcalf, *Cathedrals of England*, 243), the appearance of arch mouldings with 'sunk quadrants' date the arcade to the last decade or two of the thirteenth century ('building program was dragging on into ...').

195 It will be recalled that Tatton-Brown, as pointed out above, chap. 4, n. 156, has advanced an early date for the start of work in brief comments made in print at various times during the past decade, most specifically, recently, in 'Eastern Crypt,' 18–20, but he has not considered the implications of the early starting date for the chronology of the choir, aisles, and major transept.

CHAPTER 6 **Later Gothic Alterations and Additions**

1 A. Oakley, 'Rochester Priory, 1185–1540,' in N. Yates, ed., with P.A. Welsby, *Faith and Fabric: A History of Rochester Cathedral, 604–1994* (Woodbridge 1996), 49

2 M.C. Buck in C.S. Nichols, ed., *Dictionary of National Biography, Missing Persons* (Oxford 1993), 286–7. C. Johnson, ed., *Registrum Hamonis de Hethe Diocesis Roffensis AD 1319–1352*, 2 vols. (Oxford 1948). The bishop's family name was Noble. Hamo apparently suffered from ill health. He actually resigned the see in May 1352, shortly before his death. An earlier attempt to resign in 1349 because of failing health was refused by the pope (Clement VI, 1342–52).

3 Oakley, 'Rochester Priory,' 32: 'The bishopric was one of the smallest and poorest dioceses in the country and depended for support on the personal wealth of its bishops ... [Hamo] used his own wealth to embellish the cathedral church.' According to Buck (see above, n. 2), Hamo was hard pressed by debt in 1319–21, and between 1331 and 1336 he was engaged in a bitter dispute with the bishop of Norwich, William Ayremynne (1325–36).

4 S. Denne, 'Memorials of the Cathedral Church of Rochester,' in J. Thorpe, ed., *Custumale Roffense, from the Original Manuscript in the Archives of the Dean and Chapter of Rochester* (London 1788), 184 and 185

5 A.M. Oakley, 'The Cathedral Priory of St. Andrew, Rochester,' *Arch. Cant.* 91 (1975), 54, and 'Rochester Priory,' 34

6 W.H.St.J. Hope, *The Architectural History of the Cathedral and Monastery of St. Andrew at Rochester* (London 1900 = *Arch. Cant.* 23 [1898], 194–328, and 24 [1900], 1–85; hereafter cited as Hope [1900]), 111: according to him the heraldic motif of the diaper is derived from the royal arms of Edward III (1327–77) first adopted in 1340.

7 Hope (1900), 112; for the stalls, see above, chap. 5, n. 153.

8 Oakley, 'Rochester Priory,' 52 and 51

9 See above, chap. 3, p. 28 and n. 18.

10 Oakley, 'Rochester Priory,' 52–5; C.S. Knighton, 'The Reformed Chapter, 1540–1660,' in Yates, ed., *Faith and Fabric*, 57–61.

11 This area was identified as such first by Denne, 'Memorials,' in Thorpe, *Custumale Roffense*, 174. For St William of Perth and his shrine in the north arm of the minor transept, see above, chap. 5, pp. 88–9, 138, 142.

12 The public might possibly have gained less restricted entrance to the crypt from a portal replacing a window in its north end wall. There is a portal in such a position now, but it is not clear if it reflects an older or original arrangement.

13 Hope (1900), 75–6; he dated (cf. 166–7) these portals (and the choir screen doorway, fig. 30) to the early fourteenth century, which seems much too late.

14 Hope (1900), 75 and 101; G.H. Palmer, *The Cathedral Church of Rochester: A Description of Its Fabric and a Brief History of the Episcopal See*, 2nd ed. (Bell's Cathedral Series: London 1899), 115, described this small aisle portal as belonging to the 'Early English period.'

15 Hope (1900), 166–7 and fig. 39: date, early fourteenth century (76: 'same date and character' as the aisle screens).

16 Hope (1900), 30 and 81–2 (and n. †, for Latin text of agreement, a document in the Dean and Chapter records, dated 14 June 1327): 'quod dicti Religiosi facient dictis parochianis unum Oratorium in angulo dicte navis ecclesie juxta hostium boriale cum hostio et fenestra, ex parte exteriore dicte ecclesie.' On the relationship between the monks and parishioners, which generally seems to have been difficult, see R.C. Fowler, '[Religious Houses:] Cathedral Priory of St. Andrew, Rochester,' in *VCH: Kent*, II (London 1926), 123; and Oakley, 'Cathedral Priory,' 56, and 'Rochester Priory,' 35–6.

17 Profile: Hope (1900), fig. 32 (82)

18 It leads to a 'room' defined by wooden panelling on top of the vault of the remaining (east) bay of the south aisle of the Romanesque crypt (fig. 78); according to Palmer, *Cathedral Church*, 112, the enclosure was used as a vestry. Also see C. Tracy and C. Hewett, 'The Early Thirteenth-Century Choir Stalls and Associated Furniture at Rochester Cathedral, with Drawings and Carpentry Notes,' *Friends of Rochester Cathedral: Report for 1994/5* (1995), 17–20 and 21, pl. X and fig. 3; the authors accept a thirteenth-century date for it, although the polygonal angle shaft and its capital are not at all typical thirteenth-century forms and would fit more comfortably into the fourteenth century (as is

indeed true of the choir screen and stalls, for similar reasons: see above, chap. 5, nn. 152 and 153).

19 Hope (1900), 71

20 These are probably to be identified as 'the windows in the S. Isle of the Steeple Cross' that Charles Sloane (1690–1764) in his 'Report of several needfull Repairs to be don at the Cathedral Church,' December 1754 (Holbrook, 'Repair and Restoration of the Fabric since 1540,' in Yates, ed., *Faith and Fabric*, 192: RMSC, DRc/FTv 110), recommended should be bricked up.

21 One window appears in a view of 1822 ('Part of Rochester Cathedral & Castle') by C.J. Hullmandel (1789–1850). The pattern is similar to that in the east clerestory of the south arm of the major transept (restored by Scott in the 1870s: see above, chap. 5, n. 75). In 1801, Daniel A. Alexander (1768–1846) recommended that the decayed 'enriched work' of the three aisle windows should be removed and replaced by 'Y' tracery: RMSC, DRc/Emf 40, 'Specifications of Repairs to be made at the Cathedral, Rochester. March 1801,' p. 4. Hullmandel's view suggests this may not have been done. The tracery may have been removed by Scott during the restoration in the 1870s, but see B.C. Worssam, 'A Guide to the Building Stones of Rochester Cathedral,' *Friends of Rochester Cathedral: Report for 1994/5* (1995), 25: 'Three Portland stone lancet windows, replacements of larger late Medieval windows are probably the work of Daniel Alexander in 1801.'

22 It is fully described by A. Ashpitel, 'Rochester Cathedral,' *Jnl BAA* 9 (1854), 284; Hope (1900), 82–3; and Palmer, *Cathedral Church*, 107. The portal, sometimes described as 'much restored,' has been generally ignored in recent literature: it was only briefly mentioned by J. Evans, *English Art, 1307–1461* (Oxford History of English Art: Oxford 1949), 51 (where it was [mis?]attributed to Bishop John de Sheppey [whose dates of office were incorrectly given as 1332–60, rather than 1352–60] and dated 1352 [a misprint for 1342?]), and only in a passing comparison of a minor feature by L. Stone, *Sculpture in Britain: The Middle Ages* (Harmondsworth 1955), 160 n. 14 (on p. 258). It also appears in E.S. Prior and A. Gardner, *An Account of Medieval Figure Sculpture in England* (Cambridge 1912), fig. 393; S. Gardner, *A Guide to English Gothic Architecture* (Cambridge 1922), 130; and A. Gardner, *A Handbook of English Medieval Sculpture* (Cambridge 1935), fig. 263.

According to Worssam, 'Guide to Building Stones,' 31, the stone is Reigate.

23 Hope (1900), 107–8, 165–6, 167–8, and 169–70. The traceried window

and portal now in the south wall at ground level do not belong and have been put together and inserted at some later date.

24   Hamo is supposed to have carried out work in the dormitory and refectory: BL, Cotton MS Faustina B.V ('Willelmi de Dene [Notarii Publici] Historia Roffensis ab anno MCCCXIV ad annum MCCCL'), f. 89[88]v (Wharton, ed., *Anglia Sacra*, I, 375: 'Anno xvi regni Regis Edwardi III [1342]. Episcopus Refectorium, Dormitorum, et alios defectus in ecclesia sumptibus suis pro majori parte fecit reparare.')

25   The existing tracery in the south window is the work of John Lough-brough Pearson (1817–97): see above, chap. 5, n. 25.

26   J. Storer, *History and Antiquities of the Cathedral Churches of Great Britain*, 4 vols. (London 1814–19), IV (1819), pl. 5 (1816) (Hope [1900], fig. 34 [91]); Palmer, *Cathedral Churches*, 90

27   Hope (1900), 85, suggested that these windows with their varied patterns 'verging on the Perpendicular,' along with similar ones in the north choir aisle, 'probably' dated to the episcopate of Brinton (1373–89). The variety of patterns would seem to assure that they belong to the fourteenth century.

28   See above, chap. 5, n. 17. The original patterns are shown in several pre-restoration views of the interior: an anonymous watercolour (RDCL, Portfolio 15; NMR, neg. no. AA77/2442); another signed by G. Gunning (RDCL [missing]: NMR, neg. no. AA77/2448); and an early ?photograph (RDCL [missing]: NMR, neg. no. BB68/3499).

29   Hope (1900), 117–18, identified the arms as those of Rochester, Canterbury, and Bishop Brinton; cf. Palmer, *Cathedral Church*, 95, who identified the arms of the canopies as those of the see of Rochester, the priory of St Andrew, and 'that [of the priory or see?] of Christ Church, Canterbury'; date, 'late Perpendicular.'

30   Hope (1900), 85 (not sexfoil as he states)

31   See above, p. 151 and n. 16. J.T. Irvine (1825–1900), RMSC, DRc/Emf 77/77 and 77/133, 'An Account of the Church of St. Andrew at Rochester, otherwise the Cathedral of the Castle of the Kentishmen,' Notebook no. 2, p. 14 (DRc/Emf 135 [a typed transcript prepared by G.M. Livett (1859–1951)], p. 10), reported he found evidence of a porch in front of this bay during the underpinning of the aisle wall in 1875, but gave no suggestion as to its date.

32   This tracery pattern may date only to the 1780s, when the window was removed and a new 'gothic' window was inserted; the tracery was mostly renewed by Cottingham in the 1820s: see D. Holbrook, 'Repair and Restoration,' 196 and 204. Also see above, chap. 5, n. 17.

33 Both transept arms (and the choir aisles) were cleaned and repaired in the early 1920s (the north vault in 1924) under the supervision of W.R. Lethaby (1857–1931; surveyor to the cathedral, 1920–7): F.H. Duffield and H.T. Knight, with S.W. Wheatley, *A Sketch of the History of the Diocese of Rochester with a Short Account of the Cathedral and Precinct* (Chatham 1926), 51. The vaults were cleaned and repaired again in the 1970s when Emil Godfrey was surveyor to the fabric (1952 to death in 1982): the north vault was restored in 1972 (RMSC, DRc/DE 209/VII), the south arm between 1973 and 1975 (DRc/DE 209/VIII, IX[1]), at which time gold leaf was applied to the ribs and the bosses were coloured and gilded: previously they had been plain. See Holbrook, 'Repair and Restoration,' 213 and 215.

34 In his memoirs, *Personal and Professional Recollections by the Late Sir George Gilbert Scott, R.A.* (London 1879), 351, Scott remarked: 'The interior of the south transept, with its timber groining, has been repaired, as has been a projecting building on its eastern side.' The extent of any replacement of timber is not clear, but was apparently necessary; according to RMSC, DRc/Emf 64/5/2 (Holbrook, 'Repair and Restoration,' 208), 'The vaulting of this Transept has oak ribs much decayed and threatening to fall ... spaces between them, formerly boarded, are now of lath and plaster.'

35 I wish to thank Nicola Coldstream for looking at photographs of these and the other bosses to be discussed below, in order to confirm their late date on the basis of style.

36 For photographs of the transept bosses by C.J.P. Cave, see NMR, neg. nos. AA52/6515–18 (north), and AA52/6519–23 (south). The bosses were photographed again after the restoration of the 1970s by Leonard Hill, but the photographs seem to be missing from the cathedral library.

37 P. Brieger, *English Art, 1216–1307* (Oxford History of English Art: Oxford 1957), 184: *Close Rolls of the Reign of Henry III (Preserved in the Public Record Office), A.D. 1242–1247* (London 1916), 39

38 Brieger, *English Art*, 184 n. 3, referred to it as 'the only remaining example of this kind' (a wooden vault with moulded ribs and carved bosses in the manner of a stone vault), by which he presumably meant the *earliest* remaining of its kind.

39 E. Gee, 'Architectural History until 1290,' in G.E. Aylmer and R. Cant, eds, *A History of York Minster* (Oxford 1977), 136–41

40 J. Harvey, 'Architectural History from 1291 to 1558,' in Aylmer and Cant, eds, *History of York*, 158. F. Bond, *An Introduction to English Church Architecture from the Eleventh to the Sixteenth Century*, 2

vols. (London 1913), 840–1, cited, in addition to York (and St Albans), the 'chancels' of Winchester Cathedral and Selby Abbey, the Lady chapel of St Albans, the cloister of Lincoln Cathedral, the towers of Exeter and Winchester cathedrals, and the nave of the parish church of Warmington (Northamptonshire).

At the Cistercian abbey of Byland, completed in the early 1190s, the transept and nave were covered by a wooden barrel vault: see P. Fergusson, *Architecture of Solitude: Cistercian Abbeys in Twelfth-Century England* (Princeton 1984), 80 and nn. 41, 73, and 82. In a paper presented at the British Archaeological Association Conference held in Glasgow in 1997, 'Glasgow Cathedral and the Wooden Vault in Twelfth- and Thirteenth-Century Architecture in Scotland,' M. Thurlby suggested that others may have existed at Cistercian Fountains Abbey and Ripon Minster, and in Scotland, at Dornoch, Dunblane, Elgin, St Andrews, and Glasgow cathedrals and at Paisley Prior and Holyrood Abbey. Now also see M.F. Hearn and M. Thurlby, 'Previously Undetected Wooden Ribbed Vaults in Medieval Britain,' *Jnl BAA* 150 (1997), 48–58.

41 BL, Cotton MS Faustina B.V, f. 90[89]v (Wharton, ed., *Anglia Sacra*, I, 375: 'Anno xviii regni Regis Edwardi III [1343]. Episcopus [tunc] Campanile *novum* ecclesiae Roffensis petris atque lignis altius fecit levare & illud plumbo cooperire, necnon & quatuor companas novas in eodem ponere, quarum [*sic*] nomina sunt haec, Dunstanus, Paulinus, Itamarus, atque Lanfrancus.')

Four bells are recorded as being placed in a major tower ('in majori turri') at various times before ca. 1300: two by Prior Reginald (1155–60); one named Thalebot after the sacrist, late twelfth century; and one named Bretun, in the time of Ralph de Ros, sacrist (before 1193–1203/ 8): MS Cotton Vespasian A.XXII, f. 87[89]r–v. See Hope (1886), 326, and (1900), 8–10, where the *majoris turris* is identified as 'Gundulph's' Tower. In the mid-sixteenth century, the north tower was identified as the three-bell steeple, the central tower as the six-bell steeple: see above, chap. 2, n. 5 (lease of 1545).

42 Holbrook, 'Repair and Restoration,' 186–7 (RMSC, DRc/Ac2/4, 8a; DRc/Ac 2/3, 14a; and DRc/FTb 16, 17, and 18)

43 Ibid., 188 and 189 (RMSC, DRc/FTv 37 and 46; FTv 44 and 45)

44 Denne, 'Memorials,' in Thorpe, ed., *Custumale Roffense*, 183; Palmer, *Cathedral Church*, 30 ('Mr. Sloane'). See also Holbrook, 'Repair and Restoration,' 192 (RMSC, DRc/FTv 97 and 99), who identifies him as John Sloane, while crediting (191) Charles Sloane with the refitting of

the choir in 1741 and the design of the bishop's throne. H. Colvin, *A Biographical Dictionary of British Architects 1600–1840* (London 1978), 739, includes an entry only on Charles Sloane, to whom the Rochester spire is attributed.

45 Holbrook, 'Repair and Restoration,' 196 (RMSC, DRc/Emf 37; DRc/FTv 139[1] and 153)

46 RMSC, DRc/Emf 34, 'A Survey of the Cathedral Church of Rochester. Anno 1760' (unpaged [27 pp.], [pp. 15–16])

47 Hope (1900), 90 and 92; Palmer, *Cathedral Church,* 39–40; M.R. Covert, 'The Cottingham Years at Rochester,' *Friends of Rochester Cathedral: Report for 1991/2* (1992), 7–8 and 10; Holbrook, 'Repair and Restoration,' 203–4 (RMSC, DRc/FTv 1871). 'Fragments of richly carved marble' were found in the tower casing: see L.N. Cottingham, *Some Account of an Ancient Tomb, etc., Discovered at Rochester Cathedral* (London n.d.), pl. VI. Hope (1900), 117, attributed them to Hamo's shrines for saints Paulinus and Ithamar; he did not explain when or how fragments from Hamo's shrines came to be reused in the tower's casing. C. Miele, 'The West Front of Rochester Cathedral in 1825: Antiquarianism, Historicism and the Restoration of Medieval Buildings,' *Arch. Jnl* 151 (1994), 404–9, accepted them as fragments of Hamo's tower without seeming to realize that it was Hamo's tower that Cottingham had removed. Misled by Cottingham's caption to his pl. V (Miele, illus. 4), 'Elevation of the Towers, as restored with sundry fragments found in the modern casing of the old one,' Miele (406 and 409) failed to detect that the style of the tower was indeed not Perpendicular of the late fourteenth or fifteenth centuries (as Cottingham dated the fragments), but – except for the pinnacles – rather simple Decorated; even the pinnacles, which seem not to have any ogee curves to the blind arches, could be dated to the late thirteenth century. See also Cottingham's watercolour of the west elevation before its restoration (RDCL [missing]: NMR, neg. no. BB65/3736).

48 Holbrook, 'Repair and Restoration,' 211–12 (RMSC, DRc/Emf 144)

49 Few examples of the use of brick in medieval buildings remain from before 1300; the most celebrated are the gatehouse (ca. 1170) and chapel (ca. 1225) at Little Coggeshall Abbey (Essex) and Little Wenham Hall (Suffolk), ca. 1270/80. In the north, a brickyard was established at Hull (Yorkshire) ca. 1303, so it is not surprising that bricks were employed in the chancel and transept of Holy Trinity, Hull, ca. 1315–45, and in the nave vault webs of Beverley Minster, from the 1330s and 1340s. Other early-fourteenth-century examples seem to be the vaults of the under-

crofts of St Olave's Priory, Herringfleet (Suffolk) and of Bridewell Museum, Norwich. Most remaining brickwork in Kent dates from after 1400: A. Clifton-Taylor, 'Building Materials,' in J. Newman, *BE: West Kent and the Weald*, 2nd ed. (1976), repr. & corr. (Harmondsworth 1980), 26–7. Also see J.A. Wight, *Brick Building in England from the Middle Ages to 1550* (London 1972), pls. 3–8; L.S Harley, 'Bricks of Eastern England to the End of the Middle Ages,' *Essex Journal* 10/4 (1975/6), 134–41; R. Brunskill and A. Clifton-Taylor, *English Brickwork* (London 1977), 13 and 17; and P.J. Drury, 'The Production of Brick and Tile in Medieval England,' in D.W. Crossley, ed., *Medieval Industry* (Council of British Archaeology, Research Report no. 40: London 1981), 126–42.

50 Hope (1900), 85, dated these alterations to the north choir aisle to the mid- to late fourteenth century, of about the same period as the tracery 'verging on Perpendicular' inserted into the lower presbytery windows (ca. 1373–89, episcopate of Thomas Brinton). For a fuller discussion of the alterations to the north aisle, now see J.P. McAleer, 'Rochester Cathedral: The North Choir Aisle and the Space between It and "Gundulf's" Tower,' *Arch. Cant.* 112 (1993), 127–63. Since writing that paper, I now wonder if the north aisle was left incomplete like the south aisle in the thirteenth century (see above, chap. 5, pp. 114–19 and 145–6), and whether the refacing (thickening?) of the wall was not due to 'structural problems,' but rather to the addition of the vault.

51 Hope (1900), 100, claimed that 'the present doorway is modern, but replaces an early one'; however, it appears 'genuine' to me. This portal now opens into a tunnel cut through rubble debris leading to an opening in the west end of the south wall of the so-called Gundulf's tower. The existence of the portal, which is not earlier than the second half of the thirteenth century, strongly suggests that the debris now filling the space between aisle wall and tower was not there in the thirteenth or fourteenth centuries and was the result of the demolition of the upper stage of the tower in the early nineteenth century. See McAleer, 'The Space,' 147 and pls. VIIB and VIIIB; also above, chap. 2, pp. 19–20 and esp. nn. 18 and 19.

52 McAleer, 'The Space,' 147 and pls. VIB and VIIIA

53 See above, chap. 2, p. 20 and fig. 22

54 According to Dean Robert Stevens (1820–70), RDCL, 733.3 COT, 10, '[t]he ceiling of St Edmunds Chapel, which was in a very bad state, has been entirely renewed, with the exception of the curious woodwork,

which has been restored and brought clearly into view with all its grotesque figures.' This apparently had been done on the recommendation of [Sir] Robert Smirke (1781–1867): see his 'Remarks on the State of Rochester Cathedral at a Survey made on March 11, 1825,' RMSC, DRc/Emf 52/1 (13 pp.), pp. 6–7 (also typescripts, DRc/Emf 135 and RDCL, 733.3 COT [5 pp.], p. 3).

55 However, the bosses have attracted little if any scholarly attention. Both Hope (1900), 75, who dated the ceiling to the early fourteenth century, and Palmer, *Cathedral Church*, 112, who dated it to the late thirteenth, failed to mention them. C.A. Hewett, *English Cathedral and Monastic Carpentry* (Chichester 1985), 89 and fig. 85 (also *English Cathedral Carpentry* [London 1974], 54 and fig. 43, and *English Historic Carpentry* [London and Chichester 1980], 138 and figs. 121 and 257), uncritically accepted Hope's date of ca. 1322; however, a fourteenth-century date seems to be confirmed by the use of angled tying timbers and jowls.

56 Photographs of them by C.J.P. Cave are in the NMR, neg. nos. AA52/6530–42, but they were neither discussed nor illustrated in his *Roof Bosses in Medieval Churches: An Aspect of Gothic Sculpture* (Cambridge 1948). The actual sequence on the south rib, reading from east to west, is oak leaves, fleur-de-lis, rose, dragon, and rose with small hooded heads. On the north rib, again reading from east to west, the sequence is head in foliage, rose with foliage, head with tongue sticking out, winged Green Man, and rose.

57 Carden & Godfrey, Architects, 130/3 (23 December 1953)

58 Robert Willis (1800–75) in Hope (1900), 85–6 (CUL, Add. MS. 5128, f. 42), described the windows as work 'of the plainest and meanest character ... awkwardly arranged, so that no one window stands above the centre of a pier arch, each being more or less to the west of it.' J. Harvey, *The English Cathedrals*, 2nd ed. (London 1956), 167, dated the clerestory twenty years (ca. 1490) later than the west window (ca. 1470).

59 The roof was completely rebuilt in 1804: see Holbrook, 'Repair and Restoration,' 200–1 (RMSC, DRc/Emf 43, 45, 46, 47, and 48/1; DRc/Ac 9/34; DRc/FTv 134, 135, and 161).

60 The west window was completely rebuilt by Cottingham: see Covert, 'The Cottingham Years,' 8; Miele, 'West Front,' 410; Holbrook, 'Repair and Restoration,' 204.

61 In the 1804 view of the cathedral from the northwest by J. Buckler (1770–1851), BL, Add. MS 36.368 (Buckler Architectural Drawings, XIII.

Kent[E-W]-Lancaster), ff. 81v–82r, the central mullion is depicted as heavier than the others, thus emphasizing the verticality of the two major arched subdivisions rather than the horizontality of two registers of eight sub-lights. However, earlier engravings, i.e., that by J.C. Schneb-belie of 1788 in Thorpe, ed., *Custumale Roffense*, pl. XXXV, do not show a thicker central mullion; nor does Buckler's 1805 watercolour view (BM, PS136595, based on BL, Add. MS 36.368, f. 84r, of 1804) of the interior of the nave to the west.

62 See J. Harvey, *The Perpendicular Style 1330–1485* (London 1978), illus. 177 and 181.

63 See Harvey, *Perpendicular Style*, 130 and illus. 38; he attributed the building with its variety of window traceries and mouldings to Henry Yevele (ca. 1320/30–1400) and a 'competent site architect.'

64 Hope (1900), 86: London, Lambeth Palace, MS Registrum Chichele, I, f. 462v (E.F. Jacob, ed., *The Register of Henry Chichele, Archbishop of Canterbury, 1414–1443*, 4 vols. [Canterbury and York Society, 46: Oxford, 1937–47], II [1937], 556–8: 'ad reparacionem tecti navis ecclesie nostre Roffensis'), and MS Registrum Stafford, f. 132 ('ad fabricam navis ecclesie cathedralis Ruffensis ... Proviso quod opere fabrice hujusmodi aliquod memoriale fiat per sculpturas armorum meorum et nominus mei'), respectively. I am grateful to Victoria Peters, Assistant Archivist, for the correct date of the will of Bishop Thomas (*not* 28 October 1455, as given by Hope [1900], 86).

65 The chapel served as the consistory court (since 1681 at the west end of the south nave aisle) from ca. 1741: Holbrook, 'Repair and Restoration,' 191. The exterior, particularly the parapets and windows, was exten-sively repaired in 1801: see Holbrook, 198–9. The chapel was originally built out of Kentish rag, with Caen stone used for window frames and tracery and for the buttresses: see Worssam, 'Guide to Building Stones,' 26–7.

66 The space is 26 ft (7.9248 m) wide between the wall faces and 28 ft 2 in. (8.5852 m) high to the top of the capitals of the wall shafts (from which the ribs would have sprung): Carden & Godfrey Architects, Rochester Cathedral, sheet 130/3, 23 December 1953.

67 Ashpitel, 'Rochester Cathedral,' 284, 'a chapel called by tradition St. Mary's chapel'; Hope (1881–5), 226, 'It is also equally certain that the Perpendicular extension was never called the Lady Chapel until modern times'; Palmer, *Cathedral Church*, 70, 'The so-called Lady Chapel was really built as a choir [*sic*] to the Lady Chapel proper in the south transept.' Its site was part of the precinct of the Bishop's Palace (see above, chap. 3, n. 105).

68 The first reference to an altar of the Virgin Mary dates from the early
fourteenth century (ca. 1305?: Thorpe, ed., *Custumale Roffense*, 3) and
did not specify its location: 'Lucas de Honeberwe vi d. de terra de
Monekedone ad altare beate Marie in novo opere.' The south major
transept arm would have been the most recent work at the time,
although hardly new, unless the alterations in its east wall were the
'novo opere' to which reference was made.

Two later references to an altar or a chapel 'de novo constructa' are
sixty years apart. One is a grant in 1322 for a lamp to be placed at the
altar, recorded in the chapter records (J. Thorpe, ed., *Registrum Roffense: or A Collection of antient records, charters, and instruments of
divers kinds, necessary for illustrating the ecclesiastical history and
antiquities of the diocese and cathedral church of Rochester* [London
1769], 546 [Cartae Elyanorae Coman]); the second dates from 1389, the
will of Bishop Thomas Brinton (Registrum Courtney, f. 231a), who
desired to be buried in the chapel. If the altar existed as early as ca.
1305, it is difficult to understand how the same altar or chapel could be
considered 'de novo constructa' in 1322 or, especially, in 1389. Does the
latter reference confirm an earlier structure than the one now existing,
one opening off the arm to the west? There was an altar dedicated to
the Virgin in the Infirmary chapel from 1240: Ashpitel, 'Rochester
Cathedral,' 281.

Hope (1900), 102–4, cited many other references to a chapel of St.
Mary, primarily in wills of the fifteenth century – usually requesting
burial. None, however, specifies its location.

69 Society of Antiquaries, Dr Thorpe's Collection, MS 178.7, f. 147. See
J. Harvey, *English Medieval Architects: A Biographical Dictionary
down to 1550*, rev. ed. (London 1984), 25, and *English Cathedrals*, 137,
ca. 1500–12.

70 With regard to the exterior, it is sometimes said (e.g., Holbrook, 'Repair
and Restoration,' 198) that it formerly had a high western gable (and,
therefore, presumably, a steeply pitched roof). But this cannot have been
the case, for a high roof, not only out of character for a late Perpendicular building, would have blocked the west clerestory windows of the
south arm of the transept. In work to be done on the chapel, D.A.
Alexander specified in his survey of 1801 (RMSC, DRc/Emf 40, 'Specifications of Repairs to be made at the Cathedral, Rochester. March 1801,'
p. 3) that the gable was to be demolished to the level of the bottom
cornice 'and to be rebuilt from this level to its present height of the top
of the angular Coping 18 inches thick, in Rag masonry ... The top to be
coped with same portland coping well bedded & clamped, no cornice

here.' Alexander's words do not suggest a high gable: he implies that the new gable should equal the old. (According to Holbrook, 198, the builder apparently lowered the height by 14 in. [35.56 cm]!) There is now no gable, as a low parapet runs uniformly along the nave aisle and the chapel west and south walls.

71 The doorway in the west bay leading into the south aisle was cut through only in 1889: Holbrook, 'Repair and Restoration,' 210.

72 Hope (1900), 87–8; Palmer, *Cathedral Church*, 51. The chancel aisles of All Saints, Maidstone, were also intended for fan vaults that were never built. Because the vaults would have been supported by piers on one side, Bond, *An Introduction*, I, 339, compared them to the outer north (Dorset) aisle at Ottery St Mary (Devon), ca. 1503/30 (N. Pevsner, *BE: South Devon* [Harmondsworth 1952], 221), and the outer south (Lane) aisle at Cullompton parish church (Devon) of ca. 1525–6 (Pevsner, 96 and 97, and pl. 17).

73 The bases are now dark in colour, giving the impression of Purbeck. But they appear to have been given a coat of plaster and dark varnish. Traces of a similar application can be seen on some of the round shaft-like plinths below them and on some of the vaulting shafts above: see particularly the plinths of the west mid-wall shafts and the southwest respond. This treatment is similar to that given to the bases and shafts in the area of the crossing and the Gothic bays of the nave (see above, chap. 5, nn. 81, 83, 120–2, and 127).

74 Has the pattern been altered? See Holbrook, 'Repair and Restoration,' 199: the top half of this window was to receive new mullions – sketched in Alexander's specification, with the Gothic heads reworked 'as before,' but the builder noted that it was 'executed different; head taken out.' In addition, the eastern and western windows on the south were 'to be formed anew by taking down the Mullions of the whole opening with the enriched work above the springing of the arch'; the middle window 'having had new mullions does only require new saddle bars' (RMSC, DRc/Emf 141).

75 Could this arch relate to the chapel, 'de novo constructa,' mentioned in the will of Bishop Thomas Brinton (see above, n. 68)?

76 See F. Woodman, *The Architectural History of Canterbury Cathedral* (London 1981), fig. 124, type 2, and fig. 123. This general base/plinth type, in a number of closely related variations, had a long currency at Christ Church from about 1360 to 1450: see Woodman, 162. At Rochester, a base type anticipating Woodman's type 1 appeared in the portal attributed to Bishop Hamo (see above, pp. 152–3).

77 For the base profile, see Woodman, *Architectural History*, fig. 124, type 5.

78 I wish to thank Richard Morris for looking at my primitive profiles, directing me towards Canterbury for comparisons with the entrance arch, and gently seconding my suspicion that the main body of the chapel *might* be of a later date than the entrance arch.

EPILOGUE

1 Perhaps the debate may begin as a consequence of the publication of C. Flight, *The Bishops and Monks of Rochester, 1076–1214* (Kent Archaeological Society, Monograph Series, no. 6: Maidstone 1997), which was received by this author too late to be taken into consideration during the final stages of the preparation of this study.

Essential Bibliography

Primary Sources

Manuscripts

'Custumale Roffense': (perhaps compiled by John de Westerham, prior 1320–1, ca. 1300) Rochester upon Medway Studies Centre, MS DRc/R2; formerly Rochester, Dean and Chapter Library, MS A3/7). See J. Thorpe, ed. [under *Published Chronicles*, below]

'Registrum Roffense': (thirteenth century) British Library, Cotton MS Vcspasian A.XXII, ff. 60[63]r–117[121]r ('Registris ecclie S. Andrej Roffensis'). See J. Thorpe, ed., 1–143

'Registrum Temporalium Ecclesiae et Episcopatus Roffensis': (mid?-fourteenth century) Centre for Kentish Studies, DRb/Ar 2 (formerly DRc/R3; formerly Rochester, Dean and Chapter Library. See Thorpe, ed., *Registrum Roffense*, 1–13

'Textus Roffensis' (register of cathedral priory compiled in the early twelfth century, ca. 1123/4): Rochester upon Medway Studies Centre, MS DRc/R1 (formerly Rochester, Dean and Chapter Library, MS A.3.5). See P. Sawyer, ed. [under *Published Chronicles*, below]

'Vita Gundulfi episcopi Roffensis' (twelfth century): British Library, Cotton MS Nero A.VIII, ff. 42[39]r–86[83]r. Published in Wharton, ed., *Anglia Sacra*, II, 273–92; also as *Life of Gundulf*, trans. the nuns of Malling Abbey (Malling 1968); and R. Thomson, ed., *The Life of Gundulf, Bishop of Rochester*, Toronto Medieval Texts, VII (Toronto 1977); also see J.B. Hall, 'Critical Notes on Three Medieval Latin Texts: "Vita Gundulfi," "Carmen de Hastingae Proelio," "Vita Merlini,"' *Studi Medievali*, 3rd ser., 21 (1980), 899–916, esp. 899–903

British Library, Cotton MS Nero D.II, ff. 2[1]r–199[198]: (early fourteenth century). Published in H. Wharton, ed., *Anglia Sacra* (see under *Published Chronicles*, below), I, 341–55 (attributed to Edmund of Haddenham); = MS 'N' in H.R. Luard, ed., *Flores Historiarum*, 3 vols., Rolls Series, 95 (London 1890); also see [Sir] T. Duffus Hardy, *Descriptive Catalogue of Materials Relating to the History of Great Britain and Ireland*, 3 vols., Rolls Series, 26 (London 1862–71), vol. III, 289–90
– Cotton MS Faustina B.V, ff. 2[1]–101[100]. Published in Wharton, ed., *Anglia Sacra*, I, 356–77 ('Historia Roffensis,' attributed to William de Dene)

Published Chronicles, etc. (arranged chronologically)

Wharton, H., ed. *Anglia Sacra, sive collectio historirum, partim antiquitus, partim recenter scriptarum de archiepiscopis & episcopis angliae, a prima Fidei Christianae susceptione ad Annum MDXL.* 2 vols. London 1691 (Rochester: I, 327–94 [329–40: Ernulfi episcopi Roffensis Collectanea De Rebus Ecclesiae Roffensis. A prima Sedis Fundatione ad sua Tempora; 341–55; 356–77]; II, 273–92)
Hearne, T., ed. *Textus Roffensis. Accedunt, Professionum antiquorum Angliae Episcoporum Formulae, De Canonica obedientia Archiepiscopis Cantuariensibus praestanda. Et Leonardi Hutteni Dissertatio Anglice conscripta, de Antiquitatibus Oxoniensibus. E Codicibus Mss. descripsit ediditque Tho. Hearnius.* Oxford 1720
Thorpe, J., ed. *Registrum Roffense: or, a collection of antient records, charters, and instruments of divers kinds, necessary for illustrating the ecclesiastical history and antiquities of the diocese and cathedral church of Rochester.* London 1769
– *Custumale Roffense, from the original manuscript in the archives of the Dean and Chapter of Rochester.* London 1788 (*Custumale*, 1–37; Samuel Denne, 'Memorials of the Cathedral Church of Rochester,' 153–246)
Thorpe, B., ed. *The Anglo-Saxon Chronicle.* 2 vols. Rolls Series, 23. London 1861
Stubbs, W., ed. *The Historical Works of Gervase of Canterbury.* 2 vols. Rolls Series, 73. London 1879–80
Lehmann-Brockhaus, O. *Lateinische Schriftquellen zur Kunst in England, Wales und Schottland, vom Jahre 901 bis zum Jahre 1307.* 5 vols. Munich 1955–60 (Rochester: II [1956], 390–404 [nos. 3708–74])
Sawyer, P., ed. *Textus Roffensis: Rochester Cathedral Library Manuscript A.3.5.* Early English Manuscripts in Facsimile, VI (Part I) and XI (Part II). Copenhagen 1957 and 1962

Whitelock, D., ed., with D.C. Douglas and S.I. Tucker. *The Anglo-Saxon Chronicle: A Revised Translation*. London 1961

Le Neve, J. *Fasti Ecclesiae Anglicanae, 1066–1300*. Vol. II: *Monastic Cathedrals (Northern and Southern Provinces)*, 75–82. Compiled by D.E. Greenway. University of London, Institute of Historical Research. London 1971

Campbell, A., ed. *Charters of Rochester*. British Academy, Anglo-Saxon Charters, 1. London 1973

Compilations and Indexes (arranged chronologically)

Oakley, A.M. 'The Archives of the Dean and Chapter of Rochester, *c.* 1100–1907.' Unpublished catalogue of documents held in the Rochester upon Medway Studies Centre, Civic Centre, Strood (compiled 1963–70)

Holbrook, D., collator and ed. 'A Chronological Record of Maintenance, Repair, Alteration, Restoration, Decoration, Furnishing and Survey of the Fabric of Rochester Cathedral, 1540–1983.' Extracts from the Dean and Chapter Records, Rochester upon Medway Studies Centre (1994)

Secondary Sources

Historical Background

Brown, A. 'The Financial System of Rochester Cathedral Priory: A Reconsideration.' *Bulletin of the Institute of Historical Research* 51 (1977), 115–20

Cheney, C.R. 'King John's Reaction to the Interdict in England.' *Transactions of the Royal Historical Society*, 4th series, 31 (1949), 129–50

Denne, S. 'Memorials of the Cathedral Church of Rochester.' In Thorpe, ed., *Custumale Roffensis*, 153–246

[Denne, S., and Shrubsole, W.] *The History and Antiquities of Rochester and Its Environs*. London 1772; 2nd ed., 1817

Oakley, A.M. 'The Cathedral Priory of St. Andrew, Rochester.' *Arch. Cant.* 91 (1975), 47–60

Rowlands, I.W. 'King John, Stephen Langton and Rochester Castle, 1213–15.' In C. Harper-Bill, C. Holdsworth, and J.L. Nelson, eds, *Studies in Medieval History Presented to R. Allen Brown*, 267–79. Woodbridge 1989.

Rudd, M. 'Monks in the World: The Case of Gundulf of Rochester.' *Anglo-Norman Studies*, 11: *Proceedings of the Battle Conference 1988* (1989), 245–60

Smith, F.F. *A History of Rochester*. London 1928

Smith, R.A.L. 'The Financial System of Rochester Cathedral Priory.'
English Historical Review 56 (1941), 586–95 (*Collected Papers*, London
1947, 42–53)

– 'The Place of Gundulf in the Anglo-Norman Church.' *English Historical
Review* 58 (1943), 257–72 (*Collected Papers*, 83–102)

– 'The Early Community of St. Andrew at Rochester, 604–c. 1080.' *English
Historical Review* 60 (1945), 289–99

Warren, W.L. *King John*. 2nd ed. London 1978

Yates, N., with P.A. Welsby. *Faith and Fabric: A History of Rochester
Cathedral, 604–1994*. Kent History Project, 4. Woodbridge 1996

KENT

Fisher, T. *The Kentish Traveller's Companion*. Rochester and Canterbury
1776; 2nd ed., 1779; 4th ed., 1794 (Rochester, 92–5)

Glynne, S.R. *Notes on the Churches of Kent*. London 1877 (Rochester,
315–18)

Hasted, E. *The History and Topographical Survey of the County of Kent*. 4
vols., Canterbury, 1778–99; 2nd ed., 12 vols., Canterbury 1797–1801
(Rochester, 1st ed., vol. II [1782], 22–30; 2nd ed., vol. IV [1798], 86–112)

Ireland, W.H. *England's Topographer, or A New and Complete History of
the County of Kent*. 4 vols. London 1830 (Rochester, vol. IV, 328–36)

Works on English Medieval Architecture

GENERAL

Clapham, (Sir) A.W. *English Romanesque Architecture*. Vol. I, *Before the
Conquest*; vol. II, *After the Conquest*. Oxford 1930 and 1934; repr., 1964

Fernie, E. *The Architecture of the Anglo-Saxons*. London 1983

Taylor, H.M., and J. Taylor. *Anglo-Saxon Architecture*. 2 vols. Cambridge
1965

Taylor, H.M. *Anglo-Saxon Architecture*. Vol. III. Cambridge 1978

Webb, G. *Architecture in Britain: The Middle Ages*. Pelican History of Art:
Harmondsworth 1956

KENT

Livett, G.M. 'Early-Norman Churches in and near the Medway Valley.'
Arch. Cant. 20 (1893), 137–54

ROCHESTER CASTLE

Brown, R.A. *Rochester Castle*. Official Guidebook: London 1969
Brown, R.A., and H.M. Colvin. 'The Royal Castles, 1066–1485.' In R.A.
Brown, H.M. Colvin, and A.J. Taylor, eds, *The Middle Ages* (H.M.
Colvin, gen. ed., *The History of the King's Works*). 2 vols. London 1963
(Rochester, II, 806–14)
Flight, C., and A.C. Harrison. 'Rochester Castle, 1976.' *Arch. Cant.* 94
(1978), 27–60

Studies Relating to Rochester Cathedral

GENERAL

Ashpitel, A. 'Rochester Cathedral.' *Jnl BAA* 9 (1854), 271–85
Hope, (Sir) W.H.St.J. 'Chronological Table of the Architectural History of
Rochester Cathedral Church.' *Arch. Cant.* 17 (1887), xli–xliii (including
'Historical Ground Plan' between xlii and xliii); also *Proceedings of the
Kent Archaeological Society* (1886–7), xxxvii–liv, and Kent Archaeologi-
cal Society, *Twenty-Ninth Annual Report: Second Annual Meeting [at
Rochester]*, *August 1889*, xxxviii–xliv; published yet again in F.F. Smith
(1928), 274–7 [see under *Historical Background*, above]
– 'The Architectural History of the Cathedral Church and Monastery of
St. Andrew at Rochester.' *Arch. Cant.* 23 (1898), 194–328, and 24 (1900),
1–85; also London 1900 (references are made to this edition)
– 'Notes on the Architectural History of Rochester Cathedral Church.'
Transactions of St. Paul's Ecclesiological Society 1 (1881–5), 217–30
Newman, J. *The Buildings of England: West Kent and the Weald*.
Harmondsworth: 1st ed., 1969; 2nd ed., 1976; repr. & corr., 1980 (Roches-
ter, 451–69 [1st ed.]; 470–88 [2nd ed.])
Palmer, G.H. *The Cathedral Church of Rochester: A Description of Its
Fabric and a Brief History of the Episcopal See*. Bell's Cathedral Series.
London 1899
Spencer, C. *A Walk through Rochester Cathedral*. London 1840
Tatton-Brown, T. 'Three Great Benedictine Houses in Kent: Their
Buildings and Topography.' *Arch. Cant.* 100 (1984), 171–88 (Rochester,
185–8)
– 'Archaeology and Rochester Cathedral.' In T. Tatton-Brown and
J. Mumby, eds, *The Archaeology of Cathedrals*, 103–14. Oxford Univer-
sity Committee for Archaeology, Monograph no. 42. Oxford 1996

Ward, A. 'Excavations at Rochester Cathedral, 1990–1995.' Canterbury Archaeological Trust (unpublished archival report), 1997

VIEWS (arranged chronologically)

Storer, J. and E. *History and Antiquities of the Cathedral Churches of Great Britain.* 4 vols. London 1814–19 (Rochester, vol. IV [1819] [unpaginated]: 1. 'Rochester Cathedral from the Canons Gate' [view from Prior's Gate toward the south transept]; 2. 'West Front'; 3. 'Entrance to the Chapter House, Rochester Cathedral'; 4. 'N.W. View of Rochester Cathedral' [north wall of nave and northwest view of north transept]; 5. 'S. Eastern Transept, Rochester Cathedral' [gable wall of southeast transept and chapter room]; 6. 'S.E. View' [view from garth towards south main transept including corner of 1805 prebendiary house]; 7. 'Part of the Choir' [view into choir crossing]; 8. 'Part of the Nave & Transept, Rochester Cathedral' [view across main crossing towards northwest crossing pier and north transept]; plan by Wm. Espin Jr.)
Winkles, H. and B. *Winkles's Architectural and Picturesque Illustrations of the Cathedral Churches of England and Wales.* 3 vols. 1838–42 (Rochester, vol. I [1838]: [facing] 105, 'Northwestern View'; 106, Ground Plan; 113, 'Western Doorway'; 115, 'View of Nave' [looking west]; 117, 'View of the Crypt'; 118, 'View of the Doorway Leading into the Chapter-House'; 120, 'Northern Transept' [view to north across main transept])
King, R.J. *Handbook to the Cathedrals of England: Southern Division.* 2 pts. London 1861 (Rochester, pt. II: title page, 'West Door'; frontispiece, 'West Front'; I. [facing 499] 'Interior of Nave / Nave from the South-East'; II. [506] 'Tomb of Bishop Glanville / Bishop Glanville's Tomb'; III. [507] 'Door of [present] Chapter House'; IV. [508] 'Oak Roof in the North Transept / Roof of South-East Transept' [actually south choir aisle ceiling]; V. [508] 'The Crypt'; VI. Remains of [the] Norman Chapter-house' [view of the east walk of the cloister and the chapter house])

PRE-CONQUEST

Fairweather (1929) [see under ROMANESQUE, below], 192 and plan (pl. I) facing p. 187
Hope, 'Architectural History' (1900) [see under GENERAL, above], 1–4 and 19–22
Livett, G.M. 'Foundations of the Saxon Cathedral Church at Rochester.' *Arch. Cant.* 18 (1889), 261–78

Peers, C.R. 'On Saxon Churches of the St. Pancras Type.' *Arch. Jnl* 58
(1901), 402–34 (Rochester, 418–19)
Radford, C.A.R. 'Rochester Cathedral: A New Fragment of Pre-Conquest
Wall.' *Annual Report of the Friends of Rochester Cathedral* (1969), 13–16
Taylor and Taylor (1965) [see under *Works on English Medieval Architec-
ture*, GENERAL, above], II, 518–19, fig. 252
Taylor (1978) [see under *Works*, GENERAL, above], III, 992
Ward [see under GENERAL, above], [1–6]

ROMANESQUE

Ashpitel (1854) [see under GENERAL, above], 273–8
Fairweather, F.H. 'Gundulf's Cathedral and Priory Church of St. Andrew,
Rochester: Some Critical Remarks on the hitherto Accepted Plan.' *Arch.
Jnl* 86 (1929), 187–212
Gem, R. 'The Origins of the Early Romanesque Architecture of England,'
545–56. PhD thesis, Cambridge University, 1973
Hope, W.H.St.J. 'Gundulf's Tower at Rochester, and the First Norman
Cathedral Church There.' *Archaeologia* 49 (1886), 323–34 (most of this
paper is repeated in Hope, 'Architectural History' [1900] [see under
GENERAL, above], 8–19)
– 'Architectural History' (1900) [see under GENERAL], 8–19 and 22–4
(Gundulf's building); 24–36 (second Romanesque building)
Livett (1889) [see under PRE-CONQUEST, above], 269–76, and 278
McAleer, J.P. 'The Significance of the West Front of Rochester Cathedral.'
Arch. Cant. 99 (1983), 139–58
– 'Some Observations on the Building Sequence of the Nave of Rochester
Cathedral.' *Arch. Cant.* 102 (1985), 149–70
– 'The West Front of Rochester Cathedral: The Interior Design.' *Arch.
Cant.* 103 (1986), 27–43
Palmer (1899) [see under GENERAL, above], 6–11, 41–50, and 64–70
Tatton-Brown, T. 'Observations Made in the Sacrist's Checker Area beside
"Gundulf's" Tower at Rochester Cathedral – July 1989.'*Arch. Cant.* 107
(1989), 390–4

GOTHIC

Ashpitel (1854) [see under GENERAL, above], 279–85
Brodie, A. 'Rochester Cathedral: The Chronology of the East End.' M.A.
report, University of London (Courtauld Insitute), 1982
Hope, 'Architectural History' (1900) [see under GENERAL, above], 40–88

McAleer, J.P. 'Rochester Cathedral: The North Choir Aisle and the Space between It and "Gundulf's" Tower.' *Arch. Cant.* 112 (1993), 127–65

Palmer (1899) [see under GENERAL, above], 12–18, 50–6, 70–5, 81, 84–8, 107–8, and 112–16

ANNALES AMICORUM CATHEDRALIS ROFFENSIS / ANNUAL REPORTS OF THE FRIENDS OF ROCHESTER CATHEDRAL

Arnold, A. 'The Shrine of St. Paulinus at Rochester.' *Report for 1988,* 16–21
– 'The Lapidarium.' *Report for 1990/1,* 21–2
Blair, J. 'The Limoges Enamel Tomb of Bishop Walter de Merton.' *Report for 1993/4,* 28–33
Churchill, I.J. 'The See of Rochester in Relation to the See of Canterbury during the Middle Ages.' *Third Annual Report* (1938), 31–7. Repr. in *Report for 1991/2,* 24–7
Cleggett, D.A.H. 'The Central Tower and Spire.' *Report 1996/7,* 4–10
Cobb, E.F. 'Explorations on the South Side of the Nave.' *Third Annual Report* (1938), 22–4
Covert, M. 'An Exciting Find.' *Report for 1988,* 10–11
– 'The Cottingham Years at Rochester.' *Report for 1991/2,* 6–14
Forsyth, W.A. 'Rochester Cathedral: Restoration of the Norman Cloister.' *Fourth Annual Report* (1939), 20–2
Geddes, J. 'Some Doors in Rochester Cathedral.' *Report for 1989/90,* 19–22
McAleer, J.P. 'The Cathedral West Front: Form, Function, and Fashion.' *Report for 1990/1,* 23–36
– 'Rochester Cathedral: The West Range of the Cloister.' *Report for 1992/3,* 13–25
Radford, C.A.R. 'Rochester Cathedral: A New Fragment of Pre-Conquest Wall.' *Annual Report* (1969), 13–16
Swanton, M.J. 'The Decoration of Ernulf's Nave.' *Report for 1989/90,* 11–18. Repr. from *Arch. Jnl.* 136 (1979), 125–35 ('A Mural Palimpsest from Rochester Cathedral')
Tatton-Brown, T. 'The Chapter House and Dormitory Facade at Rochester Cathedral Priory.' *Report for 1993/4,* 20–8
– 'The Eastern Crypt of Rochester Cathedral.' *Report 1996/7,* 18–22
– 'The East Range of the Cloisters.' *Report for 1988,* 4–8
– '"Gundulf's" Tower.' *Report for 1990/1,* 7–12
Tracy, C., and C. Hewett. 'The Early Thirteenth-Century Choir-Stalls and Associated Furniture at Rochester Cathedral, with Drawings and Carpentry Notes.' *Report for 1994/5,* 10–23

Ward, A. 'Excavations at Rochester Cathedral.' *Report for 1990/91*, 13–15

West, J. 'A Stone Rejected, Retained, and Reconsidered.' *Report for 1995/6*, 31–5

Worssam, B.C. 'A Guide to the Building Stones of Rochester Cathedral,' *Report for 1994/5*, 23–34

Index

Offices held in the diocese and priory of Rochester are indicated in bold. Counties are those existing in Britain before 1974. Earlier persons are generally indexed under their forenames; bishops and others are indexed under their family names after 1400. Churches are indexed under the towns, cities, or districts in which they are situated. Subject headings for Rochester Cathedral are found throughout the index (rather than under 'Rochester').

Adam (**sacrist**), 106

Aethelberht I (king of Kent), 8, 10, 11, 17, 168 n2; building of, 10, 13, 16–17, 173 n44, 174 n47, 188 n17

Aethelberht's building, 10, 11–13, 16–17, 173 n44, 174 n47; burials, 10, 13, 14, 17; destruction of, 10–11, 17; location of altar, 13; secretarium, 10, 17, 188 n17; use as chapter house, 17. *See also* pre-conquest structure(s)

Aethelred, king of Mercia, 10

Aethelred the Redeless (king of Wessex), 9, 11

aisle walls, 60; excavations, 12, 22, 30–2; identification by Willis, 42; restoration, 71, 212 n12

aisles. *See* nave

Aldington (Kent) 207 n145

Alexander, Daniel Asher, 31, 42, 211 n10, 214 n20, 275 n21, 283 n70

Alexander, William, 39, 253 n75

Alfred (king of Wessex), 9

altar(s): crypt, 94, 132, 142, 246 n38; first Romanesque church, 45, 47–8; Gothic building, 132, 267 n155; infirmary chapel, 283 n68; location in Aethelberht's building, 13; matutinal, 75; parochial, 45; second Romanesque church, 75; transept (major), 110, 117, 132, 138, 161, 261 n131, 267 n155; transept (minor), 132–3

ambulatories, rectangular, 50

Amiens Cathedral (Picardy: Somme), 264 n152

Andrew, Saint (apostle), 10